The Doctrines of Grace in an Unexpected Place

The Doctrines of Grace in an Unexpected Place

*Calvinistic Soteriology in
Nineteenth-Century Brethren Thought*

Mark R. Stevenson

FOREWORD BY
Tim Grass

☙PICKWICK *Publications* · Eugene, Oregon

THE DOCTRINES OF GRACE IN AN UNEXPECTED PLACE
Calvinistic Soteriology in Nineteenth-Century Brethren Thought

Copyright © 2017 Mark R. Stevenson. All rights reserved. Except for brief quotations in critical publications or reviews, no part of this book may be reproduced in any manner without prior written permission from the publisher. Write: Permissions, Wipf and Stock Publishers, 199 W. 8th Ave., Suite 3, Eugene, OR 97401.

Pickwick Publications
An Imprint of Wipf and Stock Publishers
199 W. 8th Ave., Suite 3
Eugene, OR 97401

www.wipfandstock.com

PAPERBACK ISBN: 978-1-4982-8109-6
HARDCOVER ISBN: 978-1-4982-8111-9
EBOOK ISBN: 978-1-4982-8110-2

Cataloguing-in-Publication data:

Names: Stevenson, Mark R., author | Grass, Tim, foreword.

Title: The doctrines of grace in an unexpected place : Calvinistic soteriology in nineteenth-century Brethren thought / Mark R. Stevenson ; Foreword by Tim Grass.

Description: Eugene, OR: Pickwick Publications, 2017 | Includes bibliographical references and index.

Identifiers: ISBN 978-1-4982-8109-6 (paperback) | ISBN 978-1-4982-8111-9 (hardcover) | ISBN 978-1-4982-8110-2 (ebook).

Subjects: LCSH: Brethren (Brethren churches). | Calvinists—Europe—History.

Classification: BT265.3 S75 2017 (print) | BT265.3 (ebook).

Manufactured in the U.S.A.   03/06/17

Dedicated with gratitude

to my wife Tonya—*fellow heir of the grace of life*

and

to the memory of my father, John (Jack) Wallace Stevenson (1932–98),

who loved both the Brethren and the doctrines of grace.

Contents

Foreword by Tim Grass | ix
Acknowledgments | xi
Abbreviations | xv

1 Introduction | 1
2 Calvinistic Soteriology: A Historical Survey—Part 1: From the Restoration through the Evangelical Revival (1660–1800) | 16
3 Calvinistic Soteriology: A Historical Survey—Part 2: The Nineteenth Century Context | 43
4 "The Total Ruin of Man": Fallen Human Nature in Brethren Thought | 67
5 The Brethren and the Doctrine of Predestination | 112
6 The Extent of the Atonement: Universal and Particular | 165
7 "What Must I Do to Be Saved?": Brethren Perspectives on Saving Faith, Repentance, and Assurance | 201
8 Evaluation and Conclusion | 253

Bibliography | 263
General Index | 291
Scripture Index | 303

Foreword

WHILST A NUMBER OF theses have explored Brethren thinking regarding such matters as the last things and the church, their understanding of the doctrine of salvation has not received anything like so much coverage. In the light of their development into a movement which had the proclamation of the gospel at home and abroad at its heart, this means that our understanding of what made nineteenth-century Brethren "tick" has been incomplete and potentially seriously distorted. Mark Stevenson's exploration of Brethren teaching (and preaching) about salvation is therefore to be welcomed as filling a significant gap in our understanding of the movement. Not only so, but the author offers a confident, competent and wide-ranging account of the views of leading teachers within the movement. As "the book of the thesis," one might expect what follows to be dense and unintelligible; Mark certainly packs in a great deal of content, but in a style which makes for much easier reading than with most books of this nature. Its conclusions are likely to spark further debate within and beyond Brethren circles, but he takes great care to ground them in the evidence offered by the sources. Supervising his research was a pleasure as well as an education, and I am delighted to commend this work. May it be widely read and digested!

Dr. Tim Grass
Senior Research Fellow
Spurgeon's College, London

Acknowledgments

THE COMPLETION OF THIS book would not have been possible without the help of others. There are many people I wish to thank—perhaps too many to name, but I will nevertheless acknowledge some here and offer my sincere apologies to any I may neglect to mention.

Along the way, a number of people have provided helpful advice, answered queries, assisted with sources, or supplied me with published or unpublished material. Among them are David Bebbington, the late Edwin Cross, Neil Dickson, Donald Fairbairn, Jack Fish, Ken Fleming, Crawford Gribben, David MacLeod, Thomas Marinello, Nigel Pibworth, Ian Randall, Roger Shuff, Kenneth Stewart, Timothy Stunt, Neil Summerton, Graham Watts, and Stephen Wright. In addition to his help with several sources, I am grateful to Neil Dickson for inviting me to participate in the Brethren Archivists and Historians Network, from which I have greatly benefited. Special thanks are due to Pieter Lalleman and Sue Tyler, who proof-read the entire manuscript and offered many helpful suggestions and corrections. Errors that remain, of course, are my responsibility.

This book began life as a PhD thesis, initially under the supervision of Donald Tinder at the Evangelische Theologische Faculteit (ETF) in Leuven, Belgium, and I am grateful for his encouragement. Don generously gave me a copy of Tim Grass's history of the Brethren, *Gathering to His Name*, and as Don was retiring from ETF, it was Tim who agreed to take me on as a research student at Spurgeon's College in London. It has been a privilege to work under Tim's supervision. I am deeply grateful for his scholarship, guidance, and wisdom throughout the course of this project—and for the warm hospitality that Tim and his wife Ann extended to me during a most delightful visit to their home on the Isle of Man.

Some of the material in this thesis was presented at various conferences and seminars, and I am grateful for the feedback and interaction with others that grew out of those presentations. In every case my thinking was sharpened. I am thankful to Gary Brady, who invited me to deliver the 2013 Annual Lecture at the Evangelical Library in London. Out of that experience the title for this thesis was born.

A number of libraries and archives have been consulted in the process of research, but I would like to acknowledge especially the kind and ready assistance of Graham Johnson, archivist of the Christian Brethren Archive in the John Rylands Library, University of Manchester. Graham always makes visits to the Archive an enjoyable experience. But far and away my greatest debt along these lines is to John Rush, Director of Library Services at Emmaus Bible College. Not only did John willingly track down my many requests, but he frequently provided me with sources he knew I ought to consult. His own knowledge of Brethren history and literature has been invaluable. I also appreciate his patience, as I have held library resources hostage in my office for far too long!

I wish to express my sincere gratitude to William Coyle and the board of Stewards Ministries for their generous academic scholarship, which enabled me to carry out this research. I would also like to thank the administration of Emmaus Bible College, where I am privileged to serve, for their gracious support at multiple levels, without which I would never have been able to undertake or complete this project. I am especially grateful to Lisa Beatty, Dean for Academic Affairs, for her understanding and encouragement—and for occasionally excusing me from faculty meetings!

A number of student assistants have provided valuable help in hunting down references, including Ryan D. Thompson, Jonathan Schulz, Adam Mostert, Elizabeth Cravillion, Joel Carter, and Khellan Fletcher. Students from my Theological Research Seminar have allowed me to think through the research process with them, and their work has often stimulated my own thinking. I am also grateful to my colleagues at Emmaus for their encouragement. Frank Jabini graciously assisted with formatting issues on a number of occasions. Dave MacLeod has followed this research with great interest, having considered the subject before I formally tackled it. I have valued our many conversations and appreciate our friendship. Another friend who has encouraged me from start to finish is Tom Marinello. From providing hospitality while in Europe, to traveling the English countryside together, to supplying me with A4 paper, Tom's camaraderie has been an abiding joy.

Most of all, I am thankful to my family for sharing this journey with me. My children, Jonathan, Emma, Katelyn, and Sophia, displayed remarkable understanding while Dad was away working on his book. They have often been the ones to bring me back from the nineteenth century, and their love has helped me appreciate the joys of the present. I am grateful beyond words for my wife Tonya. Through this whole process, her love, support, encouragement, patience, dedication to our family, and able management of our home have been nothing short of awesome. It is to her that this book is affectionately dedicated.

I am ever grateful for the formative influence of my parents, Jack and Marion Stevenson. I consider growing up in their home in Canada one of the happy providences of my life. My father passed long before this book was even conceived, but I daresay he would have liked to read it. His life and example shape me still. Along with my wife, I dedicate this book his memory.

Finally, in a study devoted to "the doctrines of grace," I cannot fail to acknowledge my deepest gratitude to the God of all grace. His grace to me is more than academic; it is life itself.

Soli Deo Gloria

Abbreviations

BC	*The Barley Cake*
BDE	*Biographical Dictionary of Evangelicals*
BDEB	*Blackwell Dictionary of Evangelical Biography*
BHR	*Brethren Historical Review*
BM	*The Believer's Magazine*
BQ	*Baptist Quarterly*
BT	*The Bible Treasury*
CBA	Christian Brethren Archive, John Rylands University Library, University of Manchester
CF	*The Christian's Friend*
CH	*Church History*
CO	*The Christian Observer*
CTJ	*Calvin Theological Journal*
CW	*The Collected Writings of J. N. Darby*
CWit	*The Christian Witness*
DNB	*Dictionary of National Biography*
DSCHT	*Dictionary of Scottish Church History and Theology*
EQ	*The Evangelical Quarterly*
GS	*The Gospel Standard*
JR	*Journal of Religion*
JTS	*Journal of Theological Studies*

NEI	*The Northern Evangelistic Intelligencer*
NI	*The Northern Intelligencer*
NIDCC	*The New International Dictionary of the Christian Church*
NPNF	*Nicene and Post-Nicene Fathers*
NW	*The Northern Witness*
ODNB	*Oxford Dictionary of National Biography*
OR	*Our Record*
SBET	*Scottish Bulletin of Evangelical Theology*
SBJT	*The Southern Baptist Journal of Theology*
TNO	*Things New and Old*
VE	*Vox Evangelica*
W	*The Witness*
WCF	Westminster Confession of Faith
WTJ	*Westminster Theological Journal*

Biblical quotations are taken from the King James Version.

1

Introduction

"Calvinism . . . when it treats of actual salvation, is almost wholly right."

—F. W. Grant[1]

"At the level of theology, the earliest Brethren were Calvinists to a man."

—Harold H. Rowdon[2]

DOES GOD SOVEREIGNLY ELECT some individuals for salvation while passing others by? Do human beings possess free will to embrace or reject the gospel? Did Christ die equally for all people or only for some? These questions have long been debated in the history of the Christian church. They belong to the field of soteriology—the division of theology concerned with the Christian doctrine of salvation. Answers to these questions typically fall into one of two main categories that were known by the seventeenth century in the Western church as "Calvinism" and "Arminianism." The focus of this book is to establish how nineteenth-century Brethren responded to these and other related questions. This introductory chapter will justify the need for such a study and will orient the reader to the central issues, sources, and methodology engaged throughout the book.

The Brethren movement emerged in the late 1820s in Ireland, but soon afterward its largest assembly formed in Plymouth, England. Thus the movement was dubbed "Plymouth Brethren," although its adherents refused

---

1. [Grant], "The Sovereignty of God in Salvation," 180. The essay was reprinted in Grant, *Leaves from the Book*, 152.

2. Rowdon, *Who Are the Brethren?* 35.

any label except those found in the New Testament, preferably, "brethren."[3] These Christians were evangelical in conviction, but they have also been characterized as *radical* evangelicals.[4] They were disillusioned with existing churches and ecclesiastical forms, and longed to return to the simplicity of New Testament patterns of church practice and fellowship. Brethren ideals were shaped in part through the influence of Romanticism, which reacted to the rationalism of the Enlightenment by stressing imagination, feeling, and awe.[5] Brethren adaptation of Romantic values manifested itself in a number of ways,[6] including a penchant to exalt faith above reason; an almost mystical devotion to the authority and sufficiency of Scripture; and an overarching pessimism in light of the failures of the church, all the while maintaining an abiding hope in the imminent return of Christ and the supernatural work of the Holy Spirit in calling out a people for God in the present evil age.[7]

In the late 1840s, tensions mounted when some leading personalities clashed over Christological matters. Consequently, the movement experienced a major division that resulted in two streams: the Open Brethren, who asserted the autonomy of each local assembly; and the Exclusive Brethren, who, by contrast, were "tightly connexional with a high degree of interdependence within a network of assemblies."[8]

The Brethren movement, though never large, exerted a significant influence on other evangelicals in the nineteenth century.[9] Brethren writers published a substantial amount of material in the form of magazines, evangelistic literature, and biblical exposition that was appreciated beyond the confines of Brethrenism. The "faith principle" exemplified in the missionary endeavors of Anthony Norris Groves and the orphanage work of George Müller had a wide impact.[10] Particularly after the 1859 revivals, the movement placed a high priority on evangelism and produced a number of influential evangelists. D. L. Moody testified that after listening to Brethren

---

3. Donald Akenson has recently suggested that "Wicklow Brethren" would be a more fitting descriptor to indicate the Irish roots of the movement. Akenson, *Discovering*, 14, 51.

4. E.g., Stunt, *From Awakening*.

5. See for example, Bebbington, "Evangelicalism," 243–48.

6. For an extended discussion see Bebbington, "Place of the Brethren Movement," 248–60.

7. Cf. Roger Shuff, *Searching for the True Church*, 2–3.

8. Ibid., 3. Shuff prefers the term "connexional Brethren" for the Exclusive stream and "independent Brethren" for the Opens.

9. Bebbington, "Place of the Brethren Movement," 257–60.

10. For Müller's influence on Spurgeon see Randall, "'Ye Men of Plymouth,'" 74–75.

evangelist Henry Moorhouse, his own gospel preaching underwent transformation.[11] Theologically, perhaps the most distinctive contribution the Brethren have bequeathed to the broader evangelical world has been the development of dispensational premillennialism—although this has also drawn a fair share of criticism, not least from Calvinists.

The Need for the Present Study

For these and other reasons, the Brethren movement has attracted significant enquiry from historians. By and large, however, scholarly interest has focused on matters related to historical development and influence, as well as sociological issues. Investigation of the theology of the movement naturally tends to focus on matters of dispensationalism,[12] ecclesiology,[13] and eschatology,[14] since these have been its distinguishing features, and it is in these fields that Brethren have exerted the most influence. Other studies concentrate on the thought of John Nelson Darby,[15] the dominant personality of the movement, or missiology,[16] or the concept of "living by faith."[17]

To date, what has been lacking is an in-depth study of the soteriology of the early Brethren. In a 2006 article for the *Brethren Archivists and Historians Network Review* (now called *Brethren Historical Review*), Tim Grass wrote in regard to Brethren studies, "One issue has not generally been discussed in detail, and that is the thinking among early Brethren concerning soteriology. Some form of Calvinistic teaching seems to have been fairly generally accepted among them." He adds, "Early Brethren soteriology would thus appear to be an area worthy of further research . . . A book or thesis cries out to be written on Brethren evangelistic proclamation—a topic

---

11. Needham, *Recollections*, 105–11.

12. Sweetnam and Gribben, "J. N. Darby," 569–77; Henzel, "Darby, Dualism"; MacLeod, "Walter Scott," 155–78; Crutchfield, *Origins of Dispensationalism*.

13. Bass, "The Doctrine of the Church"; Callahan, *Primitivist Piety*; Clarke, "A Critical Examination"; Dann, *Primitivist Ecclesiology*; Grass, "The Church's Ruin"; Yeager, "The Roots of Open Brethren Ecclesiology."

14. Akenson, *Discovering*; Coad, *Prophetic Developments*; Ward, "The Eschatology of John Nelson Darby."

15. Some examples include: Burnham, *Story of Conflict*; Dixon, "Pneumatology of John Nelson Darby"; Elmore, "A Critical Examination"; Krapohl, "A Search for Purity"; Nebeker, "Hope of Heavenly Glory"; Schwarz, *Leben im Sieg Christi*.

16. Dann, "Primitivist Missiology."

17. Larsen, "'Living by Faith,'" 67–102.

of unquestionable contemporary relevance."[18] The present thesis seeks to rectify this gap in Brethren research.

The focus of this study is not the whole field of soteriology, but more narrowly on some of the central issues in the Calvinism/Arminianism debate, such as total depravity and the question of the freedom or bondage of the will (chapter 4); election and predestination (chapter 5); and the extent of the atonement (chapter 6).[19] An additional chapter will investigate Brethren views on the nature of saving faith, repentance, and assurance (chapter 7), since these were areas that attracted criticism from Reformed opponents; they also illustrate how Brethren could be critical of elements within the Calvinist tradition while advancing their own brand of Calvinistic soteriology. We do not consider other important soteriological doctrines, such as justification and imputed righteousness, though this book lays the groundwork for other researchers to pursue these questions.

The topics featured here—often affectionately known to Calvinists as "the doctrines of grace"—are of perennial interest and debate to students of theology. Furthermore, questions about the relationship between divine sovereignty and human responsibility, the atoning work of Christ, and the nature of saving faith all touch the gospel and thus remain at the center of evangelical theological reflection. But this study is also needed because in the Brethren movement at present, the issue of Calvinism has emerged as a significant matter of concern. A number of writers, largely from the Open stream of the movement, have gone into print warning of the perceived dangers of Calvinism.[20] Many of these writers seem unaware that the early leaders of the movement were Calvinistic and advocated some of the very doctrines current leaders consider harmful. Others have recognized the prevalent position of many Brethren as a departure from the movement's Calvinistic roots,[21] yet no study to date has described in any kind of sufficient detail the nature of those roots. This book, therefore, endeavors to provide some much-needed historical perspective on the contemporary debate.

---

18. Grass, "Thomas Dowglass," 20–21.

19. We do not employ the popular acronym TULIP as a descriptor of Calvinistic soteriology. Not only is it woefully reductionistic, promoting misunderstanding and misrepresentation of Calvinist doctrine, but the acronym itself did not come into use until the twentieth century and was thus unknown to nineteenth-century Brethren (or anyone else, for that matter). See Stewart, *Ten Myths*, 75–95, 291–92.

20. E.g., Dunlap, *Limiting Omnipotence*; de Silva, *Calvinism*. For more examples see Stevenson, "Early Brethren Leaders," 2–6.

21. Davidson, "Reformation and the Brethren," 3–5.

Scope and Limitations

The geographical concentration of this study is limited primarily to England, Scotland, and Ireland, since "Britain was the chief epicentre of Brethrenism"[22] in the nineteenth century. As observed above, the movement originated in Ireland and quickly spread to England. In the latter half of the century, Scotland emerged as a remarkable base of growth and activity, especially for Open Brethrenism.[23] Some attention will be devoted to Brethren leaders who emigrated from Britain to North America, since they essentially transplanted British Brethren principles to Canada and the United States. The doctrinal convictions of these leaders were formed in the context of British Brethrenism. Furthermore, Brethren in North America looked to the writings of their British brothers as formative and often reprinted them in their magazines.

Chronologically, the purview of this study is restricted to the nineteenth century. Given the space limitations of a work of this nature, a later *terminus ad quem* would fail to do justice to the abundant early source material. Changes in Brethren perspectives on some of the issues addressed here began to emerge in the twentieth century. These modified views demand full-scale analysis in their own right and would need to be traced out considerably into the twentieth century—thus truncating research of the earlier period. By focusing on the nineteenth century, this study provides the foundation for further investigation of developments that took place in the new century.

Sources

Soteriology

Two studies have explored the soteriology of individual Brethren leaders. First, John Goddard's 1948 ThD dissertation arranged aspects of Darby's soteriology along the lines of systematic theology. While Goddard noted the Calvinistic tenor of Darby's view of sin and election, he did not connect Darby's positions to the larger context of nineteenth-century debate; nor did he comment on the impact of Darby's soteriology on the Brethren movement at large.[24] Second, James Harvey's essay "Donald Ross: A Sote-

---

22. Bebbington, "Place of the Brethren Movement," 242.

23. Dickson, *Brethren in Scotland*.

24. Goddard, "The Contribution of John Nelson Darby." Dixon has a discussion of Darby's soteriology as it related to the work of the Holy Spirit. See Dixon, "Pneumatology of John Nelson Darby," 211–35.

riological Retrospective"[25] successfully demonstrates that Ross maintained Calvinistic soteriology, even though he, like other Brethren, eschewed the label. While Harvey makes some reference to the views of other Brethren[26] and is sensitive to the historical context, his focus is narrowly on Ross.

Two works by the modern-day Darby apologist Roy Huebner[27] are worth noting. These books do not offer scholarly analysis of Brethren soteriology; they essentially restate the positions of Brethren writers such as Kelly, and especially Darby, in light of recent controversies over "the doctrines of grace."[28] The first, entitled *The Work of Christ on the Cross and Some of Its Results* (2002), seeks to explain and uphold Darby's distinction between universal propitiation and particular substitution. The second volume, *God's Sovereignty and Glory in the Election and Salvation of Lost Men* (2003), responds to contemporary Arminian writers such as Norman Geisler and Dave Hunt. Huebner argues that "unconditional election of the saints is taught in Scripture, along with the fact that man is totally lost." Yet he also rejects "the Calvinistic doctrine of an eternal decree of reprobation."[29] Huebner relies heavily on quotations from Darby. Both of these works are valuable in highlighting primary source material on issues investigated in the present study. Huebner's volumes also illustrate that the soteriological views of early Brethren writers still hold sway among some loyalists.

Calvinism in Historical Context

Tim Grass's PhD thesis, "The Church's Ruin and Restoration: The Development of Ecclesiology in the Plymouth Brethren and the Catholic Apostolic Church, c.1825–c.1866," (King's College, London, 1997), argues that the approach of the Brethren (and the Catholic Apostolic Church) to ecclesiology was "an outworking of their reappropriation of Calvinist thought with its stress on divine sovereignty and human inability."[30] Grass's work is valuable in demonstrating how the fabric of nineteenth-century British Calvinism helped shape the ecclesiology of the two groups. However, his focus is ecclesiology, not soteriology.

---

25. The essay is posted on Harvey's blog: http://impact59.files.wordpress.com/2010/01/donald-ross-soteriological-retrospective-dec09.pdf.
26. Primarily Darby, Kelly, and Mackintosh.
27. Huebner died February 18, 2008.
28. Huebner, *The Work of Christ*, v.
29. Huebner, *God's Sovereignty*, vi.
30. Grass, "The Church's Ruin," 6.

Two important works that illuminate the dynamics animating evangelicals vis-à-vis the Established Church are Grayson Carter, *Anglican Evangelicals: Protestant Secessions from the Via Media, c.1800–1850* (Oxford, 2001) and Timothy C. F. Stunt, *From Awakening to Secession: Radical Evangelicals in Switzerland and Britain 1815–35* (T&T Clark, 2000). Both works identify Calvinism as a central issue in the theological debate. Both works also discuss influences on the thinking of early Brethren leaders. And both works set the origins of the movement in the larger context of the fervor of radical evangelical secession. Stunt's contribution demonstrates that such activity was preceded and influenced by the Swiss *Réveil*. Also noteworthy is Robert Dann's *The Primitive Ecclesiology of Anthony Norris Groves*. Chapter 2, "A Calvinistic Evangelical Anglican," not only highlights Groves's Calvinism, but the Calvinism of a significant number of his contemporaries. Dann provides another voice demonstrating that in the larger historical context, Calvinism was an issue very much on the minds of evangelical churchmen and seceders.

Ian Rennie, in an essay entitled "Aspects of Christian Brethren Spirituality," suggests that hyper-Calvinism was a shaping influence in the formative assembly at Plymouth. While it may be questioned whether Rennie has marshalled enough evidence to make his case, the suggestion is certainly provocative.[31]

Brethren Source Material

The severance of the movement into two factions, Open and Exclusive, adds a layer of complexity to any study of the Brethren. While the Open Brethren would ultimately attain greater numerical strength, for many years the Exclusive Brethren possessed the more influential and prolific teachers. Open Brethren continued to read popular Exclusive writers, and thus on many themes, Open and Exclusive Brethren were indistinguishable.[32] Since soteriology was not the crux of the original division, both streams must be stud-

---

31. Ian Randall believes Rennie "has over-estimated the influence of 'hyper-Calvinism' . . . among the Brethren." See Randall, *Evangelical Experiences*, 143. Yet Randall's focus is on the movement a century after its founding when any hyper-Calvinist influence—if even present to begin with—would have waned. Indeed, Randall is able to document examples of the diminishing of Calvinism among the Brethren by the 1920s and 30s.

32. Rowdon, "The Brethren Concept of Sainthood," 91–92. Grass observes, "Expository works by Exclusive authors such as Bellett, Darby, Kelly, and Mackintosh were manifestly superior to anything by Open authors," and were frequently quoted and advertised in Open magazines. Grass, *Gathering to His Name*, 199.

ied. Yet because Exclusive writers produced more material, they will feature more prominently in the present study,[33] particularly the most prominent and prolific of the Exclusive writers, Darby, Kelly, and Mackintosh.[34]

Central to any historical study is the primary source material. It is necessary to investigate how the Brethren understood and discussed the doctrines of grace, and how they employed—or avoided—Calvinist terminology. Although the Brethren displayed great interest in Bible doctrine, they did not as a rule produce major works of theology, and they shunned systematic theology on principle.[35] Instead, they spent their energies on producing devotional works, biblical commentaries, doctrinal expositions, periodical literature, and a seemingly endless supply of pamphlets and tracts.[36]

In terms of specific material, a good portion of what John Nelson Darby wrote made its way into print.[37] Darby's *Collected Writings* run thirty-four volumes, and his *Letters*, three volumes.[38] Through the recent publication, *Dates of J. N. Darby's Collected Writings*, it is now possible to pinpoint when many of the essays in the *Collected Writings* originally appeared.[39] Additional works include five volumes of *Synopsis of the Books of the Bible*, seven volumes of *Notes and Comments on Scripture*, five volumes of *Notes and Jottings from Various Meetings with J. N. Darby* (later compiled into one volume), and two volumes of *Additional Writings of J. N. Darby*, which consist mainly of magazine articles that were not reprinted in the *Collected Writings*. Thus from doctrinal articles, to exposition of specific

---

33. Rowdon speaks of the "paucity of influential Open Brethren expositors of scripture and, particularly, of doctrine." Rowdon, "The Brethren Concept of Sainthood," 92.

34. Again Grass notes, "Exclusive writers such as Kelly, Mackintosh, and Darby were widely read among Open Brethren (and even published by them)." Grass, *Gathering to His Name*, 4.

35. E.g., [Brenton], "Thoughts on System in Religion," 310–12.

36. A substantial collection of Brethren writings is found in the library of Emmaus Bible College (Dubuque, Iowa, USA), the largest Brethren institution of higher education. However, the most extensive collection of Brethren material world-wide is the Christian Brethren Archive (CBA) housed at the University of Manchester's John Rylands University Library.

37. For an extended bibliographic discussion of Darby's works see Akenson, *Discovering*, 487–98. This is a highly insightful piece, even if Akenson's conclusions seem, at times, overly skeptical.

38. Two additional volumes of letters have recently been released: Darby, *Letters: Supplement*.

39. Although Akenson urges caution with this resource due to the lack of explanation for the dates assigned to each item. Akenson, *Discovering*, 495.

Scripture passages, to candid opinions expressed in letters, there is no shortage of material from the most influential of early Brethren writers.

William Kelly's output is equally impressive. Considered to be the finest exegete among the Brethren,[40] Kelly produced expositions or lectures on virtually every book of the Bible. He also authored numerous doctrinal articles.

C. H. Mackintosh was one of the most popular and prolific writers among nineteenth-century Brethren. Mackintosh himself was not an original thinker but was influenced significantly by Darby's thought. As a writer, however, he was far more lucid than Darby and was thus able to mediate "Darbyite theology to the wider world."[41] His *Miscellaneous Writings* and *Short Papers*, most of which first appeared as magazine articles, offer a wealth of doctrine reflection at a popular level that appealed broadly to readers both inside and outside the movement.

When we turn to the Open wing of the movement we discover there is less material available from early leaders like Anthony Norris Groves and George Müller. Much of their writing was autobiographical in nature, although some of Müller's sermons were published.[42] The increase of itinerant evangelists after the 1859 revival spawned more Open literature, mostly in the form of magazines and gospel tracts, although some doctrinal works appeared, like Sir Robert Anderson's *The Gospel and Its Ministry*, which was first published in the 1870s.[43]

At least two methodological challenges arise from this material. First, many Open Brethren evangelists—like Donald Munro, for example—did not publish much. They were preachers and activists first and foremost, and their writing usually consisted of reports of their ministry in the magazines. The second challenge relates to the gospel tract genre of which the Brethren were so fond. These often consisted of a presentation of the gospel with stories and anecdotes, along with appeals to the readers to turn to Christ, but the theology behind their appeals was not always obvious. Furthermore, the Brethren did not believe that difficult theological questions like election should be discussed in evangelistic contexts.

While the primary sources will be cited throughout this study,[44] a word on Brethren magazines as an important source of historical data seems in

---

40. See, for example, Cross, *Irish Saint and Scholar*, 113–14.
41. Grass, *Gathering to His Name*, 151 n.27. cf. Cross, *Life and Times*, 44.
42. Müller, *Sermons and Addresses*; Müller, *Jehovah Magnified*.
43. Anderson, *The Gospel and Its Ministry*.
44. Since numerous works by a variety of Brethren will be studied, the reader is directed to the footnotes and bibliography for the specific material consulted.

order. Not only were the Brethren prolific in producing periodical literature, but a large portion of the material was devoted to biblical and doctrinal themes. Most of the magazines entertained questions from the readership, and occasionally enquiries related to Calvinism surfaced.

The earliest Brethren magazine was *The Christian Witness* (1834–41), edited by J. L. Harris.[45] After the split of 1848, the Exclusive Brethren were the first to publish their own magazines. Three are especially noteworthy for their theological content and influential editors: *Things New and Old* (1845–90, edited by C. H. Mackintosh and later Charles Stanley); *The Present Testimony* (1849–81, edited by G. V. Wigram); and *The Bible Treasury* (1856–1920, edited by William Kelly). Grass suggests that Open Brethren were likely influenced by these magazines "simply because for many years there were no other periodicals for them to read" from a Brethren perspective.[46] The two most prominent Open Brethren magazines were *The Witness* (commenced in 1887 but preceded by earlier versions: *The Northern Evangelistic Intelligencer* [1871–72], *The Northern Intelligencer* [1873–74], and *The Northern Witness* [1875–86]) edited by Donald Ross and then J. R. Caldwell, and *The Believer's Magazine*, which was launched in 1891 and edited by John Ritchie. These publications—and others like them, such as *The Golden Lamp* (1870–90)—served as pacesetters for acceptable doctrine and practice and were widely circulated.

On the North American scene, the key Exclusive periodical was *Help and Food for the Household of Faith*, which commenced in 1883 and was edited by F. W. Grant. The first Open Brethren magazine was *The Barley Cake*. Edited by Donald Ross, it first appeared in January 1881; the name changed to *Our Record* in 1887. It was not unusual to find articles by Exclusive writers in these publications, illustrating again that the line between Exclusive and Open thinking on some doctrinal subjects was not clearly marked.

In terms of manuscript material, one of the more important items available to Brethren researchers is a collection that has come to be known as the "Fry Manuscript." This material consists of letters and recollections of B. W. Newton, one of the most important and controversial leaders in the early years of the movement.[47] As we shall see, this material provides a fascinating glimpse into Newton's conversion to Calvinism, as well as the theological milieu of Oxford and Plymouth in the late 1820s.

---

45. Of this magazine Grass states: "Articles on prophecy formed a significant part of the contents and the call to separation was frequently sounded." *Gathering to His Name*, 63.

46. Ibid., 152.

47. For a history of the Fry material see Stunt, *From Awakening*, 313–14.

Histories of the Brethren

Several histories of the movement are important for understanding Brethren development.[48] While it is not necessary to list all the available histories, five deserve particular notice: W. Blair Neatby's *A History of the Plymouth Brethren* appeared in 1901 and was the first serious history of the relatively young movement; the work of Harold H. Rowdon on the origins of the movement (1967)[49] and F. Roy Coad's history (1968)[50] applied a level of scholarship previously unseen in Brethren historiography; and finally, Neil Dickson on Scotland (2002)[51] and Tim Grass on Britain and Ireland (2006)[52] made use of previously unknown or unavailable material and have set a new standard of meticulous research for Brethren history-writing. Significantly, both Dickson and Grass discuss the theological issues that were important in Brethren development, and both note throughout their respective histories questions related to Calvinism and Arminianism as they touched the Brethren.

Less work has been done on the history of North American assemblies. Robert Baylis's *My People: The History of Those Christians Sometimes Called Plymouth Brethren* focuses largely on North America, but does not offer much by way of theological analysis. The most important work is Ross McLaren's M.A. thesis for Vanderbilt University entitled, "The Triple Tradition: The Origin and Development of the Open Brethren in North America" (1982). McLaren provocatively argues that the so-called Open Brethren in North America lack direct historical connection to the English Open Brethren "fathers" such as Anthony Norris Groves, George Müller, Henry Craik, and those aligned with the Bethesda assembly in Bristol following the 1848 division. Instead, he maintains that the Open Brethren in North America are directly linked to the so-called "Revival Brethren" (led by evangelists like Donald Ross and Donald Munro) that emerged from the 1859–60 revivals in Scotland and Ireland. While McLaren raises some important historiographical issues, his thesis does not ultimately affect the topic of this study. Therefore, the traditional categories of Open and Exclusive Brethren will be retained, while acknowledging that, in some cases, these categories function more as points on a continuum than designating two isolated camps.

---

48. For a discussion of Brethren historiography see Grass, "The Quest for Identity," 11–27.
49. Rowdon, *Origins of the Brethren*.
50. Coad, *History of the Brethren*.
51. Dickson, *Brethren in Scotland*.
52. Grass, *Gathering to His Name*.

At this point, it is worth highlighting how frequently historians have described the early Brethren movement as Calvinistic in its soteriological orientation. Neatby, in a chapter entitled "The Theological Position of Brethrenism," wrote, "Briefly stated, the theology of the Brethren is the ordinary theology of Evangelicals of a firmly but moderately Calvinistic type."[53] For Rowdon, a Calvinistic understanding of the gospel was one of the common theological convictions that marked the movement. He wrote, "Although certain convictions, such as the supreme authority of Holy Scripture, the evangelical gospel with a Calvinistic complexion, and the expectation of a pre-millennial, personal return of Christ, were held firmly and universally, other matters of a practical as well as a doctrinal nature remained subjects of discussion."[54] In a later work describing Brethren identity, Rowdon makes an intriguing comment regarding Calvinism's status through the history of the movement: "At the level of theology, the earliest Brethren were Calvinists to a man. In the process of time they adopted the dispensationalist approach to Scripture . . . and greatly modified their Calvinism. Eventually, it became little more than a memory, maintained by a few, rediscovered by some, but largely a thing of the past."[55]

Peter Embley, in his 1966 doctoral thesis, spoke of "the moderate Calvinist theology" of the early leaders.[56] Yet occasionally Brethren theology was described as hyper-Calvinist. In 1881, Henry King wrote for the *Baptist Review*, "It may be said that in general the Plymouth Brethren have held to the essential articles of orthodoxy, the inspiration of the Scriptures, the depravity of man, the necessity of regeneration by the Holy Spirit, and the atonement by the sufferings and death of Christ. Indeed, they have been distinguished by an excessive orthodoxy, a Calvinism that has been hyper rather than moderate."[57]

In his work on the ecclesiology of the early Brethren, James Callahan asserts, "Evangelical and Calvinistic in soteriology, the Brethren functioned as the nagging conscience of British Christianity that, according to the Brethren, had departed from biblical fidelity in ecclesial doctrine, constitution,

---

53. Neatby, *History*, 230.

54 Rowdon, *Origins*, 227.

55. Rowdon, *Who Are the Brethren?* 35.

56. Embley, "Origins," 1. Embley further claimed: "If the Plymouth Brethren gained the majority of their earliest adherents from the established church, it is equally clear that they gained most of their doctrines and ecclesiastical practices from those sections of the church which might be generally described as Calvinistic Dissent" (27). Cf. Embley, "Early Development," 214.

57. King, "The Plymouth Brethren," 443.

and practice."[58] Callahan argues that the emerging principles of Brethren ecclesiology were "a consistent byproduct of Calvinistic soteriology."[59] In his monograph on the relationship between Darby and Newton, Jonathan Burnham concurs. He links the Brethren doctrine of separatism to "the movement's inherent strict Calvinism: as the 'elect' body of Christ, they became convinced that they should gather for worship only with those who could be likewise identified."[60]

The entry on the Brethren in the *Oxford Dictionary of the Christian Church* includes the statement: "Their teaching combines elements from Calvinism and Pietism."[61] The 1879 *Cyclopædia of Biblical, Theological, and Ecclesiastical Literature* concluded its summary of the Brethren this way: "As to the remainder of their creed, they seem to agree most with the Calvinistic system, and are said to be zealous in good works."[62] Also writing in 1879, church historian William Blackburn could say of the Brethren, "Many of them are Calvinist in theology."[63]

Other examples could be multiplied,[64] but the evidence cited above is sufficient to demonstrate that historians have recognized Calvinistic soteriology as one of the fundamental convictions of the early movement. Yet for all this recognition, no study has yet pursued this lead in evaluating the nature and scope of Calvinistic thought in the movement. What shape did Brethren Calvinism take? To what extent did the movement accept or reject elements of the Reformed tradition? Again, this book addresses these questions and endeavors to fill a gap in Brethren studies.

The fact that historians have noticed the Calvinistic tenor of early Brethren thought may appear to challenge the title of this thesis: The Doctrines of Grace in an *Unexpected* Place. Unexpected for whom? There are at least three groups that would find early Brethren Calvinism surprising: (1) Nineteenth-century Reformed critics who often assumed the movement was Arminian in its soteriological principles.[65] (2) Contemporary Reformed critics who believe the dispensationalism of Brethrenism necessarily leads

---

58. Callahan, *Primitivist Piety*, xi.

59. Ibid., 43.

60. Burnham, *Story of Conflict*, 85.

61. *ODCC*, 3rd ed., s.v. "Plymouth Brethren."

62. M'Clintock and Strong *Cyclopædia*, 8:306.

63. Blackburn, *History of the Christian Church*, 646.

64. See for example, Eaton, "Beware the Trumpet," 122; Sellers, *Nineteenth-Century Nonconformity*, 10; McDowell, "Influence," 211; Lineham, "The Significance of J. G. Deck," 15; Gundry, *Love Them In*, 142.

65. E.g., Porteous, *Brethren in the Keelhowes*, 159–61.

to Arminian soteriology.[66] (3) Contemporary Brethren who reject Calvinism and believe its doctrines to be a threat to the gospel.[67] Thus a contribution of the present study is its examination of a dimension of Brethren theology that historians have sensed was important yet to date have not analyzed, and in the process, the thesis offers historical perspective on contemporary impressions that often do not accurately reflect the thought of the early movement.

Organization and Methodology

A brief overview of the organizational structure of the book is appropriate at this point. Following a historical orientation to Calvinistic soteriology (chapters 2 and 3), chapters 4 through 7 examine Brethren thought on human depravity, election, the extent of the atonement, and saving faith and assurance. One possible approach would be to identify relevant biblical texts and analyze how Brethren interpreted those passages. Another would be to systematically examine how Brethren handled specific doctrines—for example, through the nineteenth century, what did the movement teach about reprobation? Despite the merits of this methodology, we have adopted a different approach. The soteriology of the movement on the issues listed above is scrutinized biographically; we explore the perspectives of the leading personalities of the movement, beginning with the earliest leaders and moving chronologically to important writers functioning at the close of the nineteenth century. Although the Brethren vehemently rejected the concept of clergy and had no place for the clergy/laity distinction, they nevertheless greatly esteemed gifted leaders who arose among them. Indeed, it was the teachers, preachers, writers, and evangelists who shaped the thought of the movement and gave valued counsel to individuals and local assemblies. One biographer felt inclined to justify his work as follows: "We note that the Scripture not only warrants but commands the remembrance of those whom God has given as leaders of His people [Heb 13:7]. To forget them means too often to forget the truth they brought."[68] For many years, a standard biographical work, *Chief Men among the Brethren*, offered sketches of the

---

66. E.g., Gerstner, *Wrongly Dividing*; Kimbro, *Gospel According to Dispensationalism*, 147–79; Mathison, *Dispensationalism*, 45–84. Additionally, the influential Calvinist preacher Martyn Lloyd-Jones, for example, blamed the practice of lay-preaching in the church on the Arminianism of nineteenth-century Brethrenism and Methodism. Lloyd-Jones, *Preaching*, 101.

67. E.g., Hunt, *What Love Is This?*

68. Reid, *F. W. Grant*, 14.

lives and contributions of many of the early leaders, keeping their memory alive for new generations of Brethren.[69] A number of these "chief men" took on legendary status in Brethren circles. For this reason, it appeared best to arrange the chapters around the leading personalities and writers of the movement. Tracing the thought of individual leaders across the spectrum of nineteenth-century Brethrenism will allow patterns of consistency (or inconsistency) to emerge. This in turn will enable us to determine whether or not there was a basic commonality to Brethren soteriology, and if it can be rightly designated "Calvinistic."

The aim of this book is not to consider Brethren thought in isolation, but to evaluate it against the broader context of historical theology. Accordingly, chapters 2 and 3 examine historical developments within the Calvinist tradition and highlight how the key soteriological questions were discussed (readers who are primarily interested in Brethren thought may wish to proceed directly to chapter 4). Each subsequent chapter offers a historical orientation of the issues addressed in the chapter. This approach will enable us to evaluate Brethren thought against the larger backdrop of Reformed theology. The conclusion (chapter 8) brings the various strands of thought together in order to offer final evaluation of the nature and character of nineteenth-century Brethren soteriology.

Finally, my hope in bringing this thesis to publication is that our understanding of early Brethren thought will be enhanced. But there is more. I also entertain the hope that this book will bring some much needed clarification to the anti-Calvinistic mood that pervades some groups of contemporary Brethren (and other evangelicals). These often believe that Calvinism stands for an unloving God, who forces people to sin and predestines them to hell. Under this impression they naturally view Calvinistic thought as a threat to the gospel. But this is a most unhappy caricature, as the following chapters will reveal. Yet sadly, it is one that seems to endlessly reappear in popular-level books and blogs. Perhaps the present study, which demonstrates that early Brethren advanced their own brand of Calvinistic soteriology while being lovers and proclaimers of the gospel will help to expose the straw man and produce a greater sense of unity toward those who love the doctrines of grace.

---

69. Pickering, *Chief Men*.

2

Calvinistic Soteriology: A Historical Survey

Part 1: From the Restoration through the Evangelical Revival (1660–1800)

"The doctrines of grace, in all their fullness, freeness, and particularity, were never dearer to me than now."

—Anthony Norris Groves[1]

Historical Background and Context

THROUGHOUT THE HISTORY OF the church, the relationship of God's sovereignty to human responsibility in salvation has been a topic of earnest debate. Well-known interlocutors such as Augustine and Pelagius, Gottschalk and Hincmar, Luther and Erasmus, Gomarus and Arminius, the Puritans and Laud, and Whitefield and Wesley have proven to be colorful sparring partners, giving the issues in question a measure of visibility and prominence in polemical theology. The theological shorthand describing the two opposing camps has come to be known within Protestantism as Calvinism and Arminianism. What these labels actually entail varies considerably, and a number of scholars protest the use of such terms as misleading.[2] Nevertheless, the labels have had extraordinary staying power

---

1. [Groves], *Memoir*, 250–51.
2. E.g., Muller, *Calvin*, 53–62; Stewart, *Ten Myths*, 40. In his 1855 translation of Calvin's *A Treatise on the Eternal Predestination of God*, Henry Cole wrote, "There are, in the religious world, almost as many different shades, phases, kinds and degrees, of Calvinism as there are Calvinists." Calvin, *Calvin's Calvinism*, 7.

in the English-speaking world and are embedded within the primary and secondary literature.[3]

The goal of this chapter and the next is to canvass in broad strokes the historical context of Calvinism and Calvinistic debate through the nineteenth century in order to gain perspective on the theological milieu out of which the Brethren movement emerged. The focus is not on Calvinism in the broadest sense, but on the soteriological features that were central in evangelical debate, such as the bondage or freedom of the will, predestination, the extent of the atonement, and the nature of faith. How were the issues discussed? What kinds of reaction did they provoke? Acquiring a sense of the development of these key doctrinal issues will place us in a better position to evaluate nineteenth-century Brethren thought. Each subsequent chapter will provide additional background material specific to the topic of that chapter. The goal of the present chapter is to gain a broad sense of Calvinistic soteriology in evangelical history through the eighteenth century. The next chapter will focus particularly on the nineteenth century context.

Setting the Stage: Pre-Nineteenth-Century Developments

In his landmark study, *Evangelicalism in Modern Britain*, David Bebbington argues that the early nineteenth century witnessed a renewed interest in Calvinism.[4] In order to understand this renewal it becomes necessary to survey previous developments. We trace here the theological discussion primarily in Britain, since this was the most prominent stage for the growth of the Brethren movement—particularly England, Ireland, and Scotland. Again, the goal is not to attempt exhaustive coverage of British Calvinism, but to highlight important and representative trends that illustrate the nature of Calvinistic soteriology.

The Later Seventeenth Century: The Impact of the Restoration[5]

An exploration of Calvinistic soteriology—frequently known as "the doctrines of grace"—might properly begin with the contribution of Augustine of Hippo, or perhaps John Calvin and the early Reformers. In the English

---

3. For a helpful discussion of the term "Calvinism"—with reference to both its limitations and unavoidability—see Wallace, *Shapers of English Calvinism*, 9–13.

4. Bebbington, *Evangelicalism in Modern Britain*, 77–78.

5. For a more comprehensive history of the origins, development, and spread of Calvinism see Hart, *Calvinism*, although this work does not focus on the theology of Calvinism.

context it would be useful to consider Thomas Cranmer, the Thirty-Nine Articles, or William Perkins, the English Puritans, and the Westminster Confession of Faith (WCF). Some reference to the Synod of Dort (1618–19) is important, since it was at Dort[6] that the key elements of Reformed soteriology were defined. In 1610 the followers of Jacob Arminius presented the Estates of Holland with a five-point Remonstrance arguing the Arminian position. Debate over these points eventually led to the Synod of Dort which, in addition to national religious leaders, hosted delegates from outside of the Netherlands. Thus the results of the Synod represented an international Calvinism. The Canons of the Synod of Dort provided the answer to the Arminian soteriology of the Remonstrance in five sections, or "heads of doctrine." These were: "of Divine Predestination"; "of the Death of Christ, and the Redemption of Men Thereby"; "of the Corruption of Man, His Conversion to God, and the Manner Thereof" (heads three and four are combined here); and "of the Perseverance of the Saints." Thus the so-called five points of Calvinism were born, and the issues they addressed form the heart of Calvinistic soteriology.

However, we begin our historical survey with the Restoration era, because it is here that many historians have marked the demise of Calvinism in England.[7] Traditional historiography of the post-Restoration Church of England portrays Calvinism as rapidly giving way to a more fashionable Arminianism. After the Restoration of the monarchy in 1660, and the passage of measures such as the Act of Uniformity (1662) and the subsequent exit of some two thousand Anglican ministers on St. Bartholomew's Day, Calvinism's star had fallen.[8] While Puritan worthies such as Bunyan, Flavel, and Owen continued to write, and other Nonconformists endeavored to keep Calvinism alive, the identification of Calvinism with the revolutionary movement largely discredited it on a national scale. The Puritan revolution had failed to win over the English people, and with no credible leader after Oliver Cromwell, the revolution had run its course.[9] Writing in 1950, Cragg pronounced the "eclipse" and "overthrow of Calvinism," arguing that the Restoration "drove from power the exponents of Calvinism, and by the

---

6. Dort is the typical English way of referring to the Dutch city of Dordrecht, also known as Dordt.

7. For example, Chadwick states, "With the restoration of King Charles II, the Calvinist tradition in England suffered an almost mortal blow." Chadwick, "Arminianism in England," 551. For an updated account of pre-Civil War Arminianism in England see Tyacke, *Anti-Calvinists*.

8. For a discussion of pre-Restoration theology see Letham, *Westminster Assembly*, especially chapter 3 "The English Context."

9. Cragg, *The Church*, 50.

same token it restored to positions of influence men who on the whole were favourable to Arminianism."[10]

More recent historians have demonstrated, however, that Cragg and others have overstated their case. For example, writing in 1991, John Spurr noticed, "the Church of England's strong Calvinist tradition did not die out . . . in 1662. Despite its associations with Presbyterianism, rebellion and king-killing, Calvinism retained its hold over some Restoration churchmen."[11] More recently still, Dewey Wallace, in an important study of the Calvinist tradition in Restoration England, argues that Calvinism "was far from an entirely spent force in the later seventeenth century."[12] We will return to this point shortly, but first it is important to recognize that although the traditional account may have exaggerated the demise of Calvinism, all agree that there was no shortage of hostility to Calvinism during this period. Moreover, opposition to Calvinism cannot be reduced to political and ecclesiastical unrest. Theological objections were frequently raised. Opponents claimed Calvinistic doctrines made God the author of sin, promoted fatalism, and produced antinomianism. Its strong doctrine of depravity was perceived to undercut human dignity and denigrate humankind's God-given rational powers. This was particularly grievous at a time when the appeal to reason was increasingly viewed as more noble than the narrow claims of dogmatism. Calvinism's doctrines were viewed as rigid, divisive, and dangerous. Thus Charles II gave the following directives to the archbishops for preachers: "None are in their sermons to bound the authority of sovereigns . . . nor to argue the deep points of election, reprobation, free will, etc."[13]

In the later years of the seventeenth century the frequency and force of these criticisms were not lost on a number of dissenting divines—particularly the Presbyterians—who endeavored to soften some of the perceived hard edges of Calvinism. Among them were Richard Baxter, Joseph Alleine, John Howe, and Matthew Henry.[14] It was not that Calvinism was a monolithic movement until Restoration forces caused fissures to finally emerge. There had clearly been more than one trajectory of Reformed thought in pre-Restoration British Calvinism, as debates over the order of divine

10. Cragg, *From Puritanism*, 13, 18.
11. Spurr, *Restoration Church*, 315.
12. Wallace, *Shapers of English Calvinism*, 4.
13. "Charles II—volume 61: October 1662," *Calendar of State Papers Domestic: Charles II, 1661–2* (1861), 517. Cited in Cragg, *From Puritanism*, 33.
14. For an extended study see Field, *Rigide Calvinism*. For the adaptation of the Calvinist heritage in the new climate see Wallace, *Shapers of English Calvinism*.

decrees and the extent of the atonement plainly show[15]—to say nothing of differences in ecclesiastical polity.[16] But in the new ideological context, writers like Howe were attempting to offer a *via media* between strict Calvinists (as represented by WCF) and the growing chorus of anti-Calvinist voices.[17]

Thus Calvinism found itself in a defensive posture. As David Field contends, "The rejection of Calvinism" was "the single most important feature on the theological landscape of England in the later seventeenth century."[18] The sentiment expressed by the Cambridge Platonist Henry More (1614–87) is seen as typical: "Antinomianism and Calvinism (I mean that dark Dogma about Predestination) are such horrid Errours, that they seem the badges of the Kingdome of Darknesse, rather than of the Kingdome of God."[19]

New intellectual winds were blowing, as embodied in the Cambridge Platonists and the so-called Latitudinarians. Both groups exalted reason, natural theology, and moralism over against what they perceived as the narrow dogmatism of Calvinism. John Passmore argues that "Cambridge Platonism . . . was primarily a rejection of Calvinism as being dogmatic, irrational, and therefore opposed to the true interests of both religion and morality."[20] Latitudinarianism was a term originally used of the Platonists,[21] but it took on its own identity as it moved into the eighteenth century. Spurr argues that the most obvious affinity between the Latitudinarians "was pastoral and theological, a shared distaste for the puritan doctrine of salvation

---

15. See for example Wallace, *Puritans*; Moore, *English Hypothetical Universalism*.

16. On the variegated nature of Puritanism over against popular evangelical impressions of the movement see Coffey, "Puritanism," 255–70.

17. Field, *Rigide Calvinisme*, 4–8, 18–19. Field identifies Amyraldianism, Neonomianism, opposition to antinomianism, "liberal rationalism," and reluctant dissent as the defining features of "Moderate Presbyterianism" (18–29).

18. Field, *Rigide Calvinisme*, 4.

19. Henry More, *Divine Dialogues* (1668), Dialogue IV, 68. Cited in Field, *Rigide Calvinisme*, 2–3. More viewed Calvinist doctrine as "demonic": Crocker, *Henry More*, 82. For an account of More's repudiation of Calvinism while a student at Eton see Lichtestein, *Henry More*, 3–4.

20. Edwards, *Encyclopedia of Philosophy*, 2:10. Passmore adds, "The Calvinists had conceived of God as operating in an arbitrary manner. For the Cambridge Platonists, in the sharpest possible contrast, God was essentially rational."

21. On the origins of Latitudinarianism see Spellman, *The Latitudinarians*. Spellman writes, "As seventeenth-century labels go, 'Latitudinarianism' is as broad and as problematic a term to define as 'Puritanism'" (1).

and its implications."[22] Indeed, they engaged "in a hard-fought campaign against puritan or calvinist soteriology."[23]

John Tillotson, who became Archbishop of Canterbury in 1691, provides a sample of the characteristic revulsion to perceived Puritan Calvinism, as well as illustrating the central role of reason in evaluating doctrine:

> Nothing can be admitted to be a revelation from God, which plainly contradicts his essential perfection, and, consequently, if any pretends divine revelation for this doctrine, that God hath from all eternity absolutely decreed the eternal ruin of the greatest part of mankind, without any respect to the sins and demerits of men, I am as certain that this doctrine cannot be of God, as I am that God is good and just; because this grates upon the notion that mankind have of goodness and justice. This is that which no good man would do, and therefore cannot be believed of infinite goodness . . . For every man hath greater assurance that God is good and just, than he can have of any subtle speculations about predestination and the decrees of God.[24]

The doctrine of reprobation, which Tillotson here decried, was frequently the target of criticism and caricature by Arminian opponents. It was also a cause of intramural debate among Calvinists, typically in connection with the *ordo decretorum Dei* (order of God's decrees), with supralapsarians pitted against infralapsarians. Calvin held a more rigid form of reprobation.[25] However, key Calvinist documents such as the Lambeth Articles (1595)[26] and the Westminster Confession of Faith[27] are more nuanced and

---

22. Spurr, "'Latitudinarianism,'" 69. Spurr identifies the key Restoration Latitudinarians as Simon Patrick, Edward Fowler, Joseph Glanvil, John Wilkins, John Tillotson, and Edward Stillingfleet.

23. Ibid., 76.

24. Tillotson, *Works*, 8:14–15.

25. E.g., "Election itself could not stand except as set over against reprobation . . . therefore, those whom God passes over, he condemns; and this he does for no other reason than that he wills to exclude them from the inheritance which he predestines for his own children." *Institutes* 3.23.1.

26. Article 4: "Those who are not predestinated to salvation shall be necessarily damned for their sins."

27. WCF 3:7 "The rest of mankind, God was pleased, according to the unsearchable counsel of His own will, whereby He extendeth or withholdeth mercy, as He pleaseth, for the glory of His sovereign power over His creatures, to pass by, and to ordain them to dishonour and wrath for their sin, to the praise of His glorious justice." This statement is repeated in the Savoy Declaration (1658). The London Baptist Confession (1677, 1688, 1689) revised WCF slightly but retained the essence.

include sin as a factor in reprobation (contra Tillotson).[28] The Canons of the Synod of Dort expressly reject Tillotson's version as a misrepresentation of the doctrine.[29] John Bunyan stated, "The simple act of reprobation ... is a leaving or passing by, not a cursing of the creature."[30] And while Bunyan affirmed that reprobation is not due to sin, he was careful to distinguish between reprobation and condemnation. Whereas reprobation is "a simple leaving of the creature out of the bounds of God's election," condemnation is a product of God's justice and is entirely connected to sin. "God damneth not the man because he is a man, but a sinner; and fore-appoints him to that place and state, by fore-seeing of him wicked." Despite these efforts at clarification, reprobation continued to be a sticking point in the debate.

It is true, however, that among some dissenters a more extreme form of Calvinism emerged that was characterized by a harsher view of reprobation, theoretical Antinomianism, and, by the early eighteenth century, a restriction on the free offer of the gospel.[31] Although this "hyper-Calvinism" did hold sway among some groups through Spurgeon's day and beyond,[32] it was easy for opponents like Tillotson to present the extreme version as normative Calvinism.

Tillotson's perspectives on theology, and specifically his negative view of Calvinism, represent what was fashionable in the post-Restoration

---

28. Horton claims that "Reformed orthodoxy tolerated supralapsarianism but favored infralapsarianism." Horton, *The Christian Faith*, 316.

29. See Article 15 under the first head of doctrine. The conclusion to the Canons of Dort took pains to repudiate a caricatured version of reprobation (similar to Tillotson's statement above). The misrepresentation of the Reformed position was articulated as follows:

> That the doctrine of the Reformed churches concerning predestination, and the points annexed to it, by its own genius and necessary tendency ... teaches that God, by a mere arbitrary act of His will, without the least respect or view to any sin, has predestinated the greatest part of the world to eternal damnation; and has created them for this very purpose; that in the same manner in which the election is the fountain and the cause of faith and good works, reprobation is the cause of unbelief and impiety; that many children of the faithful are torn guiltless from their mothers' breasts and tyrannically plunged into hell; so that neither baptism nor the prayers of the Church at their baptism, can at all profit by them.

Dort viewed the above statement as a gross misrepresentation and renounced it in the following words: "and many other things of the same kind which the Reformed Churches not only do not acknowledge, but even detest with their whole soul."

30. Bunyan, *Works*, 2:338.

31. See Toon, *Emergence of Hyper-Calvinism*.

32. See Murray, *Spurgeon v. Hyper-Calvinism*.

church.³³ In fact, it has been argued that beginning in the Restoration era, the whole tenor of Anglican theology moved away from its roots. Chadwick contends,

> It has not always been realized sufficiently how since 1662 the Calvinist or Evangelical tradition has labored in England under the imputation of being not quite an authentic version of the Anglican faith and polity. And in the realm of theology it may be said that increasingly such doctrines as justification by faith alone, the doctrine of assurance, the doctrine of predestination, the doctrine that the elect cannot finally fall from grace, labored under great difficulties and slowly became the beliefs of the minority of convinced persons within the Church of England rather than a common or official exposition of the articles of religion laid down in the reign of Queen Elizabeth.³⁴

As the eighteenth century approached, historians have understood Calvinism to be eclipsed as the Age of Reason dawned. Yet once again Cragg did not account for all the evidence when he concluded of the early eighteenth-century situation: "seldom has a reversal of fortune been so complete. Within fifty years Calvinism in England fell from a position of immense authority to obscurity and insignificance."³⁵ Gordon Rupp did not see the situation as being quite so drastic. While he acknowledged that Calvinist theology continued among dissenters,³⁶ he also surmised that there must have been "a persistence of Calvinism within the Church of England, whose descendants would emerge in the eighteenth century as the non-Wesleyan, anti-Arminian, Calvinist wing of the Evangelical Revival."³⁷ Historians must have "underestimated" the Anglo-Calvinist tradition.³⁸

---

33. The Evangelical Revival challenged the fashionable religion of the time. George Whitefield could say "Archbishop Tillotson knew no more about true Christianity than Mahomet." Whitefield claims the expression was originally uttered by John Wesley in private. Tyerman, *Life of the Rev. George Whitefield*, 1:360–61.

34. Chadwick, "Arminianism in England," 552.

35. Cragg, *From Puritanism*, 30.

36. For more on Calvinistic thought in its various forms among Restoration Dissenters see Wallace, *Shapers of English Calvinism* and Field, *Rigide Calvinisme*. The most outstanding spokesmen of orthodox Calvinism among dissenters was John Owen, although he died in 1683. On Owen in his historical and theological context see Gribben, *John Owen*, and Trueman, *The Claims of Truth*. For a summary of Calvinist-Arminian interaction among Nonconformists during this period see Sell, *Great Debate*, 27–43.

37. Rupp, *Religion in England*, 111.

38. Ibid., 326.

Bebbington concedes the plausibility of such a theory but concludes "there is scant evidence for so inherently likely a hypothesis."[39]

Rupp's instincts, however, were correct. Recent ground-breaking research by Stephen Hampton has revealed that there is in fact evidence to demonstrate more continuity with Calvinism within the Church of England than historians have previously recognized.[40] Hampton compiles an impressive assortment of scholars and churchmen who maintained a Calvinistic soteriology and held positions of influence in the post-Restoration Church of England.[41] Thus he contends, "the Reformed theological tradition remained a potent force within post-Restoration Anglicanism."[42]

This is not the place to chronicle Hampton's findings at length. Suffice it to say that contrary to the assumptions of many historians, the Reformed tradition was not dead but indeed lived on.[43] It is true that Arminian theology had become the majority position and garnered powerful support within the Church of England. It is also true that anti-Calvinist sentiment was not in short supply—"in certain quarters, Reformed theology evoked quite visceral hostility."[44] Nevertheless, as Hampton maintains,

> Despite the active opposition of several primates, despite the increasing influence of systematic Arminian thinking, despite its polemically disadvantageous associations with lawlessness, rebellion, and regicide, the Reformed tradition retained a significant level of support within the Church of England well into the eighteenth century. It still provoked hostility in certain quarters, but that is precisely because it remained a compelling and credible alternative to the majority view.[45]

One important conclusion from Hampton's work is that the Evangelical Revival of the eighteenth century should not be viewed as the recovery of an abandoned Reformed soteriology.[46] Indeed, this makes the Calvinistic character of a significant part of the Revival more intelligible.

---

39. Bebbington, *Evangelicalism in Modern Britain*, 36.
40. Hampton, *Anti-Arminians*.
41. Ibid., 10–22.
42. Ibid., 22.
43. Hampton's work has been positively reviewed in a number of journals, including *CH* 78:3 (2009) 689–91; *CTJ* 45:2 (2010) 390–93; *Fides et Historia* 42:2 (2010) 83–85; *Journal of Anglican Studies* 9:1 (2011) 120–21; *Journal of Ecclesiastical History* 61:4 (2010) 864–65; *WTJ* 71:2 (2009) 511–13.
44. Hampton, *Anti-Arminians*, 28.
45. Ibid., 274.
46. Ibid., 272.

Eighteenth-Century Developments: The Early Decades

As Hampton has demonstrated, there were important voices advocating a broadly Reformed theology within the Established Church in the early years of the eighteenth century.[47] Further evidence that Calvinism[48] was not dead is found in the fact that it continued to receive polemical attention. The most significant attack came from the pen of Daniel Whitby (1637/8–1726),[49] particularly in his book *A Discourse Concerning the True Import of the Words Election and Reprobation* (1710). This work, sometimes known under the title *Discourse on the Five Points*, was "considered by some the definitive critique of Calvinist thought."[50] The book addresses the following subjects: (1) election and reprobation; (2) the extent of Christ's redemption; (3) sufficient and effectual, common and special grace; (4) the freedom of the will of man; and (5) the perseverance of saints.[51]

Whitby's book responded to perhaps the most vigorous defender of traditional Calvinistic soteriology of the time, John Edwards (1637–1716).[52] Edwards, for his part, was responding to Whitby's denial of original sin (which was more Pelagian than Arminian) and unconditional election found in his *Paraphrase and Commentary on the New Testament* (1700–1703).[53] In 1707 Edwards published *Veritas Redux*, which defended the points of Calvinism. The title page of the book read: "*Veritas Redux: Evangelical Truths Restored namely those concerning God's eternal decrees; the liberty of men's will; grace and conversion; the extent and efficacy of Christ's redemption, and perseverance in grace.*" The work was abbreviated in 1715 under the title

---

47. For example, Oxford elected a Reformed theologian, William Delaune (1659–1728), to its Lady Margaret chair of Divinity in 1715. Delaune could still expound a Calvinistic version of the divine decrees in a collection of sermons published in 1728. Hampton, *Anti-Arminians*, 266–69.

48. Stewart qualifies the use of the term "Calvinism" as follows: "any discussion regarding the influence of Calvinist theology in eighteenth-century England must reckon with the fact that the use of such a term may not be understood to imply a predominance of the Genevan reformer's own distinctive thought. 'Calvinist theology' had become a generic term descriptive of all European Protestant theology emanating from the South German and Swiss Reformation." Stewart, *Restoring the Reformation*, 10.

49. *ODNB*, s.n. "Daniel Whitby," speaks of Whitby's "extreme Arminianism" which "engaged him in a violent controversy with both John and Jonathan Edwards."

50. *BDE*, s.n. "John Gill."

51. Whitby, *Discourse*.

52. For more on the significance of the Edwards-Whitby debate see Stewart, "Strange Reemergence." Hampton labels Edwards "one of the most productive Reformed authors of the post-Restoration Church." *Anti-Arminians*, 21. Edwards receives a chapter-length treatment in Wallace, *Shapers of English Calvinism*, 205–42.

53. Stewart, "Strange Reemergence," 3–4.

The Scripture Doctrine of the Five Points. Its impact was still felt in 1740, when George Whitefield, in a letter responding to John Wesley's anti-Calvinist sermon "Free Grace," commended *Veritas Redux* as "unanswerable."[54] But Whitby's work also made its impact, attracting responses from such eighteenth-century luminaries as the Baptist minister and theologian John Gill, and in America, Jonathan Edwards in his *Freedom of the Will* (1754).[55] Whitby was still being drawn upon in the nineteenth century by Bishop Tomline in his *Refutation of Calvinism* (1811), and Whitby's discourse against the five points of Calvinism was enthusiastically reprinted by James Nichols in 1817.[56]

To get a sense of the impact of Whitby's polemic against Calvinism, it is worth noting Gill's account of his decision to respond to Whitby. In the preface to a revised edition of his *The Cause of God and Truth*, Gill wrote:

> It should be known by the reader, that the following work was undertaken and begun about the year 1733 or 1734, at which time *Dr. Whitby's Discourse on the Five Points* was reprinting, judged to be a masterpiece on the subject, in the English tongue, and accounted as an unanswerable one; and it was almost in the mouth of every one, as an objection to the Calvinists, Why do not ye answer Dr. Whitby? Induced hereby, I determined to give it another reading, and found myself inclined to answer it, and thought this was a very proper and seasonable time to engage in such a work.[57]

Even allowing for overstatement on Gill's part, it is clear that the Calvinist-Arminian debate was not dead. *The Cause of God and Truth* would become one of Gill's best-known writings. Timothy George says, "The

---

54. The letter is reprinted in Dallimore, *George Whitefield*, 2:549–69.

55. For a helpful discussion of Whitby and Edwards's response, see Paul Ramsey's introduction to Edwards, *Freedom of the Will*, 81–89.

56. As an ardent Arminian Nichols could assert, "It is no inconsiderable honour to the Established Church, and must prove a high gratification to every true member of her, to know, that the best defenders of the truths of God against the assumptions of Calvinism, have been clergymen in communion with her." Nichols celebrated the paucity of Anglican Calvinist defenders in his day: "It is also greatly to the credit of our national establishment, that she has of late years produced no writers of eminence in favour of pure Calvinism. Toplady, Hervey, and Scott, (to omit the mention of a few others of inferior note,) are the only clergymen who have, in modern times, distinguished themselves by their attempts in its defence." Editor's "Advertisement" in Whitby, *Discourse*, 5–6.

57. Gill, *Cause of God*, iv.

Gill-Whitby exchange was widely discussed and deserves to be counted among the classic debates on the doctrine of election."[58]

The Marrow Controversy in Scotland

The history of Calvinism in Scotland is a story all of its own, but we cannot trace all those contours here.[59] A few highlights must suffice. By the first quarter of the eighteenth century—even though the Westminster Confession and Catechisms were the doctrinal standards of the Church of Scotland—a number of Scottish ministers were concerned that the Kirk had strayed from authentic Reformed teaching. On the one hand, tendencies toward legalism and hyper-Calvinism had developed, and on the other, inroads of Enlightenment thinking and even Arminianism were emerging.[60] Thus the so-called Marrow Controversy (1718–23) may be viewed as an attempt by an outspoken minority—the "Marrow men"—to reclaim the purity of the gospel.[61]

The controversy began in 1718 in response to the republication of *The Marrow of Modern Divinity*,[62] written by Edward Fisher in 1645. By 1719 a formal complaint against the book's contents was brought to the General Assembly. In 1720 the Assembly issued an Act condemning the book and forbidding ministers to endorse or promote it. This decision was appealed by supporters of *The Marrow*, who believed that by the Assembly's Act, "gospel truth has suffered, and it is likely will suffer more in the rising and succeeding generations, unless a remedy be timely provided."[63] Nevertheless, the Assembly reaffirmed its original decision in 1722. The controversy continued for several years and eventually contributed to the secession movement in the 1730s.[64]

Three key theological issues stood at the forefront of the controversy: the extent of the atonement, the gospel offer, and saving faith and assurance.

58. *BDE*, s.n. "John Gill."

59. For general theological surveys see (from a Confessional perspective) Macleod, *Scottish Theology*, and (from a Barthian perspective) Torrance, *Scottish Theology*.

60. VanDoodewaard, *The Marrow Controversy*, 22–24; Hart, *Calvinism*, 144–53.

61. Defenders of *The Marrow of Modern Divinity* included ministers such as James Hog (c.1658–1734); Thomas Boston (1676–1732); Ebenezer Erskine (1680–1754) and his younger brother Ralph Erskine (1686–1752), along with others. For an account of the contemporary significance of the Marrow Controversy see Ferguson, *The Whole Christ*.

62. Hereafter *The Marrow*.

63. Cited in VanDoodewaard, *The Marrow Controversy*, 59–60.

64. For the role of Marrow theology in the Secession churches see ibid., 113–274.

In regard to the atonement, the Assembly charged *The Marrow* with teaching "universal atonement and pardon." In response, the defenders of *The Marrow* argued the book reflected the biblical teaching that there is warrant for offering Christ to all and warrant for all to receive Christ, even though the application of redemption is effective only for the elect.[65] "Thus, the argument for a full and free gospel offer was presented in harmony with, and holding to, the doctrine of particular atonement."[66] By this point in the eighteenth century, there was a tendency among Church of Scotland ministers toward a conditional gospel offer—that is, the offer of salvation in Christ should only be given to those who evidenced some mark of election, such as conviction of sin, repentance, or concern for holiness. Some feared that an unconditional free offer of the gospel rested on universal atonement and would encourage antinomianism.[67] Again, the Marrow men defended the free offer of the gospel while upholding particular atonement. Indeed, "a relentless emphasis on the free offer of the gospel" became a mark of Marrow preachers like Thomas Boston.[68]

On the nature of faith, the Church of Scotland Assembly objected that *The Marrow* had made assurance the essence of saving faith, in departure from the Westminster Confession and Catechisms.[69] The Assembly maintained "a true believer is not at all times, even when he is acting in faith unto salvation, assured of his present being in a state of grace, and that he shall be saved; but that he may wait long to obtain this assurance."[70] In response, the Marrow men made a distinction between two aspects of assurance. The assurance of faith (*fiducia*) amounted to confidence in Christ and the gospel to save. All believers possess this assurance to some degree, and on this the Reformers, the Westminster standards, and *The Marrow* were all in essential agreement. A second aspect of assurance relates to the internal persuasion that one is truly saved. Defenders of *The Marrow* conceded that this

---

65. One of the controversial phrases from *The Marrow* was the following: "Go and tell every man, without exception, that here is good news for him; Christ is dead for him." This expression was taken from John Preston (1587–1628). While Thomas Boston argued that the expression was compatible with particular redemption, Jonathan Moore has demonstrated that Boston was mistaken, and the phrase was part of Preston's hypothetical universalism. Moore, *English Hypothetical Universalism*, 116–24.

66. VanDoodewaard, *The Marrow Controversy*, 60.

67. Ibid., 35.

68. Ryken, *Thomas Boston*, 306. Cf. Lachman, *The Marrow Controversy*, 135–36, and Murray, "The Marrow Controversy," 34–56.

69. It is worth noting that Joseph Caryl (1602–73), a member of the Westminster Assembly of Divines, wrote the original commendatory preface to *The Marrow*.

70. VanDoodewaard, *The Marrow Controversy*, 33.

assurance was not essential to saving faith and was held in varying degrees, often on the basis of evidences of grace within the life of a believer.[71]

All these issues continued to be matters of debate down to nineteenth-century Brethren discussion. In fact, as will be explored in later chapters, Brethren often distanced themselves from the Reformed tradition partly because they discerned a tendency in it to restrict the gospel offer and to base assurance on human works rather than on the work of Christ.

Calvinism in Eighteenth-Century Dissent

A spectrum of theological belief existed within eighteenth-century dissent which is often broken down by historians into at least two general categories. On the one hand, there was the progressive or liberal wing that imbibed Enlightenment ideals and rejected Calvinist doctrines. Many Presbyterians, once champions of Reformed theology, went in this direction, advancing anti-Trinitarian views that eventually led them to Unitarianism.[72] A number of General Baptists who had from their inception rejected Calvinism also followed the path to Unitarianism.[73] The conservative Presbyterians often turned to Calvinist Congregationalism.[74] The second category was the more conservative wing, populated by Congregationalists and Particular Baptists. These groups continued to maintain orthodox Trinitarianism and Calvinist teaching. Within this camp, however, there was a wide range of Calvinist thought.

In 1689 the Particular Baptists adopted a confession of faith—sometimes called the Second London Confession—which essentially was "a Baptist adaptation of the *Savoy Declaration* drawn up by the Independents in 1658, which in turn was a slightly edited revision of the *Westminster Confession* of 1647."[75] The Confession clarified that, unlike the General Baptists, Particular Baptists were Calvinists. In the eighteenth century, however, there was movement beyond the 1689 Confession to a more extreme form of Calvinism, later called hyper-Calvinism.[76] Essentially, hyper-Calvinism

---

71. Ibid., 65.

72. Watts, *The Dissenters*, 371–82; 464–71. Watts notes of the Presbyterians "that the process by which many meetings passed from Calvinism through Arminianism to Unitarianism was one of slow evolution, not revolution, and that although the development had begun well before 1730, the outcome was by no means obvious by that date" (381).

73. Hayden, *English Baptist History*, 45–54.

74. Rupp, *Religion in England*, 108; Watts, *The Dissenters*, 467–68.

75. Oliver, *History*, xviii.

76. Roger Hayden has argued that an evangelical Calvinism continued among

maintained that since God did not choose all and Christ did not die for all, preachers should not offer the gospel to all. To urge the non-elect to repent and trust Christ implied that the sinner had the ability to contribute to his or her salvation, as in Arminianism. These notions were first advanced by the Congregational minister Joseph Hussey in his 1707 publication of *God's Operations of Grace but No Offers of His Grace*.[77] Hussey's hyper-Calvinism was mediated to the Particular Baptists through one of his converts, John Skepp (1675–1721). Skepp, a London pastor, influenced fellow Baptist ministers John Gill (1697–1771) and John Brine (1703–65). Hyper-Calvinism prevailed among Particular Baptists for much of the eighteenth century,[78] largely through the influence of Brine, and especially the prolific Gill.[79] Toward the end of the century, however, hyper-Calvinism was challenged from within by a number of younger Particular Baptist ministers, most significantly, Andrew Fuller (1754–1815).[80] Fuller's advocacy of an evangelical Calvinism vis-à-vis hyper-Calvinism deserves further treatment, and we will return to it shortly.

Congregationalists (or "Independents," as they were also called[81]) generally maintained Calvinist doctrines in the eighteenth century,[82] although a moderate Calvinist position, sometimes called "Baxterian," developed among some—most notably the Independent minister Philip Doddridge (1702–51).[83] Doddridge is often presented as a bridge-builder between rigid Calvinism and the heterodox wing of Dissent. This notion has been challenged in a recent doctoral thesis by Robert Strivens, who argues that "Doddridge was not a bridge between two wings of English Dissent"

---

the Particular Baptists connected with Bristol Academy that was devoid of the hyper-Calvinism of London ministers John Gill and John Brine. However, as Oliver points out, Hayden downplays the significant influence of Gill and Brine outside the London area. Oliver, *History*, xix. See Hayden, *Continuity and Change*.

77. For more on Hussey see Toon, *Emergence of Hyper-Calvinism*, 70–85.

78. Morden, *Offering Christ*, 15–16.

79. "Towards the end of the eighteenth century most Particular Baptists had come to accept Gill's works as the final word on orthodox interpretations of Scripture. He produced an entire theological library which became standard reading material for the constituency." Naylor, *Picking up a Pin*, 147.

80. Others in Fuller's circle included John Ryland, Jr. (1753–1825), John Sutcliff (1752–1814), Robert Hall, Jr. (1764–1831). For the friendship and influence of Ryland and Sutcliff with Fuller see Morden, *Offering Christ*, 38–40.

81. However, Watts views Congregationalism as only one branch of Independency. See Watts, *The Dissenters*, 94–99.

82. Rupp, *Religion in England*, 127; Watts, *The Dissenters*, 376–79.

83. See especially Strivens, "Thought of Philip Doddridge," 80–111, and Muller, "Philip Doddridge," 65–84.

but a leader among those who "focused on central evangelical doctrines and heart religion."[84] Doddridge's moderate Calvinism has been variously described[85] but clearly stands within the Calvinist tradition,[86] even though it stood against mandatory subscription to standards such as the Thirty-Nine Articles or the Westminster Confession.[87] In sentiments remarkably similar to those championed by the later Brethren movement, Doddridge expressed his disapproval of those who harbored an "unhappy attachment to human phrases," desiring instead that "all the *party-names*, and *unscriptural phrases* and *forms*, which have divided the *Christian world*, were forgot."[88] Several theological issues were associated with this moderate Calvinism, such as a more optimistic view of the "salvability of the heathen," the rejection of unconditional reprobation (although this was true of many confessional Calvinists as well), clear opposition to any form of antinomianism, and a concern to emphasize that Christ died, in some sense, for all, even if particularly for the elect.[89]

In contrast, Arminianism was maintained among the General Baptists and, of course, Wesleyan Methodists, although it was not until the later part of the eighteenth century that Wesley's chapels were registered as dissenting meeting houses.[90] Many General Baptists moved toward Unitarianism, but some remained evangelical and were strengthened by the Evangelical Revival, to which we now turn.[91]

The Evangelical Revival

David Bebbington has argued that the evangelical movement in Britain was born out of the Revival which began in the 1730s.[92] While Bebbington's thesis has been challenged at various points,[93] the Revival unquestionably shaped evangelicalism—including its doctrinal emphases and debate. This

---

84. Strivens, "Thought of Philip Doddridge," 225–26. Strivens's thesis has now been published in the Ashgate Studies in Evangelicalism series (2015), however I am quoting from the original thesis.
85. See ibid., 80–81 and the literature cited there.
86. Muller, "Philip Doddridge," 83.
87. Strivens, "Thought of Philip Doddridge," 89.
88. Cited in ibid., 92.
89. Ibid., 89–111.
90. *NIDCC*, 653.
91. Hayden, *English Baptist History*, 51.
92. Bebbington, *Evangelicalism in Modern Britain*.
93. See the collection of essays in Haykin and Stewart, *Advent of Evangelicalism*.

is particularly true in regard to soteriology; after all, evangelicals were inexorably linked to the *evangel*, the gospel itself. Thus it is no surprise that the Calvinism-Arminian debate moved into center stage during the time of the Evangelical Revival.

The history of the Evangelical Revival is well served. Our purpose here is not to recount the broad contours of the Revival but to focus more narrowly on the Calvinism-Arminian debate. The story here begins in Wales with the preaching of Daniel Rowland (1713–90) and Howel Harris (1714–73). Sell claims that the reason "Wales did not suffer a drastic and widespread polarisation of antinomian-Arminian views is owing to the emergence of that missionary-minded brand of Calvinism"[94] pioneered by Rowland and Harris, which resulted in Welsh Calvinistic Methodism.[95]

When tensions began to rise in 1739 between Wesley and Whitefield over predestination, Harris sought to maintain a measure of peace, but not at the expense of his Calvinist convictions. In 1740 he wrote to John Cennick, a Methodist lay preacher who embraced Calvinism and would be expelled by Wesley for it in 1741.[96] The letter reveals that for Harris, the gospel was at stake in this debate. He wrote:

> I have been long waiting to see if Brother *John* and *Charles* should receive farther Light, or be silent, and not *oppose Election* and *Perseverance*; but finding no Hope thereof, I begin to be stagger'd about them what to do. I plainly see that we preach two Gospels, one sets *all on God*, the other *on Man*; the one on *God's Will*, the other on *Man's Will*; the one on *God's chusing*, the other on *Man's chusing*; the one on *God's Distinguishing Love, making one to differ from another*; the other on *Man's being better than another, and taking more pains, and being a better husband of his Grace than another, more* passive *under the Hand of the Spirit than another*; and if both shou'd come to Heaven they cou'd not harmonise in Praises.[97]

Whitefield and Wesley

While Rowland and Harris in Wales were important voices in shaping the Calvinistic stream of the Revival, it was the international prominence of

---

94. Sell, *Great Debate*, 59.

95. See Jones and Jones, *Calvinistic Methodist Fathers*. Originally published in Welsh as *Y Tadau Methodistaidd*, vol. 1, 1890; vol. 2, 1897.

96. *BDEB*, s.n. "John Cennick."

97. Cited by Sell, *Great Debate*, 61–62.

George Whitefield and John Wesley that thrust the Calvinism-Arminianism debate into the spotlight. In order to appreciate the central doctrinal issues in the debate, we must look in some detail at the Whitefield-Wesley exchange.

The split between the two preachers over the doctrines of grace is well known.[98] The breach began in 1739 when Wesley preached a sermon against predestination entitled "Free Grace."[99] In the sermon, Wesley declared predestination "is a doctrine full of blasphemy" and spoke of "the horrible blasphemies contained in this horrible doctrine." He argued that predestination "represents the most holy God as worse than the devil, as both more false, more cruel, and more unjust."[100]

Wesley published the sermon and it received wide circulation in both England and America.[101] The tone, rhetoric, and misrepresentation of his opponents' position[102] ensured that Wesley's sermon would spark heated controversy—and indeed it did! In a letter to Wesley, Whitefield observed, "I find your sermon has had its expected success; it has set the nation a-disputing; you will have enough to do now to answer pamphlets."[103]

The controversy that ensued shaped the theological discussion for evangelicals throughout the British Isles and the American colonies.[104] Luke Tyerman wrote, "The difference between Wesley and Whitefield was really one of the greatest events in the history of Wesley and even of the religion of the age."[105] More recently scholarship has not differed substantially from

---

98. "The doctrines of grace" was and still is a common way of describing Calvinistic soteriology. Dallimore says of Whitefield: "Though he sometimes used the word *Calvinism*, he did not give great place to it. He made much more of the fact that the views he held were those he had discovered in the Bible and he more frequently referred to them as the *doctrines of grace*." Dallimore, *George Whitefield*, 1:409.

99. The sermon may be found, among other places, in Wesley, *Works*, 7:371–86. Tyerman said "Free Grace" "in some respects, was the most important sermon that he ever issued." Tyerman, *Life and Times of the Rev. John Wesley*, 1:317.

100. Ibid., 381–82. Coppedge suggests that Wesley, with his strong denunciations of reprobation, was reacting to hyper-Calvinism represented by the writings of John Gill. See Coppedge, *John Wesley*, 48–49.

101. Dallimore, *George Whitefield*, 1:579.

102. Whitefield lamented the Wesleys "dressing up the doctrine of Election in such horrible colours." Whitefield, *Letters*, 256.

103. Ibid., 212.

104. For a summary of the Calvinistic controversy among Irish evangelicals, see Whelan, *Bible War in Ireland*, 11–13. See also Hempton and Hill, *Evangelical Protestantism*, 15–16.

105. Tyerman, *Life and Times of the Rev. John Wesley*, 317.

this assessment. Henry Rack, for example, has argued that the split over predestination "was of great significance in the history of the Revival."[106]

John Wesley was joined by his brother Charles in the campaign against predestination. A correspondent of Howell Harris reported: "Mr. Charles goes on in the most strong manner, constantly railing at either the Predestinarians or the Moravians."[107] John Cennick spoke of dining with Charles Wesley on one occasion when Wesley "began to dispute about election." Cennick reported that Wesley "fell into a violent passion and affrighted all at the table, and rising from the table, he said he would go directly and preach against me, and accordingly did. He called Calvin the first-born son of the Devil and set all his people into a bitter hatred of me."[108]

These statements illustrate not only the intensity of the controversy, but also the fact that the primary issues were soteriological in nature, especially "the doctrines of election and final perseverance."[109] In a letter to Wesley dated August 25, 1740, Whitefield said, "Only give me leave, with all humility to exhort you not be strenuous in opposing the doctrines of election and final perseverance." Whitefield went on to add, "Perhaps the doctrines of election and of final perseverance hath been abused (and what doctrine has not,) but notwithstanding, it is children's bread, and ought not in my opinion to be with-held from them, supposing it is always mentioned with proper cautions against the abuse."[110]

Another related point of contention was the extent of the atonement. Wesley held to universal redemption; Whitefield, to particular redemption. In response to Wesley's assertion that the doctrine of election was blasphemy, Whitefield wrote, "Judge whether it is not a greater blasphemy to say, 'Christ died for souls now in hell.'"[111] Wesley was concerned that the doctrines of election and particular redemption undercut the universal offer of the gospel. This, however, Whitefield strenuously denied. He wrote to Wesley, "Though I hold to particular election, yet I offer Jesus freely to every individual soul."[112]

---

106. Rack, *Reasonable Enthusiast*, 199.

107. Cited in Dallimore, *George Whitefield*, 2:70.

108. Ibid., citing *The Moravian Messenger*, Vol. XVI.

109. See for example Whitefield, *Letters*, 101, 140, 182, 206, 212; Whitefield, *Works*, 4:58.

110. Whitefield, *Letters*, 204–5.

111. Ibid., 212. See also Whitefield's comments in his official reply to Wesley's sermon, "A Letter to the Rev. Mr. John Wesley in Answer to His Sermon Entitled 'Free Grace.'" The entire piece is reprinted in Dallimore, *George Whitefield*, 2:549–69. On the issue of the design of the atonement see especially p. 568.

112. Whitefield, *Letters*, 331.

Wesley's main objection to the Calvinistic scheme was the doctrine of reprobation. He believed "the implication of reprobation lurked within every aspect of Calvinism."[113] He declared, "Unconditional election I cannot believe . . . because it necessarily implies unconditional reprobation," which is "utterly irreconcilable to the whole scope and tenor both of the Old and New Testament."[114] Indeed, Wesley considered unconditional reprobation to be "that millstone which hangs about the neck" of Calvinistic soteriology.[115] Whitefield perceived that reprobation was the root issue for Wesley, but only because Wesley did not understood the doctrine properly. Whitefield wrote, "You will not own election because you cannot own it without believing the doctrine of *Reprobation*. What then is there in reprobation so horrid? I see no blasphemy in holding that doctrine, if rightly explained. If God might have passed by all, He may pass by some."[116] However, Whitefield was willing to be silent on the issue in the interests of maintaining peace. He wrote to Wesley in September 1747, "As for *universal redemption*, if we omit on each side the talking for or against reprobation . . . and agree as we already do in giving an universal offer to all poor sinners that will come and taste of the water of life, I think we may manage very well."[117]

The impact of this controversy was monumental, putting a permanent stamp on the theological spectrum of evangelicalism. Mark Noll asserts that George Whitefield's response to Wesley's sermon against predestination "inaugurated the most enduring theological conflict among evangelicals, the conflict between Arminian and Calvinist interpretations of Scripture on the nature, motive powers and implications of salvation."[118] Noll later reiterates, "For doctrinal controversy nothing in the eighteenth century was as important, or has survived over the centuries since with more force, than the questions about personal salvation that are usually described as pitting Calvinists against Arminians."[119]

The trans-denominational and international prominence of both Whitefield and Wesley during the years of the Evangelical Revival brought the Arminian-Calvinism debate into sharp focus for evangelicals. More than that, it defined the concept of Calvinism around soteriological

---

113. Nettles, "John Wesley's Contention," 2:314.
114. "Predestination Calmly Considered," in Wesley, *Works*, 10:210–11.
115. Ibid., 10:255.
116. Whitefield, *Letters*, 212.
117. Cited in Dallimore, *George Whitefield*, 2:239.
118. Noll, *Rise of Evangelicalism*, 122.
119. Ibid., 268. Cf. McInelly, *Textual Warfare*, 180–212.

doctrines like predestination, free will, the design of the atonement, and final perseverance.

Augustus M. Toplady

Even before Whitefield's death in 1770, the controversy over Calvinism and Arminianism was kept alive in a rather vitriolic manner between Wesley and the Anglican minister Augustus Toplady (1740–78).[120] Toplady is sometimes viewed as the principal champion of Calvinism following the death of Whitefield.[121] In response to Wesley's Arminianism, Toplady was determined to defend the Calvinistic character of Anglicanism. Paul Helm says Toplady "became a fierce and unrelenting critic of John Wesley's intention to advance Arminianism as a legitimate theological position into the Church of England. Indeed," Helm states, "his interest in Wesley borders on the obsessive. It might even have *been* obsessive."[122]

In 1769 Toplady published *The Church of England Vindicated from the Charge of Arminianism* in which he "set out five principles—original sin, election, particular redemption, effectual calling, and final perseverance—as characteristics of Calvinism and illustrated them from the Liturgy and articles."[123] In 1774 Toplady published *Historic Proof of the Doctrinal Calvinism of the Church of England,* which was directed largely against Wesley and his followers. Helm summarizes Toplady's Calvinism as follows:

> He called it "doctrinal Calvinism" to indicate that it was distinct from the polity of the various denominations in which Calvinists were found, himself holding tenaciously to the polity of the Church of England. Such Calvinism was, in essence, the soteriology of Calvin . . . as it had been affected by the Arminian conflict and the Puritan movement in England. The themes of the bondage of the will to sin, free and unmerited election, the particular or definite character of Christ's atonement, the

---

120. For a helpful discussion of the Calvinist controversy in the 1770s see Rack, *Reasonable Enthusiast,* 450–70.

121. E.g., *ODNB,* s.n. "Sir Richard Hill."

122. Helm, "Calvin, A. M. Toplady," 214. Nettles says, "The exchanges with Toplady produced some of the most remarkable outrage in the history of controversial literature." Nettles, "John Wesley's Contention," 2:311.

123. *BDEB,* s.n. "Augustus Montague Toplady." Toplady drew particular attention to the Synod of Dort claiming, "Of all the councils that ever sat since the apostles' days, this was, perhaps, taking every thing into the account, by far the most respectable." Toplady, *Works,* 633.

imputation of Christ's righteousness, the effectual call by grace and the grace of perseverance in the faith were prominent.[124]

Thus Toplady's Calvinism was primarily focused on soteriology, and most evangelicals would have employed the term "Calvinism" in reference to the doctrines in Helm's list.

Toplady is significant for defending a strong form of Calvinism within the Church of England at a time when Calvinism generally remained unfashionable within the Establishment and was viewed as one of the peculiarities of dissenters. Although he is sometimes perceived to be the lone Calvinist voice in the Church of England, this overstates the case. There were other important advocates of Calvinism—usually much more irenic (and often more moderate) than Toplady—such as James Hervey (1714–58), William Romaine (1714–95), John Newton (1725–1807), Thomas Haweis (1734?–1820), Rowland Hill (1744–1833), and Henry Venn (1724–1797). Anglican clergyman John Fletcher (bap. 1729–85) kept up polemics on the Arminian side, producing two works responding to Toplady in 1776–77.[125]

Later Eighteenth-Century Developments: Andrew Fuller and "Hyper-Calvinism"

The nature of the gospel offer is another important factor in understanding the shape of evangelical Calvinism. This issue came into focus through Andrew Fuller's conflict with hyper-Calvinism. Fuller (1754–1815) was a Particular Baptist minister and theologian whose writings had a profound impact on nineteenth-century evangelicalism and missiology.[126]

In the memoir published by his son, Fuller recounted a conversation with three clergymen on the topic of the "different shades of Calvinism" in the latter half of the eighteenth century. He stated, "There are three by which we commonly describe; namely the *high*, the *moderate*, and the *strict* Calvinists." He then explained that the *high* are "more Calvinistic than Calvin himself." The *moderate* is "one that is a half Arminian, or as they are called with us, Baxterians," and the *strict*, "one that really holds the system of Calvin." Fuller went on to add, "I do not believe every thing that Calvin

---

124. Helm, "Calvin, A. M. Toplady," 216–17.

125. For the responses to Toplady as well as a defense of Wesleyan doctrine see Fletcher, *Works*.

126. See especially Morden, *Offering Christ*.

taught, nor any thing because he taught it; but I reckon strict Calvinism to be my own system."[127]

Ian Shaw, in his monograph on the activity of high Calvinists in the nineteenth century, says Fuller's categories "provide a helpful summary of the range of Calvinist positions found in Britain at the turn of the nineteenth century."[128] The terminology, however, is not uniform. The label "hyper-Calvinism" was not used until the nineteenth century; "high Calvinism" was more standard in eighteenth-century usage. Nevertheless, because "high" Calvinism could also refer to supralapsarianism without attachment to the aberrations later dubbed "hyper," it seems best to retain the term hyper-Calvinism to describe what Fuller was rejecting.[129] Furthermore, Fuller himself used the term "hyper-Calvinism" in the nineteenth century. He wrote of "the Hyper-Calvinists, who set aside the invitations of the gospel to the unregenerate."[130]

The controversy with hyper-Calvinism—which Fuller sometimes called "false Calvinism"—involved several doctrinal issues, but the heart of the matter was a view of divine sovereignty which virtually denied human responsibility. Antinomianism was one entailment of this stance.[131] The elect were under grace, not law, and the command was to "believe," not "work." Thus the moral law had no binding force over the believer. As Carter summarizes, "The true believer knew that he was one of the predestined elect not from any signs of increasing holiness in his life, but from the assurance of an interior conviction that he was God's chosen one."[132]

What was distinctive to hyper-Calvinism, as noted above, was the notion that human depravity meant sinners were unable to respond to the gospel, and thus preachers did not need to exhort their hearers to repent and trust in Christ. Since saving grace is irresistible and only operative in the elect, grace should not be offered indiscriminately. Another consideration—the so-called "Modern Question"—had to do with whether the

---

127. Fuller, *Works*, 1:77.

128. Shaw, *High Calvinists*, 10.

129. "Hyper-Calvinism" is the term used by Fuller's son in the memoir. Fuller, *Andrew Fuller*, 38, 189.

130. Fuller, *Complete Works*, 5:563; also 5:583 where he indicates that "high" and "hyper" Calvinist can be synonymous.

131. There have been several controversies over Antinomianism. For the debate that occupied much of the 1690s see Toon, *Emergence of Hyper-Calvinism*, 49–69. For a discussion of Antinomianism in the latter part of the eighteenth century see Oliver, *History*, 112–31.

132. Carter, *Anglican Evangelicals*, 51.

unconverted had a duty to believe the gospel.[133] Hyper-Calvinists answered that since the non-elect did not have the power to respond to the gospel, neither did they have the duty to respond.

As we have seen, hyper-Calvinism received widespread support among the Particular Baptists during a significant part of the eighteenth century. Gill, an esteemed Baptist minister and theologian, was more careful than some on these issues.[134] Nevertheless, in his book *The Doctrine of Predestination Stated* Gill wrote, "That there are universal offers of grace and salvation made to all men, I utterly deny; nay I deny that they are made to any; no not to God's elect."[135]

These ideas were challenged in 1785 when Fuller published his landmark work, *The Gospel Worthy of All Acceptation*.[136] Fuller argued that it was the duty of all men who hear the gospel to believe in Christ, and that ministers were obligated to exhort, command, and invite sinners to repent and believe. But Fuller was quick to clarify that he was in no way falling into the error of Arminianism. He wrote, "There is no dispute about the doctrine of election, or any of the discriminating doctrines of grace . . . it is granted that none ever did or ever will believe in Christ but those who are chosen of God from eternity."[137] In the third section of the book, Fuller responded to objections and defended specific doctrines, such as particular redemption,[138] human inability, and the efficacious work of the Holy Spirit enabling sinners to believe.[139] Fuller was greatly influenced by the American Calvinist Jonathan Edwards[140]—particularly Edwards's classic treatise, *Free-*

---

133. The issue was first raised in print by the Congregational minister Matthias Maurice in his 1737 pamphlet *A Modern Question Modestly Answer'd*. See Nuttall, "Northamptonshire," 101–23.

134. For a "correction to modern caricatures and misrepresentations" of Gill see Nettles, *By His Grace*, 21–54. However cf. Morden, *Offering Christ*, 13–15.

135. Oliver, *History*, 9.

136. See Nettles, "The Passion and Doctrine," 20–42.

137. Fuller, *Works*, 2:330–31.

138. Naylor points out, "Fuller is at his most weak when attempting to reconcile the doctrine of particular redemption with his conviction that all who hear the gospel should, as a matter of duty, believe in Christ for their salvation." This led Fuller to reject the view that Christ's death was "the literal payment of a debt . . . according to the number of those for whom he died." Naylor, *Calvinism*, 212. Fuller was influenced by the governmental theory of the atonement, but did not repudiate the substitutionary view. See Oliver, *History*, 163–65.

139. Fuller, *Works*, 2:373–82.

140. For more on Edwards's influence in England and among Particular Baptists ministers like Fuller, John Ryland, Jr., John Sutcliff, and Robert Hall, Jr. see Hindmarsh, "Reception of Jonathan Edwards," 40–51.

dom of the Will. From Edwards, Fuller came to understand that all sinners had a natural ability to hear and believe the gospel; what they lacked was the moral ability to do so. They simply did not desire to obey the gospel, and thus they bore responsibility for their unbelief. Hence all men had a duty to believe, and all gospel ministers were obliged to exhort sinners to repent and believe the gospel.

Fuller's focus was clearly on soteriology,[141] and yet he classified himself as a strict Calvinist. This illustrates that the term "Calvinism" among evangelicals was increasingly tied to the soteriological points of Calvinism, or "the doctrines of grace," and not the whole system of the Reformed tradition. James Garrett in his *Baptist Theology* speaks of Fuller's commitment to "Dortian Calvinism."[142] The term has some merit. For example, in a letter to John Ryland in 1803, Fuller said in regard to the Canons of Dort, "I would not wish for words more appropriate . . . to express my sentiments."[143]

Fuller's *Gospel Worthy of All Acceptation* contributed significantly to Calvinist thought as the nineteenth century dawned. E. A. Payne contends that Fuller's work produced "a theological and practical revolution in most of the Calvinist Churches."[144] That revolution "opened a door for Baptists and others onto the vast world of gospel-preaching to the nations."[145] Thus Fuller's theology helped to anchor the dissenting missionary societies which began to emerge in the 1790s.[146]

Fuller, who died in 1815, continued to exercise an important influence in the nineteenth century. "Edward Steane, joint secretary of the Evangelical Alliance in the United Kingdom, estimated in 1872 that Fuller's writings had exerted the greatest influence in shaping the characteristics of modern Calvinism."[147] Nevertheless, hyper-Calvinism continued to cast its shadow over nineteenth-century discussion of soteriology.

The Soteriological Spectrum

As we bring our survey of the eighteenth century to a close, it will be useful to outline the various positions vis-à-vis Calvinism and Arminianism among

---

141. See Clipsham, "Andrew Fuller," 99.
142. Garrett, *Baptist Theology*, 180.
143. Fuller, *Works*, 2:712.
144. Cited in Nuttall, "Northamptonshire," 101.
145. Nettles, "Andrew Fuller," 97.
146. Bebbington, *Holiness*, 33; Morden, *Offering Christ*, 128–56.
147. Bebbington, *Dominance of Evangelicalism*, 132.

evangelicals.[148] Of course, any attempt to categorize theological viewpoints carries with it the danger of reductionism; individual proponents are typically more nuanced than summary statements allow. Nevertheless, notable distinctions appear on the spectrum of beliefs regarding divine sovereignty and human freedom, and some attempt to sketch those distinctions will help bring a measure of clarity to the present study.

What follows is drawn largely from Bruce Hindmarsh's research of English evangelical theology in the mid-eighteenth century.[149] Some modifications have been incorporated, most significantly in distinguishing between high Calvinism and hyper-Calvinism. Hindmarsh's focus is on the eighteenth century, when the term "hyper Calvinism" was not yet in use.[150] What follows below, therefore, brings Hindmarsh's taxonomy into the nineteenth-century setting.

1. **Evangelical Arminianism** taught that election is conditional, based on God's foreknowledge of human choices; the atonement is unlimited and universal in scope; and final salvation is contingent upon sustained faith and co-operation with sanctifying grace. The free offer of the gospel is based on Christ's universal atonement for every person—original sin and inability having been removed by common grace. Those who held this position were often charged by Calvinists with advocating Pelagianism and justification by works.

2. **Moderate Calvinism** believed in unconditional election based upon God's sovereign will and irresistible grace. Reprobation, however, was denied. The atonement is unlimited, at least in terms of provision; it is ultimately efficient only for the elect. Final perseverance was viewed as a corollary of election, but the process of sanctification was still necessary. Like Arminianism, the free offer of the gospel was linked to universal atonement.

3. **Strict Calvinism** maintained unconditional election and irresistible grace. Reprobation was softened or denied altogether. The atonement is particular, limited to the elect. Final perseverance and the process of sanctification were affirmed. The free offer of the gospel was based upon the general sufficiency of Christ's death for sinners, whose duty it is to repent and believe.

---

148. This section has been updated from Stevenson, "Early Brethren Leaders," 6–9.

149. Hindmarsh, *John Newton*, 124–25. Hindmarsh's work is also summarized in Burnham, *Story of Conflict*, 54–55.

150. The earliest use of the term "hyper-Calvinism" I have found to date is 1806 in H. K. "Remarks on Romans," 258.

4. **High Calvinism** based unconditional election on a supralapsarian scheme of divine decrees, which included a strong doctrine of reprobation. In addition, high Calvinism often viewed justification as eternal, with Christ's righteousness imputed to the elect from eternity before the actual exercise of faith. This feature often produced some form of theological antinomianism.

5. **Hyper-Calvinism** mirrored high Calvinism at most points, with the exception that hyper-Calvinists were unwilling to offer the gospel freely to all people. They took divine sovereignty to such an extreme that they denied it was the duty of all sinners to repent and believe the gospel—hence the restriction on gospel preaching. While high Calvinism is often equated with hyper-Calvinism, it is clear that not all high Calvinists placed such limitations on preaching.

While the positions outlined above provide a basic summary of Calvinistic and Arminian soteriology operative in the nineteenth century, it must be stressed that the terminology used in the literature is not uniform. For example, early Brethren theology is often dubbed "moderately Calvinistic,"[151] yet many Brethren held some version of particular redemption (often with their own nuance). Thus "moderate" may embrace strict Calvinism in the above taxonomy; the term "moderate" in this case appears to be intended to distinguish the Brethren from high or hyper-Calvinism (especially in regard to the objectionable doctrine of reprobation). It may also have reference to the tone and relative emphasis placed on Calvinism among the Brethren.[152]

In any case, we turn now to survey nineteenth-century developments as the direct backdrop for the emergence of the Brethren movement.

---

151. Neatby, *History*, 230.

152. Stewart rightfully says, "The inherent difficulty with such terminology is that the meaning of the term "moderate" must always be determined by the extremes it seeks to avoid." Stewart, *Restoring the Reformation*, 12–13.

3

Calvinistic Soteriology: A Historical Survey

Part 2: The Nineteenth Century

> *"The knowledge of God in Christ is a divine work and gift... we owe all to sovereign grace."*
>
> —*J. N. Darby*[1]

The Nineteenth Century Context

Continuity and Change

THE PREVIOUS CHAPTER BRIEFLY surveyed the state of Calvinistic soteriology in the evangelical world from the time of the Restoration through the eighteenth century. We are now in a better position to evaluate Bebbington's suggestion that the nineteenth century brought a "renewed interest in Calvinism."[2] Perhaps "renewed" may be something of an overstatement, for as we have seen, the debate over Calvinism and Arminianism highlighted by popular evangelists Whitefield and Wesley and sustained by the churchman Toplady; the presence of hyper-Calvinism among Baptists; and the work of Andrew Fuller spawning a brand of evangelistic Calvinism[3]—all ensured that "the doctrines of grace" were never far from evangelical discussion. Even outside the ranks of evangelicalism, Calvinism attracted atten-

---

1. Darby, *Letters*, 1:376.
2. Bebbington, *Evangelicalism in Modern Britain*, 77.
3. William Carey's *An Enquiry into the Obligations of Christians to Use Means for the Conversion of the Heathen* (Leicester, 1792) was also an important work in advancing evangelical Calvinism.

tion.⁴ Thus Bishop George Pretyman Tomline, building on his earlier work, *Elements of Christian Theology* (1799), in which he sought to "repudiate the Calvinist interpretation of article 17,"⁵ published in 1811 *A Refutation of Calvinism*. The work was "widely read"⁶ and went through eight editions, the final one appearing in 1823. Tomline's *Refutation* attracted significant responses from Thomas Scott, *Remarks on the Bishop of Lincoln's Refutation of Calvinism* (1812),⁷ and the Independent minister and tutor Edward Williams, *A Defence of Modern Calvinism: Containing an Examination of the Bishop of Lincoln's Work Entitled a Refutation of Calvinism* (1812), as well as responses from anonymous writers.

Within Anglicanism there was disagreement over the character of the Thirty-Nine Articles. The debate was frequently tied to the question of how Arminian clergy could subscribe to the Articles in good conscience. For example, John Overton (1763–1838) argued that the evangelicals were the ones who upheld the true sense of the Articles and the Book of Common Prayer. In the process, Overton sought to demonstrate—contrary to many contemporary writers—that the Anglican reformers were Calvinistic in their theological convictions, and this fact was clearly reflected in the Articles.⁸ Overton was opposed by Charles Daubeny (*bap.* 1745–*d*. 1827), who argued that the original English reformers were not Calvinists at all— in fact, they intentionally sought to exclude Calvinistic interpretations of the Articles and liturgy.⁹ The controversy was highlighted at length in the *Christian Observer*.¹⁰

---

4. In terms of the denominational breakdown in England, Bebbington writes, "The groups that drew their theology from Calvinist sources in the nineteenth century were the Evangelical Anglicans, the Congregationalists [or Independents] and the Baptists." Many of the Presbyterians had been strongly influenced by rationalism and veered into Unitarianism. Bebbington, *Holiness*, 29–30.

5. *ODNB*, s.n. "Sir George Pretyman Tomline." In 1822 Tomline issued *A Scriptural Exposition of the Seventeenth Article*.

6. *DNB*, s.n. "Sir George Pretyman Tomline."

7. Scott also published *The Articles of the Synod of Dort* in 1818. Significantly for the present study, Grass suggests that Scott may have been a source of John Nelson Darby's Calvinism. See Grass, "The Church's Ruin," 97; cf. 28.

8. Overton, *True Churchmen*. Cf. reviews defending the Calvinistic character of the Church of England in the *Evangelical Magazine* 14 (1806) 38–39; 34–37.

9. Daubeny, *Vindiciae Ecclesiae Anglicanae*.

10. *CO* 3 (1804), 425–39; 483–91; 488–96; 569–78; 629–40; 687–93. Interestingly, Darby sought to demonstrate that the English Reformers taught what would later come to be known as Calvinism in "The Doctrine of the Church of England at the Time of the Reformation, of the Reformation Itself, of Scripture, and of the Church of Rome, Briefly Compared with the Remarks of the Regius Professor of Divinity," in *CW*, 3:1–43.

Yet Bebbington's assessment is not entirely off the mark. Thomas Scott, in his response to Tomline, worried that the Bishop's *Refutation of Calvinism* had "revived" the controversy and brought it before the public again. Scott himself was hesitant "to commence a controversy" but could not in good conscience avoid it, since "many doctrines which belong to our common christianity are deeply involved in the argument, the contest is no longer about unessential matters, but *pro aris et focis* [for home and hearth]."[11]

John Wolffe has argued that for evangelicals, "the theological controversies of the mid-eighteenth century, which had divided evangelicalism sharply on Arminian-Calvinist lines, were receding by the 1790s."[12] There is truth to this. As long as evangelicals remained centered on the gospel, the Calvinist-Arminian doctrinal issues would bubble beneath the surface. For many, however, the heat of the early years was cooling, and a tendency toward moderation characterized the new atmosphere.[13] Thus in the opening years of the nineteenth century, "while some Arminian-Calvinist tensions remained, especially within the Baptist and Independent communities, the issue had now lost the divisive potential it had had in the early decades of the evangelical movement."[14] We shall see, however, that before too long, tension over Calvinism would be an important factor in evangelical secession from the Establishment.[15]

We turn now to examine some of the trends and features of nineteenth-century Calvinism.

Moderate Calvinism

The Calvinist tradition has never been monolithic, and on the spectrum of its theological tenets, moderate voices have always claimed a place. However, the nineteenth century witnessed a distinct movement toward a moderate Calvinism by many evangelicals.[16] The title of Edward Williams's response to Bishop Tomline's *Refutation* is suggestive: *A Defence of Modern Calvinism*. With the term "modern," Williams wanted to distinguish a moderated brand of Calvinism from some of the harsher elements often attributed (not

---

11. Scott, *Remarks*, iii–iv.
12. Wolffe, *Expansion of Evangelicalism*, 39.
13. See for example, Ingenuus, "Conciliatory Remarks," 8–12 and W. H., "Suggestions for Reconciling," 211–14.
14. Wolffe, *Expansion of Evangelicalism*, 39.
15. See Carter, *Anglican Evangelicals*, and Stunt, *From Awakening*.
16. Bebbington, *Evangelicals in Modern Britain*, 63–65. For a discussion of moderate Calvinism among Anglican Evangelicals see Carter, *Anglican Evangelicals*, 49–50.

least by Tomline) to traditional Calvinism. Williams's brand included a rejection of antinomianism, limited atonement, and reprobation. "Positioned between high Calvinism on the one hand and Arminianism on the other, the moderate or 'modern' Calvinism espoused by Williams became accepted as Dissenting orthodoxy for much of the nineteenth century."[17] Moderate Calvinism was also acceptable among some evangelical clergy within the Establishment and was normative for Irish evangelical churchmen.[18]

This move toward moderation was not lost on Arminian writers of the day. The Arminian publisher James Nichols spoke of Williams's version of Calvinism "as that which is in most fashionable repute." Writing in 1817, Nichols commented on the new Calvinism:

> No other system of religious doctrines has so changed its scenery as Calvinism has done. In the last age, this old hag was remarkable for her unblushing effrontery in preaching up absolute reprobation, infant-damnation, and the other horrible consequences of her unscriptural dogmas. In the present age, conforming herself to the advancement made in knowledge, she has by various expedients tried to cast a veil over her ugly features; and by means of certain modern refinements, she has partially succeeded.

In a footnote Nichols added, "To smooth down the unsightly asperities of Calvinism, appears now to be the order of the day. This system of refinement is carried into every department of literature into which a Calvinist is capable of conveying it."[19] Nichols's assessment is colorful and hyperbolic, but it does represent a fairly common nineteenth-century impression of Calvinism—namely, that the term was associated with a harsh version of reprobation. As we shall see, this is one reason why Brethren writers wanted to distance themselves from the term "Calvinism," even though they affirmed several of its basic soteriological tenets.

Avoiding Antinomianism

Though high Calvinists did not encourage practical antinomianism, it was often perceived to be the logic of their preaching—and actual examples among their congregants only added fuel to the fire.[20] Thus moderate Cal-

---

17. *BDE*, s.n. "Edward Williams."
18. Carter, *Anglican Evangelicals*, 61.
19. James Nichols's advertisement to Whitby, *Discourse*, 7–9.
20. In 1860, the editor of a hyper-Calvinist magazine, J. C. Philpot decried "the

vinists took pains to distance themselves from antinomianism, which was frequently attached to the label of Calvinism. Writing in the later years of the eighteenth century, Henry Venn expressed sentiments very much alive among nineteenth-century moderates: "Though the doctrines of grace are clear to me, I am still no friend to high Calvinism. A false, libertine Calvinism stops up every avenue: sin, the Law, holiness, experience, are all nothing. Predestination cancels the necessity of any change, and dispenses at once with all duty."[21]

Moderate Calvinists were sensitive to the charge of antinomianism and were diligent to prove their doctrines did not entail it.[22] Writing in 1812, Thomas Scott could say, "At present, I am persuaded, that the evangelical clergy *in general* are very careful to caution their congregations against every antinomian perversion of the doctrine of grace."[23] Brethren likewise were vocal in their opposition to antinomianism.[24] Yet antinomianism was sometimes a real problem in hyper-Calvinist circles.

Unlimited Atonement

Moderate Calvinism, like Arminianism, typically affirmed a universal, or general, atonement. Again Scott, to take one representative example, in his response to Bishop Tomline's *Refutation of Calvinism*, stated the following: "It seems to be the established opinion of his Lordship, that the evangelical clergy, especially such of them as believe the doctrine of personal election, hold what is called *particular redemption*; whereas in fact very few of them adopt it. The author of these remarks . . . above twenty-four years since, avowed his dissent from the doctrine of particular redemption."[25]

The Morning Watch, the voice of the circle of prophetic students associated with the Albury Conferences of 1826-30, complained that the five

---

loose, Antinomian spirit so widely prevalent in the Calvinist churches." He added, "Doctrinal preaching in many pulpits has become crystallised into a regular form, so that were the preacher to diverge from the established round to insist upon the vital experience of truth in the heart, and the fruits of the Spirit as manifested by a holy, godly walk in the life and conduct, a suspicion would be spread from pew to pew that he was wavering in his creed, and was secretly introducing free will and Arminianism." [Philpot], "Address," 10-11.

21. Venn, *Life*, 34.

22. Nuttall observes, "Antinomianism is not Calvinism; but it is Calvinism's peril." Nuttall, "Calvinism," 425.

23. Scott, *Remarks*, 291.

24. E.g., [Mackintosh], "'Accepted,'" 249-50.

25. Scott, *Remarks*, 332.

points of Calvinism presented a woefully inadequate summary of Christian truth, and that the doctrine of particular redemption was "directly in opposition to the plain words of the Scriptures."[26]

By 1850 the *Wesleyan Methodist Magazine* claimed a decisive victory in the doctrinal battle over the extent of the atonement. "That Christ died for all," it claimed, "is on all hands admitted."[27] The atonement question was one that exercised Brethren writers such as Darby and Kelly, and they offered their own nuance to the discussion. We will return to this question at length in chapter 6.

Rejecting Reprobation

Moderate Calvinists were adamant in their rejection of reprobation. Their defensiveness on this point arises from the fact that an extreme view of reprobation—that God predestined the majority of the human race to hell without reference to their sin—was a frequent target of opponents.[28] Thus at one level the moderates set out to rescue Calvinism from the stigma of association with the "dreadful doctrine" of reprobation. Writing of modern Calvinists, especially those of the Established Church, Scott challenged, "Let our opponents prove, if they can, that one in ten, or twenty of those, who have committed themselves, by publishing their sentiments, hold that God decreed to consign any portion of mankind to everlasting misery, without regard to their foreseen conduct as deserving it. This at least, I avow, and a large majority of my brethren will join with me; that I wholly disclaim all such nominal Calvinists, as deliberately maintain that sentiment."[29]

Moderate Calvinists often pointed out that the terms "reprobate" and "reprobation" did not occur in Scripture.[30] This observation leads to another common feature of evangelical theology in the nineteenth century.

---

26. "Calvinism Not the Whole," 376.

27. *Wesleyan Methodist Magazine* (July 1840), 741. Cited in Bebbington, *Dominance of Evangelicalism*, 138.

28. The term "reprobation" continued to be used within the Calvinist tradition to denote different ideas, as Williams acknowledges (*Defence of Modern Calvinism*, 209–10). However, anti-Calvinists were convinced the logic of unconditional election made unconditional reprobation the only legitimate conclusion.

29. Scott, *Remarks*, 451.

30. E.g., ibid., 395, 439–40, 456.

Scripture over Systematic Theology

Bebbington has argued that one product of the Enlightenment's influence on evangelicals was an aversion to metaphysical systems.[31] As a result, they tended to eschew systematic theology, which they believed imposed an artificial structure on the Bible. The systems of Calvinism and Arminianism were often the victims of this attitude. Specifically, moderate Calvinists had little appetite for speculation over the order of divine decrees, something Scripture did not address.[32] They preferred to take their doctrine directly from the Bible. Isaac Milner (1750–1820) said, "Calvin is much too systematical for me: though, perhaps, the hardest things he says may have some foundation; but I am sure it is not the system of Scripture to speak as he speaks in many instances."[33] Hannah More (1745–1832) was more blunt: "How I hate the little narrowing names of Arminian and Calvinist. Christianity is a broad basis. Bible Christianity is what I love."[34] Charles Simeon quipped, "Be Bible Christians not system Christians."[35] In the preface to his homiletical commentary on the Bible, Simeon wrote, "The Author is no friend to systematizers in Theology. He has endeavoured to derive from the Scriptures alone *his* views of religion; and to them it is his wish to adhere, with scrupulous fidelity; never wresting any portion of the word of God to favour a particular opinion, but giving to every part of it that sense, which it seems to him to have been designed by its great Author to convey."[36] Unlike proponents of human systems—and here he named Calvinists and Arminians—Simeon determined to be true to the whole of Scripture.[37]

In 1804 the Anglican clergyman George Stanley Faber (1773–1854) issued *Thoughts on the Calvinistic and Arminian Controversy*. The piece was a plea for a more moderate tone in the debate, which was another characteristic feature of the new Calvinism. But Faber also identified the allegiance to

---

31. Bebbington, *Evangelicalism in Modern Britain*, 57–60.

32. Stewart says of the Calvinistic preachers during the Evangelical Revival: "If this Calvinism was often presented as Scripture truth rather than as systematic dogma, this should be understood as the strategy for an age when all systems and articles of faith had fallen into oblivion or contempt." Stewart, *Restoring the Reformation*, 14.

33. Cited in Elliot-Binns, *Early Evangelicals*, 196.

34. Cited in Haykin, "Evangelicalism and the Enlightenment," 42.

35. Cited in ibid.

36. Simeon, *Horae Homileticae*, 1:xxiii.

37. Though often considered a moderate Calvinist, Simeon "decided in 1822 to try to disarm anti-Evangelical prejudice by publically disavowing Calvinism altogether." Bebbington adds, "Thereafter, many Anglican Evangelicals regarded themselves not as indebted to Calvin but as simple 'Bible Christians.'" Bebbington, "Calvin and British Evangelicalism," 284.

"systems" as the place where both sides go astray. After endeavoring to show the abuses which systems inevitably produce, he concluded:

> So long as men are determined to fabricate systems for themselves, and cannot rest contented with the simple word of God: we must not be surprised, if, on the one hand, we should occasionally find a Calvinist, wallowing in the mire of Antinomianism, or locked up in the immoveable ice of Fatalism; nor if, on the other hand, we should sometimes have reason to bewail the heretical pravity of an Arminian, inflated with the vain idea of his own sufficiency, and rushing madly into all the philosophising errors of determined Pelagianism.[38]

Thus "the simple word of God" was the antidote to high (and hyper-) Calvinism on the one hand and the Pelagian tendencies of Arminianism on the other.

High and Hyper-Calvinism

Although moderate Calvinism was a common theological stance among evangelicals, it was not the only stream found among them. Hyper-Calvinism was primarily confined to Nonconformist groups,[39] but toward the end of the eighteenth century and into the nineteenth century it was also making its presence felt among some evangelical Anglicans.[40] In an important study of evangelical secession in the first half of the nineteenth century, Grayson Carter demonstrates that "high and hyper-Calvinists were strongly represented among Evangelical clergy seceding from the Church of England."[41] What is notable for the present study is the fact that a number of the evangelical clergy who seceded joined the Brethren,[42] and in some important cases had been influenced by high or hyper-Calvinists.

In the early nineteenth-century context, William Huntington (1745–1813) was perhaps the most notable hyper-Calvinist among dissenters.[43] Some of the more militant variety viewed themselves as the true heirs of

---

38. Faber, *Thoughts*, 40.
39. See Toon, *Emergence of Hyper-Calvinism* and Nuttall, "Calvinism."
40. Carter, *Anglican Evangelicals*, 50–54.
41. Ibid., 53.
42. See Grass, *Gathering to His Name*, 520–23.

43. See *BDEB*, s.n. "William Huntington." Iain Murray suggests that "Huntington was probably the first London preacher to show that one could be both a popular preacher and a vigorous upholder of Hyper-Calvinism." Murray, *Spurgeon v. Hyper-Calvinism*, 133–39. Cf. Shaw, *High Calvinists*, 16–17.

the Calvinist tradition and were not averse to referring to the moderates as "bastard Calvinists."[44] High Calvinism featured prominently among the Walkerites in Ireland and the Western Schism in England.

Walkerites in Ireland

While Reformed Presbyterianism was firmly established in Ulster,[45] by the early nineteenth century moderate Calvinism was common among evangelicals in Ireland—although Arminianism had a vocal presence especially through Wesleyan Methodists.[46] However, a more extreme version of Calvinism marked a controversial separatist group known as the "Walkerites"—"the first indigenous Irish Dissenting body."[47] John Walker (1768–1833) was a fellow at Trinity College, Dublin and an ordained priest in the Church of Ireland. In the late eighteenth century he developed "a reputation within Dublin's burgeoning Evangelical movement as a popular and effective clergyman."[48] By 1804, however, Walker became convinced of the unscriptural nature of the Established Church and seceded from the Church of Ireland, as well as resigning his fellowship at Trinity. He also separated from the various evangelical societies he had been connected with and established his own congregation in Stafford Street, Dublin, which he designated as the "Church of God." Walker and his followers, with their radical position on separation, were viewed as extremists; they came to be known as the "separatists," or simply Walkerites. They believed that they alone had recovered the apostolic pattern of New Testament Christianity.[49] Mainstream evangelicals believed the spectacle of Walker and his separatists, having attracted public attention, was a blow to their quest for acceptance, respect, and a united Protestant reformation in Ireland.

One of the unsavory features of the Walkerite position was their "extreme Calvinism."[50] Carter argues that "Walker's high Calvinism tended

---

44. E.g., Goulding, *Series of Letters*, 66; I. K., "Morsel," 152–53; cf. Bebbington, "Calvin and British Evangelicalism," 283.

45. For developments see especially Holmes, *Shaping*. For a general survey of Calvinism and Ulster Presbyterianism in Ireland, especially in connection with revivals, see McKee, "Revivals," 87–100.

46. For a glimpse into the development of the Reformed church in Ireland see Gribben, *Irish Puritans*. See also Bowen, *History*. For the nineteenth century milieu see Bowen, *Protestant Crusade*.

47. Carter, *Anglican Evangelicals*, 77. Cf. Rowdon, "Secession," 76–78.

48. Carter, *Anglican Evangelicals*, 77–78.

49. Ibid., 88.

50. *BDEB*, s.n. "John Walker." Neatby called Walker "a Calvinist of an extreme, not

(at least in public perception) to dominate the theological orientation of the 'Church of God.'"[51] And while Walker was not a hyper-Calvinist,[52] his intense opposition to Arminianism warrants categorizing his position as one of extreme Calvinism. For example, Walker asserted that a true Arminian was not a real believer in the gospel, since "the essential character of Arminianism stands in direct opposition" to the gospel. Therefore, Walker announced, *"no real Arminian is a real believer."*[53] He was convinced that Arminian doctrines were "anti-christian, and opposite to the truth of God's word," and unless those who held such doctrines repented, "they will perish in their unbelief."[54] Neatby, the early Brethren historian, claimed to have it on good authority that Walker proposed union with another separatist group, led by Thomas Kelly, on the condition that the Kellyites affirm that John Wesley—the Arminian—was in hell.[55]

It is worth noting that in its "radical primitivism,"[56] some features of the Walkerites resembled the later Brethren movement, such as the weekly practice of "the Breaking of Bread." William Kelly, however, disavowed any connection between the groups, calling the Walkerites "the very antipodes of 'Brethren'" in certain matters.[57] Indeed, for some evangelicals, extremists like Walker gave Calvinism a bad name. They often felt compelled to qualify their adherence to the doctrines of grace in order to distance themselves from what were commonly viewed as harsh and unfashionable varieties of Calvinism.

The Western Schism in England

"Western Schism" was the label attached to the secession from the Church of England of a group of clergymen and their followers in several Western

---

to say a rabid type." Neatby, *History*, 26.
51. Carter, *Anglican Evangelicals*, 90.
52. E.g., Walker, *Essays and Correspondence*, 1:439–40.
53. Ibid., 1:51–52. Emphasis original.
54. Ibid., 1:44.
55. Neatby, *History*, 27.
56. Carter, *Anglican Evangelicals*, 83.
57. Kelly, "The Archdeacon of Durham," 96. Cf. Kelly, *Christian Worship*, 12. Grass observes, "there are parallels between Walker's ecclesiology and Darby's but no evidence of dependence, and Darby himself was not converted until around 1820, after Walker left Dublin." Grass, "The Church's Ruin," 27. In a letter to Darby in 1836, A. N. Groves warned that Darby's increasing separatism was dangerously akin to the Walkerites: "your Shibboleth may be different, but it will be as *real.*" The letter is reproduced as an Appendix in Coad, *History of the Brethren*, 291–95.

counties around 1815. In some ways, what the Walkerites were to Ireland, the Western Schism was to England. Anglican evangelicals were the most critical of the Western Schism; they were concerned to distance themselves from the doctrinal extremes associated with the schismatics—including Trinitarian heterodoxy and high Calvinism. For example, one of the leading lights of the Schism, George Baring, advocated a form of Sabellianism and the hyper-Calvinist idea of the elect's eternal sanctification—along with the antinomian implications connected to such a position. His hyper-Calvinism was illustrated in a sermon preached in Salisbury in 1817 in which it was reported that "he preached and prayed for the elect only."[58] Although there was some variation among the schismatics on points of doctrine, Stunt suggests, "in most cases their High Calvinism was the principal issue on which they found themselves at variance with their Anglican superiors."[59] A contemporary critic of the Schism, clergyman Richard Warner, "claimed that the seceders' high Calvinism had rapidly divided the local community [of Milford] and undermined social order by its rigoristic separation of the elect from the reprobate."[60]

The attention the Walkerites and the Western Schism attracted meant that "Calvinism" was not infrequently connected to extremism in the public mind. Thus again, mainstream evangelicals were often wary of identifying themselves as Calvinists outright. When they did embrace the doctrines of grace, they were often at pains to demonstrate their moderation.

The early Brethren movement in its formative stage crossed paths with hyper-Calvinist advocates in Plymouth and Oxford. It is therefore appropriate to sketch some of the background at this point.

Plymouth and Oxford

The story of the crucial role Plymouth played in the history of the Brethren movement is well documented and need not detain us here.[61] What is significant is the strong presence of hyper-Calvinism in Plymouth through the

---

58. Carter, *Anglican Evangelicals*, 118–19.

59. Stunt, *From Awakening*, 288.

60. Carter, *Anglican Evangelicals*, 113. It is worth noting that the Open Brethren leader Robert C. Chapman was converted though the preaching of James Harington Evans (1785–1849). Evans was recognized as the most able theologian of the clergy who seceded as part of the Western Schism. We will recount that story and its significance in chapter 5.

61. See for example, Rowdon, *Origins*, 74–85; Embley, "Origins," 67–78; Grass, *Gathering to His Name*, 34–39; Burnham, *Story of Conflict*, 75–100; Stunt, *From Awakening*, 287–304.

influence of Robert Hawker (1753–1827), vicar of Charles Church. Hawker was "the most prominent hyper-Calvinist in the Church of England."[62] He influenced the theology of a number of evangelical clergy who seceded in connection with the Western Schism, though he himself remained in the Church of England.[63] Whenever Hawker preached at the Lock Hospital in London, William Wilberforce took his family elsewhere, being eager to protect them from Hawker's antinomian "poison."[64]

Hawker died in 1827, and his successor, James Carne, died in 1832—around the time the new Brethren assembly in Plymouth was formed. Thus many of Hawker's high Calvinist congregation made their way to the Brethren meeting, which was "only a stone's throw from Charles Church."[65] To what extent the Brethren were influenced by hyper-Calvinism is difficult to determine with any kind of precision. Ian Rennie has suggested several ways in which hyper-Calvinist ideas were reflected in Brethren spirituality,[66] but in terms of soteriology, nineteenth-century Brethren were consistently critical of hyper-Calvinism's extremes. Instead, their soteriology ranged between strict and moderate Calvinism, as subsequent chapters will demonstrate.[67]

Hawker's Calvinism made its presence felt at Oxford, particularly through Henry Bellenden Bulteel (1800–1866). Born in Plymouth, Bulteel

---

62. Rennie, "Aspects," 203. That Hawker may rightly be called a hyper-Calvinist is seen in his belief that invitations in the Bible were made to the elect, or to those God made willing: "To preach Christ, [the Apostles] knew to be their province; to persuade to the acceptance of Christ, they knew to be His." Cited in Shaw, *High Calvinists*, 18.

63. *BDEB*, s.n. "Robert Hawker." For more evidence of Hawker's hyper-Calvinism and a contemporary criticism of his theology see "Modern Antinomianism," 508–28. The piece also criticizes the high Calvinism of Edward Thomas Vaughan (1772–1829) of Leicester—another Anglican clergyman who did not secede.

64. Wilberforce and Wilberforce, *Life*, 3:473. This is somewhat ironic since Hawker was a strong advocate of the anti-slavery movement and published a letter in 1823 supporting Wilberforce's work. Hawker, *Works*, 10:486–506. Dann notes that Hawker "established a fund for purchasing plantations, and by paying the negroes for their work, enabled them within a few years to buy their freedom." Dann, *Primitivist Ecclesiology*, 45.

65. Rennie, "Aspects," 203; Grass, *Gathering to His Name*, 34. It is worth noting that Bethesda Chapel in Bristol, where George Müller and Henry Craik ministered, had previously been led by Thomas Cowan, a high Calvinist, Western Schism man. Carter, *Anglican Evangelicals*, 132. Furthermore, "In North Devon, a Particular Baptist church at Barnstaple was gradually transformed into a Brethren assembly, through the work of Robert Cleaver Chapman (1803–1902)." Grass, *Gathering to His Name*, 39.

66. Rennie, "Aspects," 204–5.

67. One of Hawker hymns, "Abba, Father, thus we call Thee," (or "Abba, Father! we adore Thee") with a decidedly Calvinistic tone was included in at least two popular Brethren hymnals, *A Few Hymns and Some Spiritual Songs for the Little Flock* (1856, 1881), and *The Believer's Hymn Book* (1884).

graduated BA in 1822 from Brasenose College, Oxford. In 1823 he was elected a fellow of Exeter College and was ordained the following summer. In 1826 he served as tutor and bursar at Exeter.[68] After a conversion experience he became more serious, and his evangelical convictions grew.[69] In December 1826 he was appointed curate at St. Ebbe's, where he quickly established himself "as one of the most popular preachers in Oxford."[70] Whenever he visited Plymouth, Bulteel went to hear Robert Hawker. On one occasion he urged his friend and Exeter fellow, Benjamin W. Newton, to "come and hear Hawker." Newton replied, "No . . . I never will; he is a Calvinist."[71] Newton went, nevertheless, and was blessed by what he heard. He then commented, "I soon returned to Oxford but Bulteel remained for ten days longer in Dr. Hawker's company."[72]

Both Bulteel and Newton adopted Calvinist principles, but Newton rejected Hawker's high Calvinism which Bulteel would champion at Oxford.[73] The Bulteel-Newton connection is an important one, for Newton would go on to be a key leader in the influential Brethren assembly at Plymouth. Eventually it was Newton's teaching (on issues unrelated to Calvinism) that would become the focal point of the controversies in the 1840s which led to the severance of the Brethren movement into the Exclusive and Open branches.[74]

Bulteel's Calvinistic sentiments quickly advanced, and his impact at Oxford was immediate. Carter comments, "His sermons had a new fire and a sharp, dogmatic cutting edge. Some seventy-four young men were soon converted under his preaching."[75] Bulteel was attracting such crowds that expansion plans were drawn up for St. Ebbe's. Not everyone approved of Bulteel, however. Thomas Byrth, who had been considered for St. Ebbe's along with Bulteel, wrote, "Mr. Bulteel who was the successful competitor for St. Ebbe's has created a most powerful sensation here by preaching ultra-Calvinism and circulating Dr. Hawker's tracts. If you knew how slowly true and spiritual religion makes its way through the cold atmosphere and deep-rooted prejudice of this place you would feel how much such a mis-

68. ODNB and BDEB, s.n. "Henry Bellenden Bulteel."

69. Fry MS, 115, 137–38.

70. Carter, Anglican Evangelicals, 254.

71. Fry MS, 99, cf. 137–38. Burnham dates this incident to January 1827. Burnham, Story of Conflict, 56n81.

72. Fry MS, 99.

73. The development of Newton's Calvinism is traced in chapter 5. Cf. also Stevenson, "Early Brethren Leaders," 18–22.

74. For a book-length treatment see Burnham, Story of Conflict.

75. Carter, Anglican Evangelicals, 259.

take is to be deplored."[76] Byrth, perhaps still somewhat bitter from Bulteel's preferment, went on to claim that "many are sorry they did not support me, and most look on me as something of a prophet, as I foretold the consequences of his appointment."[77]

The buzz around St. Ebbe's only increased when the Vice-Chancellor sanctioned an attempt to prevent undergraduates from hearing Bulteel. The effort was unsuccessful, and Newton recalled the excitement: "It was a wonderful movement; it roused and even terrified the University, and the authorities tried to put it down, forbidding attendance at St. Ebbe's church, and ordering the names to be taken of those who persisted." Newton boasted, "My name was the first!"[78]

J. C. Philpot,[79] who would secede in 1835 and join the Strict Baptists—eventually becoming the editor of the hyper-Calvinist magazine the *Gospel Standard*—witnessed with delight Bulteel's bold assertion of high Calvinism. He would later recall,

> Mr. Bulteel had for some years embraced the doctrines of grace, and preached them with much fervour of mind and strength of expression. This was a new sound at the learned university, and a thing almost unheard of, that a fellow and tutor of one of the colleges . . . should embrace so thoroughly and above all proclaim so boldly, the obnoxious doctrines of the Calvinistic creed. His church was crowded with hearers, and among them were seen many of the university students, and now and then a master of arts, myself being one of them, some of whom became his attached and regular hearers.[80]

The tensions came to a head when Bulteel delivered the university sermon at St. Mary's in February 1831. The sermon was highly anticipated. Edward Burton, the Regius Professor of Divinity, noted, "It will be known that an audience was attracted such as never perhaps was witnessed for numbers within the walls of St. Mary's."[81] The sermon, based on 1 Cor 2:12, was a bold articulation of Calvinistic doctrines and a rebuke of the Established Church on several points, not least for its departure from the Calvinism

---

76. Cited in Stunt, *From Awakening*, 197.

77. Cited in Burnham, *Story of Conflict*, p. 56. Both Stunt and Burnham are quoting from Moncreiff, *Remains*.

78. Fry MS, 135.

79. Darby claims to have played a role in Philpot's conversion. Darby, *Letters*, 3:167.

80. Philpot, *William Tiptaft*, 43. Also cited in Carter, *Anglican Evangelicals*, 262.

81. Burton, *Remarks*, 3; cited by Stunt, *From Awakening*, 254n52.

of the Thirty-Nine Articles. Bulteel charged, for example, "Whereas the doctrinal Articles of the Church are all in favour of Free grace and against Free will, and man's work in the whole matter of our salvation; yet it is notorious that the great majority both of prelates and preachers neither teach nor preach according to those Articles, but boldly disavow them, and brand those that hold them with the name of *heretic*."[82]

The ensuing controversy produced many responses. Burton's official university response was not viewed as particularly strong.[83] He charged that Bulteel had confused justification with salvation, which Burton argued was based on free will, obedience, and repentance. Burton also argued that the English Reformation was inherently Lutheran and not Calvinistic.

One of the more popular responses to Burton was written by John Nelson Darby, who had been in attendance at St. Mary's for Bulteel's sermon.[84] Darby defended the Calvinistic nature of the English Reformation. In the process he assembled numerous quotations from the likes of Martin Bucer and Peter Martyr Vermigli, who clearly advanced a Reformed view of predestination as reflected in the 17th Article. Darby revealed his own convictions when he wrote, "For my part, I soberly think Article XVII to be as wise, perhaps I might say the wisest and best condensed human statement of the views it contains that I am acquainted with."[85]

After a controversial preaching tour in the West Country, Bulteel's license as curate of St. Ebbe's was withdrawn, and by the autumn of 1831 he seceded from the Church of England. The Bulteel episode was a significant development. Moderate Calvinists within the Establishment had been working for years to gain a measure of respectability for evangelicalism; Bulteel seemed to have reversed any progress that had been achieved. Carter summarizes the impact as follows:

> The Bulteel affair not only widened a long-standing tension between the Oxford Evangelicals and their critics in the university, but exposed some of the fractures opening up within the Evangelical world itself. The strain of high Calvinism which had largely been marginalized among the more obscure of the "Gospel clergy" now emerged in the citadel of the Anglican Church, and in a provocative and energetic form which ensured high visibility.[86]

---

82. Bulteel, *Sermon*, 47–48. Emphasis original.
83. See Burnham, *Story of Conflict*, 67–68 and Stunt, *From Awakening*, 255.
84. Darby, *CW*, 3:1–43.
85. Ibid., 3:3.
86. Carter, *Anglican Evangelicals*, 266.

For the present study, the Bulteel affair provides clear evidence that two of the most important early Brethren leaders, Newton and Darby, had close connections to high (and hyper) Calvinism.[87] However, neither man accepted the more extreme Calvinism of Bulteel or Hawker.

By the mid-1830s most hyper-Calvinists in the Church of England had seceded. They were now mainly confined to the Strict and Particular Baptists and voiced their version of Calvinism through several magazines, most notably the *Gospel Standard,* which achieved a circulation of over seventeen thousand after 1857.[88] Hyper-Calvinists drew attention through their criticism of the evangelical luminary, C. H. Spurgeon (1834–92).[89]

Spurgeon was a strict Calvinist, but also a powerful evangelist. He was a vocal critic of the hyper-Calvinist restriction on offers of the gospel.[90] By 1874 Spurgeon described the state of hyper-Calvinism as "on the wane." He wrote, "Its leading ministers have fallen of late like leaves in autumn, and their successors are not forthcoming."[91] Yet by this date, even Spurgeon's evangelical Calvinism was on the wane.

Calvinism in Nineteenth-Century Scotland

The state of Scottish Calvinism in the nineteenth century is complex and merits a book-length treatment in its own right. Nevertheless, it is worth tracing a few developments here, since Scottish Brethren—particularly of the Open variety—played a crucial role in the ongoing development of the movement as the century progressed.[92]

The Westminster Confession of Faith (WCF) was the doctrinal standard for Calvinist orthodoxy in Scotland. From 1647 onward all ministers of the Church of Scotland were required to subscribe to the Confession, and that commitment was strengthened in the 1690s and again in 1711. Even the various seceding bodies upheld the doctrinal core of the Confession

---

87. A third important Brethren leader, George Vicesimus Wigram (1805–79), who would be crucial to the development of the Plymouth assembly, was also at Oxford from 1826, though he did not graduate. Wigram was a valuable friend to Newton at Oxford; however, his formative spiritual experience came earlier in Geneva in connection with the *réveil*. Stunt, *From Awakening,* 198–200.

88. Carter, *Anglican Evangelicals,* 302.

89. See Murray, *Spurgeon v. Hyper-Calvinism,* and Oliver, *History,* 342–52.

90. See, for example, his sermon on Acts 3:19 in *Metropolitan Tabernacle Pulpit,* 14:194.

91. *Sword and the Trowel,* (Feb. 1874), 50.

92. See Dickson, *Brethren in Scotland.*

through the eighteenth century.[93] Yet the nineteenth century witnessed a drift away from that doctrinal core in some quarters, so that by 1879 strict subscription to the Confession was no longer required in the United Presbyterian Church. In order to accommodate "liberty of opinion," ministers were required to subscribe only to a nebulous "substance of the faith" in connection to the WCF.[94] A similar Declaratory Act was passed by the Free Church in 1892, although this provoked strong resistance among Highland conservatives who remained loyal to the Confession.[95]

Of most relevance to the present study are developments connected with James Morison (1816–93), "Scotland's most prominent Arminian preacher and theologian."[96] After attending Edinburgh University (1830–34), Morison trained for ministry at the Theological Hall of the United Secession Church (1834–39), where he became close to Professor John Brown. Brown would play a prominent role in the atonement controversy in the United Secession Church (1841–45) for advocating a wider view of the extent of the atonement than was traditionally understood in the WCF.

Licensed to preach in 1839, Morison was sent to the north of Scotland, where he observed some revivals with great interest. He read Charles Finney's *Lectures on the Revival of Religion* and it had a profound influence on him—so much so that he declared in a letter to his father, "I have reaped more benefit from the book than from all other human compositions put together."[97] He began to modify his views accordingly, including a universal view of the extent of the atonement. Morison was called to Clerk's Lane Church, Kilmarnock, but questions about his Calvinistic orthodoxy quickly surfaced. He was summoned to answer for his views in March 1841 before the Kilmarnock Presbytery, and in turn was suspended from the ministry. He appealed the decision to the United Secession Church Synod, which met in June. The appeal was dismissed and Morison was removed from his ministerial office. Subsequently, many of Morison's congregation followed him into secession. His former professor, John Brown, publicly dissented from the Synod's decision to dismiss Morison's appeal, a stance taken by some as

---

93. Although there was dissent from the Confession's teaching on the role of the civil magistrate in church affairs.

94. See Hamilton, *Erosion*, 137–60. For doctrinal trends of the period, see also Cheyne, *Transforming of the Kirk*, 60–87.

95. See MacLeod, *The Second Disruption*, 179–232.

96. *DSCHT*, s.n. "James Morison." Morison's dates are wrongly listed here as 1816–63; he lived until 1893. Useful summaries of Morison may also be found in *BDE*, *BDEB*, and *ODNB*.

97. Adamson, *Life*, 55.

approval of Morison's views. This launched a prolonged controversy in the United Secession Church over the extent of the atonement.[98]

By 1843 Morison's adoption of Arminian theology was complete and he, along with three other suspended ministers who supported his views (including his father),[99] formed the Evangelical Union—an association of churches united by evangelistic zeal along Finneyite lines and a rejection of Calvinism.[100] Their version of Arminianism—often dubbed "Morisonianism"—included an emphasis on the love of God for all, conditional election, universal atonement, and the universality of the Holy Spirit's work in all people, although that work was ultimately dependent on the free will of humans to accept or reject the message of salvation. Morison's contribution was significant. He helped make Arminianism acceptable in a country that had long been dominated by Calvinism. Foster notes, "His teaching had considerable influence beyond the boundaries of the Evangelical Union, especially among Scottish Congregationalists and Baptists. In the latter part of his life, Morison saw his ideas gain widespread acceptance in Scotland; even in Presbyterian circles, he was respected."[101]

In 1851, Morison moved from Kilmarnock to minister to the Evangelical Union congregation in Glasgow. The work flourished, and a chapel was built on North Dundas Street in 1853. Morison continued his ministry there until poor health compelled him to retire in 1884. One of the active families in North Dundas Street Church was the Marshall family. John Wallace Marshall was a lay preacher and an elder. When his son, Alexander Marshall (1847-1928), was converted in his teens, he too became actively involved in the Evangelical Union. Alexander Marshall developed gifts as an evangelist and eventually served as a director of the Evangelical Union's Home Mission. He was soon recognized as "one of its most ardent

---

98. For an extended discussion of the controversy see Hamilton, *Erosion*, 43–81.

99. Morison wrote a biographical sketch of his father, Rev. Robert Morison (1782-1855), in Morison, *Worthies*, 9–23.

100. See *DSCHT*, s.v. "Evangelical Union"; Ferguson, *History*. Cf. Dickson, *Brethren in Scotland*, 41–47.

101. *BDEB*, s.n. "James Morison," 792. This is not to suggest that Morison and his circle represented the lone voice for Arminianism. John McLeod Campbell (1800-1872) and Thomas Erskine (1788-1870) had provoked an earlier atonement controversy (1828-31) for their advocacy of universal atonement, and Erskine published a book-length repudiation of the Calvinistic doctrine of election in 1837. Campbell came to reject penal substitution and advocated a view of Christ's suffering as vicarious repentance on the behalf of humanity. Both Campbell and Erskine played a role in liberalizing Scottish theology. For important studies see, Stevenson, *God in Our Nature* and Horrocks, *Laws of the Spiritual Order*. On both Erskine and Campbell see Torrance, *Scottish Theology*, 263–317.

preachers."[102] As a member of North Dundas Street Church, Marshall enjoyed Morison's friendship. Morison personally recommended him as a counsellor to the Moody campaign in Glasgow in 1874 and printed some of Marshall's articles in Evangelical Union publications.[103] However, Marshall resisted the encouragement of friends to enroll in the Evangelical Union's theological school, and around 1874 he began meeting with a small group of Brethren. He was drawn to the Brethren's biblicism, primitive ecclesiology, and zeal for evangelism. By 1876 he had become a full-time evangelist among the Brethren and continued as a valued worker and popular author into the early decades of the twentieth century.[104] Significantly, Marshall did not abandon his Arminianism when he joined the Brethren; instead, he brought it to the movement. Subsequent chapters will interact with Marshall's thought on key soteriological doctrines and how they meshed with a largely Calvinistic movement.

Despite this drift by some, Westminster Calvinism was still the "reigning theology" among conservative evangelicals. Cheyne claims, "Even in the 1860s and 1870s, the weight of numbers in every Presbyterian communion was still very much on the conservative side, theologically speaking."[105] During the mid-nineteenth century, the Free Church, for example, demonstrated its Calvinism by its "strict adherence to the doctrines of predestination and the Divine Decrees."[106] Thomas Chalmers was an important voice representing a more moderate Calvinism; he contributed to softening Calvinism's "doctrinaire character so that it would serve the practical needs of contemporary evangelism."[107] A vigorous Calvinism remained dominant in certain Highland communities, defended by the most influential Highland minister of the later nineteenth century, John Kennedy (1819–84).[108] Kennedy fiercely opposed new trends in ecclesiology, liturgy, preaching, and doctrine.[109] This was especially evident in his objection to the Moody campaign of 1873–74 in Scotland. He disliked the new methods and was sure

102. Hawthorn, *Alexander Marshall*, 27.
103. Ibid., 30, 115.
104. Pickering, "Home-calling of a True Gospel Warrior," 411–12.
105. Cheyne, "The Place of the Confession," 22.
106. Drummond and Bulloch, *The Church in Victorian Scotland*, 21.
107. Ibid., 17.
108. Macleod called Kennedy "the great preacher of his generation in Scotland" and claimed, "the great Puritans had no more eminent successor in the Scottish ministry in the 19th century." Macleod, *Scottish Theology*, 327. William Cunningham (1805–61) was another important voice for traditional Calvinism in the Free Church.
109. See especially Sell, *Defending and Declaring*, chapter 2 "John Kennedy of Dingwall (1819–1884): The Old Paths," 17–38.

the enthusiasm of revivalism would not produce lasting results.[110] But he was particularly concerned that the innovations of the campaign were undermining Calvinist orthodoxy. He believed the new evangelism "ignores the sovereignty and power of God in the dispensation of His grace." Writing of evangelists like Moody, he declared,

> Men, anxious to secure a certain result, and determined to produce it, do not like to think of a controlling will, to whose sovereign behests they must submit, and of the necessity of almighty power being at work, whose action must be regulated by another will than theirs. Certain processes must lead to certain results. This selfish earnestness, this proud resolve to make a manageable business of conversion-work, is intolerant of any recognition of the sovereignty of God.[111]

The phenomenon of "sudden" conversions was also suspect and smacked of human manipulation rather than the sovereign work of God. Kennedy was challenged in his protest by fellow Free Church minister and Calvinist, Horatius Bonar. Bonar pointed out that the conversions described in the New Testament were sudden, and thus produced by the sovereign work of God. Furthermore, God was free to accomplish his work in different ways, as was evident in the Evangelical Revival of the eighteenth century: "He wrought not only by the Calvinist Whitefield, but the Arminian Wesley."[112]

Kenneth Ross suggests that part of the difference in perspectives lies in the fact that traditional patterns of ministry were still relatively effective in conservative Highland communities like Dingwall where Kennedy ministered, while such methods were ineffective in the Lowland urban centers where Bonar labored. Thus "to organise special evangelistic campaigns was not, for Bonar, to deny the sovereignty of God but rather, in humble dependence upon that very sovereignty, to seek to meet the missionary demands of changed times."[113] Highland Calvinism had its own character, ethos, and tradition, all of which was incompatible with the Moody campaign.[114] This is not to suggest that Highland Calvinism was necessarily hyper-Calvinism. Kennedy practiced and defended the free offer of the gospel to all. Sell explains, "Kennedy offered Christ to all comers. He did not encourage undue introspection; he did not suggest that the gospel was only for 'sensible sin-

---

110. Ross, "Calvinists in Controversy," 53.
111. Kennedy, *Hyper-Evangelism*, 13.
112. Bonar, *The Old Gospel*, 10.
113. Ross, "Calvinists in Controversy," 55.
114. Ibid., 60.

ners'; and he was no antinomian. A High Calvinist he was; a Hyper-Calvinist he was not."[115] The perspectives of Kennedy and Bonar illustrate that within Westminster Calvinism there was a spectrum of traditional and progressive approaches operative in the later part of the nineteenth century.

This background connects with the Brethren in at least two ways that anticipate discussion in further chapters. First, John Nelson Darby, an ardent Calvinist, was critical of Moody's Arminianism and skeptical of the campaign in Scotland, doubting the work would produce lasting results. He wrote, "I fully judge it will foster worldliness in saints; it will foster heresy and false doctrine." He did believe that real conversions had occurred, and rejoiced in this, but he thought the percentage of genuine conversion was quite low—"seventy five out of fifteen hundred alleged conversions."[116] Second, understanding something of the ethos of Highland Calvinism helps explain why Brethren evangelists such as Donald Ross, Donald Munro, and especially Alexander Marshall, encountered such opposition to their preaching there, a theme to which we will return in chapter 7.

The 1859–60 Revivals

The revivals in Ulster and the North-East of Scotland were an important catalyst for evangelical—and more specifically, Brethren—growth in the second half of the nineteenth century.[117] Many Brethren leaders either participated or were converted in the revivals.[118] Others rode the wave of the revivalist tide and became full-time evangelists, which did much to spread the movement in Britain and beyond. The revivals also shaped the ethos of the Brethren movement, particularly the Open branch, which Coad describes as a "gospel mission,"[119] complete with itinerant evangelists preaching either in the open-air or in tents and rented halls.

But what of the theology spawned by the revivals? As we will see in chapter 7, there were many critics from the Reformed tradition who objected not only to the new methods, but also to the Arminian character of the

---

115. Sell, *Defending and Declaring*, 33–34.

116. Darby, *Letters*, 2:257–59 (1874).

117. See Grass, *Gathering to His Name*, 117–28; Dickson, *Brethren in Scotland*, 59–75; Bebbington, *Evangelicalism in Modern Britain*, 116–17. See also Jeffrey, *When the Lord Walked the Land*.

118. The Brethren magazine *The Harvester* calculated that about 80 percent of the leaders sketched in Henry Pickering's *Chief Men among the Brethren* "were 'impressed' in conversion or Christian service by the Awakening." Mills and Sookhdeo, "Revival and the Brethren," 262.

119. Coad, *History of the Brethren*, 185.

preaching.[120] On the other hand, many Calvinists participated in the revivals and maintained a strong grasp of their principles, including the doctrines of human inability and unconditional election. Describing the situation in Ulster, McKee points to "a considerable amount of evidence of orthodox Calvinist teaching in this Revival and, more than that, the emphasis which was so often laid upon the sovereign grace of God may betoken a widespread orthodox Calvinist ethos which was present among large numbers of Presbyterian people who were involved in the Revival."[121] Carson suggests, "the work was so much the work of God that it owed comparatively little to the gifts of outstanding preachers."[122] Throughout this book we will explore the soteriology of Brethren evangelists and how it impacted their preaching.

Calvinism in the Later Nineteenth Century

As the century wore on, Calvinism seemed to fade. It was kept alive among conservative groups and from obscurity by Spurgeon, evangelicalism's brightest star. Yet even with Spurgeon's influence, the doctrines of grace seemed to be increasingly marginalized by evangelicals.[123] As early as 1858, Silas Henn published *Spurgeon's Calvinism Examined and Refuted*, in which he viewed the renowned preacher's defense of Calvinism as something of an oddity. He wrote,

> By many, the Calvinistic controversy has been considered as long since settled, and comparatively few in these times, amid such enlightened views of Christianity, dare to proclaim openly and without disguise, the peculiar tenets of John Calvin. Even in many professedly Calvinistic pulpits, the doctrines are greatly modified, and genuine Calvinism is kept back. But there are some who hold it forth in all its length and breadth, and among these, the Rev. C. H. Spurgeon, the notorious preacher at the Music Hall, Royal Surrey Gardens, is the most prominent.[124]

This opinion was shared some fifteen years later by R. W. Dale, a leading Congregationalist minister who represented a more progressive evangelicalism. Writing in the *Daily Telegraph* in December 1873, Dale offered

---

120. E.g., Hamilton, *Inquiry*, 174–76.

121. McKee, "Revivals," 98.

122. Carson, *God's River in Spate*, 112.

123. J. C. Ryle (1816–1900) was the most outstanding evangelical Calvinist within the Church of England. See especially Ryle, *Light from Old Times*.

124. Quoted in Murray, *Forgotten Spurgeon*, 53–54.

his assessment "that Calvinism would be almost obsolete among Baptists were it not still maintained by the powerful influence of Mr. Spurgeon."[125]

Spurgeon wrote a response to Dale in *The Sword and the Trowel*—"The Present Position of Calvinism in England"—in which he expressed a more optimistic outlook. "Our own judgment is the very reverse of that of Mr. Dale . . . we are persuaded that the Calvinism which it is our delight to preach, so far from being an obsolete theory, is growingly operative upon the minds of a large section of Christian people."[126] However, Spurgeon's optimism proved to be misguided. Murray observes, "By the 1880s Spurgeon came to see that the tide was not for Calvinism, but against it. When Dale, in 1881, repeated his belief that 'Mr. Spurgeon stands alone among the modern leaders of Evangelical Nonconformity in his fidelity to the older Calvinistic creed,' Spurgeon did not attempt to refute it."[127] He would confess in 1884, "In theology I stand where I did when I began preaching, and I stand almost alone . . . I could preach my earliest sermons now without change so far as the essential doctrines are concerned. I stand almost exactly where Calvin stood . . . [but] that position is taken by few."[128]

By the second half of the nineteenth century, the advancing liberal theology of the times was making an impact on evangelicalism.[129] For example, in 1859 the London Congregationalist minister James Baldwin Brown published *The Divine Life in Man*. The book argued "for a break with the doctrinal inheritance of moderate Calvinism," and instead focused on themes of the Fatherhood of God, the freedom of man, and the responsibility to pursue righteousness."[130] Other issues were occupying the attention of evangelicals, such as higher biblical criticism, a milder version of the atonement, a softer stance toward eternal punishment, and Darwinian evolution.[131] In the Down Grade controversy of 1887–88, Spurgeon stood firm against the encroaching liberalism in his own denomination, yet he felt it necessary to withdraw from the Baptist Union.[132] The Down Grade was not a protest against Arminian theology; it was more fundamental still. Spurgeon was "criticizing those who, swayed by contemporary intellectual currents, were

125. Ibid., 170.
126. Spurgeon, "Present Position," 50.
127. Murray, *Forgotten Spurgeon*, 176.
128. Spurgeon, *Autobiography*, 2:393. For Spurgeon's "Defence of Calvinism," Spurgeon, *Autobiography*, 1:163–75.
129. See Bebbington, *Dominance of Evangelicalism*, 163–83.
130. Ibid., 166.
131. Ibid., 259.
132. On the Down Grade Controversy see Hopkins, *Nonconformity's Romantic Generation*, 193–248, and Nettles, *Living by Revealed Truth*, 541–78.

'giving up the atoning sacrifice, denying the inspiration of Holy Scripture, and casting slurs upon justification by faith.'"[133]

By the close of the century the Calvinist-Arminian debate had essentially run aground, so that in 1891 the traditionally Calvinistic Baptist Union was able to merge with the evangelical Arminians of the New Connexion.[134] For our purposes, we note that the Brethren remained staunchly resistant to the liberal tendencies of the "new evangelicalism," yet subsequent chapters will explore whether or not the trend away from Calvinism would evidence itself in Brethren theology as well.

Conclusion

Although the present and previous chapters have covered much ground, they are by no means exhaustive. The goal has been to establish some background into the nature of Calvinistic soteriology; to get a broad sense of Calvinistic debate among evangelicals from the seventeenth century on; and to highlight some trends in nineteenth-century Calvinism as the backdrop to Brethren discussion. We have observed that the Calvinist-Arminian debate was a central theological feature of evangelical theology and that within the Calvinist tradition there was a significant spectrum of thought. Yet these were not issues relegated to the ivory towers of scholarship; they were crucial to understanding the very gospel evangelicals cherished. Central to the debate was the nature and extent of divine sovereignty, predestination, and the work of Christ in redemption, as well as the role of human responsibility in view of human sinfulness and depravity. All of these issues had immediate relevance in the practical ministry of preaching and evangelism and thus could not be avoided.

Although the Brethren often presented themselves as aloof from the influences of the world, and even of other evangelicals ("the sects and the schisms"), they nevertheless manifested characteristics of both the moderate and high Calvinism to which we have drawn attention in these opening chapters. In the chapters that follow we will endeavor to establish that Calvinistic soteriology was indeed a characteristic of Brethren thought, and we will explore the precise shape Brethren Calvinism took in the nineteenth century.

---

133. Bebbington, "Evangelicalism," 248 citing *The Sword and the Trowel* (April 1887), 195.

134. Sell, *Great Debate*, 95.

4

"The Total Ruin of Man"

Fallen Human Nature in Brethren Thought

For what were we whom Thou didst save
But helpless victims of the grave?
Our outer life o'erspread with sin,
And not a jot of good within.

—William Kelly[1]

Man has . . . no heart to love God, no power to understand God, no will to obey God. He is incurably, irremediably bad; his only moral power is power to act according to the dictates of his nature, and therefore to hate God, to disobey God, and to disbelieve God continually.

—John Eliot Howard[2]

Historical Background

IN MANY WAYS, THE question of the degree to which the fall has affected human nature is the foundational issue in the Calvinism-Arminianism debate. Do people retain a moral or spiritual ability to turn to God? Or has sin so

1. Kelly, *Hymns and Poems*, 13.
2. Howard, *"New Views,"* 7.

impacted the human will that all spiritual ability has been lost? Under its own power, can the human heart receive or only reject God? In historical theology, three basic positions have been prominent in discussions of human sinfulness and the condition of the will. The positions are briefly summarized here in order to set the stage for an examination of Brethren teaching on these issues.

Pelagianism

In the fifth century Pelagius taught that humans possess absolute free will, which includes the ability to obey God and refrain from sin. According to Pelagius, it is absurd for God to command obedience if humans are unable to obey those commands. While God's grace in the form of the law and the teaching of Christ is available as an external aid, it is not strictly necessary, for humans have the innate ability to obey God perfectly. On the question of original sin, Pelagius taught that Adam's sin harmed only himself. No one inherits a corrupt nature from Adam or an inclination to sin; rather, each person is born in the same state as Adam before the fall. Pelagianism was condemned at the Council of Carthage in 418, the Council of Ephesus in 431, and again at the Council of Orange in 529.

Augustinianism

Augustine vigorously opposed Pelagianism. He affirmed that as a result of the fall, the human will was irreparably damaged. Through Adam's sin, humans inherit a corrupt nature and are inclined to sin. Indeed, the condition of fallen humanity is *non posse non peccare* (not able not to sin). Humans still possess free will in the sense that they are able to make voluntary choices. In their fallen condition, however, their will is bent away from God and toward sin. Left to their own power, they would never embrace Christ. Thus in salvation, God chooses to save some by granting them prevenient grace—that is, grace that comes *before* any response of the sinner. This grace is effectual in the sense that it always accomplishes its purpose: the conversion of the will. God's grace awakens the elect sinner and transforms the will so that he now *willingly* embraces Christ.

Semi-Pelagianism

Not everyone who condemned Pelagianism was happy with all of the Augustinian alternatives. The chief spokesman of what would later be called 'semi-Pelagianism'[3] was John Cassian, abbot of the monastery of Massilia. Critics of Augustine like Cassian affirmed that in the fall, humans lose neither free will nor the ability to choose the good. Nevertheless, contrary to Pelagius, they held that the grace of God is necessary to assist the will. In some, grace precedes and promotes a good will; in others, it comes to the aid of a good will already present.[4] For Cassian, "the grace of God always co-operates with our will for its advantage, and in all things assists, protects, and defends it."[5] In semi-Pelagianism the human will is weakened by the fall (*infirmitas liberi arbitrii*) and must cooperate with the grace of God for salvation. Thus there is a synergistic relationship between the will and the grace of God. The Synod of Arles (473) rejected Augustinian monergism and affirmed this semi-Pelagian synergism: "Man's effort and endeavor is to be united with God's grace; man's freedom of will is not extinct but attenuated and weakened."[6] However, the advance of semi-Pelagianism was checked by the Council of Orange (529). It denied that humans can take the initiative in salvation and affirmed: "The sin of the first man has so impaired and weakened free will that no one thereafter can either love God as he ought or believe in God or do good for God's sake, unless the grace of divine mercy has preceded him."[7]

---

3. The actual term was not coined until the sixteenth century. Pelikan wryly comments, "The penchant for tagging every doctrinal position with a party label has led to the invention of the name Semi-Pelagianism, which is even less useful than most such designations." Pelikan, *Emergence*, 318. Some prefer the label "Semi-Augustinian" for Augustine himself, while he charged that they were still "in darkness on the question concerning the predestination of the saints," nevertheless referred to them as "brethren of ours." Furthermore in Augustine's mind, their acceptance of original sin and the necessity of grace "abundantly distinguish them from the error of the Pelagians." Augustine, *Treatise on Predestination*, 498.

4. "When [God] sees in us some beginnings of a good will, He at once enlightens it and strengthens it and urges it on towards salvation, increasing that which He Himself implanted or which He sees to have arisen from our own efforts." Cassian, *Third Conference*, 426.

5. Ibid., 430.

6. Bettenson and Maunder, *Documents*, 66.

7. *Canons of the Council of Orange*.

Later Church History

These positions continued to be debated to varying degrees throughout the history of the Western church. The Reformation saw a renewal of the Augustinian position with Luther defending the bondage of the will against, most notably, Erasmus's defense of free will.[8] Indeed, Luther saw this as a core issue of the Reformation.[9] He wrote: "I hold that a solemn and vital truth, of eternal consequence, is at stake in the discussion; one so crucial and fundamental that it ought to be maintained and defended even at the cost of life, though as a result the whole world should be, not just thrown into turmoil and uproar, but shattered in chaos and reduced to nothingness."[10]

This was not literary hyperbole for Luther. He was convinced that the condition of the will was right at the heart of the Reformation. In his conclusion, Luther thanked Erasmus for raising the issue because, in Luther's words, "You alone, in contrast with all others, have attacked the real thing, that is, the essential issue. You have not wearied me with those extraneous issues about the Papacy, purgatory, indulgences and such like—trifles, rather than issues—in respect of which almost all to date have sought my blood . . . you, and you alone, have seen the hinge on which all turns, and aimed for the vital spot."[11]

Luther was not alone here. In the introduction to their translation of Luther's *Bondage of the Will*, J. I. Packer and O. R. Johnston assert:

> Historically, it is a simple matter of fact that Martin Luther and John Calvin, and, for that matter, Ulrich Zwingli, Martin Bucer, and all the leading Protestant theologians of the first epoch of the Reformation, stood on precisely the same ground here. On other points, they had their differences; but in asserting the helplessness of man in sin, and the sovereignty of God in grace, they were entirely at one. To all of them, these doctrines were the very life-blood of the Christian faith.[12]

Calvinistic soteriology was defined at the Synod of Dort in 1618–19. Regarding the nature of fallen humanity, Dort stated: "All men are conceived

---

8. Rupp and Watson, *Luther and Erasmus*.

9. Highlighting the importance of this issue for the Reformation, B. B. Warfield said of Luther's *Bondage of the Will*: "It is the embodiment of Luther's reformation conceptions, the nearest to a systematic statement of them he ever made. It is the first exposition of the fundamental ideas of the Reformation in comprehensive presentation, and it is therefore in a true sense the manifesto of the Reformation." Warfield, *Works*, 9:471.

10. Luther, *Bondage of the Will*, 90.

11. Ibid., 319.

12. Ibid., 58.

in sin, and are by nature children of wrath, incapable of any saving good, prone to evil, dead in sin, and in bondage thereto; and without the regenerating grace of the Holy Spirit, they are neither able nor willing to return to God, to reform the depravity of their nature, nor to dispose themselves to reformation."[13]

Likewise, the Westminster Confession of Faith (1647) reiterated the orthodox Calvinist position, affirming that fallen man "hath wholly lost all ability of will to any spiritual good accompanying salvation" (9:3).

As evangelicalism developed in the eighteenth century, George Whitefield and John Wesley highlighted the difference between the Calvinist and Arminian positions that formed the boundary markers of orthodoxy for the movement. Wesley maintained a strong view of depravity and even denied that fallen humanity possessed free will in relation to God. He could say, "I believe that Adam, before his fall, had such freedom of will, that he might choose either good or evil; but that, since the fall, no child of man has a natural power to choose anything that is truly good. Yet I know . . . that man has still freedom of will in things of an indifferent nature."[14] And again, "such is the freedom of his will; free only to evil; free to 'drink in iniquity like water;' to wander farther and farther from the living God."[15] Nevertheless, Wesley veered away from the Calvinist position at this point through his doctrine of prevenient grace. For Wesley, although the natural man is spiritually dead and unable to make the slightest move toward God, prevenient grace restores the freedom of will lost in the fall and thus enables people to choose or reject God. Wesley wrote, "There is a measure of free-will supernaturally restored to every man, together with that supernatural light which 'enlightens every man that cometh into the world.'"[16] Prevenient grace is God's gift to all people, leaving the ultimate determination of salvation to human decision.[17]

The American Calvinist Jonathan Edwards sought to refute Arminian ideas in his work *Freedom of the Will*.[18] First published in Boston in 1754, the book made a significant contribution to the Calvinist-Arminian debate on both sides of the Atlantic. As noted in chapter 2, Edwards's work had a

---

13. Canons of the Synod of Dort, Third and Fourth Heads of Doctrine, Article III.
14. Wesley, *Works*, 10:350.
15. Ibid., 5:104.
16. Ibid., 10:229–30.
17. For an evaluation from a Calvinist perspective see Schreiner, "Does Scripture Teach," 2:365–82.
18. The full title is: *A Careful and Strict Enquiry into the Modern Prevailing Notions of that Freedom of Will, which Is Supposed To Be Essential to Moral Agency, Virtue and Vice, Reward and Punishment, Praise and Blame.*

profound impact on Andrew Fuller and his circle as they developed an evangelistic Calvinism that challenged the hyper-Calvinism of their Particular Baptist heritage.[19] Edwards's exposition of the distinction between natural and moral inability "was the key that unlocked the question of duty faith" for Fuller and his friends.[20] Edwards described moral inability as consisting "in the want of inclination; or the strength of a contrary inclination; or the want of sufficient motives in view, to induce and excite the act of the will, or the strength of apparent motives to the contrary."[21] For Fuller and others this meant that sinners could be invited to respond to the gospel, contra hyper-Calvinism, since they lacked no *natural* ability to comply with its terms. The problem was identified in the fact that all people, as a result of original sin, lacked *moral* ability to embrace the gospel. Fallen humans simply did not desire to repent and follow Christ; their inclinations to sin were greater, and thus they bore responsibility for their unbelief. This insight enabled evangelical Calvinists to maintain their doctrine of depravity and yet offer the gospel freely to all people.

As observed in chapter 3, by the nineteenth century, Calvinism and Arminianism remained prominent in evangelical polemics, and the question concerning the freedom or bondage of the will took on heightened significance by mid-century in light of new methods utilized in revival evangelism. The most influential and controversial figure for the transatlantic evangelical movement was Charles Grandison Finney (1792–1875). Finney believed that conversion and revivals were the product of careful planning and the use of proper techniques. His methods were often opposed by Calvinists, but they appealed to evangelicals eager for results; by 1850 over eighty thousand copies of Finney's *Lectures on Revivals of Religion* had been sold in Britain.[22] Finney's success as an evangelist made him a pragmatist when it came to theological questions. Indeed, "his theology was patterned to fit his career as a revivalist"; consequently he displayed little patience with "the Calvinistic theological system."[23]

Finney claimed to be "embarrassed" by the traditional Calvinistic doctrine of human depravity—specifically, the teaching which insisted that fallen human beings possess an inherited sinful nature and a will plagued by moral inability. Upon subsequent study he judged such doctrines to be

---

19. See Hindmarsh, "Reception of Jonathan Edwards," 207–12.
20. Ibid., 208.
21. Edwards, *Freedom of the Will*, 159.
22. Carwardine, *Transatlantic Revivalism*, xiv.
23. Johnson, "Charles G. Finney," 338.

unbiblical.[24] In his *Lectures on Systematic Theology*, Finney set out his own unique position, distinguishing between physical and moral depravity. Physical depravity refers to deterioration of the faculties of the human body and mind through sickness or age. This sort of depravity "can have no moral character in itself, for the plain reason that it is involuntary, and in its nature is disease, and not sin."[25]

Moral depravity, on the other hand, consists in an individual's free moral choice. Finney explained, "Moral depravity is the depravity of free-will, not of the faculty itself, but of its free action. It consists in a violation of moral law." He argued that while all people are morally depraved, this does not mean individuals possess an inherently sinful nature. Nor is the will in itself depraved, for that would involve physical depravity, which is, by definition, amoral. "Moral depravity, as I use the term, consists in selfishness; in a state of voluntary committal of the will to self-gratification."[26] Lucas summarizes Finney's position and its impact for evangelism as follows: "A sin nature is non-existent; rather sin consists solely in sinning, the decisions of the will to satisfy self rather than glorify God. Therefore, in order to have a conversion, it is necessary to convince an individual to cease making decisions to satisfy self and to begin making decisions to glorify God."[27] Not everyone influenced by Finney adopted his Pelagianistic view of depravity, but his ideas certainly presented a challenge to traditional Calvinism.

Charles Finney was by no means the only one seeking to overturn the Calvinist view of human moral inability.[28] By the 1820s in Scotland, for example, where Calvinism had long reigned, Thomas Erskine was advancing notions of free will and other Arminian doctrines.[29] By the end of the century, trends in evangelism, theology, and science resulted in the decline of Calvinistic anthropology, even among evangelicals.[30]

---

24. Finney, *Lectures on Systematic Theology*, ix.

25. Ibid., 229.

26. Ibid., 231.

27. Lucas, "Charles Finney's Theology," 203. Cf. Smith, "Theology of Charles Finney," 75–76.

28. Yet as Carwardine notes, "at the popular, less intellectually sophisticated level, Finney had no rival." Carwardine, *Transatlantic Revivalism*, 97.

29. See Horrocks, *Laws of the Spiritual Order*, 154–55, 168–69, 173.

30. For a discussion of scientific views of the will and the impact of Darwinism on theology see Livingston, *Religious Thought*, 150–229.

The Brethren on "The Total Ruin of Man"

We turn now to examine how Brethren writers handled the question of human sinfulness and the condition of the will. We begin with three of the most prolific and influential Brethren writers of the nineteenth century: Darby, Kelly, and Mackintosh. Since all three were Exclusive Brethren, their ecclesiology was not followed by the Open branch of the movement.[31] Yet on other doctrinal subjects they were highly regarded and widely read even by Open Brethren.[32] The present section will also examine a representative sample of other influential teachers in the movement before we turn our attention to some key Brethren evangelists.

Influential Brethren Teachers

John Nelson Darby (1800–1882)

Darby is perhaps best remembered in the wider theological world for his development of dispensationalism. What is less known is the foundation on which his dispensational scheme rested, namely, Calvinism. George Marsden could say, "Darby was himself an unrelenting Calvinist. His interpretation of the Bible and of history rested firmly on the massive pillar of divine sovereignty, placing as little value as possible on human ability."[33]

Darby's favorite expression to describe the nature of fallen humanity was "the total ruin of man,"[34] by which he meant "total depravity" in contemporary Calvinist parlance. This was a doctrine he held strongly—so much so, that he often expressed concern over what he perceived as a drift toward Arminianism among evangelicals on this point.[35] In a letter dated October 23, 1861, Darby responded to an enquiry about "free will." He answered, "This fresh breaking out of the doctrine of free-will ministers to the pretension of the natural man not to be entirely lost, for that is just what

---

31. E.g., [Ritchie], "Young Believer's Question Box," (1893), 70.

32. See Grass, *Gathering to His Name*, 4, 199.

33. Marsden, *Fundamentalism*, 46. Marsden adds, "John Nelson Darby puzzled over how [D. L.] Moody could on the one hand accept the prophetic truths concerning God's sovereignty in history, and yet inconsistently allow room for a non-Calvinist view of human ability when it came to personal salvation. But Moody was more American ... He preferred action to intellectual systems, and freedom to authoritarianism." Ibid.

34. In addition to examples that will be cited in this section, see Darby, *Additional Writings*, 2:248; Darby, *Synopsis*, 4:392; Darby, *CW*, 13:296; 14:352; 34:264. He also employed similar phrases, such as "the utter ruin of man." See Darby, "Utter Ruin," 258.

35. E.g., Darby, *Letters: Supplement*, 2:320.

it amounts to." He added that free will is "the dogma of the Wesleyans, of all reasoners, of all philosophers," but for Darby this doctrine "completely changes the whole idea of Christianity, and entirely perverts it."[36] Clearly this was no secondary matter.

Instead, Darby believed that the human heart "is so corrupt, and his will so determined not to submit to God . . . that nothing can induce him to receive the Lord, and to forsake sin." Regarding the Wesleyans, Darby charged that "their confidence in their own strength makes confusion in their teaching, and leads them not to recognize the total ruin of man."[37] By contrast, he asserted: "As for me, I see in the word, and I recognize in myself, the total ruin of man. I see that the cross is the end of all the means that God has employed to gain the heart of man, and, consequently, that it proves the thing impossible. God has exhausted all His resources; man has shewn that he was wicked, past recovery; the cross of Christ condemns man—sin in the flesh."[38]

Regarding the condition of the will, Darby affirmed that man is free *to* will, in the sense that there is no external constraint or compulsion forcing his choices. However, man is not free *in* will, "because the law in his members brings it into captivity, which is merely saying he has a sinful nature."[39] The sin nature inclines the will to evil, and thus it is right to say the will is in bondage. Darby went so far as to deny that man before the fall possessed will, in the sense of standing independently from God: "Morally, man unfallen had no will, for creature perfection is obedience; man, fallen, is governed in disobedience by corrupt motives, and thus is merely a sinner, and his will is *under* sin."[40] Thus for Darby the concept of free moral will is "pure nonsense." Freedom simply means that "God does not hinder [man] choosing good, or force him to choose evil."[41] But since the fall, the will is inclined toward evil and chooses accordingly.[42] Consequently, fallen

36. Darby, *Letters*, 1:314. This letter is reproduced with slight alterations as "Letter on Free-Will" in *CW*, 10:185–87.

37. Darby, *Letters*, 1:315.

38. Ibid.

39. Darby, *Notes and Comments*, 1:162.

40. Ibid. Similar sentiments were expressed in Newberry "God's Will," 125. Newberry (1811–1901) left Exclusivism for Open assemblies in 1866.

41. Darby, *Notes and Comments*, 1:163.

42. Darby's view is akin to what is commonly known today as "compatibilism" or "soft determinism." See Feinberg, *No One Like Him*, 637. Paul Helm explains compatibilism as follows: "people perform free acts when they do what they want to do, not when they have the power of self-causation, or some other version of indeterminism. That is, they are not constrained or compelled in their actions, but what they do flows unimpededly from their wants, desires, preferences, goals and the like." Helm, *Providence of*

humans have no desire for Christ. He wrote, "When Christ is presented, man is free to receive Him . . . but his actual state is proved by his seeing no beauty in Him to desire Him."[43] What is necessary to change this condition is divine and sovereign grace.

In Darby's view, advocates of free will denied the necessity of grace in conversion. It was incomprehensible to him how sinners, of their own fallen accord, could embrace Christ. He asserted, "Arminianism, or rather Pelagianism, pretends that man can choose, and that thus the old man is ameliorated by the thing it has accepted. The first step is made without grace."[44] Darby's equating of Arminianism with Pelagianism shows how much he disliked Arminian doctrine, and how serious an issue this was for him.[45]

In another letter, dated April 17, 1872, Darby returned to the topic of the will. His comments are worth repeating at length for their clarity.

> Where the Lord says, "No one can come to me except the Father which hath sent me draw him;" it is not that God prohibits or hinders, but that man is so wicked in will and corrupt, that unless a power outside himself act on him he cannot come—he is never morally so disposed. Man is perfectly free to come now as far as God is concerned, and invited to come, yea, besought . . . But then there is the other side, man's own will and state. There is no will to come, but the opposite . . . Man does not wish to be with God . . . The crucifixion of the Lord is the proof that man would not have God . . . To say he is not inclined to evil, is to deny all scripture and all fact; to make him free to choose he must be as yet indifferent, indifferent to—having no preference for—good and evil, which is not true, for evil lusts and self-will are there, the two great elements of sin . . . I have learned by experience under divine teaching that I am *not* free and cannot free myself.[46]

So humans do not have "free will"; their wills are enslaved to sin. This was not the case in the beginning, but is a consequence of the fall.[47] In

---

God, 67. It is noteworthy that Darby uses both terms "constraint" and "compulsion" in precisely the same way that contemporary compatibilists use the terms.

43. Darby, *Notes and Comments*, 1:164. "Man in the flesh cannot see beauty in Christ, any more than keep the law." Darby, *Letters*, 2:502 (1879).

44. Darby, *Letters*, 1:315–16.

45. Cf. Darby, *CW*, 3:19. In another place Darby strongly rejects the Pelagian presupposition: "People say, God cannot give you a rule you cannot attain to. But I say, God never gives you a rule which you can attain—never!" *CW*, 27:275 (1875).

46. Darby, *Letters* 2:164–65.

47. Ibid., 2:166–67.

their fallen state, human beings have a fundamental disposition of hostility toward God. They are not neutral but "disposed to follow that which is evil."[48] Therefore, when faced with a choice, the will of a fallen human rejects God every time.[49] Commenting on Rom 8:6–7, Darby described "the mind set on the flesh" in no uncertain terms: "The mind of the flesh is enmity against God, resists His authority, rejects His will, rises up against Him and His authority, does not like it should exist, and consequently hates Him. It is not hence subject to the law, nor can be. Its lusts will not have what [the law] claims, nor its self-will bow to the claim itself. God comes in by law, asserts authority, and forbids lust; but the flesh knows no obedience, loves its will and its lust, and hates God."[50]

Darby argued that man never wishes to believe, "because the object of faith is hateful to him."[51] He frequently referenced John 1:13 and Jas 1:18, which emphasize that salvation is produced through the will of God, not the will of man.[52] In response to the notion that faith is simply a matter of opening one's hand to receive God's gift of salvation, Darby responded, "But hearts are not so disposed; they will not open the hand."[53] He continued:

> Observe that Jesus says, "You will not come" [John 5:40]. I believe fully that they are responsible for it; but where do you find, You will? The word of God expressly says, No. "There is none that seeketh after God." He came to seek them, thank God, but when He came He was rejected; He was not received save by those who are born of God . . . Now certainly God does not hinder any one from coming, but such is the disposition of the heart of man that he will not. This is why the work of God is necessary, and why it is said, "No man can come unto me except the Father which hath sent me draw him" [John 6:44].[54]

Despite his assertion that people are responsible to come to Christ, some would argue that Darby's strong view of human inability leads to an abrogation of moral responsibility. He vehemently rejected the notion,

---

48. Ibid., 1:316.

49. "God has presented to him the choice, but it was to convince the conscience of the fact that, in any case, man would have neither good nor God." Ibid.

50. Darby, *Exposition*, 79.

51. Darby, *Letters*, 2:478, (February 1879).

52. E.g., On one occasion, after quoting John 1:11–13 (v. 13 reads "who were born, not of blood nor of the will of the flesh nor of the will of man, but of God"), Darby said, "John's Gospel is thoroughly what men call Calvinistic." Darby, *CW*, 26:249 (1871).

53. Darby, *Letters*, 2:479. A few months later, in May 1879, he made the same point but added that only grace enables one to open the hand. Ibid., 2:503.

54. Ibid., 2:479–80.

however, and stated bluntly, "I deny that morality depends on freedom of choice."[55] Human freedom consists in acting in conformity to one's nature. Darby could say, "Man has in one sense made himself free, but it is free from God, and thus is in moral apostasy and the slave of sin. From this Christ wholly delivers, and sanctifies us to obedience, having borne the penalty of the fruits of our free will."[56]

Moral responsibility still exists, even if our moral ability has been lost in the fall. Darby argued that "in the reasoning of Arminians there is a totally false principle, namely, that our responsibility depends on our power."[57] To illustrate the point, Darby suggested that a man who owes him a thousand pounds is not relieved of the responsibility because he is a spendthrift and has no money left to fulfil the obligation. Nor is the creditor forced to release the claim.[58] But surely, one might counter, the situation is different for those who were born with inability. Darby responded as follows:

> Man takes another ground of reasoning against God I know, that God put him into this place, or he was born in it, and therefore he is not responsible. This raises another point, that moral responsibility attaches to will, not to power. We do what our own consciences condemn because we like it. My child refuses to come when I call him to go with me; I am going to punish him because he would not: he pleads that he was tied or could not open the door. But I punish him because he refused as to his will to yield to the obligation: I had a knife ready to cut what bound him, a key to open the door: he by his will refused the claim. In a word, responsibility flows from the claim on us arising from the relationship in which we stand.[59]

Darby believed the question of responsibility "lies at the root of Calvinism and Arminianism,"[60] and he left no doubt that he was on the side of the Calvinist on this question. The natural human response is to make one of two errors: either to affirm human ability even after the fall, thus denying the full effects of original sin; or to deny human responsibility altogether. He wrote, "Man is responsible to keep the law perfectly, but by the fall he has lost the power. This the natural heart cannot understand. One man denies

55. Ibid., 2:167, (April 17, 1872).

56. Ibid.

57. Ibid., 2:501, (May 9, 1879).

58. Ibid., 2:168 (date uncertain). He used a similar illustration in his letter of May 9, 1879 (p. 501), but increased the debt to £100,000.

59. Ibid, 2:168; cf. Darby, *CW*, 25:242 (1871).

60. Darby, *Letters*, 2:477, in a letter dated from Elberfeld, [Germany] 1869.

his responsibility, and another assumes his power; grace, and this only, puts a man right on both points."[61]

Darby's convictions regarding the "total ruin of man" ran deep and show no evidence of change over time. Indeed, these convictions were basic to his theology—so much so, that on occasion he clashed with people over the issue. In his biography of Darby, W. G. Turner relates the following account of a dispute Darby had with the American evangelist D. L. Moody in Chicago:

> Mr. Darby was invited by D. L. Moody to give a series of Bible readings in Farwell Hall. These were attended by many lovers of the Word of God, but unfortunately suddenly came to an abrupt end as the two clashed over the question of the freedom of the will. Mr. Darby held to what Mr. Moody considered extreme Calvinism on this point, affirming that so perverted was man's will he could not "will" even to be saved . . . Mr. Moody insisted that man as a responsible person was appealed to by God to turn to Him and would be condemned if he did not . . . The controversy became so heated one day that Mr. Darby suddenly closed his Bible and refused to go on.[62]

H. A. Ironside claimed that after the clash with Moody, Darby had a similar exchange with a prominent leader of the Exclusive Brethren in North America, F. W. Grant—although, unlike the Moody affair, this was a private disagreement.[63]

In many ways, Darby's position on the ruin of man reveals the foundation on which his dispensational scheme rested. Each dispensation was a divine test which man failed, thus demonstrating human inability to obey God.[64] R. A. Huebner, a modern Darby apologist, states, "Up to the cross God put fallen man under probation, under testing, to see if fallen man is recoverable . . . The epoch of probation, that ran from Adam fallen to the cross, was not to educate God concerning what result there might be

---

61. Darby, *CW*, 12:276n (≤1846).

62. Turner, *John Nelson Darby*, 21–22. The account is also found in Veitch, *Story of the Brethren*, 65–66; Ironside, *Historical Sketch*, 81; and Findlay, *Dwight L. Moody*, 126–27. Cf. Darby's references to Moody's Arminianism in Darby, *Letters*, 2:193; 2:257–59; 2:327–28.

63. Ironside, *Historical Sketch*, 81. John Reid's account in *F. W. Grant*, 57–63 is not altogether reliable as Darby and Grant differed on the doctrine of the atonement more than Reid suggests. According to Ironside, Darby also clashed with the American Methodist leader Daniel Steele over "the doctrines of grace" (Ironside, *Historical Sketch*, 82). This is confirmed in Steele, *Substitute for Holiness*, 131.

64. Darby, *CW*, 1:124–30.

... it was to fully demonstrate that fallen man was not recoverable, and to conclude that he was 'lost.'"[65] Darby's view, argues Grass, that "each dispensation was doomed to failure may be seen as an application of radical Calvinist soteriology, and in particular of the doctrines of divine sovereignty, original sin and human inability, to the realms of salvation-history and ecclesiology."[66] This is an important insight, for it demonstrates that both dispensationalists and Reformed critics who think that dispensationalism and Calvinism are incompatible have not understood the foundation on which the superstructure of Darby's dispensational scheme rested.[67]

Furthermore, Darby's understanding of the ruin of man also lies at the root of his ecclesiology, as manifest in his doctrine of the "ruin of the church."[68] He said, for example, "The church has not escaped the effect of that principle in poor human nature, that the first thing it does is to depart from God, and ruin what He has set up."[69] Therefore, in Darby's doctrine of the total ruin of man we discover a key to his theology.

William Kelly (1821–1906)

Though not a founding brother, William Kelly became one of the most important figures in the history of the Brethren movement. Edwin Cross suggests that Kelly "may be regarded as the foremost author and editor among the Brethren."[70] If Darby was the Luther (bold activist) of the Brethren movement, Kelly was the Calvin (biblical scholar and teacher).[71]

Kelly, like many Brethren, eschewed the labels of Calvinism and Arminianism because he believed both systems went beyond what Scripture taught. He wrote, "Like other systems [Calvinism and Arminianism] are in

---

65. Huebner, *God's Sovereignty*, 15. This theme also appears in other Brethren, e.g., Kelly, *Lectures . . . Minor Prophets*, vii; Kelly, *Lectures on the Church*, 8; [Trotter], "No Man," 308–18.

66. Grass, "The Church's Ruin," 96. Cf. Clarke, "A Critical Examination," 260.

67. E.g., Dunlap, *Limiting Omnipotence* and Gerstner, *Wrongly Dividing*.

68. The ruin of the church is a frequent theme in Darby's voluminous writings. See for example, Darby, *CW*, 32:392–407. For analysis of this theme see Grass, "The Church's Ruin," chapter 4 "The Ruin of the Church," 96–128.

69. Darby, *CW*, 32:381. Grass asserts Darby's belief in the church's ruin was "rooted in an essentially Calvinist anthropology." Grass, "The Church's Ruin," 100.

70. Cross, *Irish Saint and Scholar*, 114.

71. "Whereas Darby was a pioneer church planter, evangelist and visionary, Kelly was primarily a scholar and Bible teacher." Critchlow, "William Kelly," 37. Critchlow has just published her doctoral thesis on Kelly: *Against the Trend*. Unfortunately, it was released after the present volume was in the hands of the publisher and thus I was unable to consult it.

part true and in part false—true in what they believe of scripture, false in yielding to human thoughts outside scripture: happy those, who are content as Christians with the truth of God and refuse to be partisans on either side of men! Our wisdom is to have our minds open to all scripture, refusing to go a hair-breadth farther."[72] Nevertheless, despite Kelly's repudiation of the label, his soteriology on the whole may be described as Calvinistic.

Like Darby, Kelly's favorite expression for human depravity was the "total ruin of man."[73] He was convinced that humans have no power to move toward God, but are in a hopeless state apart from grace. Commenting on 1 Cor 15:50–58 ("flesh and blood cannot inherit God's kingdom, neither doth corruption inherit incorruption"), he wrote, "Here man breaks down utterly. He revolts from what makes nothing of his power or his merits, yea, what exposes his total inability and demonstrates his ruin through sin, while it reveals the free and full and triumphant grace which saves."[74] The Law is of no help here, for it serves to demonstrate "the abject, thorough, hopeless bondage to sin in which our nature is held."[75] This is the state of all who are outside of Christ. Kelly asserted, "To be in the flesh then is hopeless ruin, its mind being at variance with God, and in utter insubjection to His law; and this is the sad condition of all the sons of fallen Adam."[76]

Kelly's clearest statement on the condition of fallen human beings came in his comments on Eph 2:1–3, where Paul describes those whom God has "quickened" as formerly being "dead in trespasses and sins." He wrote:

> It is not merely a question of disease in the moral state of man; but they are "dead." What a blow to all the thoughts of man . . . that he is in a mere sickly state of soul; and if you only soothe and comfort and educate him, after all he is not so bad! Some people think there is a difference between believers and unbelievers in

---

72. Kelly, *Notes . . . Romans*, 220. Cf. Kelly, *Lectures . . . Minor Prophets*, 9–10. Similar sentiments were expressed by the Exclusive writer F. G. Patterson in Patterson, "Editor's Preface," vi–viii.

73. The epistle to the Romans describes "the total ruin of man and his need of this mighty intervention of God in the gospel." Kelly, *Notes . . . Romans*, 2. Other places where Kelly used the expression include: Kelly, *Lectures . . . Minor Prophets*, vi, x; Kelly, *Exposition of the Gospel of Luke*, 119; Kelly, *Exposition of the Gospel of John*, 95, 114; Kelly, *Exposition of the Acts*, 22, 50; Kelly, *Notes on the First Epistle . . . to the Corinthians*, 24, 132, Kelly, *Lectures . . . Ephesians*, 2; Kelly, *Lectures . . . Colossians*, 63; Kelly, *Exposition of the Epistles of John*, 281, 310, 365; Kelly, *Lectures on the Church*, 168; [Kelly], "Early Chapters of Genesis," 210; [Kelly], "The Intermediate State," 80; Kelly, "Synoptical Study," 30.

74. Kelly, *Notes on the First Epistle . . . to the Corinthians*, 282.

75. Kelly, *Notes . . . Romans*, 107.

76. Ibid., 127.

their unconverted state: this I deny. As to men being born, some of them more worthy of having mercy shown them than others, the idea is contrary to every word of God that treats of the subject. On the contrary, what the Holy Ghost insists upon is the real death and equal ruin of all. In Romans it is said that we were "without strength," but here we were "dead"... It was the expression of God's mind about the extreme ruin in which we lay. We have both Jews and Gentiles... man as such—morally dead; so that it becomes a question of what God can do... and if man is dead, thanks be to God! He raises the dead, and can and does quicken souls... However, what Scripture calls "life" is not bare existence, but a blessed spiritual nature given to a man who naturally was without it and merely felt or acted after a nature under sin. Such is the condition of every person until the Spirit of God has wrought this good work upon the soul.[77]

Elsewhere, Kelly described fallen humanity as those who were "positively dead Godward." He continued, "They had no sense of their own state; they had no acquaintance with God; and in their moral ruin they were wholly indifferent to either. Intellectual notions of man's mind might be there, but not a pulse of life toward God."[78]

The only hope for fallen humanity lies in "the mighty intervention of God's grace."[79] This grace produces faith in Christ. For Kelly, such faith does not rise out of a fallen and sinful heart, but is a result of the operations of the Holy Spirit. Reflecting on the work of grace in the heart, Kelly wrote, "It is when Christ has begun to dawn on the soul that you begin to realize that you have been lying in all that is dark and loathsome, though a glimmer of hope may break through the clouds. You are seriously conscious of evil things to which you were insensible before. This is an effect of God's mighty and gracious operation." When new feelings of hatred of sin and longing for God come, they are produced not by human free will but by Christ through the Spirit of God, and nothing else.[80] Commenting on Eph 2:8–9, Kelly clarified, "The Spirit shuts out all thought of man's contributing the faith or taking any credit because [sic] coming to Christ; for He says immediately after, 'And that not of yourselves; it is the gift of God.' This probably refers, not only to the salvation, but to the faith; it was all the gift of God, and not man's production."[81]

77. Kelly, Lectures... Ephesians, 64–65.
78. Kelly, Exposition of the Epistles of John, 280.
79. Kelly, Lectures... Ephesians, 76.
80. Ibid., 92–93.
81. Ibid., 94.

Although Kelly repeatedly criticized the Calvinist system as such, in his understanding of the fallen human condition he clearly stood in the Augustinian/Calvinist tradition.

Charles Henry Mackintosh (1820–96)

C. H. Mackintosh, commonly known simply as CHM, was one of the most popular and prolific writers among nineteenth-century Brethren. Mackintosh himself was not an original thinker but was influenced significantly by Darby's thought. As a writer, however, he was far more lucid than Darby and was thus able to mediate "Darbyite theology to the wider world."[82] It is not surprising, therefore, that Mackintosh's understanding of fallen human nature resembled Darby's. He wrote, "As to our true state by nature, the word of God presents it as one of total and irrecoverable ruin."[83]

Mackintosh agreed with Calvinists that the Bible taught "man's utter powerlessness—that he will not, and cannot, come if left to himself—that it is only by the mighty power of the Holy Spirit that any one ever does come—that, were it not for free, sovereign grace, not a single soul would ever be saved—that, if left to ourselves, we should only go wrong, and never do right."[84] Yet Mackintosh emphatically denied the inference hyper-Calvinists made that since humans are powerless, they are not responsible before God. Rather, he believed the Bible taught "with equal force and clearness . . . the solemn and weighty truth of man's responsibility."[85]

Mackintosh was happy to embrace the tension between these two strands of biblical thought and saw no point in attempting to harmonize them. This may have disappointed his more theologically inquisitive readers, but his counsel to them was simple: "It is none of our business to reconcile [man's powerlessness and man's responsibility]. God has done that for us by placing them side by side, in His own eternal word. It is ours to submit

---

82. Grass, *Gathering to His Name*, 151n27. Biographer Edwin Cross describes Mackintosh as "the arch communicator of the teaching of J N Darby and others to an audience that might not otherwise have grasped the profounder ministry of the leading Brethren teachers. He was the man most responsible for popularizing Darby's teachings throughout the world. He was not an originator of any new line of teaching . . . but he could explain in simple terms what he had embraced and enjoyed at the feet of men like Darby and Bellett." Cross, *Life and Times*, 44.

83. Mackintosh, *Miscellaneous Writings*, 1:4 ("Regeneration"). NB since the pagination in *Miscellaneous Writings* is tied only to each individual essay, the title of the pertinent essay will follow the volume and page number cited.

84. [Mackintosh], "Responsibility and Power," 57. That Mackintosh was the author of this piece is confirmed by its inclusion in Mackintosh, *Short Papers*, 1:108–12.

85. Ibid., 59.

and believe, not to reason."[86] Nevertheless, he did offer an illustration, borrowed from Darby, to show that inability does not negate responsibility. The illustration states that a man who has a debt of one hundred pounds, but is unwilling and unable to pay it, is still responsible for it and will rightly bear the consequences for not paying it.[87]

For Mackintosh, before a sinner can grasp the love of God, he must be "brought to see his own total and absolute ruin, his hopeless wretchedness, his guilt and misery, the utter vanity and worthlessness of all within and around him."[88] But the anxious sinner should not worry about the question of election. Instead, he should approach the cross of Christ from the standpoint of "conscious ruin." Mackintosh stated, "The grace of God meets him as a lost, dead, guilty sinner; not as an elect one. This is an unspeakable mercy, inasmuch as he knows he is the former, but cannot know that he is the latter until the gospel has come to him in power."[89] This does not undermine the truth of election, but simply puts it in its proper place—a comfort for believers, not a stumbling block for the unconverted.[90]

The job of the evangelist or preacher is to meet sinners where they are, "on the broad ground of our common ruin, our common guilt, our common condemnation." The preacher holds out "a message of full, free, present, personal, and eternal salvation."[91] Mackintosh had no patience for any who restricted the free offer of the gospel and refused to urge people to repent and believe. In his mind, such an approach was a grievous misapplication of human inability and the doctrines of grace.[92] While, by his own

---

86. Ibid., 60. Cf. Mackintosh, *Miscellaneous Writings*, 4:5 ("Great Commission").

87 Mackintosh, "Responsibility and Power," 62. In an earlier article I suggested Darby borrowed the illustration from Mackintosh [Stevenson, "Early Brethren Leaders," 33]. Upon further investigation, however, it would appear that the reverse is true. Darby used the illustration (in a slightly different context) in an article entitled "The Rule of Life: What Is It?" in 1867 (*CW*, 10:172). He used it again in a letter grouped with others from the year 1872 (Darby, *Letters*, 2:168). Mackintosh employed the illustration in "Responsibility and Power" which appeared in 1874. Darby offered the illustration again in a letter dated May 9, 1879 (Darby, *Letters*, 2:501). Since Darby used the illustration before 1874, and since Mackintosh was so dependent on Darby's thought, it seems better to surmise that Mackintosh borrowed the illustration from Darby.

88. Mackintosh, *Miscellaneous Writings*, 4:15 ("Glad Tidings"). Originally published in five parts in *TNO* 10 (1867). For further statements of the fallen human condition in the same piece see, pp. 10–12. See also Mackintosh, *Miscellaneous Writings*, 1:3 ("The All-Sufficiency of Christ").

89. Mackintosh, *Miscellaneous Writings*, 4:24 ("Glad Tidings").

90. Ibid., 26–27.

91. Ibid., 22.

92. See especially [Mackintosh], "One-Sided Theology," 10–16 and Mackintosh, *Short Papers*, 2:264–72. Cf. Mackintosh, *Miscellaneous Writings*, 4:28–29 ("Glad

admission, he embraced the five points of Calvinism "so far as they go,"[93] he labored hard to maintain biblical balance between divine sovereignty and human responsibility.

John Gifford Bellett (1795–1864)

An important leader from the earliest days of the Brethren was John Bellett.[94] Bellett's brother George, a high churchman and an Arminian,[95] spoke of differing with John in the 1820s over doctrinal points. He wrote of John: "His views had become more decidedly Calvinistic, and the friends with whom he associated in Dublin were all, I believe, without exception, of this school."[96] Like Darby, Kelly, and Mackintosh, Bellett affirmed a Calvinistic view of human depravity. In an essay simply entitled "Man," he asserted that human beings are "past moral correction." If Darby's preferred description of human depravity was "total ruin," Bellett's seems to have been "incorrigible and incurable"[97]—a phrase which appears throughout his brief essay.[98] He wrote further:

> It has been said of him, "Man is prone to evil, and this arises from the impotency of the will, which, when it turns to evil, is rather passive than active. Through the grace of Christ alone is it free." Very just. Not only has man fallen from God, and become a sinner, but he is the *bondman of sin*. Having been overcome of Satan, he has been brought into bondage to him . . . Man has shown himself to be in full bondage to sin, so that he will go in the way of it, in defiance of every argument and every influence which may be used with him.[99]

For Bellett, man's incorrigibility "tells us of the necessity of sovereign grace and the interference of divine power."[100]

Tidings").

93. [Mackintosh], "One-Sided Theology," 11.
94. On Bellett see Pickering, *Chief Men*, 30–32; and Bellett, *Recollections*.
95. Stunt, *From Awakening*, 153–54.
96. Bellett, *Memoir*, 42. Weremchuk suggests Darby "was certainly one of the friends" referred to. Weremchuk, *John Nelson Darby*, 237n25.
97. Although Bellett could also speak of "ruined sinners." E.g., Bellett, *Paul's Apostleship*, 66, 87.
98. Bellett, *Miscellaneous Papers*, 104, 105, 107, 108. This essay originally appeared anonymously in *BT* 2:29 (Oct. 1858), 154–55.
99. Bellett, *Miscellaneous Papers*, 104–5.
100. Ibid., 108.

Robert Cleaver Chapman (1803–1902)

One of the most respected Open leaders of the nineteenth century was R. C. Chapman. He was widely revered for his warm-hearted piety—Spurgeon called him "the saintliest man I ever knew."[101] The assembly he established in Barnstaple bore the fruit of his labors for many years and consistently numbered some four hundred members.[102] Although he is not typically noted as a theologian, he was esteemed as a preacher with a profound grasp of the Scriptures.[103] He was also an active evangelist[104] whose passion for gospel work was further manifested by his burden for foreign missions. He has been called the father of the Spanish Brethren movement and made several mission trips to Spain (1834, 1838, 1863–65, and 1871).[105] Grass adds, "He preached about the need for mission to Spain; he kept in constant touch with missionaries once they arrived there . . . and the movement's establishment has been regarded as an answer to his prayers."[106]

His views of sinful human nature are consistent with those of the other Brethren explored thus far. For example, he wrote, "The natural man has no apprehension of the Gospel. 'What must I do?' is ever his cry. Man has done his work perfectly—that of self-destruction. He is wholly bent upon evil, altogether ruined."[107]

In a brief reflection on "The Natural Man and his Religion," Chapman stated, "It is natural to the corrupt heart of man to deny its weakness and sinfulness, and to boast of its strength and righteousness." But, he added, "If Adam in his state of uprightness could not uphold himself, how shall we, his corrupt seed, by native strength rise up out of our fall?" For Chapman, the only answer to human inability was God's grace.[108]

A person may not always appear corrupt, and may indeed seem upright to his or her neighbors. Nevertheless, the heart is full of self-will in opposition to God.[109] Chapman explained, "Man's will is always in opposition to the will of God. Thus we read: 'The carnal mind is enmity against God.'

---

101. Peterson, *Robert Chapman*, 14.

102. Beattie, *Brethren*, 54.

103. Peterson, *Robert Chapman*, 15, 190.

104. See ibid., chapter 14 "The Constant Evangelist," 119–28.

105. Reports from his labors abroad appear in, for example, *The Missionary Echo* (1872), 8–9, 24, 30–31, 42–43.

106. Grass, *Generations*, 16. See also Peterson, *Robert Chapman*, 65–71.

107. Chapman, *Choice Sayings*, 2.

108. Ibid., 9–10.

109. Chapman, "Self-will and Sovereign Grace," 113–14. Cf. Bennet, *Robert Cleaver Chapman*, 135.

A man may be most amiable, most commendable, and full of good works, as between himself and his neighbour, but the root of all within is enmity against God."[110]

The doctrine of human depravity is, of course, the bad news—a necessary prerequisite to the gospel of grace, which Chapman loved to unfold. He also delighted to expound the believer's high calling in Christ. This led one biographer to write of Chapman, "No one ever taught more plainly the utter ruin of all men in Adam; none could ever have dwelt more upon the high estate to which the redeemed are raised in Christ."[111]

Henry Craik (1805–66) and George Müller (1806–98)

Another important early leader was Henry Craik.[112] Müller, of course, is remembered beyond the Brethren movement as a man of remarkable faith.[113] Craik and Müller will be forever linked in Brethren history as the leading teachers of the Bethesda meeting in Bristol. The actions of this meeting gave rise to the infamous "Bethesda question" which, in turn, divided the movement.[114] We gain insight into Craik's view of fallen humanity in his published comments on Matt 4:16 ("the people which sat in darkness saw great light; and to them which sat in the region and shadow of death light is sprung up"). Craik applied the text "to all that are living without God, and destitute of the knowledge of the gospel of Christ." He described such persons in the following terms:

> Their hearts are as depraved as their minds are unenlightened. They are destitute of any spark of spiritual life; and the gloom of present sinfulness and eternal misery hangs over them . . . The body is the slave of sensual impulse, and degrading or Satanic enjoyment; the heart is filled with the very seeds of every evil thing; and the mind, ignorant of good is skilful only in sin . . . Such is man without God—such is the sinner without a Saviour.[115]

---

110. Bennet, *Robert Cleaver Chapman*, 137.

111. Ibid., 68.

112. On Craik see Pickering, *Chief Men*, 84–87 and *BDEB*, 1:266.

113. See, for example, Harvey, *George Müller*; Miller, *George Muller*, Piper, *A Camaraderie of Confidence*.

114. For a brief overview see Grass, *Gathering to His Name*, 32–34; 43–48; 79–83.

115. Craik, *Biblical Expositions*, 108.

Craik and Müller were in agreement on "the precious doctrines of the grace of God."[116] In an address on "The First and Second Adam," Müller described those who belong to the first Adam as "dead in trespasses and sins . . . they are ruined still; they have before them still the blackness and darkness of despair."[117] As it stands, an Arminian could affirm that statement, but Müller went on to add of believers: "How is it that we do believe in the Lord Jesus . . . and trust Him for salvation? . . . Verily, brethren, we did it not ourselves. It was all of grace that it is thus,—that we have been made to believe in Jesus." Only one who affirmed a Calvinistic view of spiritual inability would state that we have been *made to believe* in Jesus by sovereign grace.[118] This, Müller came to understand, was the work of the Holy Spirit. He wrote, "the Holy Spirit alone can teach us about our state by nature, show us the need of a Saviour, enable us to believe in Christ."[119]

John Eliot Howard (1807–84)

An important nineteenth-century scientist, John Eliot Howard[120] was "recognized as the leading authority with a worldwide reputation on cinchona and quinine production."[121] But he was also a devout evangelical Christian. In the 1830s he left the Quakers, among whom he was raised, to join the Brethren. Howard planted an assembly in Tottenham, London, and eventually became an influential figure among the Open Brethren.[122]

In 1843, Howard published a second edition of a booklet he entitled: *"New Views," Compared with the Word of God*.[123] The piece was a refutation of John Guthrie's work "New Views, True Views." At the time, Guthrie (1814–78) was minister of the United Secession Church in Kendal, but in 1843 he was deposed for advocating universal atonement. Thereafter, he joined James Morison in forming the Evangelical Union. His theological

---

116. Müller's introduction to Tayler, *Passages*, xii.

117. Müller, *Jehovah Magnified*, 22.

118. For strong affirmation of both human depravity and sovereign election, see ibid., 141.

119. Müller, *Narrative*, 46.

120. He sometimes identified himself as I. E. Howard in his literary works.

121. Dickson, "The Howards," 4.

122. Howard and his family's Brethren affiliation have been the focus of recent biographical study. See Dickson, "The Howards," West, *From Friends to Brethren*, and West, "John Eliot Howard." Cf. Stunt, *Early Brethren*, 20–23, and Pickering, *Chief Men*, 202–4.

123. I am grateful to Neil Dickson for pointing me to this piece, and to Graham Johnson for securing me a copy.

views were decidedly Arminian (he would later produce a translation of *The Life of James Arminius*), and thus he had a natural affinity with Morison.[124] Howard found Guthrie's Arminian doctrine so erroneous that he was compelled to respond.

Howard's answer to Guthrie reveals his own doctrinal convictions were unmistakably Calvinistic. As the epigraph to the opening of this chapter demonstrates, he viewed the impact of the fall on human beings as total. The unbeliever, he contended, has "as little power to believe as a dead man has to walk." Yet this did not undermine human responsibility: "let us also remember that responsibility to God is *not* grounded on man's *power* to obey."[125] To be sure, God in his grace is willing to save all, and the gospel should be preached to all, "yea, pressed upon them with all affectionate longing for their souls!"[126] Nevertheless, no matter how eloquently the message is preached, the human heart will reject the Gospel. The only hope for sinners is the sovereign work of the Holy Spirit breaking through hardened and recalcitrant wills.[127]

In an appendix, Howard lamented the modern tendency to exalt "the powers of man in reference to the work of religion."[128] Particularly egregious in this regard was the influence of Charles Finney. Guthrie may not have been quite as extreme as Finney, but in Howard's view he was not far off. He charged that "Mr. Guthrie takes part with the Pelagians against Augustine, with Erasmus against Luther, and with the feelings and the pride of human nature in every age against the word of God."[129] For his own part, Howard aligned himself with Luther, quoting extensively from *The Bondage of the Will*, which he considered to be an "unanswerable Treatise." Gerald West has observed that Howard's reading of the Magisterial Reformers was influential in his coming to evangelical convictions over against his Quaker background.[130] This helps explain why he was more willing than some Brethren to appeal to Luther in a doctrinal dispute. His main arguments were rooted in Scripture, which was plainly his ultimate authority in doctrinal questions, but Howard was not reticent to find support for his biblical position in the Reformer.

---

124. Guthrie is featured prominently in Morison, *Worthies*, 265–384. The controversy with Howard is mentioned on pp. 284–86.

125. Howard, *"New Views,"* 9. Emphasis original.

126. Ibid., 16. See also 14n, where Howard grounds the universal preaching of the gospel in the fact that preachers do not know God's hidden counsels in election.

127. Ibid., 18.

128. Ibid., 37.

129. Ibid., 40–41.

130. West, "John Eliot Howard," 39. Cf. West, *From Friends to Brethren*, 94.

Benjamin Wills Newton (1807–99)

As noted in the previous chapter, one of the most controversial figures in the early years of the Brethren movement was B. W. Newton. Indeed, it was conflict between Darby and Newton that eventually led to the severance of the movement into Exclusive and Open streams.[131] Although Newton eventually left the Brethren, there can be no doubt that he was an important leader in the formative years of the movement—particularly in the influential assembly at Plymouth. Early on, Darby appointed him as the presiding elder of the Plymouth assembly.[132]

Born into a Quaker family, Newton experienced an evangelical conversion as a student at Oxford in the early part of January 1827.[133] Shortly thereafter, Newton adopted Calvinistic views of salvation.[134] In a letter to his mother he expressed concern over the current state of Christianity. He wrote, "The study of Ecclesiastical History has enlightened me more than I can describe, and proves irrefragably to my mind that Arminianism is nothing more than varnished Pelagianism."[135] One of the more explicit statements of his Calvinistic views comes in a letter to his uncle dated August 15, 1828. The statement demonstrates that Newton's Calvinism was rooted in his understanding of humanity's fallen condition. He wrote to offer his uncle "a written statement of my religious sentiments—at least those which are considered peculiar." Among such sentiments he included the following:

> It is not willingly allowed by many, but yet I cannot but think, that the grand fundamental doctrine which characterizes the system of those called Calvinists, is this: "That man is dead in trespasses and sins." And you will please to observe that we use the term *dead* in its fullest and strongest import, understanding it to mean, that man has so completely lost that spiritual life which Adam possessed, that he is not only unable to love God, but incapable of any movement of soul towards Him—in a word, as absolutely deprived of power to perform the functions

---

131. See Burnham, *Story of Conflict*.

132. Ibid., 81. Regarding the open ministry at Plymouth, Newton wrote, "I was to sit at the head of the table and rule, and anyone was allowed to speak who thought fit to do so; and if he did not speak to edification I was to silence him." Fry MS, 261. Cf. Stunt, *Elusive Quest*, 53–54; 200–201.

133. See Stunt, *From Awakening*, 194–200.

134. On this development see Stevenson, "Early Brethren Leaders," 19–22.

135. Fry MS, 143. The letter is dated January 13, 1828. No doubt it was this negative view of Arminianism that led him to say in the same letter, "Methodism is indeed a dreadful dreadful foe to gospel truth" (144).

of spiritual as the dead body is to discharge those of Animal Life.[136]

As we have seen, Darby and other Brethren writers could all affirm such sentiments, even though they would come to differ with Newton on other matters.

Hugh Henry Snell (1815–91)

H. H. Snell was not as prominent as some of the other Brethren leaders considered thus far.[137] Nevertheless, he was a valued teacher who identified with the Exclusive wing of the movement.[138] His similarity to Darby on human sinfulness is revealed in his comments on Jesus' parable of the Pharisee and the tax collector in Luke 18:10–14. He wrote:

> In that day, like the present, many erred because . . . they believed not the truth of man's total ruin and depravity; consequently they were constantly thinking of doing something to secure the favour of God, or of bringing something of creature-merit for acceptance, instead of confessing themselves to be lost, undone sinners, and justly deserving His eternal wrath. The people, therefore, could not understand Jesus; they saw no beauty in Him; they were continually mistaking His words, and perceived not that He was exactly suited to do them good, because He came to seek and to save that which was lost.[139]

For Snell, the story illustrates that when the Spirit is working in the heart and conscience, as was evidently the case with the tax collector, one becomes convinced of his own wretched sinfulness and lostness. The question then is whether there is any hope for salvation. Snell answered, "If there be, he is convinced it can only be in God Himself; for the experience he has had of his own weakness and vileness excludes all hope from himself. The only possibility is in Divine mercy."[140]

---

136. Ibid., 148.

137. On Snell see Pickering, *Chief Men*, 338–39. Snell also received notice in Noel, *History of the Brethren*, 140, 321, 434, 535–37. His writings were collected and reissued in 2003 by Present Truth Publishers.

138. Edwin Cross says Snell was "an able teacher of Biblical truth who had come over from the Open Brethren, and was a close associate and friend of Charles Stanley." Cross, *Life and Times*, 55.

139. Snell, *Streams of Refreshing*, 96.

140. Ibid., 102.

The Law was given, in part, to demonstrate the inability of fallen man to please God. Snell explained, "The law made demands on fallen, sinful man, such as he was unable to fulfil . . . it therefore proved all to be guilty, and under condemnation."[141] Hope lies alone in the fact that "God has come down to man, when a ruined, helpless sinner, in Christ, and brought a perfect and everlasting righteousness to him in the way of faith."[142] But if humans are ruined in sin and unable and unwilling to respond to God, how does faith arise within them? Snell argued, "Faith is not a work of the flesh, but a fruit of the Spirit. Faith is the gift of God. Faith is always self-renouncing; it brings a broken, empty heart to receive and welcome God's gracious gifts. Faith, therefore, gives *all* the glory to God."[143]

William Trotter (1818–65)

William Trotter was converted through the ministry of the Methodist preacher William Dawson.[144] By the age of nineteen, Trotter himself was ordained as a Methodist minister and became a successful preacher. However, he eventually "began to question the growing ecclesiasticism of the [Methodist] New Connexion, with its deepening cleavage between clergy and laity, and its insistence on subscription to creeds."[145] In due course, he associated with the Brethren and became a leader among them—indeed, Neatby claimed that Trotter "is more highly spoken of by every one that knew him than almost any other Plymouth Brother."[146]

It might be assumed that given Trotter's significant association with the Methodists, he would have Arminian sympathies.[147] But this was not the case. His own sentiments are expressed in a letter published under the title, "No Man Becomes a Child of God by an Act of His Own Will."[148] Here Trotter takes up the subject of "how a man becomes a child of God." He answers with John 1:13 and Jas 1:18, which emphasize that it is God's will,

---

141. Ibid., 59.
142. Ibid.
143. Ibid., 60.
144. Pickering, *Chief Men*, 381.
145. Rowdon, *Origins*, 175. Cf. Grass, *Gathering to His Name*, 58–59.
146. Neatby, *History*, 148.

147. Rowdon states that "Trotter was one of the few Methodists who became leading figures in early Brethren history." Rowdon, *Origins*, 175.

148. [Trotter], "No Man," 306–18. Although the piece is anonymous in the *Present Testimony*, it was reprinted as "Man's Will and God's Grace," *BT* 14 (1883), 362–64; 373–75 under the initials W. T. It is identified as authored by Trotter in the electronic collection of his writings at www.stempublishing.com/authors/trotter.

not human will, which is the ultimate cause of regeneration. Trotter was evidently writing to a friend who had, like himself, trained for the Methodist ministry. After citing the biblical texts noted above that stress God's sovereignty in salvation, he added, "Here I might leave this subject; but, knowing how the thought haunts the minds of those who have had the kind of training both you and I had—'Well, but are not life and death set before us in Scripture? And are we not called on to choose life that we may live?'—I would not thus summarily dismiss the inquiry."[149] Trotter then argued that such objections misunderstand Scripture and wrongly make the new birth dependent on human will. To the contrary, Trotter maintained the whole of Scripture demonstrates that humans refuse to respond to God. What is necessary is "Almighty grace which subdues [man's] opposition, and makes him willing to receive Christ, and the salvation He has brought. Such grace it is, and such grace alone, by which any become the children of God."[150] He then concluded, "If we are really guests at Christ's table, it is not that we have of ourselves chosen to come when invited, nor even when urged; but because we have been *brought in*, or *compelled to come*. That is, the opposition of our natural will has been overcome by that Almighty grace, which, in thus overcoming our opposition, has made us willing, and brought us in."[151]

Trotter advocated a similar position in his published reflections on John 6. He stated that although faith found no place in human hearts, nevertheless "God could give it, and would sovereignly in His grace."[152] On verse 37 ("all that the Father giveth me shall come to me"), Trotter explained the necessity of sovereign grace in predestination due to the fallen condition of men and women. He commented:

> How humiliating and heart-breaking for us, that, in the presence of incarnate life and love in the Person of the incarnate Son of God, no one would have come to Him, no one have been benefited by His mission, had there not been those who were given Him of the Father, and on whose coming therefore He could securely reckon. Man's will would, in each individual, have held out against Christ, had not the Father resolved that He should have some as the trophies of His victory, and the reward of His coming down from heaven. Alas, that our deadness to such love should have called forth such sighs as seem to breathe in these words of Jesus. Is it not as though He were accounting to Himself for the marvels of human unbelief?—as though

149. [Trotter], "No Man," 307.
150. Ibid., 317.
151. Ibid. Emphasis original.
152. Trotter, *A Full Christ*, 27.

saying... Nothing will affect man's stony heart, save where My Father's grace effectually intervenes, and on that I may securely count... "Him that cometh to Me, I will *in no wise* cast out." Precious words... but how greatly is their value enhanced when the coming to Christ is seen, not as an act of man's fickle will, but as the effect of the Father's drawing to Jesus of one given to Him in the counsels of that Father's love before the foundation of the world.[153]

Rowdon states that Trotter "became one of Darby's staunchest disciples."[154] This was noticeable in the areas of ecclesiology[155] and eschatology,[156] but it also appears to be true of the doctrines of grace—which again is particularly significant, given Trotter's background and training in Methodist Arminianism.

Edward Dennett (1831–1914)

Formerly a Baptist minister who had written a pamphlet against the Brethren, Dennett became convinced their principles were, in fact, correct, and he subsequently joined the Exclusive meetings in 1874. He was a valued author, and served as editor of the Brethren magazine *The Christian's Friend*.[157]

In a work addressed to the "anxious" and young believers wanting to understand the nature of their salvation, Dennett affirmed that every person outside of Christ "is in a state of spiritual death, having no life, and no power of life towards God."[158] What is needed, therefore, is new birth, because sinners "have an evil, corrupt, depraved nature; and this incurably corrupt nature is the tree which produces all the evil fruits of sin."[159]

Dennett then imagined an interlocutor asking, "Are we to understand that all men, without exception, are thus totally corrupt, hopelessly evil?" He replied, "Yes. Such is the verdict of God upon human nature." The interlocutor pointed to good deeds done throughout history, and objected that surely these could not have been carried out "by those who have a totally depraved nature." Dennett, however, was unmoved. As long as the works

---

153. Ibid., 28–29.
154. Rowdon, *Origins*, 175.
155. Trotter, *Origin*.
156. Trotter, *Plain Papers*.
157. On Dennett see Noel, *History of the Brethren*, 137. On his rationale for joining the Brethren see Dennett, *The Step I Have Taken*.
158. Dennett, *Fundamental Truths*, 15.
159. Ibid., 28.

are done by unregenerate people, "they are nothing but evil in the sight of God." He continued, "It is thus, as Luther said, not a question of doing, but of *being*; not a question of the character of actions, but a question of nature, and this nature God declares to be flesh, and the flesh is nothing but evil in His sight."[160] For Dennett, it was essential that sinners understand their true condition in order that they might understand their need to be saved by the grace of God alone.

Sir Robert Anderson (1841–1918)

One of the more popular books on soteriology among Open Brethren was *The Gospel and Its Ministry* by respected author, Sir Robert Anderson.[161] Originally released in the 1870s, it was in its thirteenth edition by 1907. Although Anderson would eventually leave the Brethren, his writing continued to be valued by them.[162] In *The Gospel and Its Ministry*, Anderson discussed the nature of faith in light of human fallenness. He wrote, "If, in fact, none can believe apart from the work of the Holy Spirit, the difficulty depends on no peculiarity in the faith itself. It is not a question of metaphysics, but of spiritual depravity and death . . . The hindrance lies in the apostasy of the natural heart of man."[163] Therefore, it is not that faith is an esoteric concept beyond human grasp, "but that the heart is utterly apostate, and man's natural condition is that of pure distrust of God."[164] Citing Rom 8:7 ("the carnal mind is enmity against God"), Anderson was unequivocal in his description of fallen man: "His whole spiritual being is so utterly estranged from God that not only does he not know Him, but, if left to himself, he is incapable of knowing Him. Just as a warped window-pane distorts all objects seen through it, so the human heart perverts even the very truth of God, and changes it into a lie."[165]

In this section we have seen from a variety of authors that a Calvinistic anthropology was affirmed and defended throughout the Brethren movement.

---

160. Ibid., 28–29. Similar sentiments were expressed in Ritchie, *Foundation Truths of the Gospel*, 6.

161. On Anderson see Pickering, *Chief Men*, 12–15 and *ODNB*.

162. A few months before he died, Anderson explained to Henry Pickering that his main reason for not continuing among the Brethren "was their unwillingness to provide intelligent ministry at meetings other than the Lord's Table, and their haphazard way of doing things." Pickering, "Home-Call of Sir Robert Anderson," 100.

163. Anderson, *The Gospel and Its Ministry*, 41–42.

164. Ibid., 49.

165. Ibid.

For all of these writers, the doctrine of total depravity was a fundamental teaching of Scripture, and for some—like Darby—it was a key to their whole theology.

Brethren Evangelists

As described in the previous chapter, the revival of 1859-60 in Ulster and parts of Scotland proved to be an important factor in the growth of the Brethren movement.[166] Roy Coad has suggested that the revival transformed the character and influence of independent (i.e. Open) Brethren.[167] One result of the revival was the introduction of new itinerant evangelists into the movement, many of whom engaged in pioneer evangelism. A number of these evangelists travelled abroad and were largely responsible for the development of Open assemblies in North America.[168] Grass suggests that "a considerable proportion of Open Brethren leaders were either converted during the 1859 revival or cut their teeth as part of the developing network of revivalist evangelists which grew out of it."[169] However, as will be demonstrated in chapter 7, sometimes both the content and methodology of these preachers were at variance with the thought of leading Brethren teachers. Did "the movement's increasingly revivalist theology"[170] in the latter part of the nineteenth century minimize the robust doctrine of sin advanced by the established teachers? Was the "total ruin of man" not so total in the hands of front-line gospel preachers? In this section we examine some notable Brethren evangelists with these questions in view.[171]

Andrew Miller (1810–83)

Exclusive evangelist and author Andrew Miller is perhaps best remembered now for his *Short Papers on Church History*, which was collected in one

---

166. See Grass, *Gathering to His Name*, 117–18; Dickson, *Brethren in Scotland*, 59–89.

167. Coad, *History of the Brethren*, 169.

168. See McLaren, "Triple Tradition," 25–34, and Stevenson, "Canadian Opposition."

169. Grass, *Gathering to His Name*, 236. Grass also points out that it was not until the post-1860 period that the Open Brethren became seriously involved in overseas missions (108).

170. Ibid., 119.

171. Admittedly, some Brethren evangelists were also valued as teachers and writers in the movement, just as the respected teachers and writers often engaged in evangelistic work.

volume and circulated among a wider audience.[172] He was a close friend to C. H. Mackintosh and assisted him in editing the magazine *Things New and Old*. Miller was personally responsible for financing most of Mackintosh's publications.[173] But he was also an effective and passionate evangelist. It was said of Miller that he frequently preached the gospel with tears. He thus came to be known as "the Rutherford of brethren."[174]

Miller's warm-hearted evangelism was combined with vigorous doctrinal conviction. He employed the language of "total depravity" to describe the fallen human condition. He wrote, "The more thoroughly we know the worthlessness of the flesh, the more shall we appreciate the worthiness of Christ, and the better shall we understand the work of the Holy Spirit. When the total depravity of human nature is not a settled reality in the soul, there will ever be confusion in our experience, as to the vain pretensions of the flesh, and the divine operations of the Spirit."[175]

As with other Brethren, Miller's firm belief in human ruin and moral inability through sin[176] in no way hindered the free offer of the gospel. He could say, "To hold back [the gospel], or in any way to hinder its full and free proclamation, is to rob the sinner of his only hope of heaven."[177] In his evangelistic preaching Miller urged sinners to come to Christ. For example, in a sermon on Luke 15:23 ("compel them to come in"), he pleaded: "Oh, then, destitute sinner, come! Christless, graceless, homeless sinner, come! Thy God calleth thee, 'for all things are *now* ready.' A home, a robe, a welcome, a royal feast, all await thee. Why not come? Why not come now? Remember, oh, remember, that ere long, it must either be the king's banqueting house, or the deep, dark pit of eternal despair."[178]

Yet such preaching does not imply Pelagian ability or semi-Pelagian synergism. In order to respond to such calls and invitations, the sinner must first be awakened by grace: "The heart never really desires Christ until the grace of God is at work there. The desire must come from Him."[179]

---

172. Miller, *Miller's Church History*.

173. Cross, *Life and Times*, 69. Miller followed Kelly in the division among the Exclusives in the early 1880s and this severed his relationship with Mackintosh (150).

174. Pickering, *Chief Men*, 259–60.

175. Miller, *Meditations on the Song of Solomon*, 23.

176. E.g., Miller, *Meditations on the Grace and Glory*, 196–98.

177. Ibid., x.

178. Ibid., 33. Cf. 82–83. On the same text, Stanley wrote, "On God's part no hindrance—salvation as free as the air we breathe. But what of man's free will—did one accept the invitation? Not one . . . Grace, free grace, had to go out and fetch the guests, compel them to come in." Stanley, "Free Will," 30.

179. Miller, *Meditations on the Grace and Glory*, 75.

Charles Stanley (1821–90)

In the case of the Exclusive evangelist Charles Stanley, there was great solidarity on the doctrine of human fallenness with Darby, Kelly, and Mackintosh. Stanley was a popular author whose tracts were widely distributed.[180] He also took over the editorship of the magazine *Things New and Old* from Mackintosh in 1879, and continued in this role until his death in March, 1890.[181] He, too, spoke of the "total ruin of man through sin,"[182] and in a piece criticizing the Council of Trent's view of baptismal regeneration, wrote, "We are perfectly agreed as to the utter ruin and sin, in which the whole race of Adam is born . . . By nature [man] is a child of wrath. He is born with a sinful nature. We are also agreed that the scriptures nowhere teach that the powers of human nature can deliver man from this evil nature of sin."[183]

In what would prove to be among his last published articles, Stanley addressed the subject of free will in a two-part article published in early 1890 issues of *Things New and Old*. He introduced his topic with the following words: "What angry discussion there has been on this matter, and it is said there is still much heated disputing on it, especially in the south of England."[184] It is difficult to be certain whether the angry discussion was among Brethren or outsiders. Yet it does not appear that the disputes were initiated by Brethren preachers, since he was writing "by request for the help of evangelists, local preachers, &c., who often meet with much contention on the subject."[185] In light of the fact that the magazine enjoyed "an extensive, worldwide circulation,"[186] it is likely that both Brethren and non-Brethren alike raised questions about free will to preachers who would read the magazine and welcome Stanley's counsel. In any case, Stanley's position was clear: man does not have power in himself to choose salvation. Fallen people have an evil nature and "have a constant tendency to do evil," thus in

---

180. An obituary notice for Stanley claimed that millions of his tracts had circulated and "were blessed to the salvation and deliverance of many souls. Some of his tracts have also been translated into various languages, one quite lately being published in Japanese." *TNO* 33 (1890), 139. Alexander Marshall, who wrote the entry on Stanley in *Chief Men*, asked: "What Christian worker has not heard of the "C.S." tracts?" Pickering, *Chief Men*, 352.

181. Cross, *Life and Times*, 55.

182. Stanley, *The Way the Lord Hath Led*, 91, 118.

183. Stanley, *Plain Words*, 5.

184. Stanley, "Free Will," 19.

185. Ibid., 26.

186. Cross, *Life and Times*, 53–54.

their unconverted state they are free only to follow their sinful inclinations and desires.[187] For Stanley, to exercise free will is to act independently of God; it is nothing short of disobedience. "Remember it was that very act of Adam's free will that brought in sin and all its consequences."[188]

He further argued that the invitations in Scripture demonstrate that God in no way hinders people from coming to Christ for salvation. The problem is that fallen human beings do not will or desire to come. Furthermore, they are morally unable to come, as demonstrated in John 6:44, where Jesus says, "No man *can* [Stanley's emphasis] come to me, except the Father which hath sent me draw him." From this text Stanley affirmed, "This is the true condition of fallen, utterly lost man. If our salvation depends on ourselves, on our free choice in coming, then clearly we are not lost."[189] To drive home the point, he used the following analogy:

> A man is taken prisoner, and with a great chain round his leg, he is put in a dark dungeon. Would you talk to him through a hole in the iron door, and tell him he has a free will, and he may come out if he likes? And is not our state by nature far worse than that? We were not only in the dark dungeon with sin as a chain to the leg, but *we liked it*, the darkness and the chain of sin, rather than the light.[190]

People outside of Christ are in bondage to sin—so, Stanley asked, how could they be free and a captive to sin at the same time? Free will is as far as light is from darkness. He concluded, "No man can ever talk of free will if he knows and believes in the total ruin of man through sin."[191]

Since people are so hopelessly lost, salvation cannot be of human will, but only from God (John 1:13). When sinners do come to the point where they desire to be saved, it is only because "God works in them to will. He gives them a new will, and works in them by the law of the Spirit of life in Christ Jesus."[192] Though he did not use the term, Stanley clearly viewed the new birth as monergistic.[193]

Objections naturally might be raised against Stanley's position, and he readily addressed them. For example, if there is no free will, then neither

---

187. Stanley, "Free Will," 19–20.
188. Ibid., 20.
189. Ibid., 24.
190. Ibid., 30–31.
191. Ibid., 31.
192. Ibid., 26.
193. In salvation, "man, with his boasted free will, disappears and God is all, through Jesus Christ our Lord." Ibid., 33.

is there responsibility. To this Stanley replied with two analogies. First, the man who has stolen a sheep and is apprehended by police will still be held responsible for his crime, even if he has no will or desire to give up the sheep. Second, the man who borrows a hundred pounds and squanders it recklessly is still responsible to repay the debt, even if he is unable to do so.[194]

Another common objection states that if there is no free will, why preach and say "whosoever will may come?" Stanley responded by citing several biblical texts which demonstrate the necessity of preaching and how God works through the means of Scripture to save sinners. He addressed preachers directly, saying, "God gives you the high privilege of proclaiming free forgiveness of sins, and justification from all things, through Jesus. And He gives faith by the Spirit using the water, that is the word, He gives by you. It is by the word of Him who said, 'Let there be light,' that light and life is given . . . What a privilege to be an instrument in His hands."[195]

Charles Stanley is important to the present study because he was an active and popular Brethren evangelist functioning at the close of the nineteenth century who did not deviate from the Calvinistic soteriology that Darby and other leading teachers of the movement had advanced.

George Cutting (1844–1934)

Tim Grass contends that "Open Brethren could be very positive about Exclusive evangelistic outreach, this being a vision which both sides shared."[196] This was certainly true in the case of George Cutting, author of the bestselling evangelistic booklet, *Safety, Certainty and Enjoyment*. According to *The Witness*, the booklet had run to eight million copies by 1932. The Open magazine conceded that Cutting was with the Exclusives, but declared he was "beloved by all for his work's sake."[197]

Cutting's tracts, like much Brethren evangelistic literature, pose a challenge to those interested in theological analysis: the tracts are not theological treatises; rather, they aim to state the gospel simply for unbelievers. Furthermore, as we will see in chapter 7, Brethren believed that deep theological questions like predestination should not be discussed in evangelistic

---

194. Ibid., 33–34. The similarity to Darby's (and Mackintosh's) analogy is transparent.

195. Ibid., 35–36.

196. Grass, *Gathering to His Name*, 199.

197. W 62 (1932), 188. *The Witness* carried an appreciative obituary of Cutting, W 64 (1934), 192.

contexts. This makes it difficult at times to discern whether the theological foundations of the evangelistic presentation tended in a Calvinistic or Arminian direction. Nevertheless, an author's theological proclivities occasionally rise to the surface, and such is the case in Cutting's tract, *"Good in Every Man." Is It True according to God?* He answered his own question in no uncertain terms: "The grace of God, the work of Christ, the quickening of the Spirit, are all ignored if the answer be Yes; but honoured if the answer be unhesitatingly No."[198] Cutting argued that "ruined man" possesses *"'an unsubdued will'*—the very essence of what is sinful in [God's] sight." While the unregenerate person may be "keen-sighted" in the natural realm, "he cannot discern the spiritual. He is blind to the things of the Spirit of God."[199] The whole piece is a diatribe on the sinfulness of human beings and their inability to save themselves, as well as an emphatic rejection of the Pelagian (although he did not use the term) notion that humans are good and can contribute to their own salvation.

Donald Ross (1824–1903)

When we turn to Open Brethren evangelists, it is natural to begin with Donald Ross, who helped shape the character and ethos of Open Brethren assemblies in Scotland and North America. Before he began his association with the Brethren in 1871, he led the North-East Coast Mission (NECM), whose itinerant preachers worked among the fishing communities in the Northeast of Scotland in the late 1850s and early 1860s. By 1870, however, Ross had grown disillusioned with the institutional church and the opposition of the clergy to the evangelists. He resigned from the NECM and formed the independent Northern Evangelistic Society (NES); shortly thereafter he joined the Brethren. Ross's leadership among them in pioneer evangelism, planting assemblies, and editing magazines ensured his influence was broadly felt, not least among other evangelists who looked on him with admiration.[200]

Ross's Calvinism has been recognized by Brethren historians Neil Dickson and Tim Grass[201] and is the subject of a recent study by James Harvey.[202] Growing up in a home "characterised by puritanic piety and exemplary godliness," Ross received regular instruction from the Bible and

198. Cutting, *"Good in Every Man,"* 3.
199. Ibid., 17.
200. See the recollection of Ross's "fellow-labourers" in Ross, *Donald Ross*, 98–239.
201. Dickson, *Brethren in Scotland*, 94; Grass, *Gathering to His Name*, 143.
202. Harvey, "Donald Ross."

the Westminster Shorter Catechism.[203] He was evidently a careful student, because years later his friend and fellow evangelist, Duncan Matheson, referred to Ross as "the walking Shorter Catechism."[204] Although Ross—in good Brethren fashion—would later distance himself from Catechisms and Confessions,[205] he did not appear to abandon the Catechism's basic Calvinistic soteriology.

While he was still superintendent of the NECM, Ross was charged with Morisonianism—a term used to describe the Arminianism of the Evangelical Union in Scotland. As observed in chapter 3, before James Morison formed the Evangelical Union, he had been a minister in the United Secession Church, but having been influenced by the writings of Charles Finney, Morison's theology and methods were increasingly raising opposition.[206] In 1841 he appeared before the Kilmarnock Presbytery and was charged with teaching, among other things, "that all men were able of themselves to believe the gospel unto salvation." Morison's biographer acknowledged, "This statement was accepted by Mr. Morison as accurate, and, in vindication of it, he stated that he could not maintain man's responsibility unless he firmly believed that he was able to do all that God commanded him to do. The sinner's natural and perfect ability to believe on the Lord Jesus Christ must be admitted by all who maintain that the sinner is blameable for his unbelief."[207]

After the Evangelical Union was formed by Morison, its Doctrinal Declaration took the following official position: "In opposition to the scheme of a necessitated will as held, not by Calvinists only, but (as would appear) by all classes of infidels, the Evangelical Union Conference holds tenaciously the doctrine of free will, as lying at the foundation of all religion."[208] Thus when Ross was charged with Morisonianism, it would have meant that he embraced this Arminian notion of human ability. Ross could not let the charge stand, however. He wrote directly to the minister who had made the accusation and "emphatically denied" that he was a Morisonian. He stated, "Their chief error I understand to be the following—namely, 'no special work of the Spirit.' I believe in the absolute necessity for the Holy Spirit . . . There never was and never will be a conversion without Him."[209]

203. Ross, *Donald Ross*, 14–15; Harvey, *Donald Ross*, 14–15
204. Ross, *Donald Ross*, 130.
205. [Ross], "Salvation," 44.
206. *DSCHT*, s.n. "James Morison."
207. Adamson, *Life*, 127.
208. As stated in *Doctrinal Declaration*, 9.
209. Ross, *Donald Ross*, 86. This response came in a letter dated April 12, 1867.

After responding to the other charges, Ross returned to the one he felt to be the most grievous. "Regarding the Morisonianism with which you charge me, let me add that I believe in the perseverance of saints . . . I believe in particular redemption, and, alas! there is overwhelming evidence to prove original and universal depravity."[210]

Evidence of Ross's Calvinistic anthropology is not difficult to find.[211] In an 1872 article from the *Northern Evangelistic Intelligencer*, Ross said of the unconverted, "They 'are dead'—morally—spiritually 'dead.'" In contrast, believers "have been acted upon by the mighty, quickening voice of the Son of God."[212] Later that same year he complained that the preaching in the denominations treated the unconverted as believers and "seeking, trying, doing, praying, and whatnot insisted on, as if dead people in the flesh could do anything to help themselves or please God." This was unacceptable to Ross. Instead, he believed, "The people ought to be told plainly and clearly that they are lost and already beyond the power of human help. Never shall people submit to the righteousness of God, and be brought to Christ till they learn the first lesson, viz., that they are destroyed, and that in God only is their help."[213]

Ross thought evangelists should be cautious and not assume too quickly that individuals have been truly converted. He believed, "A little more knowledge of human nature in its depth of depravity, hypocrisy, and pride would be useful as a preventive in ministering to such."[214] His own experience of conversion is instructive here. His son related: "Our father would tell how unwilling he was to be saved, and how the grace of God overcame his unwillingness and brought him to Himself. And language that conflicted with this, or that in the slightest degree weakened the truth that man was by nature an enemy of God, he would not tolerate. In his judgment it not only was untrue, but it clouded the true grace of God, and robbed Him of His glory as the alone and altogether Saviour."[215]

Ross, then, is yet another example of a Brethren preacher whose strong view of human depravity in no way hindered active evangelism and passionate gospel preaching.[216]

Ross's response was also circulated by his friend Duncan Matheson.
210. Ibid., 88.
211. See Harvey, *Donald Ross*, 36–38.
212. Ross, "Loose Him," 5–6.
213. Ross, "The Lord's Work," 59.
214. Ross, *Donald Ross*, 25.
215. Ibid., 23; cf. 35.
216. David Bebbington has concluded that Ross's belief in the possibility of sinners

Donald Munro (1839–1908)

Another pioneer evangelist closely associated with Ross was Donald Munro.[217] Munro is especially noted for planting and nurturing the first Open Brethren assemblies in Canada. John Ritchie, who was converted through Munro,[218] summarized the preaching of Munro and Ross as follows: "The evangelists brought no new doctrine, but they had the old fundamental truths of ruin by sin, redemption by Jesus Christ, and regeneration by the Holy Ghost burning in them as living realities, and preached them in full confidence that God would use His own Word to do His own work."[219]

Evidence for Calvinism in Munro is less plentiful than with others we have considered thus far. However, it is clear that he considered unbelievers to be under the power of their fallen, sinful nature with no inclination toward God. On one occasion he penned a letter to a nephew who was seriously ill and facing death, urging him to consider the facts of his spiritual condition. He wrote:

> The first of these facts, that God in His Word presses upon your attention . . . is, THAT YOU ARE A SINNER AGAINST GOD. That you were born so, and that you have lived in the practice of sin against God all your life . . . Sin is, of course, a spiritual disease, but not any the less real because it is spiritual. Your whole spiritual being has been under the power of this disease since your birth. A proof of this is, that all along you have been adverse to think about God or to speak about Him. Indeed, like all other unconverted sinners, your happiest moments have been when "God was not in all your thoughts."[220]

He then described the punishment for sin and urged his nephew to turn to Christ for salvation.

A Presbyterian minister in Canada, Rev. James Duncan, criticized the preaching of Munro and fellow evangelist John Carnie (1853–1922), observing that "there was not the most remote reference made to the need of the

---

experiencing "instant conversion and full assurance of faith" must be attributed to his "high estimate of the powers of the will." Yet the evidence above strongly suggests otherwise. It is better to conclude that Ross attributed "instant conversion" to the immediate work of the Spirit in the heart of a sinner. For Ross a long period of preparation for conversion was unnecessary. Bebbington, *Victorian Religious Revivals*, 178–79.

217. See Ritchie, *Donald Munro*.
218. Ross, *Donald Ross*, 157–58.
219. Ibid., 159.
220. Ritchie, *Donald Munro*, 66–67, emphasis original. He could also refer to the unconverted as "dead souls." *NI*, 17 (May 1873), 78.

Holy Spirit's influence to enable a sinner to see his ruined and lost condition by nature, and to enable him to believe on Christ."[221] Yet this does not mean Munro believed the work of the Holy Spirit was not essential in conversion; he simply thought his job was to preach Christ and allow the Spirit to work through the Word.[222] Furthermore, in Ross's repudiation of Morisonianism cited above, he emphatically affirmed the necessity of the work of the Spirit in conversion.[223] Ross, as superintendent of both the NECM and later the NES, oversaw Munro's evangelistic work, and it is highly unlikely that Ross would have endorsed Munro if his preaching was Morisonian, as Rev. Duncan suggested.

Munro did not publish much; his main work was preaching, not writing. In what is available by or about Munro, there is less emphasis on the doctrines of grace than there is with someone like Ross or Stanley. It is difficult to draw firm conclusions from this, given the paucity of relevant source material. Yet it may indicate a diminished focus on a distinctly Calvinist soteriology in the interests of broad evangelical appeal. It is also possible that, in reaction to his negative experience of Presbyterianism in his native Scotland and the constant criticism he faced from confessional clergy, Munro preferred to avoid Calvinist categories and preach the simple message of the gospel.[224]

Alexander Marshall (1847–1928)

Although the popular evangelist Alexander Marshall labored into the third decade of the twentieth century, he remains a relevant figure for our study of nineteenth-century Brethren because he began his full-time ministry in 1876. Furthermore, he represents a more Arminian voice in the movement, and since, as F. F. Bruce put it, Marshall's "Arminian convictions . . . were in his day exceptional among Brethren preachers,"[225] it is worth exploring those convictions.

Marshall's father, John Wallace Marshall, was a lay preacher and an ardent supporter of James Morison and the Evangelical Union—including Morison's Arminian theology.[226] John Marshall also served as an elder in

---

221. *Sarnia Observer* (Mar. 28, 1873), 2. For more on this episode see Stevenson, "Canadian Opposition."

222. E.g., Ross, *Donald Ross*, 103. Cf. Marshall, *Review*, 5–6.

223. Ross, *Donald Ross*, 86.

224. Ritchie, *Donald Munro*, 32–34.

225. *DSCHT*, s.n. "Alexander Marshall."

226. Hawthorn, *Alexander Marshall*, 10–12. See also the background on Morison

an Evangelical Union congregation.[227] After Alex Marshall's conversion as a teenager, he too took an active role in the Evangelical Union, and it was here that "the foundations of the theology which characterised his preaching and teaching" were laid.[228] His biographer, John Hawthorn, noted, "Volumes in his library with portions underlined, and annotated from the pens of Morison, Ferguson, Adamson, Guthrie of Kendal, and other of the early leaders of that movement, give some indication of the care and thought he gave to such subjects as the nature and extent of the atonement, election, and the work of the Holy Spirit."[229] In his obituary of Marshall in *The Witness*, Henry Pickering acknowledged the influence of the Evangelical Union on Marshall. He wrote, "Their main point of cleavage from others was 'the extent of the atonement,' being strong Arminians, or, 'whosoever' men. This upbringing was manifest in all Alex. Marshall's preaching and writing, and he was ever ready to contend, in a friendly way, for this view of truth."[230]

Sometime around 1874 Marshall began meeting with a small group of Brethren in Glasgow. The group included J. R. Caldwell, who would become the editor of the popular Open Brethren magazine, *The Witness*, from 1876–1914—a magazine to which Marshall frequently contributed. What is clear then, is that Marshall's Arminianism was firmly in place before he joined the Brethren.

Marshall's main contention against Calvinism was in regard to its doctrines of particular redemption and unconditional election.[231] But what did he believe about fallen human nature? One critic of the Brethren generally, and of Marshall in particular, was Rev. Richard Strachan from Ontario, Canada, where Marshall spent a significant amount of time preaching.[232] Strachan described Brethren preaching as follows:

> There is no need of contrition for sin, on the part of the sinner, in order to be saved; and no need of prayer for forgiveness, but simply to believe, as if it was possible for a sinner to believe who has not manifested the least degree of penitence. There is

---

and the Evangelical Union described in chapter 3.

227. Pickering, *Chief Men*, 249.

228. Hawthorn, *Alexander Marshall*, 21.

229. Ibid.

230. Pickering, "Home-calling of a True Gospel Warrior," 411.

231. E.g., Hawthorn, *Alexander Marshall*, 4, 22–26; Marshall, "Hindrances to Progress," 168. These doctrines will be explored in the next two chapters.

232. Strachan wrote, "In this country, a Mr. Marshall has recently taken a prominent part in pioneering and establishing [Brethrenism] throughout a wide section of Ontario, and from him his adherents have been called Marshallites." Strachan, *Wandering Lights*, 4.

nothing said of the true nature of sin, and its exceeding sinfulness . . . There is nothing said of the need of the Holy Spirit's work in awakening and convincing the sinner of his sins, and to incline his heart to seek God's mercy.[233]

In response, Marshall denied the truthfulness of the accusation, but conceded he did not preach the Holy Spirit to unbelievers simply "to appear orthodox" for ministers like Strachan. Rather, to the unconverted he preached Christ. Marshall added, "Whilst owning that man in his natural state is utterly depraved and unable to do anything to save himself, and that it is the Spirit's work to convict of sin and lead to Christ, we endeavour to remember that souls are saved, not on account of a work done *in* them by the Holy Ghost, but on account of a work done *for* them by the Lord Jesus eighteen hundred years ago."[234] While at first glance this appears to be a strong affirmation of spiritual inability, the distinction at the end of the sentence between being saved by a work done *for* sinners and not *in* sinners leaves the door open for a kind of semi-Pelagian synergism, i.e. the Spirit convicts and leads, but the sinner ultimately decides to accept the work himself.

Marshall did indeed emphasize sin in his preaching. In *God's Way of Salvation* (1888)[235] he stressed all were sinners and urged his readers to "take your place as lost and ruined in God's sight, and give up all attempts to excuse or cover up your sins."[236] Or again, "Unsaved reader, the 'best' that you can do is to admit that you are ruined, helpless, and undone."[237] Marshall repeatedly emphasized that all the reader had to do to be saved was to believe on the Lord Jesus Christ. Praying for salvation was unnecessary; all that was needed was to "stretch out the empty hand of faith and take it as *a gift* from the pierced hand of the Lord Jesus."[238]

Obviously, a gospel tract was not the place to reflect on whether or not individuals had the natural inclination or ability to "stretch out the empty hand of faith." Yet it is important to remember the influence of Morison on Marshall's thinking. Morison's position was that "the sinner's natural and perfect ability to believe on the Lord Jesus Christ must be admitted by all who maintain that the sinner is blameable for his unbelief." Furthermore, Morison "could never hold that the Spirit imparted power to believe. The

233. Ibid., 17.

234. Marshall, *Review*, 5–6.

235. This was his best known booklet, which had sold over five million copies by 1928. Pickering, "Home-calling of a True Gospel Warrior," 411.

236. Marshall, *God's Way of Salvation*, 5.

237. Ibid., 7

238. Ibid., 20.

Spirit does not enable, he 'opens the heart' of the sinner to believe by disposing him to attend to the truth as it is in Jesus."[239] Thus the Spirit's work is necessary, but it is still within the sinner's power to exercise faith.

Several comments from Marshall suggest that he followed his mentor here. For example, he declared, "A man's salvation or damnation depends on his belief."[240] And again, "If you die in your sin it will not be because God did not love you, or because Christ did not die for you, or because the Holy Spirit did not strive with you."[241] Similarly, in another piece he wrote, "What more can God do for YOU? . . . He has sent the Holy Spirit to convict you of sin, and has made known to you His glorious Gospel. If you continue keeping the door of your heart closed against His entreaties, He will not break it open."[242] Such statements suggest that God has done his part, and it is left to the individual to decide whether or not to believe—a choice that lies within his or her power. Marshall exclaimed, "It is a wonder that any remain unsaved when God has shown so clearly and fully, in His Word, how salvation is to be obtained."[243] Anyone with a strong view of spiritual inability would not make that statement. For Calvinists, the wonder is not that any remain unsaved, but that any *are* saved, given all are "dead in trespasses and sins." If the choice was left to the sinner, as Mackintosh put it, "he will not, and cannot, come . . . that it is only by the mighty power of the Holy Spirit that any one ever does come—that, were it not for free, sovereign grace, not a single soul would ever be saved."[244]

In contrast to Marshall, we have seen that Darby strongly disliked the metaphor of stretching out "the empty hand of faith." For Darby the problem with such language is that "hearts are not so disposed; they will not open the hand . . . if a man is disposed to open his hand, conversion comes from the will of man . . . This is why the work of God is necessary, and why it is said, 'No man can come unto me except the Father which hath sent me draw him.'"[245] Nevertheless, the real stress Marshall laid on human sin[246]—even the "ruin of man"—and that the only hope was to be found in Christ and his work, should have been of some consolation to Darby.[247]

---

239. Adamson, *Life*, 127–28.
240. Marshall, *God's Way of Salvation*, 13.
241. Marshall, *God's Wonderful Love*, 13.
242. Marshall, *Will a God of Love Punish?* 30.
243. Marshall, *God's Way of Salvation*, 15.
244. Mackintosh, "Responsibility and Power," 57.
245. Darby, *Letters*, 2:479–80; cf. 503.
246. See also Marshall, *Straight Paths*, 2; Marshall, *Will a God of Love Punish?* 4.
247. For example, although Darby denounced Moody's Arminianism as "false

There is evidence that one ardent Calvinist was not impressed with Marshall. In 1921 Marshall and A. W. Pink, who would become a popular evangelical author, were both preaching in Oakland, California. Marshall arranged a private meeting with Pink, and a spirited discussion over Calvinism ensued. Pink was undaunted by Marshall's challenges and reported that after about ninety minutes, Marshall closed his Bible and said, "Further conversation is useless."[248] A week later Pink heard Marshall and commented, "His address last night was exceedingly poor: took as his text Rev. 3:21—Christ knocking at door of sinner's heart: latch on the <u>inside</u>, only the sinner could open it!!"[249] Clearly, Pink understood Marshall to be advancing Arminian notions of human ability.

No doubt, Marshall had a significant influence on the soteriology of some in the Brethren movement—particularly his converts and other young preachers who were impressed with his ministry. The presence of an evangelist like Marshall is one reason Crawford Gribben's assessment, that in the later part of the nineteenth century some Brethren "began to reject traditional Calvinist orthodoxy," is not completely off the mark.[250] However, we should not assume that Marshall represented a new normative soteriological outlook. Certainly, among the Exclusives, Darby's Calvinism still held sway, but even among the Opens, Calvinism was not dead. By the end of the century, J. R. Caldwell could offer a Calvinistic answer to a question put to *The Witness* on the source of saving faith. He argued that the Holy Spirit

---

doctrine," he recognized that there were conversions through his preaching and said: "I rejoice, am bound to rejoice, in every soul converted—must do so—and saved for ever." Darby, *Letters*, 2:257–59 (1874). No doubt he would have thought similarly of Marshall's work.

248. Pink, *Letters of an Itinerant Preacher*, 43. Pink had previous knowledge of Marshall and his Arminianism. In a letter dated Feb. 21, 1919, he wrote to his publisher (I. C. Herendeen) concerning his recently published book *The Sovereignty of God* (1918): "Are you receiving any adverse criticisms on God's Sovereignty? or any commendations. [sic] I hope you did not send a copy to Alex Marshall for I'm sure it would be wasted on him." Pink, *Letters from Spartanburg*, 89. Evidently Marshall read it in any case, for Herendeen received a letter from him. Pink offered his help in responding: "If any of his arguments really trouble you, pass them on to me, maybe I could help you." Ibid., 102.

In September 1919, Pink referred disparagingly to an article in *The Witness* by Marshall. He wrote to Herendeen, "It looks as though 'God spoke to him' again on this subject [i.e. Calvinism]—but apparently in vain." Ibid., 142. The article Pink referenced is Marshall, "A Visit," 149. In the article Marshall complains of the "traditional hyper-calvinistic theology" that hindered the spread of the gospel among the Highlanders. It should be noted that Pink himself tended toward hyper-Calvinism at this point, which he would later moderate. See Murray, *Life of Arthur W. Pink*, 315–28.

249. Pink, *Letters of an Itinerant Preacher*, 47.

250. Gribben, "'The Worst Sect,'" 49.

works in such a way "as to show man his guilt and need, and so to make him willing to believe what otherwise, owing to the innate enmity of his heart against God, he would treat with indifference or contempt, and in any case with unbelief. The first motion towards salvation is, therefore, of God's grace, and not of the will of man."[251] A decade earlier, Caldwell had written, "It is evident that not only are all men lost, dead in sins by nature, but also that every man's 'free will' would decide for sin and against God . . . against Christ, against the truth, against even the Gospel."[252]

In 1890 an article appeared in *Things New and Old* decrying that comparatively few "really believe that man is a fallen creature in the sense that it is taught in the scriptures. No doubt," the author continued, "it is acknowledged as a doctrine by many who do not really believe it in its full extent."[253] The author's real concern was not with unbelievers who denied the doctrine, but with "those who profess to believe it, and yet dull its edge as much as possible."[254] Undoubtedly, this was directed at Christians who had been impacted by the theological liberalism prevalent toward the end of the century. The new emphasis on the progress and evolution of the human race meant that Calvinism's doctrine of total depravity appeared hopelessly outdated. But many Brethren held firm. In the early years of the twentieth century, *The Witness* ran an article defending "The Original Fall and Incorrigible Depravity of Man." The author, Thomas Baird, argued, "Man is now incorrigibly depraved and, from a human standpoint, irretrievably and irremediably ruined and lost. Like Israel, man is a self-destroyed being . . . and if help come not to him from God on high, then must he irrecoverably perish."[255] While Arminian voices like Marshall's could be found, the legacy of Calvinistic soteriology was still alive in the movement.

Conclusion

Central to Calvinistic soteriology is a strong doctrine of depravity wherein fallen human nature renders every individual spiritually dead and unable, apart from sovereign grace, to obey God or embrace Jesus Christ in saving

---

251. [Caldwell], "Faith: Is It Involuntary?" 68, editor's note.

252. [Caldwell], "Election," 159. Cf. B., "'The Called of Jesus Christ,'" 105–6. This piece presented a decidedly Calvinistic view of depravity, election, and effectual calling. It is significant that such an article was printed in the prominent Open Brethren missionary magazine (*Echoes of Service*).

253. "The Fall of Man," 320.

254. Ibid., 321.

255. Baird, "Original Fall," 112.

faith. Indeed, any theology that leaves room for moral ability and "free will" in spiritual matters cannot rightly be deemed Calvinistic.

In this chapter we have considered evidence demonstrating that nineteenth-century Brethren maintained a strong view of the "total ruin of man"—a view that fits squarely in the Calvinist tradition. We have also noted that toward the end of the century, some evangelists were less overtly Calvinistic (Munro), and one—Marshall—was openly Arminian. It is important to remember, however, that Marshall's Arminianism was imported from outside the movement, not nurtured from within. Thus although Marshall's views may have gained momentum among the Brethren in the twentieth century, a Calvinistic doctrine of human fallenness was still normative in the nineteenth century.

We conclude, therefore, that this chapter advances the thesis of the present study, which argues that among nineteenth-century Brethren, Calvinistic soteriology was the normative position.

5

The Brethren and the Doctrine of Predestination

Thee we praise, our God and Father,
Thou Thy love hast shewn;
Ere the world was, Thou didst choose us
For Thine own.

—Inglis Fleming[1]

As Thine, Thou didst foreknow us
From all eternity;
Thy chosen loved ones ever,
Kept present to Thine eye;
And when was come the moment,
Thou calling by Thy grace
Didst gently, firmly draw us
Each from his hiding-place.

—Samuel Prideaux Tregelles[2]

---

1. Inglis Fleming, "Thee We Praise, Our God and Father," in *A Few Hymns*, 126. Fleming (1859–1955) fellowshipped at the Park Street meeting in London and knew Darby and other leading Brethren. See Fleming, "Inglis Fleming," 109–25.

2. Tregelles, "O God of Grace, Our Father," in *Psalms and Hymns*, 337. Tregelles (1813–75) was a respected New Testament textual scholar and was active in the Plymouth assembly from 1835. He eventually left the Brethren having supported B. W. Newton (his cousin by marriage) in the disputes of the 1840s.

> *Thou God of grace our Father,*
> *We now rejoice before Thee;*
> *Thy children we, and loved by Thee,*
> *'Tis meet we should adore Thee:*
> *As Thine Thou didst foreknow us,*
> *For such was Thine election;*
> *And Thou hast shown to us, Thine own,*
> *Thy fullness of affection.*
>
> —Samuel Prideaux Tregelles[3]

Introduction and Historical Background

THROUGHOUT THE HISTORY OF the church, the doctrine of election has generated no shortage of controversy. Paul Jewett wrote, "Here is an argument that has endured so long and engendered so much feeling that the very terms *predestination, foreordination,* and *election* have become symbols of divisiveness."[4] In a recent book on the history of predestination in America, Peter Thuesen asserts, "Of all traditional Christian doctrines, few, if any, have caused as much controversy as this question of whether a person's fate in either heaven or hell is sealed from the beginning of time."[5]

The doctrine of predestination is inexorably linked to other doctrines, such as original sin and human depravity. If fallen human beings are unable and unwilling to choose God, as Calvinists assert, then it is only through God's sovereign grace in election that any are saved. Thus the brief historical introduction to the doctrine of human fallenness in chapter 4 covers similar background to that of predestination and need not be repeated here.[6]

In popular thought, John Calvin's name is the one most often connected to predestination—indeed, the very term "Calvinism" has, for many, come to stand as shorthand for a system of theology that takes God's

---

3. Tregelles, "Thou God of Grace Our Father," in ibid., 205.
4. Jewett, *Election and Predestination*, 1.
5. Thuesen, *Predestination*, 4.
6. Further historical background on these issues is covered in chapters 2–3. For useful historical surveys of the doctrine of predestination see Allison, *Historical Theology*, 453–73; Jewett, *Election and Predestination*, 5–21; and Thuesen, *Predestination*, 14–43.

sovereignty in predestination as central and foundational.[7] Calvin, however, was by no means unique among the Reformers to affirm a strong doctrine of election.[8] Neither was Calvin the most influential for English theologians; Peter Martyr Vermigli (1499–1562), Martin Bucer (1491–1551),[9] and Heinrich Bullinger (1504–75) were more prominent.[10] Indeed, Richard Muller argues that for the Reformed tradition, "Vermigli was certainly more important to the nuancing of such topics as predestination and free choice" than Calvin.[11] By the seventeenth century, Calvin's theological influence was eclipsed by the next generation of scholars and theologians.[12] For example, Calvin's influence on the definitive Canons of the Synod of Dort (1618–19) was moderate at best.[13] All this is not to slight Calvin; it simply serves to expose the myth that the doctrine of predestination was solely the notion of the Genevan reformer.

The nineteenth century, however, witnessed a revival of interest in Calvin. This was due in part to the formation of the Calvin Translation Society in Edinburgh in 1843, which produced English editions of the *Institutes*, Calvin's biblical commentaries, and a three-volume edition of Calvin's *Tracts and Treatises*. Stewart comments,

---

7. This perception is challenged by Muller, "The Placement of Predestination," 184–210.

8. For Calvin's perceived prominence in the English-speaking world, see Stewart, *Ten Myths*, "Myth 1: One Man (Calvin) and One City (Geneva) Are Determinative," 21–43, and specifically on predestination, "Myth 2: Calvin's View of Predestination Must Be Ours," 45–72. For the importance of other early theologians in the Reformed tradition on predestination see Muller, *Christ and the Decree*.

9. For Bucer's influence on Calvin see van 't Spijker, "Prädestination," 85–111. Cf. van 't Spijker, "Bucer's Influence on Calvin," 32–44.

10. "The student who has only heard of 'Calvinism' must learn that English theologians were as likely to lean on Bullinger of Zürich, Musculus of Berne, or Peter Martyr as on Calvin or Beza." Collinson, "England and International Calvinism," 214. Darby recognized this fact in his essay "The Doctrine of the Church of England at the Time of the Reformation, of the Reformation Itself, of Scripture, and of the Church of Rome, Briefly Compared with the Remarks of the Regius Professor of Divinity." Darby, *CW*, 3:1–43.

11. Muller, *Christ and the Decree*, x.

12. Stewart, *Ten Myths*, 29–30; Collinson, "England and International Calvinism," 215.

13. Sinnema, "Calvin and the Canons of Dordt," 87–103. Cf. Scott, *Articles of the Synod of Dort*, 11, 14, 28, 56. Murray observed, "Study even of Calvin's later works, including his definitive edition of the *Institutes* (1559), readily discloses that his polemics and formulations were not oriented to the exigencies of debates that were subsequent to the time of his writing." Murray, "Calvin, Dort," 150.

The net effect of this re-release of so much of Calvin's published material was a virtual Calvin renaissance. Calvin . . . was in consequence more of a force to be reckoned with in 1864 (the tercentennial of his death at Geneva) than in 1764 or 1664. His reputation now went from being the "great Reformer" on the basis of lore about him transmitted from Tudor times to being the "still-greater Reformer" whose posthumous literary influence now grew by leaps and bounds. It is in such a context that we observe Victorian Christianity exalting John Calvin to a degree not customary a century earlier.[14]

Thus for many in the nineteenth-century British context, a Reformed understanding of predestination was perceived to be rooted in the thought of John Calvin. This meant Calvin was either a hero or a villain, depending on one's view of predestination. Spurgeon, the outspoken Baptist Calvinist, gave this glowing assessment: "Among all those who have been born of women, there has not risen a greater than John Calvin; no age before him ever produced his equal, and no age afterwards has seen his rival. In theology, he stands alone, shining like a bright fixed star, while other leaders and teachers can only circle round him, at a great distance—as comets go streaming through space—with nothing like his glory or his permanence."[15]

By contrast, in the nineteenth-century American context, Calvin was presented negatively in school textbooks and popular fiction, not least because his tyrannical doctrine of predestination was viewed as the antithesis to American notions of freedom and autonomy.[16] The influential historian John Fiske confessed, "It is not easy to speak of Calvin with enthusiasm," and offered this description of the reformer:

> Among all the great benefactors of mankind the figure of Calvin is perhaps the least attractive. He was, so to speak, the constitutional lawyer of the Reformation, with vision as clear, with head as cool, with soul as dry, as any old solicitor in rusty black that ever dwelt in chambers in Lincoln's Inn. His sternness was that of the judge who dooms a criminal to the gallows. His theology had much in it that . . . the descendants of his Puritan converts have learned to loathe as sheer diabolism.[17]

---

14. Stewart, *Ten Myths*, 32–33.
15. Spurgeon, *Autobiography*, 2:29.
16. Davis, "Images of Intolerance," 234–48; Davis, "Rhetorical War," 443–56.
17. Fiske, *Beginnings of New England*, 67–68. Despite Fiske's personal distaste for Calvin and his theology ("Perhaps not one of the mediaeval popes was more despotic in temper than Calvin"), he had to concede that "the promulgation of his theology was one of the longest steps that mankind have taken towards personal freedom" (68).

This awareness of Calvin is the typical backdrop against which any study of predestination in the nineteenth-century English-speaking world must reckon. When we enter the realm of nineteenth-century Brethren, however, we find a somewhat different milieu. While the larger historical context must be kept in view, the Brethren were strict biblicists and thus approached the question of predestination without particular reference to Calvin—or anyone else, for that matter. It was not that they manifested particular hostility toward the reformer; they simply wanted to make clear their view was biblical and not the product of a system of divinity.[18] Grass notes, "For most Brethren Scripture was not merely the supreme authority, but the sole authority. Thus . . . they rarely accorded authority to creeds and confessions, and sat lightly to the Protestant tradition of biblical interpretation."[19] For Brethren historian Harold Rowdon, a radical appropriation of the principle of *Sola Scriptura* was the defining feature of Brethrenism. Rowdon states, "We shall not go very far astray if we come to the conclusion that the thing above everything else which distinguished the early Brethren was the absolute priority which they accorded to the Word of God . . . Here, if anywhere, is the essential principle of the Brethren. For man-made tradition they cared not a hoot: Scripture, on the other hand, was the voice of God."[20]

This is one reason the Brethren refused to accept the label of "Calvinist," even if their doctrine of election landed them squarely in that camp, as the present chapter endeavors to demonstrate.

Definitions

Before we turn to Brethren teaching, it may be helpful to define the key theological terms that will be used throughout this chapter. *Predestination* and *election* are often used synonymously to refer to God's sovereign choice of individuals for salvation. At times, Brethren writers distinguished between the terms, particularly when they were explaining the specific

---

18. Other evangelicals, such as Charles Simeon, could express similar sentiments, but not to the same extent as Brethren. Simeon, moreover, was concerned to "disarm anti-Evangelical prejudice" among Anglicans who viewed evangelicals with their Calvinism as extremists. See Bebbington, "Calvin and British Evangelicalism," 284.

19. Grass, *Gathering to His Name*, 84. In his book on the Bible and the Victorians, Timothy Larsen originally planned to include a chapter on the Brethren. In the end he decided against it. He concluded that since the Brethren were so obviously biblicists, there was "no need for me to try to convince the reader of this." Larsen, *People of One Book*, 290.

20. Rowdon, *Who Are the Brethren?* 33–34. Cf. Rowdon, "The Problem of Brethren Identity," 174.

meaning of each word in a given context.[21] In doctrinal discussions, however, *predestination* and *election* were typically used interchangeably, and we will generally follow that practice here.

Nevertheless, more precise definitions will provide some orientation to the historical and theological issues under review. In Reformed theology there are two dimensions to predestination: election and reprobation. One Calvinistic definition states: "Election is an act of God before creation in which he chooses some people to be saved, not on account of any foreseen merit in them, but only because of his sovereign good pleasure."[22] Likewise, reprobation is defined as "the sovereign decision of God before creation to pass over some persons, in sorrow deciding not to save them, and to punish them for their sins, and thereby to manifest his justice."[23]

As discussed at length in chapters 2 and 3, the doctrine of reprobation generated a great deal of discussion within Reformed theology, and no shortage of criticism from without. The issue was bound up with the logical order of God's decree (*ordo decretorum Dei*). *Supralapsarianism* teaches that God's decree of election and reprobation comes logically *before* his decree to create and permit the fall. *Infralapsarianism* understands the decree to save and condemn as coming *after* the decision to create and permit the fall—and thus applies to individuals who are sinful and merit divine judgment. It should be noted that infralapsarianism has been the more normative position in Reformed theology. "Infralapsarians worried that supralapsarianism risked making God the author of evil and making reprobation (election to judgment) roughly parallel to God's activity in his gracious election to salvation in Christ."[24] Most Arminians treated the issue as if supralapsarianism was normative Calvinism and unconditional reprobation[25] was the necessary corollary of unconditional election. Thus by the nineteenth century, moderate Calvinists, sensitive to Arminian criticism, upheld election but denied the doctrine of reprobation altogether,[26] and were at pains to distance themselves from hyper-Calvinists, who were unashamed of it.

The Arminian position states that God foreknows who will believe on Jesus Christ for salvation, and on that basis, he predestines them to salvation. Accordingly, the Arminian view of election is conditional; it is dependent

21. Darby, *Letters*, 1:476; Kelly, *The Purpose of God*, 20–21; Bellett, *Brief Notes*, 5.
22. Grudem, *Systematic Theology*, 670.
23. Ibid., 685.
24. Horton, *The Christian Faith*, 316.
25. I.e. God condemns individuals to damnation without any reference to their sin.
26. E.g., Scott, *Remarks*, 451. See chapter 3 for a more thorough discussion.

upon a person's faith. A variation within Arminian thought is the concept of *corporate election*, in which God chooses a people—the church—for his own. God determines to bless the corporate body, but does not predetermine who will comprise that body. When an individual believes in Christ, he or she becomes a member of the *elect*. Therefore, in Arminian thought, "predestination has an individual meaning (foreknowledge of individual choices) and a collective meaning (election of a people)."[27]

Brethren Teaching on Predestination

Critics of the Brethren were not reliable guides to Brethren thought, as evidenced by their contradictory evaluations of the movement's teaching on predestination. For example, the hyper-Calvinist J. C. Philpot could say in 1842, "Election, we believe, they universally hold."[28] Philpot had early connections to the Brethren and specifically named leaders such as Darby, B. W. Newton, George Wigram, and James Harris. On the other hand, Thomas Houston, the Ulster Presbyterian, writing particularly against Brethren evangelists in 1874, said, "Numbers of these teachers are Arminian in principle, denying vehemently the doctrine of *Eternal Election*."[29] Houston often misread Brethren teaching;[30] here he may have misunderstood the Brethren practice of avoiding the subject of election in evangelistic preaching, or their rejection of the doctrine of reprobation.[31] At any rate, we need to turn to the Brethren themselves to properly evaluate their perspective on election. We begin with Darby and then move chronologically through other important Brethren leaders, writers, and evangelists who were active in the nineteenth century.

---

27. Olson, *Arminian Theology*, 180.
28. Philpot, "Editors' Review," 80.
29. Houston, *Plymouthism*, 25.
30. For example he stated, "They insist on adult Baptism, by immersion." (Ibid., 12). While this was true of Open Brethren, it was not necessarily the case among Exclusives. See Rowdon, "Early Brethren and Baptism," 55–64. Houston was aware of Exclusive writers and referenced them in his critique.
31. It is possible that Houston heard revival evangelists and assumed they were Brethren. It is also conceivable that he heard Brethren lay preachers in his region denying election, but as we will see, these would have been out of step with the movement as a whole. Brethren preachers in post-1859 Ulster such as James Campbell and John McVicker did preach "instant salvation" (see chapter 7), but did not reject election.

John Nelson Darby

Given Darby's strong view of the "total ruin of man," it is not surprising that he should adopt a Calvinistic understanding of the sovereignty of grace in election.[32] Darby's sympathies on the question of predestination were expressed relatively early in his career. In 1831 he published a pamphlet[33] in connection with a controversy at Oxford spawned by a sermon preached by Henry Bulteel.[34] The sermon boldly rebuked the Established Church for its departure from the Calvinism of the Thirty-Nine Articles.[35]

For our purposes, what is notable is that Darby sought to prove that the roots of the English Reformation—and thus the Articles—were aligned with Reformed doctrine, and specifically, a Reformed understanding of predestination. He confessed:

> For my own part, I soberly think Article XVII to be as wise, perhaps I might say the wisest and best condensed human statement of the views it contains that I am acquainted with. I am fully content to take it in its literal and grammatical sense. I believe that predestination to life is the eternal purpose of God, by which, before the foundations of the world were laid, He firmly decreed, by His counsel secret to us, to deliver from curse and destruction those whom He had chosen in Christ out of the human race, *and to bring them, through Christ, as vessels made to honour, to eternal salvation.*[36]

Since this statement came so early in Darby's literary career, at a time when a number of his theological views were still being developed—indeed, before he had formally left the Established Church[37]—the question is raised as to whether his settled doctrinal convictions reflected a different approach

---

32. Darby's strong view of sovereignty was also seen in his belief that Christians should not "meddle in politics," since God governs and "will infallibly bring about His purposes." Darby, *CW*, 32:333.

33. Darby, *CW*, 3:1–43.

34. For more on the Bulteel controversy see chapter 3. For an extended discussion see Carter, *Anglican Evangelicals*, 252–83.

35. Bulteel, *Sermon*, 47–48.

36. Darby, *CW*, 3:3. Emphasis original.

37. Stunt puts Darby's secession at 1834 [Stunt, *From Awakening*, 275–77, 370]; Rowdon at 1833 [Rowdon, *Origins*, 97–99]; and Carter states, "there is no evidence that Darby ever renounced his Anglican orders or formally seceded ... what is more certain is that, by the mid-1830s, Darby seems to have regarded himself as being outside the Established Church." [Carter, *Anglican Evangelicals*, 217.] Likewise, Akenson asserts Darby never resigned his priesthood, "instead, he went AWOL from his parish." Akenson, *Discovering the End*, 256–57.

to predestination than the one stated above. We are, however, not left to wonder. In a letter dated March 23, 1880, some fifty years after his early endorsement of Article XVII, he wrote: "As to Article XVII., I quite admit that God's predestination is secret to us, but the seventeenth Article is not: it is very plain, and I think very good."[38] In another letter to the same recipient (also dated 1880) Darby described an unnamed Anglican vicar as being "upon ordinary evangelical Arminian or semi-Arminian ground." He then added, "I suspect the seventeenth Article tries him, and it is really a very wise statement as I remember it."[39]

In the official university reply to Bulteel's sermon, Edward Burton, Regius Professor of Divinity, argued that justification was based on free will, obedience, and repentance. He also suggested that the English Reformation was inherently Lutheran, not Reformed. In his response to Burton, Darby sought to refute the notion that the Church of England derived her doctrine from the Lutheran Church via Melanchthon. Rather, Anglican doctrine—and Article XVII in particular—was influenced by Reformed men such as Martin Bucer and Peter Martyr Vermigli, who derived their doctrine from Scripture.[40] Darby quoted Bucer and Vermigli at length on predestination[41] to demonstrate their Reformed orientation and to show "that they are equally and expressly opposed to the Arminian (so called, but properly Pelagian) notion of prospective works, or the (new and if you please Melancthonian [sic]) notion of church election, as contrasted with the individual." From Darby's endorsement of the literal understanding of Article XVII it is clear that he sympathized with the material he was quoting. He did not, however, allow the reader to equate his views with Bucer and Vermigli's, for he clarified, "I am not here arguing the point of the truth of these things; but arguing on the facts of the history of the times."[42] Perhaps Darby added this caveat to distance himself from Bucer and Vermigli's position on reprobation.[43]

In Darby's expositional writings on Scripture, we observe his consistent rejection of Arminian interpretations of election in favor of more Calvinistic ones. For example, in a discussion of Rom 8:29 ("whom he did foreknow, he also did predestinate"), he insisted that predestination was not

---

38. Darby, *Letters*, 3:70.

39. Ibid., 71. See also Darby, *CW*, 9:300 (1862). John Owen, for example, also appealed to Article 17 in his defense of a Calvinistic doctrine of election over against Arminian views. Owen, *Works*, 10:53.

40. Darby, *CW*, 3:14, 22.

41. Ibid., 4–18.

42. Ibid., 19.

43. For Darby's view on reprobation see below.

based on God's foreknowledge of human faith as in "the Arminian scheme"; rather, it was individuals as such whom God foreknew and predestined.[44] Summarizing themes in the Gospel of John, Darby commented, "Election and the sovereign action of grace, and its absolute necessity for salvation, are brought out everywhere. No one can come to Jesus, unless the Father, who hath sent Him, draw him."[45] Darby was convinced that, apart from sovereign grace, "not one soul would be saved, for none understand, none seek after God, not one of himself will come that he might have life. Judgment is according to works; salvation and glory are the fruit of grace."[46] However, he did not dwell at length on predestination, even when handling passages that directly addressed the issue.[47] It seems that for Darby—and presumably for many of his readers—predestination was not a doctrine that needed to be defended, because its truth was not in question. Thus he did not focus on predestination for its own sake, but frequently celebrated the *goal* of predestination: present adoption as God's children,[48] and ultimately, conformity to the image of Christ. His comments on Rom 8:29 illustrate his approach: "If through grace any have loved God, they were called according to His purpose. The purpose is not here, nor indeed anywhere, simply sovereignty in election. It includes that to which they were called. They were foreknown; but whom he foreknew He predestinated to a glory which was in His mind and counsels before the world began, namely, to 'be conformed to the image of his Son.'"[49]

One of his longer discussions of the subject is found in a letter to a correspondent who had raised the question of election and predestination with him. He responded as follows: "Election suppose [sic] a large number out of whom God chooses . . . Predestination is the proper purpose of God as to these individuals . . . it is a blessed idea that God had His mind thus set

---

44. Darby, *Letters*, 1:476. The letter is dated Feb. 1867. Cf. Darby, *CW*, 33:389, 398 (≤1853). In a conversation with the Methodist critic of the Brethren, Daniel Steele, Darby reportedly said, "an election, grounded upon reasons, would destroy the sovereignty of God, and that no act of the creature, no foreseen faith in Christ, conditioned election." Steele, *Substitute for Holiness*, 131.

45. Darby, *CW*, 30:272–73 (1871–72). In connection with Rom 9 he argued, "Whenever the sovereignty of God is called in question, it is the soul saying, in effect, I am to judge God, and not that God is to judge me." *CW*, 33:396.

46. Darby, *CW*, 26:108 (1862, 1868).

47. E.g., ibid., 26:102–03; 27:7–8; Darby, *Synopsis*, 4:192–93.

48. Darby, *CW*, 27:127 (1850).

49. Ibid., 26:173–74 (1871); cf. 1:243 (1843); 31:163 (1878); Darby, *Synopsis*, 5:509.

on us without thinking of others."⁵⁰ Clearly, he did not accept the Arminian idea of corporate election.

Although Darby upheld a Calvinistic view of election, he disavowed "what is called reprobation."⁵¹ He asserted that Rom 9 "speaks of the absolute sovereignty of God" and teaches that "the potter may do what he pleases with the clay."⁵² Nevertheless, he did not believe that God made people wicked—to say so would be "horrible blasphemy."⁵³ When God hardens a person, it amounts to a judicial act of giving the person over to his or her already sinful heart and desires. "God does not make man wicked, but simply gives man up to what he is."⁵⁴ Darby viewed Rom 9:21 as "the unqualified assertion of God's power to make vessels of dishonour, if He pleased, but careful avoidance of the thought that He had made any."⁵⁵ God did not fit the vessels of wrath to destruction, but "*endured with much longsuffering* the vessels of wrath fitted to destruction (Rom 9:22)." Such vessels "were evil to begin with,"⁵⁶ and that of their own doing. On the other hand, "the vessels of mercy" God "had afore prepared unto glory" (Rom 9:23). Darby explained, "the vessels of mercy were afore prepared of God unto glory, while the vessels of wrath are fitted to destruction by their iniquities having come to the 'full.' But whatever there is of good must come from God, and God only; the evil, alas! is already in us."⁵⁷

Darby had a tremendous impact on the Brethren movement. A number of aspects of his thought were revered by some and rejected by others. However, his teaching on predestination was not a subject of controversy or division among the Brethren in the nineteenth century.

---

50. Darby, *Letters*, 1:476–77 (February 13, 1867).

51. Darby, *Notes and Jottings*, 355. As we shall see, Brethren consistently rejected the doctrine of reprobation. For example, a comment that appeared in the *Bible Treasury* on 2 Pet 3:9 (God "is not willing that any should perish, but that all should come to repentance") was typical: "These words entirely set aside the horrid idea (technically called reprobation) that any man ever was made for the purpose of being cast into hell." "The Coming, and the Day," 59. It is clear that the Brethren did not display a nuanced understanding of reprobation as it was often discussed in the Reformed tradition. More often than not they were rejecting an extreme or caricatured version of it.

52. Darby, *CW*, 33:393 (≤1853).

53. Ibid., 399.

54. Ibid.

55. Darby, *CW*, 26:106.

56. Ibid., 26:181.

57. Ibid., 33:400.

James Lampen Harris (1793–1877)

James Harris, cousin of the Oxford high Calvinist Henry Bulteel, was an Anglican clergyman who seceded in 1832 and joined the Brethren at Plymouth, "where he played a leading role with [B. W.] Newton."[58] He also edited the first Brethren journal, *The Christian Witness*. He would later play a prominent part in the Newton controversy in the 1840s that led to the severance of the movement.

During the early years in the Plymouth assembly, Harris was one of the principal teachers.[59] Significantly for our purposes, a Mr. Cole, who attended the early Plymouth meeting and sat under the ministry of Harris, described him as "a very powerful exponent of the doctrines of grace."[60] This is reflected in a lecture Harris gave on Galatians 1 in which he stated, "The greatest opposers of the doctrines of grace are those who receive their religion from tradition, and not from the Word of God." The apostle Paul, Harris argued, was delivered by grace from such tradition, and as he went forward preaching the gospel, "he saw in others who received his gospel what others saw in him—an elect vessel of mercy, and gave the glory to God of [*sic*] their conversion, as others glorified God in him."[61] In the next lecture, Harris's Calvinistic soteriology is further suggested by the following statement: "It is neither personal qualification, nor the things we do, nor official character, which God regards; but that which His own grace makes any to be in Christ, and the gift He of His sovereign will confers on any. 'A man can receive (take unto himself) nothing, except it be given him from heaven [John 3:27].' Nothing could be added to this."[62] While Harris does not directly reference predestination here, the crediting of salvation to God's sovereign will and grace, without any contribution from the human subject, certainly implies unconditional election. Furthermore, it is highly unlikely that one described as "a very powerful exponent of the doctrines of grace" would have advanced an Arminian position on the doctrine of election.

---

58. *BDEB*, s.n. "James Lampen Harris," 523. It is worth noting that when Newton was developing strong convictions about the truth of Calvinism, Harris appeared to be in his inner circle. In a letter to his mother in which Newton describes Arminianism as "nothing more than varnished Pelagianism," he speaks of Harris delivering a parcel for him. Fry MS, 143. Cf. Burnham, *Story of Conflict*, 78n14.

59. Pickering, *Chief Men*, 177–78.

60. Cole, *Reminiscences*, 4.

61. J. L. Harris, *Law and Grace*, Lecture 1.

62. Ibid., Lecture 2. Harris denounced antinomianism, which both hyper-Calvinists and the Brethren were sometimes accused of in Harris, *Antinomianism and Legalism*.

John Gifford Bellett

A perception exists that a Calvinistic view of election is necessarily harsh and callous, but no such tone is found in J. G. Bellett's writings. He meditated on the eternal counsels of God wherein believers were "chosen, predestined, and written in the Book of Life"[63] with a kind of worshipful reverence and wonder. He also saw the goal of predestination as bringing one into a relationship of love with God. He wrote, "We are predestinated to a state of *gratified affections*, as well as to a place of *displayed glories*—to 'the adoption of children,' and to be 'before Him in love' . . . We are apt to forget this. We think of calling and of predestination, in connection with glory, rather than in connection with love, and relationship, and home, and a Father's house."[64]

For Bellett, "the election of grace" means that it is the Father "who gives to the Son, and draws to the Son, all who come to Him."[65] He too rejected the Arminian notion of corporate election, and insisted that the object of election and predestination is the individual.[66] He saw this illustrated in the life of Abraham:

> In our patriarch, then, we see the election and the call of God. He was of the corrupt, departed family of man, without a single claim on God. But sovereign grace (in the virtue of which all the redeemed, according to eternal counsel, stand) had made him its object; and under such grace he is, in due time, manifested as a chosen one, and is called of God to be a heavenly stranger in the world. Scripture speaks of him as the father of all them that believe. Rom. 4. We may, therefore, expect to find the life of faith exhibited in him; and so we do find it.[67]

Bellett was convinced that the doctrine of individual election to salvation is designed to be a source of joy and encouragement to the Christian. In a brief essay entitled "Election" he explained:

> The truth of the divine foreknowledge of us, of God's having elected us personally and predestinated us to most blessed destinies, is . . . for the saint as he walks in uninterrupted grace before

---

63. Bellett, *Short Meditations*, 158.
64. Bellett, *The Patriarchs*, 150. Cf. 188–89.
65. Bellett, *On the Gospel of John*, 58–59.
66. Bellett, *Paul's Apostleship*, 89. Cf. Bellett, *Short Meditations*, 118–19; Bellett, *Brief Notes*, 5.
67. Bellett, *The Patriarchs*, 99–100. Cf. 190: "Election, and the call of God, in the sovereign exercise of His grace, were exhibited in Abraham."

God. It is for the joy of his heart . . . It is for the putting of very boastful and triumphant language into his soul, by teaching him what anxious and everlasting interest God has had in all that concerns him. For it tells us . . . that we were the subject of the divine counsels—when God was all alone—before the foundation of the world; before the activities, so to speak, of creation began, we were before His thoughts.[68]

In what proved to be a common approach among Brethren, Bellett insisted the doctrine of election was a blessing for believers; it was not a subject that should trouble the unconverted. He concluded, "Thus surely does the doctrine of election set the saint down in rich and happy pastures. The sinner need not think of it. It is not for him."[69]

Anthony Norris Groves (1795–1853)[70]

In his history of the Brethren, Tim Grass says that Anthony Norris Groves "had significant contact with most of the early leaders and centres, exercising considerable influence, especially in the area of personal lifestyle. Furthermore, his life and thought epitomise much that was distinctive about early Brethrenism."[71]

As a young man of nineteen, Groves moved from London to Plymouth in order to practice dentistry. Shortly after his arrival in Plymouth, he underwent an evangelical conversion, although his widow, in her memoir of Groves, downplayed the experience. She wrote, "It was [at Plymouth], also, he was able to profess himself a disciple of Christ . . . but his entrance into the full liberty of gospel light did not take place till some time after, in Exeter."[72] Timothy Stunt understands Mrs. Groves's comments to reflect "her disapproval of the Arminianism of the circle with which Groves was then associated."[73]

In Exeter, Groves adopted views that were more Calvinistic in nature through the influence of friends like William Caldecott and Bessie Paget.

---

68. Bellett, *Showers upon the Grass*, 103.

69. Ibid., 106.

70. This discussion of Groves is adapted from Stevenson, "Early Brethren Leaders," 22–24.

71. Grass, *Gathering to His Name*, 12.

72. [Groves], *Memoir*, 3.

73. Stunt, *From Awakening*, 119. Stunt adds the circle "included Robert Lampen, a clergyman, who was later noted as an important opponent of Calvinism in Plymouth." Cf. Stunt, *Elusive Quest*, 106.

Such was the influence Paget had on Groves that he could say, "I look up to her, and love her now as my mother, in the things of God."[74] Again he wrote of Paget, "Dearest B. had, for some time, sunk the keen controversialist in the tender and kind friend." In a footnote to this rather obscure sentence, Harriet Groves commented, "This refers merely to his Arminian views, from which she was at last the means of delivering him."[75]

Some years later, after Groves had set out on his missionary endeavors, he wrote back to his friend William Caldecott confessing, "I adore God's electing love in choosing such a wretch to be the partner of His Son's throne."[76] In the same letter, Groves took pains to distance himself from the perceived antinomianism of high Calvinism.[77] Yet to reassure his friend that he had not abandoned Calvinism, he clarified: "Do you think your old friend is from a superlapsarian [sic] Calvinist become an Armenian [sic]? believe it not; the doctrines of grace, in all their fullness, freeness, and particularity, were never dearer to me than now; but because they are dear, I would desire to disentangle them from that web of selfishness and sloth by which they have too long bound the Church, till we are afraid to use God's words, or if we use them, introduce them by an apology."[78]

Groves's willingness to identify himself as a supralapsarian Calvinist is somewhat surprising; it suggests he may have affirmed the doctrine of reprobation, which most Brethren of this era rejected. Nevertheless, for Groves, the doctrine of "the sovereign grace of God, and His love entertained towards the soul before the foundation of the world" happily sustained his soul.[79]

---

74. [Groves], *Memoir*, 40.

75. Ibid. In his biography of Groves, Robert Dann asserts, "The majority of early Brethren, including Groves himself, had a decidedly Calvinistic theology." Dann, *Father of Faith Missions*, 304n16, cf., 405.

76. [Groves], *Memoir*, 249.

77. Ibid., 250.

78. Ibid., 250–51.

79. Ibid., 167–68. Cf. Groves, *Journal*, 102–3. Here Groves speaks of the "comfort and consolation of the soul" that he finds in the doctrines of "the sovereignty of God's government, and the individuality of God's election in Christ Jesus, from before the foundation of the world." Cf. 104–6 for his unequivocal endorsement of a Calvinistic view of election.

Percy Francis Hall (1801–84)

Another important leader in the early days at Plymouth was Captain Hall.[80] By the time Darby arrived in Plymouth in 1830, Hall was already "known in the villages round about the ancient seaport town as a faithful and zealous preacher."[81] Captain Hall was not a prolific writer, so it is difficult to evaluate his soteriological convictions with precision. Nevertheless, there is a hint which suggests that, like other early leaders, he maintained Calvinistic principles and would have taught unconditional election.

The hint comes in connection with the development of a Brethren meeting in Hereford. In 1832, John Venn was appointed to succeed the Calvinist Henry Gipps as vicar of St Peter's Church, Hereford. Venn "worked tirelessly to help the poor"[82] and was a faithful preacher, "but some of his people disliked the Arminian note in his preaching"[83]—including Mr. & Mrs. William Yapp and Dr. & Mrs. J. Griffiths, all of whom would join the Brethren.[84] While visiting friends in Plymouth in 1837, Mrs. Griffiths heard Captain Hall. She was so impressed that "she begged the Captain to come to Hereford, assuring him that there were many Christians who would gladly welcome such teaching."[85] Hall accepted the invitation and ended up settling in Hereford, where his preaching was well received. The meetings were attended "largely by discontented members of Venn's church."[86] A reference to the Brethren in the April 1838 edition of the *Hereford Journal* reads, "Captain Hall was the founder . . . they consist chiefly of seceders from the Church of St. Peter's; they have made a most rapid progress from the time they have been established—about six months, and scarcely a week passes without new converts being added."[87]

One recent book attributes the defection of many of Venn's congregation to his Calvinism[88]—but surely this is mistaken, especially given Gipps's (Venn's predecessor) strong Calvinism.[89] Rawson responds, "Charles

---

80. On Hall see Schneider, "'The Extravagant Side of Brethrenism,'" 17–44.
81. Beattie, *Brethren*, 22.
82. Rawson, "Barton Hall," 44.
83. Rowdon, *Origins*, 164.
84. Embley, "Origins," 129.
85. Beattie, *Brethren*, 36.
86. Rowdon, *Origins*, 165.
87. Cited in Rawson, "Barton Hall," 47.
88. O'Donnell, *John Venn*, 23 as cited by Rawson, "Barton Hall," 45.
89. On Gipps see Stunt, *Elusive Quest*, 208–13. Stunt calls Gipps's doctrinal position "decidedly Calvinistic" (211).

Brewer's manuscript account[90] of those early years refers to many in the 'inner circle of the church' being offended by John Venn's Arminianism, which in view of the Calvinism of the early Brethren and what we know of Venn, seems the more likely explanation."[91] Stunt is somewhat skeptical of this assessment. He suggests that Venn's gentle temperament and dislike of argumentation "was liable to appear as Arminianism to parishioners who were accustomed to Gipp's uncompromising Calvinism."[92] Whatever Venn's precise position, it would appear that the seceders preferred their doctrine more pronounced and found it so among the Brethren.

None of this, of course, proves Hall's Calvinism. But at the very least, it suggests that his preaching lacked the perceived Arminian tone which had offended many of Venn's former congregants. Furthermore, Hall certainly sounded Calvinistic when he declared: "faith, which is the gift of God, (Eph. ii. 8) is the work of the Holy Spirit."[93] We could wish for more evidence, but even the limited amount we possess suggests that Captain Hall's sympathies bent in a Calvinistic direction.

Robert Cleaver Chapman

Although Chapman did not publish a great deal,[94] there are several indications—beyond what was noted in the previous chapter—that his soteriology was Calvinistic. Chapman was converted through the preaching of James Harington Evans. Evans had been a clergyman in the Church of England but broke away as part of the "Western Schism" in 1815. As indicated in chapter 3, the Western Schism was a movement in which a number of clergy seceded from the Anglican Church due to, among other things, their high Calvinism.[95] Evans was recognized as "the most able theologian of the party."[96] An eloquent preacher, Evans attracted the attention of Henry Drummond, who was impressed enough to build him a chapel in London—

---

90. "The Lord's Work Amongst Early Brethren in Herefordshire." Rawson suggests Brewer wrote this "late in the nineteenth century as he quotes from eyewitness reports as far back as the 1850s." Rawson, "Barton Hall," 43n1.

91. Rawson, "Barton Hall," 45.

92. Stunt, *Elusive Quest*, 215. Cf. 217.

93. Hall, *Discipleship*, 7; cf. 11.

94. According to Peterson, this was due to Chapman's desire for people to make the Bible the focus of their reading. Peterson, *Robert Chapman*, 167. Holmes states "in later life he consistently refused to publish." Holmes, *Brother Indeed*, 76.

95. Carter, *Anglican Evangelicals*, 105–51.

96. Ibid., 123.

John Street Chapel—where Evans preached "for thirty years an evangelical Calvinism."[97]

After his conversion, Chapman became an active member at John Street Chapel and got his start as a preacher there, speaking at various meetings. Evans was a mentor to Chapman and had a significant influence on him.[98] Peterson writes, "Evans' influence on Chapman's life and attitudes toward Christian worship was profound. Chapman's confidence in the all-sufficiency of the Bible, his devotedness to a weekly observance of the Lord's Supper, his emphasis on believer's baptism . . . and his views on the unity of all Christians—earmarks of his subsequent ministry—were the same as Evans'."[99] It is not unreasonable to surmise that Evans likewise would have influenced Chapman's understanding of the gospel. Having been converted through Evans's preaching, he remained under his teaching and guidance for nine years and counted him as a friend.[100] Although Evans, much like the Brethren, did not like systems of theology or "party names, party distinctions, party separations,"[101] his soteriology was Calvinistic. In Evans's memoir, his son wrote that his father affirmed "the total and entire depravity of man by nature, without ability to turn himself to God, the free, sovereign, electing love of God, flowing through the cross of Christ, and the absolute power of the Holy Ghost to commence in regeneration and carry on in sanctification His work in the soul." Yet Evans "was fettered by no shackles of system; and while he maintained that the atonement of Christ was for the sins of His own people, he proclaimed the Gospel as free to every creature under heaven."[102]

After nine years of such a close connection with Evans, it is highly doubtful that Chapman would leave John Street Chapel with Arminian notions. In subsequent years, when Chapman was engaged in ministry in Barnstaple, Evans expressed his deep respect and love for him, and could even write of Chapman in 1846, "He is one of my stars."[103]

Another close connection Chapman formed that makes sense of his Calvinism was with Elizabeth (Bessie) Paget.[104] As noted above, Bessie

---

97. *BDEB*, s.n. "James Harington Evans," 369. For a time Evans had antinomian tendencies, as well as questionable Trinitarian views. However, he reversed both these positions by the 1820s. See Carter, *Anglican Evangelicals*, 123–26.

98. See Peterson, *Robert Chapman*, 29, 40, 195–97; Holmes, *Brother Indeed*, 18–19.

99. Ibid., 31. Cf. Grass, *Gathering to His Name*, 39.

100. Chapman was converted in 1823 and moved to Barnstaple in 1832.

101. Evans, *Memoir and Remains*, 37.

102. Ibid., 91.

103. Ibid., 76. Cf. Peterson, *Robert Chapman*, 64.

104. *BDEB*, s.n. "James Harington Evans," 851.

Paget was the one who convinced Anthony Norris Groves to abandon his Arminian views in favor of Calvinistic ones. In Groves's words, Paget "sunk the keen controversialist,"[105] which suggests Bessie was a persuasive theologian! Evidently she did not need to use those skills on Chapman. Paget joined Chapman in the assembly work in Barnstaple in the late 1830s. She initiated a Sunday School, which by 1851 averaged about one hundred students.[106] She also hosted a Thursday evening Bible study, and her home was used as part of Chapman's ministry of hospitality to Christian workers.[107] Chapman died in 1902, almost forty years after Paget's passing. Interestingly, however, arrangements had been made for him to be buried in the same gravesite as Paget. Thus, as a token of their kinship in the work of the gospel, they shared a common grave and tombstone.[108]

It is also worth noting that when Chapman initially came to Barnstaple, he did so to pastor a Particular Baptist church.[109] Particular Baptists were traditionally Calvinistic ("particular" referring to their understanding of the design of the atonement), in contrast to the General Baptists, who were Arminian. Chapman did implement some changes that caused a faction of the congregation to leave, but these changes were related to the basis for participation in communion.[110] In none of the published accounts was soteriology an issue, presumably because Chapman and the congregation were, more or less, on the same page. Furthermore, as a preacher, Chapman is said to have "habitually opened up the doctrines of grace"[111]—a shorthand term for Calvinistic soteriology.

In the little that was published of his sayings, addresses, and letters, not much surfaces on the doctrine of predestination.[112] In a meditation entitled "God's Purpose in Redemption," Chapman suggests God's grand design was to reveal his glory by exalting and delighting in Christ. In this

---

105. [Groves], *Memoir*, 40.

106. Peterson, *Robert Chapman*, 77, 74.

107. Ibid., 61, 82.

108. Ibid., 183. A day before he died, he dictated the following message, "I bow to the sovereignty of God my heavenly Father; I have no will but His."

109. Ibid., 39. The church is sometimes described as "Strict Baptist" (e.g., Holmes, *Brother Indeed*, 31), but Grass points out it did not belong to that movement. The term "strict" probably refers to their practice of restricting communion to believers baptized by immersion. Grass, *Gathering to His Name*, 40n199. Gradually the church became identified with the Brethren movement.

110. Peterson, *Robert Chapman*, 59.

111. Holmes, *Brother Indeed*, 50–51.

112. Brief references are found, for example, in Chapman, *Choice Sayings*, 129; Bennet, *Robert Cleaver Chapman*, 148, 198; Peterson, *Robert Chapman*, 167.

context, Chapman's mind turned to the doctrine of election. Citing John 1:1 and 2 Thess 2:13 ("God hath from the beginning chosen you to salvation"), Chapman wrote,

> Does it not tell that the chief purpose in the mind of God (when as yet there was not any creature in being) was the setting up of Christ to be the Head of all things ... It was the purpose of God to *reveal Himself* in Christ; not only to glorify Himself, but to provide Himself in Christ with objects of affection, in which He could delight, and in which He could rest. Does not this agree with Eph. i. 5: "Having predestinated us unto the adoption of children, by Jesus Christ, to Himself?" And is not the force of that of His own choice, for His own delight? In verse 6 it is, "To the praise of the glory of His grace;" but before mention is made of glory, we read *"to Himself."*[113]

A Calvinistic view of election in which God chooses, by sovereign grace,[114] to save some sinners on the basis of his own good pleasure is the only view that makes sense of this passage. An Arminian interpretation, in which God chooses on the basis of foreseeing who would choose him, is simply incompatible with Chapman's point. Furthermore, as noted in chapter 4, Chapman believed that "man's will is always in opposition to the will of God"[115]—thus he is not able to choose Christ apart from sovereign grace.

Henry Craik and *George Müller*

In the previous chapter we observed Craik and Müller's affirmation of a Calvinist view of human depravity. Not surprisingly, they also shared a commitment to the doctrines of grace. In his introduction to Craik's *Diary and Letters*, Müller recalls the development of his friendship with Craik. In 1829–30, when both men were in Teignmouth, Müller was discovering biblical truth about a number of doctrines, such as the second coming of Christ, the authority of Scripture, the work of the Holy Spirit, and the position of the church. During this time of dawning conviction, Müller also "had seen clearly the precious doctrines of the grace of God, about which I had been uninstructed for nearly four years after my conversion." He then commented, "As these very truths so greatly occupied the heart of Mr. Craik also, we were now soon drawn closely together; and from that time to the

---

113. Bennet, *Robert Cleaver Chapman*, 150.

114. Chapman used the language of sovereign grace in Chapman, "Self-will and Sovereign Grace," 113–14.

115. "Treasures of Grace," in Bennet, *Robert Cleaver Chapman*, 137.

day of his falling asleep in Jesus, our friendship was intimate and unbroken for thirty-six years."[116]

In his autobiography, Müller elaborated further on this formative time when his discovery of the doctrines of grace affected him in such a profound way. It is worth repeating the account at length in his own words:

> Before this period I had been much opposed to the doctrines of election, particular redemption, and final persevering grace; so much so that, a few days after my arrival at Teignmouth I called election a devilish doctrine. I did not believe that I had brought myself to the Lord, for that was too manifestly false; but yet I held, that I might have resisted finally. And further, I knew nothing about the choice of God's people, and did not believe that the child of God, when once made so, was safe for ever . . . But now I was brought to examine these precious truths by the word of God. Being made willing to have no glory of my own in the conversion of sinners, but to consider myself merely as an instrument; and being made willing to receive what the Scriptures said; I went to the Lord, reading the New Testament from the beginning, with a particular reference to these truths. To my great astonishment I found that the passages which speak decidedly for election and persevering grace were about four times as many as those which speak apparently against these truths; and even those few, shortly after, when I had examined and understood them, served to confirm me in the above doctrines.

Müller then confessed that these doctrines enabled him to live a more consistent and godly life.[117]

In his later ministry, Müller did not shy away from publicly proclaiming the doctrines of grace. For example, in an address delivered in 1871, he declared that the way those who were by nature "the children of Satan" could be born of God was traceable "to the councils and purposes of God from eternity. He did choose us in Christ . . . He predestinated us to be conformed to the image of His dear Son. He arranged from eternity for our salvation in the Lord Jesus Christ."[118] Yet he hastened to add that in order to enter into this salvation, "we have to believe the Gospel, we have to put our trust for the salvation of our souls in the atonement made by the Lord Jesus Christ."[119] Müller was attempting to strike a biblical balance between divine

---

116. Müller's introduction to Tayler, *Passages*, xii.
117. Müller, *Narrative*, 46–47. Cf. Müller, *Jehovah Magnified*, 100.
118. Müller, *Jehovah Magnified*, 141.
119. Ibid., 142.

sovereignty and human responsibility, and he recognized that some under the influence of hyper-Calvinistic teaching might object to his emphasis on the latter. He therefore clarified that a belief in predestination did not imply a sinner must wait passively until God did everything for him or her; such a notion is "Satan's trap for the poor sinner." Sinners are called by God to receive Christ. Thus for those wrestling with the tension between divine sovereignty and human responsibility, Müller counselled, "If you say, 'Oh, I wish I could believe!' well, I grant it, you cannot if left to yourself. But you can groan out to God, 'Lord, help me to believe.'"[120]

While Craik shared these doctrinal convictions with Müller, he was concerned to guard himself against falling into apathy in regard to evangelism. Under the heading, "Perversion of the doctrines of predestination and grace," Craik wrote the following in his diary in September 1837:

> The moment any doctrine so operates as to make us little in earnest about souls, either the doctrine is false, or we are perverting it. Whenever therefore I find myself sinking down into a false security respecting the souls of others, from considering that none of the elect can finally perish, I am making an unscriptural use of the doctrine of election. The same authority on which I believe the doctrine, enforces as much earnestness about the salvation of sinners, as if all depended upon our own exertions. I will then be a fool for Christ's sake. I will labour and pray, as if all might be saved; and, if any are brought to God, I will give all the glory to sovereign and distinguishing grace.[121]

This is an important passage, for it shows that Craik saw no conflict between a Calvinistic view of predestination and rigorous evangelism and evangelistic preaching. If Craik found his fervor for souls waning, it was not the fault of the doctrine of election, but rather a perversion of the doctrine. Craik here is certainly representative of nineteenth-century Brethren thought in affirming predestination *and* enthusiastic evangelism.

---

120. Ibid., 147. Neil Summerton suggests that this passage in Müller is sufficient for some Calvinists to conclude that he was not a Calvinist. While that may be true, it seems better to conclude that Müller was contesting against hyper-Calvinist notions that allowed the doctrine of election to negate human responsibility and avoid passionate calls for sinners to believe the gospel. Summerton, "Theology of George Müller," 7. I am grateful to Dr. Summerton for providing me with an unpublished draft of the paper.

121. Tayler, *Passages*, 192.

Benjamin Wills Newton[122]

Despite their later conflict, Darby and Newton shared a number of common doctrinal convictions in the early years of the movement, including a Calvinistic view of the doctrine of election.[123]

As noted in chapter 3, it was at Oxford that Newton developed a friendship with Henry Bulteel, whose Calvinistic views influenced him[124] and sparked significant controversy at the university. That Newton also embraced a Calvinistic view of election is clear from several letters to his mother. For example, in a letter dated September 3, 1827, he revealed his predestinarian beliefs by quoting a sermon from the missionary Henry Martyn on the sovereignty of God in salvation.[125] He urged his mother to read the sermon, for in it she would find his "principles and feelings portrayed fully and accurately."[126] He was careful to assure her that he had not fallen into extreme Calvinism. He declared, "I am ready to shake hands with any who preach Jesus Christ as the only name given under heaven whereby we can be saved—not by works but simply by believing in his name." He then added, perhaps in order to distance himself from the supposed antinomianism of high Calvinism, "Works follow as an effect—faith (which God only can bestow) is the cause."[127] As a postscript, Newton reassured his concerned mother: "Don't think I would press the belief in election as necessary on any one."[128]

Newton's Calvinistic convictions continued to deepen. A few weeks later he spoke of the heartfelt pleasure it would bring him to see all his

---

122. This discussion of Newton is adapted from Stevenson, "Early Brethren Leaders," 18–22.

123. Burnham, *Story of Conflict*, xv.

124. Fry MS, 138. In 1827 Newton could speak of his delight "sitting under the ministry of my darling Bulteel." Fry MS, 125.

125. It is worth noting that at approximately the same time, reading the life of Henry Martyn also had a profound effect on J. G. Bellett. See Bellett, *Recollections*, 14–15.

126. Fry MS, 109. "Sermon XIII on 1 Corinthians 1:1–3" in Martyn, *Sermons*, 226–46. In one relevant portion of the sermon, Martyn stated: "Whatever there is good in his people is God's own gift and work, and could therefore never induce him to make choice of them . . . The holiness of the elect is the effect, not the cause of their election. There is, therefore, no cause existing in ourselves to render us the objects of his choice . . . Election must be called an act of that sovereign power whereby the Almighty God acts according to the purpose of his own will, without thinking fit to render an account of it to his creatures" (229–30).

127. Fry MS, 109. In the same sermon by Henry Martyn that revealed Newton's own principles "fully and accurately" there is an explicit rejection of antinomianism. Martyn, *Sermons*, 233.

128. Fry MS, 111.

friends and relatives "sincere converts to those doctrines which I am more and more convinced are more precious than life to the soul which can receive them." He then lamented how the Established Church abhorred such principles: "The Church of England would indeed be an Apostolic Church if its members and pastors believed the Articles by which they profess to be guided. But alas! how different is the fact."[129] Newton no doubt had Article XVII ("Of Predestination and Election") specifically in view, for he had cited it in his previous letter.[130]

At the close of the same year, Newton traced the development of his evangelical convictions for his mother in a letter dated December 30, 1827. The tone of this letter was somewhat evangelistic, as Newton sought to persuade her to leave the Quakers and embrace the gospel. He described his new faith as "the free unmerited gift of God." He asked, "Did I deserve the gift [of faith] more than others? No! in no wise. Freely then has he given it to me because it was his good pleasure, therefore he hath elected me to salvation." He closed the letter marveling at God's grace: "To think that he should have chosen me, so vile and sinful!"[131]

Two weeks later, Newton became even more forthright in his Calvinistic assertions. It is worth repeating a portion of his letter at length.

> Does any one ask me "Are you saved?" I answer "Yes." Does he enquire "Why?" Because I believe on Jesus Christ, therefore I am regenerate, therefore I am sanctified . . ." Who gave you this belief?" God, for "No one can come unto me except the Father draw him . . ." "How do you know that you shall continue to the end?" Because I keep not myself, but Christ keepeth me.
>
> Such is the doctrine which I find in the Bible. Such is the doctrine of Augustine, Luther, Ridley, Latimer and all those holy men who bled for their Holy Faith. Such is the doctrine of the inestimable Articles of our Church. But where is that doctrine now? Is is [sic] not become a laughing-stock for fools to scoff at? Nevertheless the counsel of God standeth sure . . . No greater blessing do I ask than that I may, in the midst of this crooked and perverse generation be endued with grace to hold up the standard of Gospel Truth.[132]

In a letter to his uncle from August 1828, Newton affirmed his belief in total depravity and in God's sovereign grace in salvation, and in final

---

129. Ibid., 114.
130. Ibid., 111.
131. Ibid., 127–28.
132. Ibid., 143–44, dated January 13, 1828.

perseverance.[133] He quoted approvingly from John Newton as follows: "If any persons have contributed a mite toward their own salvation, it was more than we can do . . . We needed sovereign irresistible grace to save us or we had been lost for ever."[134]

Clearly, B. W. Newton's soteriology was Calvinistic,[135] but he never adopted the high Calvinism of his Oxford acquaintances. Years later, writing of his association with Bulteel, he said, "There was great blessing until a very High Calvinism was developed and then I broke my connexion with it. I remember dining with a set of three persons who were discussing the certainty of Wesley being damned."[136]

Charles Henry Mackintosh

Mackintosh frequently addressed the doctrine of election, often in an attempt to clarify its meaning and to explain how it related to other doctrines, such as God's love and human responsibility.

In 1863, he published an article in response to a number of letters he had received over the doctrine of election. Evidently, some readers of his magazine, *Things New and Old*, had not understood the doctrine in its proper place and thus were struggling with it. One reader confessed, "If I only knew that I was one of the elect I should be quite happy, inasmuch as I could then confidently apply to myself the benefits of the death of Christ."[137] But for Mackintosh, this sentiment is the work of the enemy turning the doctrine of election—"blessedly true in itself—a most valuable 'landmark'"—into a "stumblingblock [sic]." The proper place of election is for the comfort of believers; it is not to be imposed on anxious enquirers.

---

133. Ibid., 148–49.

134. Ibid., 150.

135. A later admirer of Newton claimed, "[Newton] has been aptly described as 'the John Calvin of the nineteenth century.' From the commencement of his career to the end he maintained firm and unswerving devotion to the doctrines of Reformed theology." Fromow, *B. W. Newton*, 7.

136. Fry MS, 96. The story is also recalled on pp. 135 and 139 of the Fry MS. On p. 135 Newton uses the term "hyper-Calvinism." Burnham, however, suggests that "Newton's memory on this issue was partly influenced by his involvement in controversy concerning hyper-Calvinism among the Strict Baptists." Burnham, *Story of Conflict*, 59n100.

137. [Mackintosh], "Landmarks," 142–43. This was not an uncommon struggle in the nineteenth century for those familiar with Calvinistic teaching. See for example, E. E., "I Want to Believe," 286.

To the perplexed reader he advised that the proper way to view the death of Christ is not from the vantage point of election, but of "conscious ruin."[138] We are to seek the benefits of Christ's work as lost sinners. Mackintosh wrote, "salvation—free as the sunbeams, full as the ocean, permanent as the throne of the eternal God—is *preached* to me, not as one of the elect, but as one utterly lost, guilty, and undone; and when I have received this salvation there is conclusive evidence of my election."[139] Sinners under conviction need not worry about questions of predestination; they need only concern themselves about their plight before God and the solution held out to them in the gospel. It is for sinners that Christ died, and if I know myself to be a sinner, I may receive the benefit of Christ's death.

Some might wonder if Mackintosh was setting aside the doctrine of election altogether with such counsel. He anticipated the question and responded as follows: "God forbid. We only want to see it in its right place . . . We believe the evangelist has no business to *preach* election. Paul never preached election. He *taught* election, but He preached Christ. This makes all the difference."[140] He claimed to have seen "serious damage" done by preaching election instead of Christ: "Careless sinners are made more careless still, while anxious souls have had their anxiety intensified."[141]

Four years later, in 1867, Mackintosh repeated much of what he had written in "Landmarks and Stumblingblocks" with no less fervency. He wrote, "The more we ponder the subject, the more thoroughly are we convinced that it is a mistake on the part of the evangelist or preacher of the gospel to qualify his message, hamper his subject, or perplex his hearers, by the doctrine of election or predestination."[142] Seen in their proper place, these doctrines "shine like precious gems on the page of inspiration," and are meant to comfort saints. However, "they were never intended to lie as stumbling blocks in the way of earnest seekers after life and peace."[143]

These concerns were always present in Mackintosh's discussion of the doctrines of grace, and he was careful to maintain biblical balance in contrast to "systems of theology and schools of divinity,"[144] which inevitably distorted the balance. A letter from an American correspondent produced

---

138. [Mackintosh], "Landmarks," 143.

139. Ibid.

140. Ibid., 146.

141. Ibid. It is interesting to note that Anthony Norris Groves had no scruples about preaching the doctrine of election when unbelievers were present. See Groves, *Journal*, 105.

142. [Mackintosh], "Glad Tidings," 43.

143. Ibid., 46–47.

144. [Mackintosh], "One-Sided Theology," 12.

the 1876 article, "One-Sided Theology." The correspondent was under the influence of hyper-Calvinism and could not "see the rightness of calling upon the unconverted to 'come,' to 'hear,' to 'repent,' or to 'believe.'"[145] Mackintosh's problem was not with the view of divine sovereignty that stood behind this position. He affirmed, "We believe that not a single soul would ever come to Christ if not drawn, yea, compelled, by divine grace so to do; and therefore all who are saved, have to thank the free and sovereign grace of God for it."[146] He even claimed to believe the five points of Calvinism, "so far as they go."[147] His problem was that the system of hyper-Calvinism neglected "the solemn truth of man's moral responsibility, inasmuch as it is plainly taught in scripture."[148] Furthermore, biblical texts that declare God's desire for all to repent and be saved (e.g., Acts 17:30; 1 Tim 2:4; 2 Pet 3:9) cannot be taken as they stand, but must be modified to fit the one-sided system. Thus they are interpreted to mean that it is God's desire for all *the elect* to be saved. For Mackintosh, however, such texts did not conflict with predestination. Rather, "they set forth the largeness of the heart of God, the gracious activities of His nature, the wide aspect of His love. It is not according to the loving heart of God that any of His creatures should perish."[149]

Mackintosh judged both hyper-Calvinism and Arminianism guilty of distortion and imbalance. He stated, "A disciple of the high school of doctrine will not hear of a world-wide gospel—of God's love to the world—of glad tidings to every creature under heaven. He has only gotten a gospel for the elect. On the other hand, a disciple of the low or Arminian school will not hear of the eternal security of God's people. They are only safe as long as they continue faithful. Their salvation depends partly upon Christ, and partly upon themselves."[150]

In an earlier article (1873), Mackintosh clarified that God's universal love for all people does not "deny or call into question the grand truth of predestination, election, or effectual calling." Indeed, he affirmed, "We hold these things as amongst the fundamental principles of Christianity. We believe in the eternal counsels and purposes of our God—His unsearchable

---

145. Ibid., 10. The actual letter that forms the basis for "One-Sided Theology" appears to be reprinted as "On the Sovereignty of God, the Responsibility of Man, and the Heart of God as Revealed in the Gospel," in Mackintosh, *Short Papers*, 2:264–72.

146. [Mackintosh], "One-Sided Theology," 10.

147. Ibid., 11.

148. Ibid., 10. Mackintosh also complained that this and other systems of divinity neglected many other important truths of Scripture, especially Brethren distinctives in ecclesiology and eschatology (11–12). Cf. Stevenson, "Early Brethren Leaders," 27.

149. [Mackintosh], "One-Sided Theology," 14.

150. Ibid., 12–13.

decrees—His electing love—His sovereign mercy."[151] Yet none of these truths negate God's love for the whole world. He summarized his basic position on divine sovereignty and human responsibility as follows:

> The mistake lies in supposing that, because God has His purposes, His counsels, His decrees—because He is sovereign in His grace and mercy—because He has chosen from all eternity a people for His own praise and glory—because the names of the redeemed, all the redeemed, were written down in the book of the slain Lamb, before the foundation of the world—that therefore God cannot be said to love all mankind . . . and, moreover that the glad tidings of God's full and free salvation ought not to be proclaimed in the ears of every creature under heaven. The simple fact is that the two lines, though so perfectly distinct, are laid down with equal clearness, in the word of God; neither interferes, in the smallest degree, with the other, but both together go to make up the beauteous harmony of divine truth and to set forth the glorious unity of the divine nature.[152]

For Mackintosh, part of maintaining a biblical approach to divine sovereignty and human responsibility meant rejecting the doctrine of reprobation as he understood it. He argued that no one will ever say, "I longed to be saved, but could not, because I was not one of the elect. I longed to flee from the wrath to come but was prevented by the insuperable barrier of the divine decree which irresistibly consigned me to an everlasting hell."[153] Rather, all who are finally lost have only themselves to blame for their own willful rejection of God. In his view, Scripture carefully "guards against the repulsive doctrine of reprobation."[154] For example, in the judgment of the sheep and the goats in Matthew 25, the king says to the sheep on his right, "Come, *ye blessed of my Father,* inherit *the kingdom prepared for you* from the foundation of the world."[155] But in contrast, as Mackintosh observed, to the goats on his left the king says, "Depart from me ye cursed (He does not say 'of my Father') into everlasting fire, prepared (not for you, but) the devil and his angels."[156] Likewise, in Romans 9 the vessels of mercy are prepared by God for glory, but the vessels of wrath are not said to be prepared *by God* for destruction—this they do themselves. Thus Mackintosh concluded, "the

---

151. [Mackintosh], "'God for Us,'" 31–32.
152. Ibid., 32.
153. Ibid., 33.
154. [Mackintosh], "One-Sided Theology," 16.
155. Ibid., Mackintosh's emphasis.
156. Ibid.

grand truth of *election* is fully established; the repulsive error of *reprobation*, sedulously avoided."[157]

William Kelly

Kelly also upheld the doctrine of unconditional election. He wrote, "Election is necessarily from God entirely apart from those that are the objects of it, as it means the exercise of His sovereign choice. If there is the smallest ground in the party chosen because of which God chooses, it is not His choice, but rather a moral discernment, which, far from being sovereign, is only an appraisal whether the person deserves [sic] or not."[158] In other words, God's choice is based solely on his sovereign good pleasure and not on anything he sees in the person chosen—including foreseen faith. In his comments on Rom 8:29 ("for whom he did foreknow, he also did predestinate"), he clarified, "It is important to observe that the apostle does not speak of a passive or naked foreknowledge . . . as if God only saw beforehand what some would be, and do, or believe. His foreknowledge is of persons, not of their state or conduct; it is not *what*, but 'whom' He foreknew."[159] Here Kelly, like Darby, refuted the common Arminian understanding of election. He equally rejected another Arminian position, namely, corporate election. Writing on 1 Peter, Kelly argued,

> Whatever may be found in hymns, or sermons, or theology, scripture knows no such thing as an elect church . . . The very point of Christianity is this, that as to election it is personal—strictly individual. This is precisely what those who contend against the truth of election always feel most: they will allow a sort of body in a general way to be elect, and then that the individuals who compose that body must be brought in, as it were, conditionally, according to their good conduct. No such idea is traceable in the word of God. God has chosen individuals. As it is said in Ephesians: He has chosen us, not the church, but ourselves individually. "The church," as such, does not come in till the end of the first chapter. We have first individuals chosen of God before the foundation of the world.[160]

157. Ibid., cf. Mackintosh, *Short Papers*, 2:268. His argument from Matt 25 and Rom 9 is also found in "'God for Us,'" 33–34, in which he declared, "There is absolutely no such thing as reprobation in the word of God, meaning thereby the consigning on God's part, of any number of His creatures to everlasting damnation."

158. Kelly, *Lectures . . . Minor Prophets*, 508.

159. Kelly, *Notes . . . Romans*, 153.

160. Kelly, *Lectures . . . Acts*, 224–25. Cf. Kelly, *Lectures . . . Matthew*, 338.

While Kelly happily agreed with a Calvinistic view of predestination, he could not embrace the doctrine of reprobation. He stated, "One may hold then as strongly as the stoutest Calvinist the free sovereign choice of God, but the reprobation of the wicked which the Calvinist draws from it, as an equally sovereign decree, is in my judgment a grave error."[161] For Kelly, reprobation was the product of mistaken human deduction and not divine revelation.[162] Thus when a person rejects God and refuses to believe the gospel, there may be a judicial hardening, as in the case of Pharaoh, but these are instances of God giving the individual over to an unbelief already festering in his or her heart. It is never a situation in which God predestined the individual to unbelief and damnation. In Kelly's words, God "never hardens him in the first instance that he should not believe; but after he has heard and refused to believe, God seals him up in an obdurate state. In no instance, however, is this the first act of God, but rather the last, judicial and retributive, when he has slighted an adequate and faithfully rendered testimony."[163]

The doctrine of reprobation was one reason why Kelly could not embrace "Calvinism" as he understood it. He wrote, "Calvinism clogs and obscures the gospel . . . by its decree of reprobation."[164] Yet in reality, what he was rejecting was a high or hyper-Calvinism which made a strong notion of reprobation the necessary corollary of predestination. As we have seen, Calvinists have historically been divided over the nature of reprobation, and moderate Calvinists of the nineteenth century were at pains to soften or disavow reprobation altogether.[165] In any case, Kelly's distancing himself from Calvinism does not suggest he was more sympathetic to Arminianism. In the same tract cited above, he argued, "The Arminian scheme necessarily fails by making man guilty and sinful, to go as partner with God in his own salvation. But if it be true, as scripture plainly declares, that man *is* dead in trespasses and sins . . . that question is decided. Arminianism is farther from the truth than Calvinism."[166]

As much as Kelly disliked reprobation, he marveled at the grace displayed in predestination and found beauty in the doctrine. He said, "Man belongs to a stock now wholly depraved . . . God's election is entirely independent of what He finds, and spite of all evil . . . But the fallen condition of man gives to God's election, where sinners are the only possible objects,

161. Kelly, *Lectures . . . Minor Prophets*, 508.
162. Ibid., 169.
163. Ibid., 170.
164. Kelly, *Gospel of God*, 2.
165. See the discussion in chapter 3.
166. Kelly, *Gospel of God*, 2.

an exceeding beauty and very deep moment. He chooses entirely apart from anything that deserves it, in the face of all that is out of harmony with Himself."[167] Kelly could warmly affirm God's election of depraved sinners not only because he deemed the doctrine to be explicitly biblical, but also because it displayed the glory of God. On the other hand, predestination to damnation was for Kelly not only contrary to Scripture, it was grotesque.

Charles Stanley

Among the collection of tracts by the Exclusive evangelist is one simply entitled "Election."[168] In response to an anxious enquirer, the first section of the tract takes up the question of the extent of the atonement—an issue to which we will return in the next chapter. When Stanley came to the doctrine of election, he asserted that we must bow to Scripture, and when we do, we find that human responsibility and divine sovereignty "run on together." God's love toward all people and the election of a limited number are "equally true, because both are revealed in the word of God."[169] For this reason, he enthusiastically affirmed that the gospel should be preached to all, yet he equally opposed the Arminian position which said: "As many as believe are then ordained to eternal life." Stanley countered, "But it is not so; 'As many as were ordained to eternal life believed' [Acts 13:48]. Surely we have no right to alter God's word to suit human opinions."[170]

God did not create human beings as sinful; nevertheless, they fell into sin. And now "man is so desperately wicked, that left to his own free choice, he will not believe God . . . he will not receive Christ as his Saviour."[171] Thus the doctrine of election is necessarily connected to fallen human inability to obey or choose God, or even to desire him. In the doctrine of election, "all supposed merit is taken from man." Stanley announced, "If left to his own free choice, he deliberately rejects and despises the gospel of God; and the reason why any are saved, is the sovereign choice of God. Such is the distinct teaching of the word of God, whether we believe it or not."[172] Stanley was unmistakably clear on this point and repeated it several times: "It is not man, the sinner, that chooses God, but God that chooses the sinner." And again, "God hath chosen those who never would have chosen Him . . .

---

167. Kelly, *Lectures . . . Minor Prophets*, 509.
168. Stanley, "Election," 1–38.
169. Ibid., 14–15.
170. Ibid., 18; cf. 33–34.
171. Ibid., 16.
172. Ibid., 21.

He hath chosen us when obstinate, ignorant, hell-deserving sinners; and as objects of His mercy, has brought us into His everlasting favour."[173]

Although he clearly believed the Bible taught election to salvation, like other Brethren, he did not believe the doctrine of reprobation to be a biblical one. He wrote, "But does not [election] imply that God has predestinated some to be lost? Certainly not. There is no such thought in scripture. The reason why some perish is their own deliberate rejection of the truth."[174]

Stanley pointed out that people readily acknowledge the election of Israel and that there are elect angels. But "what men do so hate is the election of the predestined children of God."[175] "C. S.," however, did not despise it. Indeed for him, the doctrine was cause for gratitude, praise, and humility. In many ways, Stanley's tract represents the quintessential nineteenth-century Brethren approach to the doctrine of election.

Henry Dyer (1821–96)

Henry Dyer was a valued teacher, preacher, and evangelist, but he is also remembered for establishing "one of the first ministry conferences in England"[176] for Brethren. Conferences became an important feature of Brethren life, and Dyer continued to devote himself to conference work for twenty-five years. He also exhibited a great interest in foreign missions and spent time abroad both in evangelistic work and in ministering to missionaries on the field.[177]

In 1885 Dyer wrote a brief devotional piece in *Echoes of Service* to encourage missionaries in their labors, particularly those who were not seeing many conversions. Significantly, it was a Calvinistic view of election that Dyer presented as an assurance that their work was not in vain. He wrote, "The sovereign purpose of God . . . is a backbone of strength to gospel labourers, and bids them expect great results from their labours, though as yet they *see* scarcely any fruit in present conversions."[178] Dyer conceded that "God's sovereignty of gospel grace has its limits," meaning preachers do not know whom God has chosen for salvation, and they must

---

173. Ibid., 25.
174. Ibid., 20; see also 37–38.
175. Ibid., 16.
176. Grass, *Gathering to His Name*, 159. The conference was in Yeovil. He was also active in a popular conference in Leominster. For more on Dyer see Beattie, *Brethren*, 72–76, and Pickering, *Chief Men*, 122–25.
177. Pickering, *Chief Men*, 124.
178. D[yer], "'Other Sheep I Have,'" 84.

bow before such sovereignty. Nevertheless, Dyer affirmed, "labour in the Lord cannot be in vain... In Acts xiii., at the very outset of Paul's preaching to the Gentiles, it is said of those at Antioch, 'as many as were *ordained* to eternal life believed.'"[179] Thus for Dyer, a Calvinistic view of election was an incentive for missionaries to keep on preaching the gospel of grace. Indeed, God's sovereignty in salvation was the grounds of hope, especially for those laboring in difficult fields.

Donald Ross

Ross was one of the leading Open Brethren evangelists in the post-1859 revival era. Chapter 4 introduced Ross's Calvinistic orientation and his rejection of Morisonianism. We turn now to his thoughts on the doctrine of election.[180]

Around the year 1865, when Ross was superintendent of the North East Coast Mission, the evangelist Duncan Matheson was preaching in the town of Nairn, Scotland. As Matheson was concluding his meetings, he introduced Ross to the people in the following manner: "I am leaving you, but there is a man coming that I can heartily commend as sound in the faith. Yes; as sound as a bell. In fact, I call him 'The walking Shorter Catechism.' I have given you the stories; he will give you the doctrine. His name is Donald Ross."[181] One man who heard Ross at this time was John Gill. Gill recalled Ross addressing the subject of election and commented, "I had never before heard anyone put things so plain and in such a matter-of-fact way, and ever after I coveted his manner and his matter."[182]

This account is significant on a couple of levels. First, it indicates that Matheson, himself a Calvinist,[183] trusted Ross's doctrine. Thus when Ross spoke on election, there would be no danger of leading people into the errors of Arminianism;[184] his position would have been consistent with the Westminster Shorter Catechism. Second, Ross's treatment of election impacted Gill and stayed with him for many years. Gill (1834–1920) would join Ross's band of evangelists and in due course, along with Ross and others, like Donald Munro, he associated with the Brethren. By the mid-1870s Gill had settled in the Boston area and was instrumental in the Brethren

---

179. Ibid., emphasis original.
180. See the discussion in Harvey, "Donald Ross," 38–45.
181. Ross, *Donald Ross*, 130.
182. Ibid.
183. On Matheson's Calvinism see Harvey, *Donald Ross*, 27–30.
184. Macpherson, *Life and Labours*, 197.

work there.[185] Yet it is noteworthy that after Ross died, it was his sermon on election that rose to the forefront of Gill's memories of Ross.

Preachers who came out of the 1859 revival were sometimes accused of holding Arminian principles—often because of their unconventional methods.[186] But Ross did not see any conflict between his Calvinistic soteriology and earnest gospel preaching.[187] He also believed the holiness of the preacher was one of the means God used to bless his preaching and bring conversions. To a young evangelist under his supervision, Ross wrote in December of 1862: "Although all is of grace, yet please notice that only persons having Christianity of the highest type are used by God for the conversion of souls. Many there are labouring for Christ and seeing no fruit, who take refuge under the sovereignty of God, whereas if they would examine their own private conduct, they would find a key to the want of success."[188]

Once Ross espoused Brethren principles in the early 1870s, his position on election did not appear to alter significantly. In 1872 he published an article upholding the Calvinistic doctrine of effectual calling. Ross asserted that the new birth is all "by the Word of God—the voice of Christ—the operation of the Holy Ghost. There is no human effort in the matter . . . the soul, 'dead in trespasses and sins,' is acted upon by the voice of Christ . . . This takes all the glory out of man's hand, and places it where it ought to be, even in the hand of the Son of God. He must bear *all* the glory, for ever blessed be His name!"[189]

After he moved to the United States, Ross launched and edited the North American Brethren magazine *The Barley Cake* (which later became *Our Record*). In the December 1885 issue, he responded to the question, "What are we to understand by the doctrines 'Election,' 'Predestination,' and 'Foreordination'?" He answered as follows:

> Election means choice; predestination means what He predestines the objects of his choice to, and foreordination the same. Israel was elected, Christ was elected and precious, all the saints are elected and predestined to be conformed to the image of His son and ordained for the same glory. If there were no elections there would never be salvation at all. It is God alone that saves, none else could or would do it . . . We believe that pride of heart alone causes opposition to the Lord's way. Wherever infidelity

185. M[uir], "Mr. John Gill," 17–20.
186. E.g., Hamilton, *Inquiry*, 174–76.
187. Ross, *Donald Ross*, 104.
188. Ibid., 78.
189. [Ross], "Loose Him," 14. Cf. 5–6.

pervades society, election, predestination, new birth, etc., are rebelled against as if, forsooth, man could or would save himself or at least help to do it,—or, in other words, lay God under some obligation to do so. There is nothing more unmistakably taught in God's word than Election, Predestination and Foreordination (Rom. ix. 10–11; Eph. i.).[190]

It is worth noting that Ross does not use the language of the Shorter Catechism here; by this period his aim was to direct people to Scripture for their doctrinal study. As early as 1872, he considered searching for the way of salvation in the Reformed catechisms and confessions akin to looking for gold in a common sewer. Such human products are "muddy streams" and "nauseous" compared with the pure fountain of the Word of God.[191] His friend Donald Munro wrote after Ross's death, "We have heard him say that in his earlier days he read and studied not a few standard works on theology. But as he went on with God and His work, these lost their attraction for him. The Word in its majesty, grandeur, and perfection commanded his whole attention."[192] This was the Brethren approach, and Ross embraced it wholeheartedly. Nevertheless, Ross's methodology did not mean he abandoned a Reformed understanding of predestination, as the passage above indicates. Indeed, in his view, rebellion against predestination was a mark of infidelity! In 1882 he complained that while Britain and North America experienced different ecclesiastical problems, there was a "Laodiceanism" that "finds its fullest expression ... in the Arminianism that pervades almost all."[193]

Yet it is clear that Ross understood the Scriptures to give equal stress to human responsibility. Answering a question on how to reconcile Acts 13:48 ("as many as were ordained to eternal life believed") with John 3:16, he explained, "There are many passages in the Word that speak of salvation as wholly of God from beginning to end, and then there are many that speak of man's responsibility to receive the salvation provided of God. Both are equally true." He continued by confessing that he was "saved wholly by grace; that God did it all—that He picked me out and brought me to himself; that if I had been left to myself, I never would have been saved." Yet at the same time, Ross affirmed the biblical teaching that "whosoever

---

190. Ross, "Notes of Questions," 184.
191. [Ross], "Salvation," 44.
192. Ross, *Donald Ross*, 103.
193. [Ross], "Creamery," 110. In the same year, he complained that the preaching in Harrisburg, Pennsylvania was in many cases "a mixture of Arminianism, Socinianism, and Ritualism." *The Missionary Echo* (1882), 55.

will may come; that salvation is for all." He was content to maintain both lines, concluding: "The reconciliation of these two truths would require an infinite mind, which we have not. We receive them both from God; we see the difficulty involved, but believe the solution of it is in Him and trust Him about it. It is well for us, we believe, to meet with truths that are beyond us; they keep us in our place as finite creatures and hide pride from man."[194]

This was typical of the way nineteenth-century Brethren approached the matter; strong on divine sovereignty in salvation, but never to the exclusion of human responsibility and the need for preaching and evangelism. They were not embarrassed by the tension this presented, because they were sure this is what the Bible taught.

William Lincoln (1825–88)

William Lincoln was the Anglican minister of Beresford Chapel, Walworth, whose preaching attracted a significant following. He grew increasingly uncomfortable with the state-church system, however, and finally seceded in 1862.[195] Grass notes that his adoption and implementation of Brethren views was gradual, but in time Beresford Chapel was recognized as a Brethren assembly.[196]

Lincoln wrote several expositions of Scripture, and when the biblical text spoke of election, he consistently took a Calvinistic interpretation. For example, on 1 Thess 1:4 ("knowing, brethren beloved, your election of God"), Lincoln acknowledged that we do not begin with election; we begin as sinners who need a savior. But once saved, we look back and discover the truth of election. Lincoln declared, "Election is the work of God. God began it, it is all of Him together." And it is cause for rejoicing: "Ah! we little knew once what God had done for us, what thoughts He had toward us; that our names were in the Book of Life, that we were given to Christ, before the world began."[197]

Like other Brethren, Lincoln considered election to be a wonderful truth for believers. He wrote in connection with 2 Thess 2:13, "When in Christ, we are not afraid of the doctrine of election. It is very precious to know, that God always intended to save us . . . It is very precious to know that we did not first choose God, but He chose us."[198]

194. [Ross], "Questions and Answers," 153–54.
195. Pickering, *Chief Men*, 221.
196. Grass, *Gathering to His Name*, 129.
197. Lincoln, *Lectures on the Epistles to the Thessalonians*, 10.
198. Ibid., 52.

Arminians frequently appealed to 1 Pet 1:2 ("elect according to the foreknowledge of God") to support their position of conditional election based on God's foresight of who will believe in Christ. Lincoln, however, rejected that interpretation. Instead, he understood the word "foreknowledge" in the sense of "fore-ordained."[199] To the question of why God would choose one person over another, an Arminian would again take recourse in a concept of election conditioned upon human choice. Yet Lincoln could not give that response; he simply replied, "I cannot answer that. No explanation can be given."[200] Furthermore, in his exposition of Ephesians 1, he refuted the Arminian concept of corporate election: "Not merely He chose the Church in Christ, but He chose each one separately in Christ. In chapter i., God deals with individuals; in chapters ii., iii., iv., collectively. Before God shows us about building a Temple, in chapter ii., a Body, in chapter iii., or a Bride, chapter v., there are the individuals in chapter i."[201]

What is surprising about Lincoln's Calvinism is that, unlike most other Brethren,[202] he appeared to favor a supralapsarian position. He argued that Eph 1:4 "gives an answer to an important question, which was much discussed about two hundred years ago. Some persons say God loved us when He saw us in our misery; others, before—which is right? Verse 4, shows that God loved us apart from our wickedness; then there was provision for our misery. He chose us before the world began . . . It assumes that predestination was the foundation of election."[203]

Lincoln was not writing a systematic theology but an exposition of Scripture—likely the substance of sermons he preached—thus he did not discuss the question of reprobation. Nevertheless, from his perspective, even supralapsarian predestination ought to evoke praise. He exclaimed, "A chain of things, all in the heart of God when the creature knew nothing about it. They were deep counsels in the heart of God, 'or ever the earth was' . . . Oh! when I get before Him, how I'll praise Him! Oh! my God, to think Thou didst look at *me* in Thy love, predestined *me* and made me holy! Oh! what cause I shall have to praise Thee!"[204]

---

199. Lincoln, *Lectures on the First and Second Epistles of Peter*, 8.
200. Lincoln, *Lectures on the Epistle to the Ephesians*, 15.
201. Ibid.
202. With the exception of Anthony Norris Groves, as noted above.
203. Lincoln, *Lectures on the Epistle to the Ephesians*, 12.
204. Ibid.

It is significant to note that in 1884, Donald Ross published Lincoln's exposition of Ephesians—with its Calvinistic view of election—in *The Barley Cake*.[205]

Emma Frances Bevan (1827–1909)

In a recent essay, Neil Dickson maintains that "Frances Bevan was the most prolific nineteenth-century woman writer among the Brethren."[206] She was respected as a poet and hymn-writer,[207] but she also authored several historical works, and even a commentary on Ezekiel. Although some have thought Bevan was connected to the Open Brethren, Dickson demonstrates she joined the Exclusives around 1860. Darby became her favorite theologian, so it is not surprising that her soteriology was Calvinistic.[208] In a biographical work on the French reformer William Farel, Bevan identified the natural tendency of fallen humans to attempt to contribute to their own salvation. But, she argued, all are dead in trespasses and sins, and therefore, "if there are any who are brought to the simple confession, 'salvation is of the Lord,' it is by the power of the Holy Ghost alone." She then produced a quotation from Farel with which she was clearly sympathetic: "God has chosen, before the foundation of the world, all those who have been, or will be saved. It is therefore impossible for them not to be saved. Whosoever upholds free-will, absolutely denies the grace of God."[209]

Although Bevan admired John Wesley enough to devote a biography to him, she was also concerned to expose his theological "errors and defects."[210] These included Wesley's doctrine of perfection and his teaching that believers might lose their salvation. On this latter point, Bevan aligned herself with Whitefield and Cennick, who taught "that salvation was entirely God's work from beginning to end—that God had chosen His own people before the world was made—that He saved them because He loved them—that although no dependence could be put in *them*, *God* could be depended upon to keep them safe for ever."[211] Bevan bluntly declared, "If you take the trouble to look into the bible, you will see that in these matters

---

205. Lincoln, "Notes on Ephesians," 167–72; 177–81.

206. Dickson, "'A Darbyite Mystic,'" 10. I am grateful to Dr. Dickson for allowing me access to an unpublished draft of the paper.

207. See Roach, *The Little Flock*, 13.

208. Dickson, "'A Darbyite Mystic,'" 17.

209. Bevan, *William Farel*, 215–16. Cf. 46.

210. Bevan, *John Wesley*, iii.

211. Ibid., 147–48. Emphasis original.

John Wesley was in the wrong."[212] While she happily endorsed the Calvinistic Methodists' teaching on election, she disagreed with any who "denied that God made any offer of mercy to sinners, except in the case of such as were chosen by Him before the foundation of the world."[213] For Bevan, such a position was contrary to Scripture. Like other Brethren, Bevan affirmed a Calvinistic view of election but rejected any hyper-Calvinistic restriction on gospel offers.

F. W. Grant (1834–1902)

Frederick W. Grant was born in England and immigrated to Canada as a young man. After serving for a time as an Anglican minister, he eventually joined the Brethren. He was soon recognized for his gifts and emerged as the key leader among North American Exclusive Brethren. From Canada, Grant moved to the United States and eventually settled in Plainfield, New Jersey, which became a center of Brethren activity.[214] H. A. Ironside wrote the following of Grant:

> In America, F. W. Grant had become by 1880 the leading figure among the Exclusive Brethren. His platform gifts were not of a high order, but as a teacher, he was unexcelled. Many consider him to this day the superior of Darby himself, in accuracy and spiritual insight, but he always held himself as a disciple greatly indebted to J.N. Darby up to the last, and the two were fast friends, though for a number of years there had been slight doctrinal differences between them, but they were in no sense fundamental.

According to Ironside, Darby and Grant had clashed over the issue of the freedom of the will.[215] Grant, like Darby, could speak of "man's ruin," acknowledging that although human beings are responsible, they are nevertheless "fallen, and become the willing slave[s] of sin."[216] Unlike Darby, however, Grant could suggest the following: "Is there not after all in [the will of man], define it as we may, some mysterious power which, spite of the fall, spite of the corruption of nature, should yet respond to these invitations,

---

212. Ibid., 149. Cf. 312–13.
213. Ibid., 323.
214. Reid, *F. W. Grant*, 15.
215. Ironside, *Historical Sketch*, 81.
216. Grant, *Leaves from the Book*, 149.

these pleadings of divine grace?"[217] For Darby, such a notion was inconceivable, but Grant seemed inclined to answer in the affirmative, conscious of the mystery of it all.

Darby and Grant did agree on the doctrine of predestination.[218] In fact, in an essay entitled "The Sovereignty of God in Salvation," Grant articulated what by now should be considered the prevalent nineteenth-century Brethren approach to the doctrine of election.[219] He began by lamenting that the sovereignty of God is not always a welcome theme among Christians—especially the sovereignty of God in *salvation*. He complained, "The truths of election and predestination, while the favourite cavil in the mouths of unbelievers, are undoubtedly, by many who receive them, received with inward shrinking—as at most necessary, rather than really approved."[220] Yet for Grant such truths are desirable, since God is full of perfect goodness and wisdom. It is fitting that all things should be molded by the counsel of His will. In fact, Grant went so far as to say that "predestination extends to everything."[221] This does not mean that God is responsible for moral evil; neither is human will negated, nor human responsibility abrogated. However insoluble these mysteries may be, "The doctrine of predestination remains our only comfort and support in this perplexity: to give it up would be to abandon ourselves to the despair of good as the final goal to which all tends."[222]

For Grant, then, predestination is comprehensive, while the doctrine of election is more narrowly focused on soteriology. He clearly rejected the Arminian interpretation of election: "Election is so plainly taught in the word that it is surely only the opposition of the heart to it that can account for its not being universally received among Christians. Nor is this election nationally or individually to privileges or 'means of grace' such as plainly Israel . . . [has] enjoyed but to salvation; and to salvation, not on account of foreseen holiness or faith, but *through*, or by means of, these."[223] Grant believed that people reject the doctrine of election not because the Scriptures are unclear on the matter—indeed, for him they could not be more clear—but because it is a "truth most humbling to man's pride of heart."[224]

---

217. Ibid., 153.
218. See Reid, *F. W. Grant*, 58–59.
219. The essay is found in Grant, *Leaves from the Book*, 146–158.
220. Ibid., 147.
221. Ibid., 150.
222. Ibid., 148.
223. Ibid., 150–51.
224. Ibid., 151.

Like many Brethren of his era, Grant was critical of the systems of Calvinism and Arminianism for their lack of biblical balance and their refusal to acknowledge any truth in the other party. He saw Calvinism centered on divine grace, and Arminianism fixed on human responsibility: "The strength of each lies in what it affirms; its weakness, in what it denies."[225] Yet Grant was more critical of Arminianism and could even concede that "Calvinism . . . when it treats of actual salvation, is almost wholly right."[226] At the same time, Grant was no hyper-Calvinist. He affirmed the love of God for all, not just for the elect, and stressed that the gospel should be preached to all. Furthermore, he denied that "there can be any contrary decree of God hindering the salvation of any."[227] But "the truth of predestination does not conflict" with these concessions "in any way."[228] Indeed, for Grant, every description of the new birth "ascribes it in the fullest to divine and sovereign power."[229]

John R. Caldwell (1839–1917)

From 1876 to 1914, J. R. Caldwell[230] served as editor of *The Witness*, which has been described as "the principal Brethren review worldwide."[231] From this strategic post, Caldwell helped to shape Open Brethren discussion on many issues, including doctrine. In the later years of the nineteenth century, the issue of election surfaced in *The Witness* on several occasions.[232]

In 1888 the question of whether or not God ordained some to be saved and some to be lost was raised. Caldwell did not answer all the questions in the "Question and Answer" section of the magazine himself, but he only published responses that he could endorse.[233] One answer Caldwell printed said, "That God has ordained that many shall be saved is clearly taught in Scripture, and this without in any wise taking from the individual respon-

---

225. Ibid., 152.

226. Ibid.

227. Ibid., 153. Grant, like many other Brethren, strongly rejected reprobation and claimed that to teach an election to damnation is blasphemy (Ibid., 157).

228. Ibid., 155.

229. Ibid., 157.

230. On Caldwell see Pickering, *Chief Men*, 50–54.

231. Dickson, *Brethren in Scotland*, 147.

232. E.g., [Caldwell], "Question 189," 32; B[ennet], "Regeneration and Election," 132; Davis, "Making Our Election Sure," 147–48; J. M., "Faith: Is It Involuntary?" 67–68 (and Caldwell's "editor's note" 68).

233. Dickson, *Brethren in Scotland*, 147.

sibility of man. That any should be saved is due to sovereign grace alone, and the judgment at the great white throne shall be on account of misdeeds wilfully persisted in." A second answer stated, "That God has ordained some to be saved is most blessedly true . . . on the other hand, it is equally certain that the doctrine of reprobation, or of God's ordaining any to be lost, has no foundation in the Word of God." Both answers provided ample biblical support for their positions. Yet Caldwell was compelled to add, "The foregoing replies demonstrate from Scripture that God has ordained some to eternal life . . . But we fail to find any such predestination of individuals to destruction." What followed was a brief exposition of Calvinistic soteriology from an infralapsarian point of view.[234] This is significant because answers to questions in *The Witness* often, as Dickson says, "established acceptable beliefs"; indeed, the pronouncements of important editors like Caldwell "were widely accepted as authoritative and aided the establishment of normative thinking."[235] Thus it is fair to say that a Calvinistic view of election, alongside a rejection of the doctrine of reprobation, was normative thinking among Brethren even as the nineteenth century drew to a close.

Henry Moorhouse (1840–80)

Born in Manchester, Moorhouse was converted after a rebellious youth that included more than one stint in jail. After his conversion, he gave himself to outreach and soon became a full-time evangelist. Roy Coad describes Moorhouse as one of the second generation revival preachers "who threw their lot in fully with Brethren."[236] Although he maintained Brethren ecclesiastical convictions and always sought to meet with Brethren to "break bread" even as he travelled, he was more open to inter-denominational gospel work than some Brethren.[237] In fact, Moorhouse is perhaps best remembered for the powerful influence he exerted over the American evangelist D. L. Moody. In 1867 Moorhouse made his first trip to the United States, and in due course, he came to Chicago. He preached seven consecutive evenings in Moody's church on John 3:16, turning over and over again the theme of God's great love for sinners. Moody, skeptical at first, was quickly drawn in and deeply moved by what he heard. He testified, "Instead of preaching that God was behind them with a double-edged sword, to hew them down, he told them God wanted every sinner to be saved, because He loved them." The follow-

---

234. [Caldwell], "Election," 159–60.
235. Dickson, *Brethren in Scotland*, 147–48.
236. Coad, *History of the Brethren*, 170.
237. For Moorhouse's Brethren principles see, Needham, *Recollections*, 196–200.

ing evening, Moorhouse "went from Genesis to Revelation to show that it was love, love, love, that brought Christ from heaven—that made Him step from the throne to lift up this poor fallen world."[238] The impact on Moody was profound. Previously the focus of his preaching centered on warning sinners about the judgment of God. Yet hearing Moorhouse proclaim the love of God transformed Moody's evangelistic approach.[239] He confessed, "I have preached a different gospel since, and I have had more power with God and man since then."[240]

With such a strong emphasis on preaching the love of God to all, some might wonder if Moorhouse's doctrinal sympathies ran in an Arminian direction. Such was not the case, however. George Needham, a friend and fellow evangelist (who was himself converted through the preaching of C. H. Mackintosh[241]), characterized Moorhouse's theological views as "sound to the core"—although, he admitted, Moorhouse was "considered by some rather too Calvinistic."[242] He certainly affirmed the doctrine of unconditional election. For example, at Princeton, a center of Calvinism at the time, he preached in a Presbyterian church crowded with seminary students and professors. His biographer recalled, "In this discourse he proclaimed the doctrines of grace, giving a striking and memorable illustration of 'election.'"[243]

The noted American Bible teacher James H. Brookes had come to know Henry Moorhouse during his visits to the United States, and he penned a tributary letter a few weeks after Moorhouse's death. In it he summarized the evangelist's soteriological views that formed the foundation of his preaching. He wrote, "The utter depravity of man's nature . . . the absolute necessity of the new birth by the Holy Ghost through faith in Christ as revealed in the Word, the atonement made by the blood shed upon the cross, the present and certain salvation of the believer, God's sovereign choice of His people . . . were constantly proclaimed with remarkable clearness and

---

238. Ibid., 109.

239. Gundry, *Love Them In*, 46. In view of Moorhouse's influence on the American evangelist, Coad calls Moody's later preaching "the most spectacular indirect result of the work of a Brethren evangelist." Coad, *History of the Brethren*, 189.

240. Gundry, *Love Them In*, 110. Moorhouse also helped Moody to see the importance of rooting his preaching in the biblical text, not his own ideas (118).

241. Cross, *Life and Times*, 122.

242. Gundry, *Love Them In*, 196. Moorhouse and Needham frequently ministered together and the latter recalled how "the precious doctrines of the vicarious atonement, the sovereignty of God, the great salvation, the complete justification of the believer . . . laid hold of our hearts and strengthened our hands for the work" (105).

243. Macpherson, *Henry Moorhouse*, 74.

force."[244] The Calvinistic emphasis is obvious, leading biographer Stanley Gundry to observe that Moody had come "under the spell of such species of Calvinism as were to be found among the Plymouth Brethren in general and Henry Moorhouse in particular."[245]

What is noteworthy for our purposes in this chapter is that Moorhouse believed the Calvinist doctrine of unconditional election was wholly compatible with passionate preaching of the love of God for sinners.

Sir Robert Anderson

As noted in the previous chapter, a popular book among Open Brethren on soteriology was *The Gospel and Its Ministry* by Sir Robert Anderson. In chapter 6, Anderson took up the topic of election and wrestled with the biblical tension between divine sovereignty and human responsibility. Like most Brethren, he did not approach the subject from the standpoint of systematic theology. In fact, again like many other Brethren, he manifested a kind of antipathy toward systems, as if they necessarily distort Scripture.[246] For example, he wrote, "The theological doctrine based upon [election] is too often pressed beyond the limits of the positive teaching of Holy Writ, and thus the divine mystery which crowns the great truth of sovereign grace, is degraded to the level of a narrow dogma, inconsistent alike with both sovereignty and grace."[247] Here Anderson was targeting a high Calvinism with its doctrine of reprobation and scant emphasis on human responsibility.[248] Nevertheless, he affirmed a Calvinistic understanding of election to salvation. He thought such a position was the obvious teaching

---

244. Needham, *Recollections*, 181–82. Cf. Macpherson, *Henry Moorhouse*, 111.

245. Gundry, *Love Them In*, 46. This is not to suggest that Moody himself became a Calvinist. See Gundry 135–43.

246. In his history of the Brethren, Grass notes, "With such an impressive line-up of textual scholars and commentators, it is significant that Brethren have not produced systematic theologians." Grass, *Gathering to His Name*, 171, cf. 374, 424. See also Stevenson, "The Brethren and Systematic Theology."

247. Anderson, *The Gospel and Its Ministry*, 76.

248. This is especially obvious in a later book entitled *The Entail of the Covenant*, in which he labored to distinguish between "the Scriptural truth, and the theological doctrine, of election." (14). He balanced election with preaching the gospel to "every creature"; but for Anderson this meant the "Scriptural truth of election must therefore be kept apart from the Augustinian doctrine" (54). The Christian can rejoice in election "without having the light of that glorious truth bedimmed by the shadow which Augustinian theology has cast upon it" (63). Unfortunately, Anderson did not display a sophisticated understanding of the Augustinian tradition, but attacked contemporary hyper-Calvinistic variations of it.

of Scripture and needed no defense. He was content to simply cite 2 Thess 2:13–14 and move on to reflect on how the truth of election did not hinder the gospel message.[249]

His primary question was: "How can grace be compatible with election?"[250] Anderson spoke of the "paradox of election and grace" and "the great mystery of divine sovereignty in relation to human will."[251] But to reject one in favor of the other "is to put reason above revelation, or in other words, to place man above God."[252] This was paramount to Anderson; both election and human responsibility are taught in Scripture, and therefore both must be embraced.

The difficulty was not limited to the question of election. The tension resurfaces in matters such as prayer, prophecy, and providence. For example, Acts 2:43 reads, "[Christ], being delivered by the determinate counsel and foreknowledge of God, ye have taken, and by wicked hands have crucified and slain." Anderson commented, "The murderers of Christ were acting in fulfilment of a divine decree, and yet their own deeds were really and absolutely their own . . . When this can be explained, that they who set up the cross on Calvary were fulfilling a divine purpose, though acting in direct antagonism to the divine will, the clew will have been found to every difficulty here alluded to."[253]

Many contemporary Calvinists appeal to the same paradigm under the term "compatibilism" in contrast to the Arminian notion of libertarian freedom.[254] But for Anderson, this was not a matter for theological debate;[255] it was an issue of submitting to the Word of God. He wrote, "To recognise and act upon the fact of our own responsibility and freedom, and yet to accept the consequences of our acts as coming from the hand of God, is the part of a spiritual Christian."[256]

So how do these tensions work out for the evangelist in gospel preaching? Anderson's answer was that the evangelist "goes forth with a proclamation which *seems* to ignore election . . . but, as he reviews his labours, his thought is, 'As many as were ordained to eternal life believed'" [Acts

---

249. Anderson, *The Gospel and Its Ministry*, 76–77.
250. Ibid., 80.
251. Ibid., 83
252. Ibid., 80.
253. Ibid., 83.
254. See, for example Helm, *Eternal God*, 144–70; Feinberg, *No One Like Him*, 625–775; Carson, *How Long, O Lord?* 177–203.
255. See his comments on how the blessing of election is often nullified through controversy over election in Anderson, *The Gospel and Its Ministry*, 75.
256. Ibid., 83.

13:48].²⁵⁷ This is similar to Mackintosh's stance that election is for the edification of believers, not the anxiety of the unredeemed, and thus should not form part of the evangelist's message.

Alexander Marshall

Alexander Marshall represents the beginning of a shift toward a more Arminian interpretation of the doctrine of election in Brethren thinking. That shift would not be substantial until the twentieth century, but the seeds of it were sown primarily by Marshall in the latter part of the nineteenth century. Chapters 3 and 4 introduced Marshall's upbringing and training for ministry in Morisonian circles. He joined the Open Brethren by 1874, but by that time his Arminianism was a settled conviction.²⁵⁸ He went on to be a tireless evangelist, primarily in Canada but also in his native Scotland and many other places around the world through his gospel campaigns.²⁵⁹ He was also valued as a popular writer, and thus his impact on the Brethren movement was significant.²⁶⁰

As to the question of predestination, Marshall was a careful student of the writings of the early leaders of the Evangelical Union—a denomination whose theological distinctives were decidedly Arminian.²⁶¹ These writers largely shaped his understanding of "such subjects as the nature and extent of the atonement, election, and the work of the Holy Spirit."²⁶² Thus his basic Arminian orientation is not surprising.

Henry Pickering points out that Marshall "almost seemed to relish" engagement with those who held Calvinistic views. According to Pickering, one of Marshall's favorite arguments against a Calvinistic interpretation of election was the following: "If all those to be saved were chosen in Christ before the foundation of the world (Eph 1:4), what did Paul mean when he said of Andronicus and Junia, 'who were *in Christ before me*'? (Rom 16:7)." Pickering, a great admirer of Marshall, added, "We never yet heard a satisfactory answer to the question."²⁶³ The question is not as irrefutable as Pickering supposed, since traditional Calvinists believe that although

---

257. Ibid., 84.
258. See the discussion on Marshall in the previous chapter.
259. Pickering, "Home-calling of a True Gospel Warrior," 411–12.
260. See Hawthorn, *Alexander Marshall*, 115–25.
261. I. T. Foster notes that "'Morisonianism,' as it became known was a fully fledged Arminian system of doctrine from 1843." *BDEB*, s.n. "James Morison," 792.
262. Hawthorn, *Alexander Marshall*, 21.
263. Ibid., 4.

individuals are chosen for salvation in eternity past, they are not born regenerate. They need to be "born again" in time by the sovereign work of the Holy Spirit through the means of the gospel.[264] However, the question does reveal that Marshall rejected the idea that "all those to be saved were chosen in Christ before the foundation of the world." Although Marshall did not write on the meaning of election, he undoubtedly embraced the position of the Evangelical Union which, in rejection of unconditional election, stated, "We believe . . . that election, 'like justification,' is conditioned on faith."[265] In other words, predestination is based on God's foreknowledge of those who place their faith in Christ—the standard Arminian position.[266]

In 1908 Marshall issued a booklet warning Open Brethren about a drift toward unhealthy sectarianism. Part of his concern was to urge forbearance on minor points of doctrine. He wrote, "To insist on agreement on minor truths as distinguished from fundamentals, such as election, free will, predestination, baptism, church government, the Lord's coming, preaching in missions, etc., would constitute a sect."[267] It is interesting that first on the list of "minor truths" for Marshall were election, free will, and predestination. Perhaps he had been opposed by other Brethren and was pleading for tolerance.[268] In any case, it does not appear that, in practice, Marshall viewed these doctrines as minor. His biographer, John Hawthorn, spoke of "the forceful way in which [Marshall] contended for what he considered to be fundamental to the whole"—Hawthorn was speaking specifically about "the nature of the atonement, election, and the work of the Holy Spirit."[269] Furthermore, on at least two occasions, Marshall complained that a strong view of predestination was a hindrance to the gospel. He argued that when a Calvinistic view of predestination is embraced, Christians become in-

---

264. However, the comment may be more useful in debate with hyper-Calvinists who advocated a doctrine of eternal justification.

265. Morison, "Apology," 77. Here Morison was quoting from the "Doctrinal Declaration" of the Evangelical Union Conference of 1858. The *Apology* was Morison's response to a published criticism of EU doctrine by "A Minister of the Church of Scotland," entitled *The Doctrinal Declaration of the Conference of the Evangelical Union reviewed and brought to the test of Scripture* (Edinburgh, 1862). See Adamson, *Life*, 351.

266. Morison, *Apology*, 79. The Evangelical Union taught that the meaning of Eph 1:4 (used by Marshall above) is: "according as he hath *purposed to choose us in Christ*, before the foundation of the world," which would support conditional election.

267. Marshall, *Holding Fast*, 33. For the date of this piece see Dickson, *Brethren in Scotland*, 173n228.

268. For example, James Campbell criticized Morisonianism at a Brethren conference at which Marshall was present. "Notes Taken," 33, 44. See also the comments on Norman Case below.

269. Hawthorn, *Alexander Marshall*, 21–22.

different about evangelism, and unbelievers become unconcerned about salvation.[270] Marshall claimed he encountered these attitudes, and that the "fetters of Calvinism" impeded his evangelistic efforts, particularly in the Scottish Highlands. He wrote, "One of the chief hindrances to the spread of the Gospel in the Highlands and Islands is the traditional hyper-calvinistic theology, in which they have been soaked. Many of them hold that God loves the elect *alone*, that Christ died for some men *only*, that the faith—necessitating 'irresistible' power of the Holy Spirit, is given to 'His own' alone; and they are strong believers in universal foreordination."[271] It was this outlook that fueled Marshall's anti-Calvinistic sentiments and makes it unlikely that he considered predestination and free will "minor" matters.

There is evidence to demonstrate that Marshall recognized the Calvinistic soteriology of nineteenth-century Brethren and was not happy with it. In a dispute over Calvinism with Arthur Pink in 1921, Pink pointed out that the Exclusive leader C. E. Stuart (1823–1903) had taken a Calvinist view of John 3:16. Marshall responded, "Yes, <u>sad</u> indeed; Stuart was a hyper-C[alvinist]."[272] Pink then added, "Wm. Kelly took the same view." Marshall replied, "Yes, I know, & Mr. K. was another C[alvinist]." Pink described the conversation in a letter to a friend, adding, "I could not resist the temptation to say—I'm glad there has been one or two Calvinists even among the Brethren!"[273]

John Ritchie (1853–1930)

In 1871 Ritchie was converted under the preaching of Donald Munro and eventually associated with the Brethren emerging in the North-East of Scotland.[274] Early on, Ritchie was an active evangelist, but he later gave himself fully to the work of writing and publishing. As a prolific author and, from

270. Marshall, "Hindrances to Progress," 168.

271. Marshall, "A Visit," 145; cf. Hawthorn, *Alexander Marshall*, 149.

272. For Stuart's Calvinistic understanding of election see, for example, Stuart, *Outline*, 121–23. In his discussion of John 6, Stuart highlighted divine sovereignty in salvation, but he equally stressed the reality of human responsibility, thus invalidating Marshall's claim that he was a hyper-Calvinist. Stuart, *Tracings*, 158–62. Other important Exclusive leaders such as J. B. Stoney (1814–97), F. E. Raven (1837–1903), and C. A. Coates (1862–1945) upheld a similar Calvinistic view of election. E.g., Stoney, *Ministry*, 5:128; Raven, *Ministry*, 3:150; Coates, *Outline*, 160–62, 166–68.

273. Pink, *Letters of an Itinerant Preacher*, 43. Pink also identified the Brethren writer W. H. Bennet (1843–1920) as Calvinistic, which Marshall conceded. See for example B[ennet], "Regeneration and Election," 132.

274. See Grass, *Gathering to His Name*, 124–26. On Ritchie, see Pickering, *Chief Men*, 306–10.

1891, editor of the important Brethren journal *The Believer's Magazine*, Ritchie's influence on the movement was substantial.[275]

On questions related to divine sovereignty and human responsibility, Ritchie maintained that "election is a truth clearly taught in the Word" that "brings blessing to the soul, and draws forth thanksgiving toward God who has both willed and wrought our salvation."[276] He acknowledged that the doctrine can engender strife, yet it should not be neglected, since it has been given by divine revelation for the spiritual health of believers. At the same time, the doctrine "is not included in God's testimony to the world, and forms no part of the evangelist's message."[277] The evangelist is instructed by Scripture to preach the gospel freely to all. "To put limitations on the grace of God, or hindrances in the way of sinners by dragging in the doctrine of election here, would be to degrade it, and to force it into a place where it is never found in Scripture."[278] Once a person is saved, the doctrine of election is designed to produce humility and gratitude, for it teaches that salvation is all of grace. "It directs our thoughts to what we were as utterly ruined, with no claim upon God, but wholly at His Sovereign will . . . and reminds us that all that we are and hope to be, is 'of Him.'"[279]

Although Ritchie upheld election to salvation, he rejected reprobation entirely. "There is not a text or a word from Genesis to Revelation to support the doctrine."[280] He believed the concept of foreordination to damnation was the product of the misinterpretation of Scripture at the hands of theologians like Augustine and Calvin. In light of these kinds of theological abuses, Ritchie—in typical Brethren fashion—refused to own the label of Calvinist (or Arminian). Reminiscent of earlier Brethren teachers, he declared: "Our safety lies, in receiving all that God has spoken, not reasoning thereon, but reverently assured that whatever may seem dark to us is clear as the sunlight to Him."[281]

J. Norman Case (1858–1913)

Dr. Case was a frequent contributor to Open Brethren magazines such as *The Witness*, *The Believer's Magazine*, and *Our Record*. He left his native

275. See Dickson, *Brethren in Scotland*, 146–48.
276. Ritchie, "Election," 76.
277. Ibid.
278. Ibid., 77.
279. Ibid., 91.
280. Ritchie, *Contested Truths*, 43.
281. Ritchie, "Election," 92.

England in the early 1880s for Canada, where he engaged in evangelism and Bible teaching in a number of cities and towns in Ontario. After earning a medical degree, he went to China as a missionary in 1891, serving there until he died of typhoid fever in April 1913.[282]

In 1885 Case wrote to Donald Ross as a fellow evangelist, stating that the doctrine of God's sovereign election provided an incentive for him to preach the gospel.[283] By the close of the nineteenth century, in 1898, Case wrote an article on the sovereignty of God in which he expressed concern over the current spiritual climate which, in Case's view, was far too anthropocentric. He began,

> The words *"divine sovereignty"* and the facts beneath them were much ofterner in the minds and on the lips of believers of a past generation than they are today. Those stern old warriors humbly and heartily confessed before heaven and earth that the chief end of man was to glorify God and enjoy Him forever. We live in different days. Influenced by our environment, we are all apt to assume the converse of this; viz., that the great business of God is to serve man and make him happy forever. Then the thoughts and plans of Christian men centered around God and His claims; now we are more occupied with man and his needs.[284]

Although Case did not focus exclusively on the sovereignty of God in salvation, it did constitute one of his major themes. In relation to the doctrine of predestination, he argued that "God is the planner and chooser, and He chooses, not from any outside compulsion, not because of any merit or worthiness in the creature, but in His own sovereign wisdom and grace."[285] His Calvinistic soteriology was unmistakable, although, like other Brethren, he avoided using the actual term "Calvinism." Nevertheless, he wrote, "As with love, so with election; we chose Him because He first chose us. The great and scriptural terms, 'foreknowledge,' 'election,' 'predestination,' take us back to the counsel of the Triune God before times eternal, and believing that the terms betoken facts we bow to and worship the God of sovereign grace, wisdom and power."[286]

It is not clear that Case had the Brethren specifically in mind when he lamented the fading emphasis on divine sovereignty; he referred more

---

282. *OR* 26 (June 1913) back inside cover; "The Falling Asleep of Dr. Case," 193, cf. 180; "Whose Faith Follow," 215 (mistakenly reports Case's death as 1912).
283. *BC* 5 (1885), 108–9.
284. C[ase], "According to God's Good Pleasure," 145.
285. Ibid., 147.
286. Ibid.

generally to the influence of the surrounding "environment" on all. But he probably had concerns about some Brethren evangelists along these lines. A decade earlier, Case had complained about the doctrinal shallowness that characterized contemporary evangelistic work.[287] Furthermore, he knew Alexander Marshall from contact in Ontario in the 1880s,[288] and certainly did not share Marshall's Arminianism. At any rate, Case—as well as editor Donald Ross, who made Case's piece the lead article in *Our Record*—was concerned about a drift away from emphasis on the sovereignty of God. He concluded his essay by arguing that all pride and "every form of self-gratulation, are, by the law of sovereign, distinguishing, electing grace, forever excluded."[289]

In urging Brethren not to forget the sovereignty of God—not least in salvation—the esteemed missionary[290] was calling on his contemporaries not to forsake an important feature of the nineteenth-century Brethren movement: Calvinistic soteriology.

Conclusion

The basic distinction between a Calvinistic and Arminian view of predestination is plain enough: either election is unconditional, based on God's sovereign choice alone (Calvinism), or it is conditional, based on human faith (Arminianism). From the evidence set forth in this chapter, the conclusion is unambiguous: nineteenth-century Brethren writers and leaders—with the exception of Alexander Marshall—affirmed the Calvinistic understanding of election.

A recent book on predestination argues that the doctrine "has been one of the most important but unacknowledged sources of discord in churches across the denominational spectrum."[291] Yet it is remarkable that nineteenth-

---

287. Case, "Evidences of the New Birth," 109–13, 121–24.

288. Marshall was centered in Orillia, Ontario and Case had spent time there. See Hawthorn, *Alexander Marshall*, 44, 50, and "Whose Faith Follow," 215. Marshall made reference to Case's work in Ontario in a report in *Echoes of Service* (1885), 160.

289. C[ase], "According to God's Good Pleasure," 149.

290. Case was not the only Open Brethren missionary upholding unconditional election toward the end of the century. In 1892, an article appeared in *Echoes of Service* advancing a Calvinistic position on election and reiterating many of the themes traced in the present chapter. After briefly surveying the New Testament support for the doctrine, the author concluded for his missionary readers that the truth of sovereign election "is well calculated to encourage those who go forth with the gospel of God." B., "'The Elect of God,'" 129–30.

291. Thuesen, *Predestination*, 4.

century Brethren—a group so noted for discord—found themselves largely in agreement on the controversial doctrine of election.

Technically, they did not view themselves as Calvinists, not least because they believed the "system" of Calvinism entailed affirming unconditional reprobation and minimizing the significance of human responsibility. Regardless of whether or not their understanding of "Calvinism" was accurate here,[292] the Brethren believed they rose above the fray by not slavishly following any human system of theology. Instead, they believed they were simply being faithful to the whole revelation of God in Scripture.[293] But whether they accepted the label or not, this chapter has demonstrated that their doctrine of election was, in fact, Calvinistic.

Common features of the nineteenth-century Brethren approach to predestination may be summarized as follows:

1. Election is unconditional, based on God's sovereign grace and good pleasure, and not on foreseen human faith, as in Arminianism. Furthermore, the objects of election are individuals, not a generic corporate body.

2. Human responsibility is equally taught in Scripture. Thus the gospel should be preached to all people, and the urgency of evangelism maintained.

3. The truth of election is for the comfort and edification of believers and is rightly taught in the assembly. However, it should not be pressed upon unbelievers and has no place in the evangelist's message.

4. Reprobation is not taught in Scripture; it is the product of human deduction. People perish not because God predestined them to that fate, but because of their own sin and rejection of God's love and grace in Christ.

---

292. Most Brethren seemed to recoil from the doctrine of reprobation because they understood it in strong supralapsarian terms, i.e. unconditional predestination to damnation is the parallel decree to unconditional election to salvation. However, as John Frame notes, "most Reformed theologians have been infralapsarian." McKim, *Encyclopedia*, 193. The Synod of Dort, for example, vehemently rejected any view that taught "God, by a mere arbitrary act of his will, without the least respect or view to any sin, has predestined the greatest part of the world to eternal damnation, and has created them for this very purpose." It also strongly rejected the notion "that in the same manner in which the election is the fountain and cause of faith and good works, reprobation is the cause of unbelief and impiety." "Conclusion" to "The Canons of the Synod of Dort," in Schaff, *Creeds of Christendom*, 3:596.

293. Bebbington, "Place of the Brethren Movement," 249.

As we have seen, Alexander Marshall stands as the exception to other nineteenth-century Brethren leaders. He did not like their Calvinism, and would help to sway the tide toward Arminianism in the twentieth century. Yet he was at home among the Brethren because he found the movement's biblicism, primitive ecclesiology, and zeal for evangelism in tune with his own convictions. And it was for these reasons he was accepted and valued in the movement, even by those who rejected his Morisonianism.

6

The Extent of the Atonement: Universal and Particular

Our heart can joy in God
By faith of Jesus slain;
His people's sins He bore away,
He died and rose again.

—Robert C. Chapman[1]

Tis finished all: our souls to win,
His life the blessed Saviour gave;
Then rising, left His people's sin
Behind Him in His open grave.

Sweet thought! we have a Friend above,
Our weary, faltering steps to guide,
Who follows with the eye of love
The little flock for which He died.

—Edward Denny[2]

---

1. Chapman, *Hymns and Meditations*, 6–7.
2. Edward Denny (1796–1889), "Tis finished all: our souls to win," #303 in *The Believers Hymn Book*.

> *The sinner who believes is free,*
> *Can say, "The Saviour died for me":*
> *Can point to the atoning blood,*
> *And say, "This made my peace with God."*
>
> —Albert Midlane[3]

Introduction

ONE OF THE DEFINING marks of evangelicalism, as David Bebbington rightly notes, is "crucicentrism."[4] In other words, evangelicals place a great deal of emphasis on the cross of Jesus Christ in their preaching, teaching, evangelism, and worship. Of course, the emphasis on the cross did not begin in the eighteenth century, the era from which Bebbington marks the rise of the evangelical movement.[5] The Reformers in particular focused on the cross. Theologian Henri Blocher has argued, "If justification by faith stands out as the heart of the Reformers' gospel, its foundation or presupposition is found in the objective work of atonement."[6]

Building on the work of Anselm, the Reformers emphasized the cross as satisfaction—not of God's honor, as Anselm had taught, but of divine justice.[7] Furthermore, Anselm's position forced a choice between satisfaction *or* punishment. By contrast, the Reformers taught satisfaction *through* punishment.[8] Indeed, the heart of the Reformers' understanding of the work of Christ has come to be called "penal substitution"[9]—that is, God's

---

3. Albert Midlane (1825–1909), "The Perfect Righteousness of God," in *A Few Hymns*, 341.

4. Bebbington, *Evangelicalism in Modern Britain*, 3, 14–17.

5. Some would challenge Bebbington's thesis that the evangelical movement began in the 1730s, and would argue that eighteenth century—and later—evangelicals viewed themselves as heirs of the Reformation. See the collection of essays in Haykin and Stewart, *Advent of Evangelicalism*.

6. Blocher, "The Atonement," 279.

7. Allison, *Historical Theology*, 398–99. Although it should be noted that Anselm did teach "that on the cross Jesus satisfied the demands of the Father's justice," yet his emphasis fell more on the concept of restitution of God's honor. Bray, *God Has Spoken*, 451–52.

8. van Asselt, "Christ's Atonement," 60–61.

9. Calvin, for example, wrote, "This is our acquittal: the guilt that held us liable for punishment has been transferred to the head of the Son of God . . . We must, above all, remember this substitution, lest we tremble and remain anxious throughout life—as

holy justice demands that sin must be punished, therefore on the cross, Christ acted as the substitute for sinners, bearing the divine punishment they deserved. In so doing, he propitiated God's wrath, satisfied his justice, and secured a righteous basis for him to justify sinners.[10] This penal substitutionary view of the cross has been the dominant view among evangelicals.[11] J. I. Packer has called penal substitution "a distinguishing mark of the worldwide evangelical fraternity."[12] This is not to suggest that evangelicals have refused to allow other motifs to nuance their understanding of the cross; it is simply to recognize what has been central in their doctrine of atonement. There have been those who dissented from the standard view, especially among Arminians.[13] The influential American revivalist Charles Finney (1792–1875), for example, rejected penal substitution,[14] as did the Methodist theologian John Miley (1813–95).[15] Nevertheless, as Bebbington points out, even if "belief that Christ died in our stead was not uniform in the Evangelical tradition . . . it was normal."[16]

Nineteenth-Century Developments

In the nineteenth century, some theological innovators were unhappy with traditional accounts of the atonement—particularly those of the Calvinistic variety—and advocated alternative theories. One contemporary theologian

---

if God's righteous vengeance, which the Son of God has taken upon himself, still hung over us." Calvin, *Institutes*, 2.16.5.

10. Evangelical scholars have argued that that the Reformers were not the first to think of the atonement in terms of penal substitution. For examples see: Ensor, "Justin Martyr," 217–32; Williams, "Penal Substitutionary Atonement," 195–216; Jeffery et al., *Pierced for Our Transgressions*, 161–85; Vlach, "Penal Substitution," 199–214.

11. Bebbington, *Evangelicals in Modern Britain*, 15; Bebbington, *Dominance of Evangelicalism*, 28.

12. Packer, "What Did the Cross Achieve?" 3.

13. John Wesley's Arminianism, however, did not prevent him from advocating penal substitution. See Wood, "John Wesley's Use of the Atonement," 55–70.

14. Finney, *Lectures on Systematic Theology*, 270–71.

15. Miley, *Systematic Theology*, 2:156–59. Both Finney and Miley affirmed the governmental view of the atonement. First advanced by Hugo Grotius (1583–1645), the governmental theory argues that God could have simply forgiven humankind of their sins, but that would make his moral government appear weak. Therefore, he accepted the death of Christ as a kind of token punishment for sin. Christ did not bear the penalty for sinners as their personal substitute; he died to honor God's law and to demonstrate God's displeasure with sin. Not all Arminians have accepted the governmental view. See Olson, *Arminian Theology*, 221–41.

16. Bebbington, *Evangelicals in Modern Britain*, 16.

argues that Finney's *Systematic Theology* "is almost entirely dedicated to expounding the moral government theory of the atonement in all of its aspects."[17] In Scotland some progressive thinkers were eager to see the old wineskins of Calvinism give way to fresh ideas more congenial to the times. John McLeod Campbell (1800–1872) was deposed from the ministry of the Church of Scotland in 1831 for teaching, among other things, that Christ died for every individual without exception. Campbell's defiance of the Calvinist tradition "set in motion a process of theological exploration which was to lead him towards a very different understanding of the whole nature of the atonement."[18] In 1856 he published what would become his best known and most controversial work, *The Nature of the Atonement*. Here Campbell set aside the forensic and penal categories that dominated Reformed discussions of the atonement in favor of a moral and spiritual approach, with a heavy emphasis on filial imagery.[19] Thus the atonement is rooted in the fatherliness of God and salvation in Christ is likened to "the experience of *orphans who have found their long lost Father.*"[20]

A central element of Christ's mission was to reveal the character of God as love. Herein lies one of Campbell's objections to the Calvinist doctrine of an atonement which is limited in its design and efficacy to the elect alone. He confessed, "I am unable to see any way out here, or any escape from the conclusion, that the doctrine of an atonement for the elect only, destroys the claim of the work of Christ to be what fully reveals and illustrates the great foundation of all religion, that God is love."[21]

In Campbell's theory, Christ came to represent God to humanity. Therefore, the sufferings of Christ were not penal but a manifestation of the holy sorrow of God over human sin. Christ's sufferings were the expression of pain endured in sympathy with God and "the expression of the divine mind regarding our sins."[22] Yet Christ also came to deal with God on behalf of humanity because, Campbell conceded, "the wrath of God against sin is a reality, however men have erred in their thoughts as to how that wrath was to be appeased."[23] For Campbell, God's wrath was assuaged through Christ's intercession for sinners. Specifically, the Son made "a perfect confession of our sins." Campbell explained, "This confession, as to its own nature, must

17. Horton, *The Christian Faith*, 505.
18. Stevenson, *God in Our Nature*, 44.
19. Ibid., 55–58. See Campbell, *Nature of the Atonement*, 166–69, 241–43.
20. Campbell, *Nature of the Atonement*, 241. Emphasis original.
21. Ibid., 74.
22. Ibid., 116.
23. Ibid., 117.

have been *a perfect Amen in humanity to the judgment of God on the sins of man.*"[24] But how does "perfect confession" appease God's wrath against sin? Campbell answered as follows:

> He who so responds to the divine wrath against sin, saying, "Thou art righteous, O Lord, who judgest so," is necessarily receiving the full apprehension and realisation of that wrath, as well as of that sin against which it comes forth into His soul and spirit . . . and, so receiving it, He responds to it with a perfect response—a response from the depths of that divine humanity—and *in that perfect response He absorbs it*. For that response has all the elements of a perfect repentance in humanity for all the sin of man . . . and by that perfect response in Amen to the mind of God in relation to sin is the wrath of God rightly met, and that is accorded to divine justice which is its due, and could alone satisfy it.[25]

Although there were other nuances to Campbell's understanding of the nature of the atonement, this concept of "vicarious repentance," as it has come to be called, was a central feature.[26]

McLeod Campbell was not alone in casting off traditional Calvinism in favor of new approaches. In fact, there is evidence that Campbell was influenced, to some extent, by his friend Thomas Erskine of Linlathen (1788–1870).[27] In Erskine's innovative reinterpretation of the atonement, he focused on Christ acting representatively for humans, but not as their substitute in some kind of penal transaction. Instead, he emphasized the subjective effects of Christ's work. He wrote, "The atonement was not a mere *opus operatum, a mere act* on account of which God blesses man, but it was and is a living principle, reproducing itself in the hearts and lives of those that receive it . . . The fact that the paschal lamb was slain within each individual house in Israel, is also a proof that the atonement must be reproduced in each heart."[28] More objectively, but no less controversially, Erskine taught

---

24. Ibid., 118. Emphasis original.

25. Ibid. Emphasis original.

26. Campbell laid great emphasis not only on the retrospective aspect of the atonement—dealing with what we were through sin, but also on the prospective aspect—what the atonement helps us become in Christ. For a thorough analysis of Campbell's *Nature of the Atonement* see Stevenson, *God in Our Nature*, 54–113.

27. "It is notable that many of Campbell's later developed views were already evident in seed form in Erskine before they met in about 1827–28, Campbell having already read Erskine's early works." Horrocks, *Laws of the Spiritual Order*, 14.

28. Erskine, *The Doctrine of Election*, 373. For an analysis of Erskine's doctrine of the atonement see Horrocks, *Laws of the Spiritual Order*, 101–25.

that through the death of Christ, a full pardon was achieved for all humanity. His doctrine of "universal and unconditional pardon" meant that each member of the human race is pardoned and forgiven by God—whether they realize it or not. This does not mean everyone is saved whether they realize it or not; each person must appropriate divine forgiveness. Nevertheless, the logic of Erskine's position led him to believe that God's universal love would eventually result in universal salvation.[29]

Another friend of both Campbell and Erskine who challenged traditional orthodoxy on the atonement was Edward Irving (1792–1834). A colorful preacher, Irving faced plenty of theological controversy in his brief life and ministry. In terms of Christology, Irving taught that in the incarnation, Christ took upon himself fallen human nature—although he never actually sinned.[30] The atonement was not substitutionary; nor did Christ die to appease God's wrath. Christ became the author of salvation not through suffering bodily on the cross, but through his perfect submission and obedience to the will of the Father. The essence of the atonement is in the fact that "Christ took our fallen nature, with all its natural and inherent propensities; and overcame these, and brought it into union with Godhead, and hath fixed it there for ever by the resurrection."[31]

Not surprisingly, these novel views of the atonement were challenged by traditional evangelicals.[32] Leaders among the Brethren who kept abreast of contemporary theological trends were among those who rejected these innovations. In an evaluation of "modern views subversive of the Atonement," William Kelly dismissed Campbell's *The Nature of the Atonement* as "ruinous departure from revealed truth." Campbell's theory that the essence of the atonement is to be found in Christ's perfect confession and repentance of human sin was nonsense; indeed, it was "to mistake the word of God, and foist a fable." For Kelly, the Scriptures clearly taught that Christ suffered on the cross as a substitute for sinners, and this alone could satisfy divine justice against sin. In his words, "Nothing but vicarious suffering for us from God can account for the profound feelings and language of our Lord when delivered for our offences, and bearing our sins in His own body on the tree."[33] John Nelson Darby considered Erskine's notion of "universal

---

29. See Horrocks, *Laws of the Spiritual Order*, 96–101.

30. On Irving's Christology see Grass, *Edward Irving*, 174–89; and McFarlane, *Christ and the Spirit*.

31. As cited in Grass, *Edward Irving*, 181.

32. E.g., Smeaton considered Campbell's theory as "extravagant and strangely constituted"; it had "no warrant or foundation in Scripture." Smeaton, *Doctrine of the Atonement*, 494.

33. Kelly, *Lectures on the Day of Atonement*, 171–73.

pardon" to be "entirely wrong, if judged properly by Scripture."[34] He also found Irving's denial of "the substitution of Christ as bearing our sins, and therefore dying for us" to be a serious error.[35] Kelly, likewise, viewed Irving's doctrine of atonement as reprehensible. In maintaining that Christ assumed fallen human nature, Irving and his followers attacked "the heart and centre of all revealed truth," and in the process, completely undermined the meaning of the cross. Kelly argued, "The bearing of their fundamental heterodoxy as to Christ's person on His atoning work is absolutely destructive of its truth . . . Hence the infinite sufferings of the cross are ignored or even decried; hence the railing and ridicule heaped on the substitution of Christ, on the imputation of righteousness to the believer, in short on all that the christian elect of God have found most solemn and precious in and through the Saviour's death."[36]

The Extent of the Atonement in Historical Perspective

For many traditional evangelicals who affirmed penal substitution, the point of contention in regard to the cross was less about the nature of the atonement and more a question of its extent or design. That is, on the cross, did Christ bear the sins of all people, or did he make atonement only for the sins of the elect? Did the Father design the cross to be a conditional provision for all people, or was his intention to actually redeem those whom he had chosen for salvation? Three main views developed in the sixteenth and seventeenth centuries that continued to be discussed and debated in the nineteenth century. It is important to briefly sketch these views in order to evaluate where the Brethren stood in the discussion—specifically, did they fall within or outside of the Reformed tradition on the extent of the atonement?[37]

34. Darby, *CW*, 2:20 (1829). Cf. 15:25–27 (1835); 29:185 (1877). In April, 1831 Anthony Norris Groves wrote in his journal: "I have lately read several of Erskine's works . . . and never did I see the pernicious effects of system displayed more legibly than in several of his most interesting, but as a whole, most delusive publications. In his view of Gospel freeness . . . there seems, to my mind, a radical defect, that nothing in so good a man accounts for but the baneful effects of a system, and a secret insurmountable repugnance to the sovereignty of God's government, and the individuality of God's election in Christ Jesus, from before the foundation of the world." Groves, *Journal*, 102.

35. Darby, *CW*, 29:186.

36. Kelly, "The Catholic Apostolic Body," 93–95. Cf. Kelly, *Lectures on . . . the Holy Spirit*, 133.

37. It is something of an anachronism to call the position "Calvinist" since the lines of debate were drawn after Calvin's time, as historians increasingly recognize. See for example, Muller, *Calvin*, and the literature cited therein. However, as Muller

Arminianism: Universal Redemption

The Arminian position affirmed that Christ died equally for all people and that his death has, in a provisional way, obtained redemption and the forgiveness of sins for all without exception. While Christ bore the sins of all people, the benefits of Christ's death are applied only to those who believe.[38] In this scheme, the human response of faith precedes election and is its cause. The view is variously called "unlimited atonement" or "universal redemption."

Reformed Theology

Within the Reformed tradition, unanimity on the extent of the atonement could not be achieved. In fact, Raymond Blacketer states that the question of the sufficiency and efficiency of Christ's satisfaction "was the most contentious issue at the great Synod of Dort (Dordrecht) in 1618–19, and continues to be one of the most controversial teachings in Reformed soteriology."[39]

Peter Lombard (c. 1100–1160) articulated what came to be a common formula in the Middles Ages on the extent of the atonement, distinguishing between the *sufficientia* and *efficientia* of Christ's work. Lombard argued that Christ offered himself "for all, with respect to the sufficiency of the ransom, but for the elect alone with regard to its efficiency, because it effects salvation for the predestined alone."[40] This formula was known to the Reformers and served as the launching point for further discussion in the post-Reformation era.[41]

---

acknowledges (55), the term Calvinism was commonly understood by evangelicals in the eighteenth and nineteenth centuries to refer to a more or less Reformed version of soteriology, particularly in regard to issues surrounding sin, grace, and predestination—and the question of the extent of the atonement. Therefore we use the terms "Reformed" and "Calvinism" synonymously.

38. See Article II of "The Five Arminian Articles, a.d. 1610," in Schaff, *Creeds of Christendom*, 3:546.

39. Blacketer, "Definite Atonement," 304. Cf. Godfrey, "Tensions." Calvin's position on the extent of the atonement has been the subject of significant debate. For an assessment see especially Muller, *Calvin*, 70–106, and the literature cited therein.

40. Peter Lombard, *Libri Quatuor Sententiarum*, 3:20 as translated in Blacketer, "Definite Atonement," 311. See also Hogg, "'Sufficient for All,'" 75–95.

41. See Rouwendal, "Calvin's Forgotten Classical Position," 319–21.

Particular Redemption

The Synod of Dort affirmed "the infinite worth and value" of the death of Christ as being "abundantly sufficient to expiate the sins of the whole world."[42] Therefore the gospel "ought to be declared and published to all nations, and to all persons promiscuously and without distinction."[43] Nevertheless, it was God's design in the cross to effectually redeem only the elect and "confer upon them faith, which, together with all the other saving gifts of the Holy Spirit, [Christ] purchased for them by his death."[44] Thus while there is no limitation on the value of Christ's work or the preaching of the gospel, the intention of the Father was to accomplish redemption for those whom he had chosen for salvation. Christ, therefore, bore the sins of all the elect on the cross; he did not bear the sins of the non-elect. This position came to be the majority view in Reformed soteriology.[45] It is called "particular redemption" or "definite atonement" to emphasize the actual achievement of the cross. It is popularly dubbed "limited atonement." However, this is a poor descriptor, since it implies some inadequacy in Christ's work, and particularists readily affirmed "the dignity, worth, preciousness, and infinite value of the blood and death of Jesus Christ."[46] Limitation comes at the point of applying the benefits of Christ's sacrifice, and here even Arminians limit the atonement, since not all are saved. Thus Calvinists typically did not prefer the term "limited atonement."[47]

The Westminster Confession of Faith, which would become the definitive doctrinal confession in Scotland, affirmed particular redemption. It stated that Christ, by his sacrifice, fully satisfied the justice of God and purchased reconciliation "for all those whom the Father hath given unto him" (8.5). Furthermore, the work of Christ on the cross is described as "the alone propitiation for all the sins of the elect" (29.2).

---

42. Canons of Dort, II.3 in Schaff, *Creeds of Christendom*, 3:586.

43. Canons of Dort, II.5.

44. Canons of Dort, II.8.

45. As noted above, however, this was a debated issue at Dort, with some British delegates affirming "hypothetical universalism." For how such a theological position could be maintained while subscribing to the Canons of Dort, see Moore, "Extent of the Atonement," 144–48.

46. Owen, *Works*, 10:295. Owen added that Christ's sacrifice is "sufficient in itself for the redeeming of all and every man, if it had pleased the Lord to employ it to that purpose; yea, and of other worlds also, if the Lord should freely make them, and would redeem them."

47. Muller points out that none of the Reformed thinkers of the sixteenth and seventeenth centuries used the term "limited atonement." Muller, *Calvin*, 60.

By the nineteenth century, some came to associate the idea of a limited atonement with the practice of hyper-Calvinism's restriction of the gospel offer, since that restriction was rooted in their belief that Christ did not die for all. Traditional Calvinists rejected such a restriction as extreme and unwarranted,[48] but some—including the Brethren—took pains to avoid any association with the hyper-Calvinist position.[49]

Hypothetical Universalism

A third view is known as "hypothetical universalism." There are several variations of this position[50] but essentially the view maintains that Christ died for all without exception, yet the benefits of his death are conditioned upon faith. Since not all believe, God's grace in predestination ensures that the elect will be granted faith and have the benefits of Christ's death applied to them. It is often assumed that hypothetical universalism is simply another name for Amyraldianism, after the teaching of Moïse Amyraut (1596–1664). However, Amyraut's views were considered problematic even among hypothetical universalists, given that his ordering of the divine decrees resulted in God having multiple, even conflicting, intentions.[51] One recent scholar suggests that Amyraldianism should not be considered hypothetical universalism.[52] Nevertheless, all forms of hypothetical universalism (including Amyraldianism) differ from Arminianism in that the efficacy of Christ's work is ultimately governed by divine election, not human response.[53]

It is important to recognize—and it is not always recognized—that there was significant diversity within the Reformed tradition on questions

---

48. E.g., Murray, *Spurgeon v. Hyper-Calvinism*.

49. [Mackintosh], "One-Sided Theology," 10–16.

50. See chapter 5 of Muller, *Calvin*, 126–60. Moore says that hypothetical universalism "was a highly complex phenomenon with no one definitive formulation or uniformity of explanation." Moore, *English Hypothetical Universalism*, 225.

51. See Muller, *Calvin*, 152–60, and Thomas, *Extent of the Atonement*, 190–91, 226–30. In Amyraut's scheme, God decreed to save all by the death of his Son, provided that they believe. Foreseeing, however that none would believe, God decreed to elect some to salvation and to apply the benefits of Christ's death to these alone.

52. Moore, *English Hypothetical Universalism*, 217–19.

53. The *Thirty-Nine Articles* may be interpreted along hypothetical universalism lines since Article 31 states: "The offering of Christ once made is the perfect redemption, propitiation, and satisfaction for all the sins of the whole world." Yet Article 17 affirms that salvation has its origin in God's decree of election. The British delegation to the Synod of Dort, however, debated whether Article 31 was "to be understood of all particular men, or only of the Elect, who consist of all sorts of men." See Muller, *Calvin*, 131–34.

related to the extent and design of the atonement. As Muller states, when carefully examined, "a rather complex picture emerges of different approaches to the issue of the value, merit, or sufficiency of Christ's satisfaction and its relationship to a limited application."[54] Thus although particular redemption was the majority view, the various forms of hypothetical universalism formed trajectories of thought within the Reformed tradition, none of which should be viewed as either authentic Calvinism or an abandonment of Calvinism, as is sometimes argued.[55] There was room for hypothetical universalism within Reformed theology as evidenced in the work of James Ussher, Moïse Amyraut, John Davenant, Pierre du Moulin, John Preston, and Richard Baxter.[56] In Reformed orthodoxy, the Arminian position was out of bounds. Hypothetical universalism, however, was considered useful by some, though unacceptable by the majority—but *not* heretical.[57]

This point needs to be sufficiently appreciated, because in evaluating Brethren thought on the extent of the atonement, we encounter a rather nuanced position. Nineteenth-century Brethren perspectives on this question do not fall into the "unlimited atonement" category, but neither do they rest precisely on "particular redemption" ground. As we shall see, the universal and particular dimensions to their view place them in the rather complex Reformed camp on this issue—although Brethren interpreters claimed no loyalty to any theological party, only to the teaching of Scripture.

Brethren Writers on the Extent of the Atonement

For the Brethren—as "evangelicals of the evangelicals"[58]—the cross was central in their teaching, worship, hymnody, and proclamation. They focused on the cross in their weekly "breaking of bread" meetings, and they heartily pointed sinners to the cross in their evangelistic preaching. They

54. Muller, *Calvin*, 279. He identifies "at least seven distinct patterns of formulation (not to mention variants within these basic patterns) among the early modern Reformed" (77n22).

55. As in, for example, Armstrong, *Calvinism*; and Clifford, *Calvinus*. Muller critiques these notions at length in *Calvin*, along with debunking the "Calvin against the Calvinists" theory as represented in, for example, Kendall, *Calvin and English Calvinism*.

56. Some have argued that even the Westminster standards do not finally exclude hypothetical universalism. See Moore, "Extent of the Atonement," 148–52 and Fesko, *Theology of the Westminster Standards*, 187–203.

57. Muller, *Post-Reformation*, 4:391. Elsewhere Muller goes so far as to say that hypothetical universalism does not represent "a fundamental departure from the formulae of the Synod of Dort and therefore can be subsumed under what had typically been called the Reformed doctrine of limited atonement." Muller, *Calvin*, 45.

58. Bebbington, "Place of the Brethren Movement," 260.

affirmed the penal, substitutionary nature of the atonement.[59] But they also held some unique perspectives on aspects of the work of Christ, particularly in regard to the extent of the atonement.[60] They did not always address this issue directly or precisely in their writings, however. Thus this chapter will not attempt to decipher the position of every Brethren writer who may have hinted at the subject, but instead will examine the views of a selection of influential Brethren—both Exclusive and Open—who addressed the extent of the atonement directly.

John Nelson Darby

In the late 1820s, Darby visited friends at Oxford University at a time when questions related to Calvinism and Arminianism were hotly debated among evangelicals at the university. According to B. W. Newton, two parties had formed, the "High Calvinists led by [Henry] Bulteel and another more Arminian led by Sibthorpe."[61] In his first conversation with Darby, Newton asked him about his views on these issues. Newton was pleased to hear that Darby had no hesitation preaching the gospel "to sinners simply as sinners"—thus he was no hyper-Calvinist. On the other hand, Newton was also satisfied that Darby did not "universalise the Atonement."[62]

It does appear that some early Brethren writers affirmed particular redemption, such as Anthony Norris Groves,[63] George Müller,[64] and John

---

59. E.g., Darby, *CW*, 7:63–86 and 7:297. See also [Caldwell], "Question 275," 192. Penal substitution was a frequent theme in Brethren hymnody.

60. The internal controversy among the Brethren over the non-atoning sufferings of Christ lies outside the focus of the present chapter. On this see Neatby, *History*, 239–64 and Grass, *Gathering to His Name*, 77–79, 163, 200–201.

61. Fry MS, 236.

62. Ibid. Early on, Newton subscribed to a universal propitiation which vindicated God's righteousness, and yet a substitution in which Christ bore the sins of the church only. [Newton], "On the Propitiation of Christ," 32–35; [Newton], "Doctrines," *121. This was essentially Darby's position. In his post-Brethren years however, Newton seems to have advocated a more traditional form of particular redemption. See Newton, *An Erroneous Mode*.

63. A. J. Scott (1805–66), who edited Groves's *Journal*, felt it necessary to add notes at the end of the book correcting Groves's "error regarding the extent of the Atonement" (288). Scott advocated universal atonement over against Groves's support for limited atonement. However, if the passages in Groves which Scott found so objectionable are studied carefully, they reveal that Groves was speaking of the doctrine of election, not limited atonement. Scott seems to have assumed that a Calvinist view of election necessarily entailed particular redemption.

64. Müller confessed that as a new Christian, he was opposed to the Calvinist doctrines of "election, particular redemption, and final persevering grace." Upon further

Eliot Howard.⁶⁵ However, most nineteenth-century Brethren advanced a nuanced and rather unique position on the extent of the atonement, shaped in large measure by the thought of John Nelson Darby. The hallmark of Darby's stance was his distinction between two aspects of the work of Christ on the cross: propitiation and substitution. In fact, he believed that "a good deal of Arminian and Calvinistic controversy, arises from not distinguishing propitiation and substitution."⁶⁶ These aspects of the work of Christ, Darby often noted, were prefigured in the great Day of Atonement (Lev 16). Aaron as priest was to take two goats, one for the Lord and one to serve as a scapegoat that would symbolically bear away the sins of the people. The goat that was the Lord's lot was to be killed and its blood sprinkled on the mercy seat as a sin offering for the people. Darby explained, "The blood was presented to God, whose holy presence had been dishonoured and offended by sin."⁶⁷ Sin made the people unclean before the absolute holiness of God, and thus blood on the mercy seat was necessary to uphold, announce, and vindicate the righteous character of God vis-à-vis sin.

In Darby's understanding, this corresponds to Christ's work of propitiation, in which God's righteous judgment against sin was displayed at the cross, and the demands of his character were thus upheld. For Darby, the glory of God was at the heart of the cross, and the removal of believers' sins, as important as that is, "was really a secondary thing to the basis of the glory of God in the universe, and the bringing all into order,"⁶⁸ which is what propitiation achieved. Thus in the cross, "God's majesty, righteousness, love, truth, all that He is, was glorified in the work wrought by Christ."⁶⁹ This work of propitiation is directed against the principle of sin in light of the holiness of God. Sin created a barrier to God's being merciful to humans, but through Christ's propitiatory sacrifice, God's righteousness was affirmed, clearing the way for him to deal mercifully with sinners.⁷⁰ As a result, propi-

---

study, however, he came to joyfully embrace these doctrines. Müller, *Narrative*, 46–47.

65. Howard argues for particular redemption as part of his refutation of John Guthrie's Arminian views, including universal atonement. Unlike most Brethren discussed in this chapter, Howard does not make a distinction between universal propitiation and particular substitution. He views propitiation as "the payment of a debt on behalf of the Church." Howard, *"New Views,"* 57. For his defense of particular redemption see pp. 24–30.

66. Darby, *CW*, 27:318 (1873). Curiously this same piece appears in *CW*, 29:286–88.

67. Ibid.

68. Darby, *Letters*, 3:101. Cf. Darby, *CW*, 19:250.

69. Darby, *CW*, 27:319. Cf. 23:241 (1873); 29:243–46 (1878).

70. Darby's view of propitiation here is similar to a governmental view of the atonement and he can use the language of "moral government" in describing part of

tiation is what enables the preacher to offer the gospel freely to all people. In a letter written in 1880, Darby explained as follows: "Propitiation alters the whole ground of God's dealings with man. It is the display of God's mercy maintaining God's righteousness, but opening the door to the sinner—the ground on which I preach the gospel, and can say to every sinner, The blood is on the mercy-seat; return to God, and it will be His joy to receive you: it is not necessary for Him to judge you if you so come, for His righteousness is fully glorified, and His love free."[71] In this sense, then, it is proper to speak of Christ as the propitiation for the whole world (1 John 2:2). This is the universal dimension to the work of Christ, and "in this aspect we may say Christ died for all."[72]

Yet propitiation is only one dimension of Christ's work. On the Day of Atonement, the goat whose blood was sprinkled on the mercy seat did not have the sins of the people confessed over its head. That was the role of the second goat. The sins of the people were transferred to the second goat and it bore those sins away to a remote wilderness. This action represents Christ's work of substitution. On the cross, Christ actually and effectually bore the sins of all those he represented, namely, the elect.[73] Therefore, Darby did not believe that Christ died as a substitute for all people.[74] He wrote, "scripture never says Christ has borne the sins of everybody." In his preaching, he preferred to say that Christ died for "our sins" (as Paul did in 1 Cor 15) since "our" refers strictly to believers.[75] Only after one has come to faith in Christ is he or she able to affirm, "Christ died for *my* sins and bore them on the cross."[76]

The practical outworking of these two dimensions of Christ's death may be seen in the following summary:

> In the blood which is put upon the mercy-seat, it is not a question of those who are saved or of election, but of the majesty of God, which demands satisfaction for sin. I can address all, and declare to them that this satisfaction has been made, and that

---

what propitiation upheld. Darby, *CW*, 29:244.

71. Darby, *Letters*, 3:101.

72. Darby, *CW*, 27:319.

73. Darby, *Letters*, 1:99. It should be noted that Darby's distinction between propitiation and substitution remained essentially the same over time. This is evident when one compares the letter here cited written in 1846 with the one cited above (3:101) written in 1880.

74. "It is never said Christ died for the sins of the world." Darby, *CW*, 21:199 (1869); 27:319. Cf. 29:270.

75. Darby, *CW*, 19:243.

76. Ibid., 31:358 (1881); 21:385 (1874).

God the Father has perfectly accepted it. But I cannot say to all that Christ bore their sins, because the word does not say it anywhere. If He had borne *their* sins, they would certainly be justified, and consequently saved by the life of Christ, and glorified.[77]

In a review of a book by Horatius Bonar on the work of Christ,[78] Darby censured the author for confounding propitiation and substitution, and for generally mishandling such an important biblical doctrine as substitution. Darby taught that substitution involved Christ taking the place of others and bearing the wrath due their sins. This work was altogether effectual, so that those for whom he died will be saved. It was inconceivable to him that many for whom Christ died as substitute would reject him and thus be judged again for their sins, as Bonar seemed to suggest. Darby wrote, "Were their sins transferred to the Substitute and the wrath borne effectually and irreversibly, and yet they reject Christ and die in their sins? Dr. B's substitution is no substitution at all, for nobody's sins were really borne, and no people really represented."[79] All those for whom Christ acted as substitute and "took the consequence in sovereign grace" are saved. "He cannot charge as a judge the sins which He has Himself borne and expiated on those for whom He Himself has already borne them."[80]

The heart of Darby's teaching on the extent of the atonement lies in this distinction between propitiation and substitution. Yet the universal and particular aspects of Christ's work are further elucidated in another distinction he made between "purchase" and "redemption." He wrote, "All the world, all mankind, even the wicked, are *bought* by Christ's blood; but none save believers have *redemption* (ἀπολύτρωσιν) through His blood, the forgiveness of sins."[81] The idea is that all people are purchased, but such purchase simply makes them Christ's property or slaves; those who believe are redeemed and set free. Darby elaborates the thought in his comments on 2 Pet 2:1, which speaks of false teachers who introduce destructive heresies

---

77. Darby, *Letters*, 1:98.

78. Bonar, *Everlasting Righteousness*.

79. Darby, *CW*, 23:241. Darby made essentially the same point in critiquing another work by Bonar, *CW*, 23:265–66 (1875).

80. Ibid., 23:242. Bonar, as a Westminster Calvinist, subscribed to—and defended—definite atonement. See Horatius Bonar in Green, *The Five Points of Calvinism*, 77–79. Darby's problem was with Bonar's muddled explanation of the doctrine: "the whole teaching is confusion and darkness." Darby, *CW* 23:243.

81. "A Letter on Atonement," Darby *Additional Writings*, 2:288. Although this distinction is less prominent in Darby than propitiation/substitution, he did criticize writers for confusing purchase and redemption. See Darby, *Letters*, 3:448–50 (January, 1877).

and deny the master who *bought* them. He explained, "It is no question here as to the title of the Lord, nor of redemption. The simile is of a master who has purchased slaves at the market, and they disown and refuse to obey him. Thus among the converted Jews there would be false teachers, who disowned the authority of Christ—His rights over them."[82] By their actions, these false teachers would prove that they were unrighteous and remained unredeemed.

Perhaps Darby's most lucid explanation of the distinction between purchase and redemption comes in his comments on the parable of the treasure hidden in the field (Matt 13:44). Jesus told a parable of a man who purchased an entire field because of the valuable treasure buried within it. The desired object was not the field, but the treasure. Darby interpreted the parable as follows: "Christ has purchased the world. He possesses it by right. His object is the treasure hidden in it, His own people, all the glory of the redemption connected with it; in a word, the Church looked at, not in its moral and in a certain sense divine beauty, but as the special object of the desires and of the sacrifice of the Lord—that which His heart had found in this world according to the counsels and the mind of God."[83] In other words, Christ has purchased the world by his blood in order to redeem the elect—those chosen by God before the foundation of the world.

Darby's position is very clear: the work of propitiation makes it possible to offer the gospel to all, but it is not proper to say to all, "Christ has borne *your* sins." This strong notion of particularity is rooted in the absolute efficacy of Christ's substitution. The fact that he believed Christ bore only the sins of his people[84] makes his position incompatible with the Arminian doctrine of universal atonement and places him squarely in the Calvinist tradition. However, he could criticize the Calvinist for not recognizing the universal aspect of the work of Christ, which his doctrine of propitiation advanced (even as he criticized Arminians for denying the particularity of substitution).[85] Darby's somewhat unique position[86] is illustrative of Brethren methodology: systems of theology do not capture the full-orbed

---

82. Darby, *Synopsis*, 5:476.

83. Ibid., 3:107–8.

84. In a sermon on "The Sufferings of Christ," he said, "There is no more sacrifice for sin—He Himself having suffered all the penalty due for all the sins of His people." Darby, *Notes of Sermons*, 158–59.

85. Darby, *CW*, 27:319–20.

86. To date I have not discovered any previous writer who maintained Darby's distinction between propitiation and substitution. Thus it would appear that this is an original contribution, though few outside the Brethren movement have taken notice of it.

teaching of Scripture, which has room for both universal and particular dimensions in the atoning work of Christ.

Many Brethren followed Darby here, and the distinction between propitiation and substitution frequently appeared in Brethren magazines—both Exclusive[87] and Open.[88] Evangelist Charles Stanley did not hesitate to explain these dimensions of the work of Christ to anxious souls.[89] He faced head-on the objection that if Christ was not the substitute for all, how can I know he was the substitute for *me*? He explained: "If the Scriptures did teach that He was the Substitute of all men, you would be far more uncertain; for it is evident many are not saved, and therefore, if He had been the Substitute of all, and yet many of these were for ever lost, then His dying for your sins would have been no security of your salvation, for after all you might be lost."[90]

Much more reassuring, argued Stanley, was the scriptural truth that Christ bore the sins of many, and for all these he has won eternal redemption. Propitiation has secured the righteousness of God, and thus mercy may be proclaimed to every sinner, "yet, as Substitute, the sins of all men were not laid on Him, and therefore it does not follow that all will be saved."[91] Only the one who believes can have the confidence that Christ has surely borne away his or her sins, and thus can enjoy peace with God.

Although Stanley did not credit Darby, his teaching was virtually identical to Darby's. Other major writers who shaped Brethren thought, such as Mackintosh and Kelly, also followed Darby here, as we shall see below.

Henry William Soltau (1805–75)

Converted in 1837 under the preaching of Captain Percy Hall, Soltau soon afterward gave up his practice of law "in order to devote himself to the study

---

87. E.g., F. K., "Expository Papers," 298–300; S[nell], "Atonement," 118–25; Stuart, "Propitiation," 244–51, 274–77; Stuart, "Substitution," 297–306. Stuart would later argue (unlike Darby) that propitiation took place in heaven after Christ's death. William Kelly attacked this teaching as significant error in "'Strange Doctrine.'" On the debate see Ironside, *Historical Sketch*, 118–20.

88. E.g., Laing, "Substitution," 27–28; J. S. D., "Question 314," 47 Ans. B; T[rench?], "Substitution," 179–80. Cf. D[yer], "Christ as 'Door,'" 193–98. Dyer used door and good shepherd, propitiation and substitution, to expound the universal and particular dimensions of the atonement.

89. Stanley, "Election," 7–14. See also Stanley, *Atoning Death*, 7–8, 15–20.

90. Stanley, "Election," 8.

91. Ibid., 11–12.

of the Scriptures and the work of the assembly in Plymouth."[92] After the division of the movement, Soltau remained with the Open Brethren and engaged in an active preaching and writing ministry.[93] He was especially known for his work on the tabernacle, which advanced an allegorical approach to the subject that became popular among the Brethren.[94]

In his book *The Soul and Its Difficulties*, Soltau responded to a number of common questions, including, "How do I know that Christ died for me?" He answered not by appealing to universal redemption, but by asking the reader if he (or she) knew that he was a sinner and had felt deep and personal conviction of sin: "It is one thing to *say*, We are all sinners, and quite another thing from the heart to acknowledge, *I* am a sinner."[95] Not until a person owned the reality of their sin could they know that Christ's death was for them (1 Tim. 1:15). He wrote, "You have but to know yourself a sinner. You have only to plead your complete ruin; and your consciousness of that very ruin is, upon God's authority, your title to say, Christ Jesus came into the world to save *me*."[96] Significantly, Soltau did not argue that Christ died for everyone. The logic of his argument was not, Christ died for all and therefore he died for you, but that Christ died for sinners, and if you know yourself to be a sinner in need of salvation, then you may be assured his death was for you.

Henry Groves (1818–91)

Henry Groves was the eldest son of Anthony Norris Groves. He was, perhaps, the first Brethren "missionary kid," having travelled with his family in their missionary endeavours to Russia, Persia, and India. By the 1860s, Henry was back in the United Kingdom, ministering widely among the Open assemblies.[97] Along with William Yapp, he served as editor of the first Open Brethren magazine, *The Golden Lamp* (1870–90). He also maintained an influence on Brethren missions by co-editing (with John Maclean) *The Missionary Echo*, which later became *Echoes of Service*, a periodical dedicated to overseas missions.

Henry Groves appears to have upheld his father's Calvinistic convictions. John McVicker (1826–1900) reported hearing Groves preach at a

92. Rowdon, *Origins*, 161.
93. *BDEB*, s.n. "Henry (William) Soltau."
94. Soltau, *The Tabernacle*; Soltau, *Holy Vessels*.
95. Soltau, *The Soul and Its Difficulties*, 44.
96. Ibid., 47.
97. See Pickering, *Chief Men*, 158–60.

Brethren conference in Leominster in 1881 and was duly impressed. He declared, "I have seldom been in a better meeting than we had last night. Mr. Groves surpassed himself in speaking on the sovereignty of the grace of God."[98]

On the issue of the extent of the atonement, Groves was clearly influenced by Brethren thought. In 1879 he published an article in *The Golden Lamp* entitled, "The Day of Atonement: Its Godward and Manward Aspects."[99] As the title indicates, he maintained the Darbyite distinction in his discussion of the two goats. The previous year, he responded to the following question posed by a reader of *The Golden Lamp*: "Is it right to say, 'Christ made an atonement for the sin of the world?'" Groves affirmed that there are both universal and particular aspects to Christ's atoning work. He explained: "The atonement is, as from God, unlimited in its extent and universal in its aspect; but as to man, it is limited and particular. The distinction observed in Scripture between the universality of the atonement in the gospel presented by God, and the limited character of the atonement in the gospel received by man, has carefully to be regarded in preaching, or else expressions are used and applied to the unregenerate hearer which belong only to the child of God."[100]

The universal dimension of the atonement ensured the gospel could be preached to all, but the particularity of it should make preachers cautious not to claim too much since, as Groves affirmed, "the sin of the believer alone is atoned for."[101]

William Kelly

Kelly followed Darby closely in applying the imagery of the two goats from the Day of Atonement to the work of Christ in propitiation and substitution. He explained, "In the first goat God has secured His majesty, and His righteous title to send forth His message of love to every creature. Again, in the second goat He has equally cared for the assurance of His people, that all their sins, transgressions, and iniquities, are completely borne away."[102]

Propitiation is of supreme importance because God must be glorified in atonement. "Sin had put shame on God, and done violence to His will,

98. McVicker, *Selected Letters*, 108.
99. G[roves], "Day of Atonement," 265–73.
100. [Groves], "Notes and Replies," 144.
101. Ibid., 143–44.
102. Kelly, *Lectures on the Day of Atonement*, 62. A very similar discussion may be found in Kelly, *Exposition of the Epistles of John*, 63–67.

nature, and majesty. God, therefore, must be vindicated in every respect about sin."[103] Propitiation first and foremost secures God's holiness and honor and thus opens the door to preaching God's love freely to all.[104] It is in this sense that the blood of Christ is not limited to the elect, for propitiation is directed toward God and announces that all who believe in Christ will be saved.

Be that as it may, the second goat, over which the people's sins were confessed, does involve a limitation. Christ bore the sins of only those who believe—and Kelly was here willing to bring in the doctrine of election. After stating that it is wrong to assume Christ's blood has no scope beyond the elect (as the first goat illustrates), he clarified: "Not that to me God's electing love is a doubtful question, but as sure as any other truth of revelation, and a spring of solid comfort to the household of faith, humbling to man's pride and glorifying to the God of all grace. One may be quite willing to allow, therefore, that election is behind the second goat . . . for there limitation comes; but the first goat typically is unlimited in its range."[105]

Again, it is this unlimited dimension that allows the gospel call to be proclaimed to all, whereas limited substitution ensures that a real atonement was accomplished for the elect. Like Darby, Kelly believed that "man is not entitled to tell an unbeliever, 'Christ bore your sins in His own body on the tree'; when one believes, God's word assures him of it."[106] If Christ had truly borne the sins of the whole world, then the whole world would be saved—such is the efficacy of Christ's atonement—and there would be no place for judgment.[107] Like traditional Calvinists, however, Kelly was quick to clarify that the limitation in no way lessens the sufficiency or value of the atonement. He declared, "Were there a thousand worlds to save, were there sinners beyond all that exist to hear God's glad tidings, there is that in the blood of Jesus which would meet every sinner of every world. Such is the unlimited value God finds in the death of His Son."[108]

103. Kelly, *Lectures on the Day of Atonement*, 41.

104. Ibid., 44–45, 57.

105. Ibid., 113.

106. Ibid., 56; also 114–15; 121. Kelly added, "No doubt if you believe the gospel, you are one of God's elect" (115).

107. Ibid., 56.

108. Ibid., 114. Cf. Owen, *Works*, 10:295. However, Kelly did not identify himself as a Calvinist, for he asked, "Why reason like a Calvinist to limit the God of grace? Would you narrow the glad tidings of God?" (115). He was evidently thinking of a hyper-Calvinist restriction of the gospel call: "Nothing can be conceived more disastrous to the unmeasured width of the gospel than to address the elect merely. The Lord commanded that it be preached to every creature" (113–14). Of course, traditional Calvinists did not limit the preaching of the gospel or the value of Christ's sacrifice.

Kelly (again following Darby) distinguished between the biblical terms "purchase" and "redemption"; and since both Arminians and Calvinists fail to make this distinction, both parties, from Kelly's perspective, have fallen into confusion.[109] By his death, Christ has purchased everyone. Of course, as Creator, he is the rightful possessor of all things. But the introduction of sin brought with it great distortion and evil. Therefore, "By His death on the cross the Lord added to His creator rights, and made every creature His by that infinite purchase."[110] For Kelly, universal purchase in no way suggests that all are saved. Indeed, there are "persons bought that are unrenewed, and they may turn out rebels against His rights Who bought them."[111] The limitation is connected to actual redemption. This redemption won by Christ is not "merely a manifestation of grace which may be despised and ineffectual; it is an unfailing work, a delivering operation, a blessing that is actually conferred and possessed," but it is limited to believers alone.[112]

In advocating universal propitiation and purchase as well as particular substitution and redemption, Kelly believed he achieved the biblical balance that had eluded both Calvinists and Arminians. In his mind, both parties preached only part of the truth. He argued that "each is partially right, and partially wrong . . . the Calvinist is as right in holding particular redemption, as the Arminian in maintaining universal purchase. But they are both in error when they fail to distinguish purchase and redemption."[113] As we have observed, key Calvinist documents and writers did emphasize the infinite value and sufficiency of Christ's sacrifice, which grounds the universal gospel offer.[114] Perhaps this did not go far enough for Kelly, or perhaps he was thinking more of hyper-Calvinism,[115] but clearly his particularist emphasis excluded him from the Arminian camp and placed him in the Calvinist tradition, even though he refused to own the label.

It is unfortunate that Kelly, who was very well-read, did not display greater nuance in describing the Reformed tradition.

109. Kelly, "Purchase and Redemption," 263.

110. Kelly, *Exposition of the Epistles of John*, 66.

111. Kelly, "Purchase and Redemption," 265. Cf. Kelly's discussion of 2 Pet 2:1 in Kelly, *Epistles of Peter*, 126.

112. Kelly, "Purchase and Redemption," 265, 280. Other Brethren writers frequently made this distinction. For example see Scott, *Exposition of the Revelation*, 140.

113. Kelly, *Exposition of the Epistles of John*, 66. Cf. Kelly, *Lectures on the Day of Atonement*, 59–60.

114. E.g., Canons of Dort II.3–6 in Schaff, *Creeds of Christendom*, 3:586.

115. In another place Kelly asserts that the Calvinist could not "understand the word which calls one to preach the gospel to every creature." Kelly, *Great Olivet Prophecy*, 15. But again, this is not the position of normative Calvinism and surely Kelly knew better.

Charles Henry Mackintosh

It comes as no surprise that CHM followed Darby and Kelly in his views of the atonement given that Mackintosh was, in the words of one recent biographer, "the arch communicator of the teaching of J N Darby."[116]

In an article on the atonement, Mackintosh spoke of its "two grand aspects," the first Godward, the second directed toward sinners.[117] The first deals with sin "in its very broadest aspect," and not with the forgiveness of individual sins. It redresses the glory and character of God, which had been "so grossly dishonoured" by human sin. This is the primary aspect of the atonement, since "it was infinitely more important that God should be glorified than that we should be saved," although both ends are realized through the work of Christ.[118] In this Godward aspect, "God has been glorified as to sin—His claims satisfied—His majesty vindicated—His law magnified—His attributes harmonized."[119] On this basis, the gospel can be freely proclaimed to all, not just to the elect. Mackintosh understood the Scriptures to teach that Christ died for the elect, but in another sense, that Christ died for all. Acknowledging these two strands of biblical teaching launched Mackintosh into one of his characteristic protests against systematic theology: "We can no more systematize God's word than we can systematize God Himself. His word, His heart and His nature, are quite too deep and comprehensive to be included within the limits of the very broadest and best constructed human system of theology that was ever framed. We shall, ever and anon, be discovering passages of Scripture which will not fall in with our system."[120]

In context, Mackintosh was targeting traditional Calvinist and Arminian approaches to the extent of the atonement. Even though he recognized that Christ died in a particular way for the elect, he loathed the practice of some Calvinists who interpreted passages that speak of Christ's death for all to mean all *the elect*. Christ's work of propitiation is universal in scope, and that is why the message goes out to all the world, not merely the world of the elect. However, "when any one through grace believes it he can be further told that not only has Christ put away *sin*, but that also He has borne his *sins*—the actual sins of all His people—of all who believe in His name."[121] In good Dar-

---

116. Cross, *Life and Times*, 44. An editor's note in an older work commented, "It is often said that 'C. H. M. is J. N. D. made easy.'" Noel, *History of the Brethren*, 158n.

117. Mackintosh, *Miscellaneous Writings*, 6:2 ("The Three Appearings").

118. Ibid., 3.

119. Ibid., 5.

120. Ibid., 7. Cf. [Mackintosh], "One-Sided Theology," 12–16.

121. Mackintosh, *Miscellaneous Writings*, 6:8 ("The Three Appearings").

byte fashion, Mackintosh summarized his position as follows: "Christ is a *propitiation* for the whole world. He was the *substitute* for His people."[122]

Given this distinction, questions were often raised about the meaning of John 1:29 ("the Lamb of God, which taketh away the sin of the world"). Mackintosh, again following Darby,[123] connected it to "the great propitiatory work of Christ in virtue of which every trace of sin shall yet be obliterated from the wide creation of God."[124] Nevertheless, "the full result of this work will not be seen until the new heavens and the new earth shall shine forth as the eternal abode of righteousness."[125] Christ's death has, however, enabled God to deal in mercy with the world. And yet Mackintosh was careful to clarify that the text does not say the Lamb takes away the *sins* of the world, as Arminians like to say. "If this were so, no one could ever be lost. Such a statement would furnish a basis for the terrible heresy of universal salvation . . . This is not scripture but fatally false doctrine."[126] He emphatically declared: "Christ is never said to have borne the *sins* of the world,"[127] only the sins of believers. Therefore, Mackintosh represents yet another proponent of universal propitiation and particular substitution. The former establishes the preaching of the gospel to all people; the latter ensures that the sins of God's people have been efficaciously borne away.

F. W. Grant

In F. W. Grant we have a writer who deviated from the standard Brethren position on the atonement while still retaining some of its emphases. Grant appeared to be uncomfortable with the full force of Darby's stress on particularity. He described the typical Brethren view as teaching, "On the cross there was a work for all and a *special* work for the elect beside—a double atonement, as it were; that it was a propitiation for all, a substitution for the elect. In other words, the Arminian atonement and the Calvinistic atonement are both considered true, and to be found together in the work of Christ."[128] Grant rejected the position as leading to "much confusion and misreading of Scripture."[129]

---

122. [Mackintosh], "One-Sided Theology," 16.
123. Darby, *Synopsis*, 3:418–19.
124. [Mackintosh], "One-Sided Theology," 16; cf. Mackintosh, *Short Papers*, 2:262.
125. Mackintosh, *Short Papers*, 2:262.
126. [Mackintosh], "One-Sided Theology," 16.
127. Mackintosh, *Short Papers*, 2:262.
128. Grant, *Atonement*, 190–91.
129. It should be noted that he did subscribe to Darby and Kelly's distinction

His own view was expressed in response to the American Methodist critic of the Brethren, Daniel Steele, who took aim at the Calvinism of the movement. Steele, an Arminian who advocated a governmental view of the atonement, argued that the penal substitutionary view inevitably led the Brethren to a limited atonement in which Christ bore the punishment only for the elect. Interestingly, Steele noticed that Brethren avoided using standard Calvinistic terminology, but this, he suggested, was by design in order to make their teaching more "palatable to those educated in the Arminian faith."[130] In response, Grant stated, "the Plymouth Brethren in general do *not* believe in 'limited atonement' in the sense in which this is usually understood."[131] He then explained his own view (not claiming to speak for all Brethren) that Christ bore the penalty and full wrath of God not for the world, for that would be universalism, nor for the elect as a definite number of people, for that would be limited atonement and "would give no basis for a universal offer of salvation."[132] Instead, Christ made atonement for his people—"a satisfaction available for *all the world upon condition of faith*; actually such *for all believers*." Thus "it is an atonement unlimited in value and availability for all men; limited only by the unbelief that slights or rejects it."[133] Grant believed his view ought to be intelligible to Arminians, for to his mind it removed all difficulties.

Grant, like other Brethren, used the imagery of the two goats from the Day of Atonement in Leviticus 16 to speak of propitiation and substitution. Unlike Darby, however, Grant did not detach substitution from propitiation by assigning propitiation exclusively to the Lord's goat and substitution to the people's goat, as was the normal approach in Brethren thought.[134] Rather, he argued that propitiation is accomplished *by* substitution; the two cannot be separated. He explained, "The goat which is the Lord's lot . . . explicitly speaks of substitution as it does of propitiation."[135] Furthermore, Grant argued that propitiation was for the sins—not merely sin in a general way—of the whole world. But if propitiation is by substitution, does this not mean that Christ is the substitute for the whole world? Here is where Grant agreed with Darby, even if he did not abide by the logical implication of his

---

between purchase and redemption. See Grant, *Numerical Bible: Hebrews to Revelation*, 183–84.

130. Steele, *Substitute for Holiness*, 130.

131. Grant, *Miscellaneous Writings*, 2:26 ("Christian Holiness").

132. Ibid., 2:27–28.

133. Ibid., 2:28.

134. For this reason, some Brethren considered his views "very questionable." Noel, *History of the Brethren*, 1:337, 339.

135. Grant, *Atonement*, 104.

argument. He wrote, "A substitute for the world the Lord could not be, or universalism would be the simple necessity, and there could be no judgment for a single soul. But this is terrible error, and not the truth in any wise; and error which is now deceiving thousands."[136] Clearly, he rejected the Arminian position, but neither was he prepared to say that substitution was only for the elect. This would mean limited atonement and would provide no ground for offering the work of Christ to all. Grant recognized that it is proper to speak of Christ's death being sufficient for the world and of the highest value, but this does not make it *available* for the world. Therefore, he concluded that Christ is "the Substitute of *His people*, but a people not numerically limited to just so many, but embracing all who respond to the invitations of His grace, though it were indeed the world for multitude."[137]

Grant's position appears to be both theologically confused and logically incoherent. He maintains that propitiation is by substitution, and Christ is the propitiation—but not the substitution—for the sins of the whole world. Christ did not bear the sins of the world, but neither did he bear the sins of a specific number of people. He bore the sins of believers. But this raises the obvious question as to whether believers constitute a fixed number of people. Calvinists and Arminians alike would argue that they do, and that they are known to God either through sovereign selection (Calvinism) or foreseen faith (Arminianism).

Grant, however, did not want to connect election with the atonement in any way. While he did believe in election,[138] he argued that "the provision made in atonement is not merely for the elect. It is the provision of a substitute, not for a definite number of people of *individuals*, but for a certain *class*."[139] Christ bore the sins of "those who will accept the Substitute, without a rigid exact number being at all implied."[140]

Essentially, Grant was saying that Christ died for a certain class (not individuals), namely, those who believe. Once an individual believes, he or she comes "into this class—among the people for whom the substitutionary sacrifice has been accepted."[141] This position seems to have an affinity with the doctrine of corporate election, which states that God did not choose individuals for salvation; he chose the church. Once a person believes, he or she becomes part of the church and is thus elect. Grant again, however, con-

---

136. Ibid., 108. Cf. Grant, *Miscellaneous Writings*, 2:24 ("Christian Holiness").
137. Grant, *Atonement*, 109.
138. E.g., ibid., 109 and 193. See also chapter 5 for Grant's view of election.
139. [Grant], "Some Further Notes," 27.
140. Ibid., 28.
141. Ibid.

tinued to affirm individual election, stating, "I have no thought of disputing the truth and necessity of election; but what I deny absolutely is that in fact provision is made only for the elect." Evidently, what drove Grant to this position was the desire to be able to offer the gospel to all: "The sufficiency of the atonement for all must be a real one to make the general call founded upon it sincere."[142] Grant described his position as "conditional atonement." He wrote, "[Christ] bare the sins of believers on the tree, and this is equivalent to what we have been saying—that the efficacy of atonement is conditional. It is conditioned upon faith, and His bearing the sins of believers is a complete negative of universalism in all its phases. Only their sins are borne, although the atonement is for the sins of the whole world; and the duty and responsibility of faith are therefore to be pressed on every creature."[143]

He argued that believers' sins were borne by Christ, but not until they actually believe. This led to the following tortured explanation:

> The sins of believers were really borne eighteen hundred years ago; but only when men become believers are their sins borne, therefore. The very man who to-day believes, and whose sins were borne eighteen hundred years ago, not only could not say yesterday that his sins were borne, but they were really not borne yesterday, although the work was done eighteen hundred years ago. But it was done for believers, and only to-day is he a believer. The work of atonement only now has its proper efficacy for him: he is justified by faith.[144]

Among Brethren writers, Grant came closest to hypothetical universalism in that he advocated a "conditionally efficacious" atonement for the whole world. It is not limited to the elect or any definite number of people, but is truly available for all who will believe. Grant's position cannot be called Arminian, because he rejected the notion that Christ bore the sins of the world. He maintained that Christ did not die to make people saveable; his death actually accomplished redemption, and this is not true of the world.[145] Furthermore, he affirmed a Calvinistic view of election, but believed election had no relation to the atonement. Although he tied himself in several theological knots, his rather confused approach illustrates how far some Brethren writers would go to ensure their position was "biblical" and

---

142. Ibid.
143. Grant, *Atonement*, 191–92.
144. Ibid., 192.
145. Grant, *Atonement*, 187.

not contaminated by systematic theology. Ironically, in Grant's mind, "all this is perfectly simple"[146] and "clears up many obscurities."[147]

Donald Ross

Previous chapters have highlighted the significance of Donald Ross to Open Brethrenism through evangelism and magazine work.[148] His Calvinistic roots and ardent gospel preaching make him a fascinating case study for the question of the present chapter. When Ross was accused of teaching Morisonianism, he emphatically denied the charge and stated plainly, "I believe in particular redemption."[149] This statement came in 1867, before he joined the Brethren. However in later years, his discussions of the extent of the atonement were less precise; nevertheless, they do reflect the Brethren emphasis on both the universal and the particular.

Although Ross no longer valued Reformed confessions nor employed the Westminster standards to explain doctrinal questions,[150] he continued to reject the Morisonian version of universal redemption. Morison had written that the sacrifice of Christ was a gift "to all men everywhere, without distinction, exception, or respect of persons" and "a true propitiation for the sins of the world," and that the Holy Spirit was active in "applying to the souls of all men the provisions of Divine grace."[151] This language was adopted as the manifesto of the Evangelical Union.[152] Yet it was precisely this language that Ross disavowed. In describing his preaching, he wrote, "We deviate somewhat from the Popery, Armenianism [sic], and Legality generally preached . . . Neither do we talk of 'The Spirit *applying* to us the redemption purchased by Christ.' This we deem quite unscriptural."[153]

After about a decade with the Brethren, Ross fielded the following question from a reader of his magazine, *The Barley Cake*: "Did Christ die for the sin and sins of all, that is, can we say to the ungodly Christ died for your sins, or is it only to the believers we can say so?" Ross's answer

---

146. Ibid., 192.

147. Ibid., 106.

148. Ross identified himself as Open Brethren and called "Mr. Muller of the Bristol Orphan Houses and of Bethesda Chapel . . . one, or perhaps chief, of our number." Ross, "A Clear Statement," 6.

149. Ross, *Donald Ross*, 86–88.

150. See the discussion in chapter 5.

151. Adamson, *Life*, 240.

152. Ibid.

153. Ross, "A Clear Statement," 5.

is not entirely lucid, but it does reflect Brethren themes. For example, he appealed to the two goats of Leviticus 16, noting that the first goat's blood was sprinkled on the mercy seat in order to satisfy God's demands. The type corresponds in the present day to the way being opened to preach the gospel to every creature.[154] The second goat had the sins of the people confessed on its head, which marked the putting away of sin by Christ (as in Heb 9:26). Ross then declared, "scripture knows nothing of a 'limited or an unlimited atonement.'" He clarified by adding, "The whole is made to turn on Faith—all who *believe*."[155] Thus Ross was not willing to say that Christ died for the sins of the world. It may be—especially in light of his appeal to the two goats of Leviticus 16—that he was upholding the Darbyite distinction between universal propitiation and particular substitution. However, he did not use that language. His answer was vague enough to also allow a Grantian interpretation—Christ did not bear the sins of the world or the elect, but of believers only.

In an 1885 article, Ross articulated the Brethren position on universal purchase and particular redemption. Based on Matt 13:44 and 2 Pet 2:1, he argued that Christ purchased the world but "redeemed only His own people—all men are not redeemed, else none would be lost."[156] He addressed the question of "the scope, intention and extent of the 'atonement'" again in 1896, but evidently his primary objective was to critique both traditional Calvinistic and Arminian answers, not to provide a clear statement of his own position.[157]

We conclude that Ross's position was significantly shaped by Brethren thought. Before joining the Brethren, he did not hesitate to affirm the Calvinistic view of particular redemption. Afterward he was more nuanced, not wanting to be identified with any theological party. This did not make him more Arminian, for he could say the idea that Christ died for every man "is not found in God's book from cover to cover."[158] Like many Brethren, he maintained the universal and particular aspects of the atonement, and in doing so believed that he was holding fast to Scripture, and not human theological systems.

---

154. [Ross], "Question 14," 79–80.

155. Ibid., 80.

156. [Ross], "His Own Blood," 116. Cf. [Ross], "Counter Truths," 66 where he said, "Christ, by dying, bought everything, even the earth itself. (Matthew xiii.44.) But a ransom He paid only for 'many.'"

157. [Ross], "The Atonement," 24–27.

158. Ibid., 26.

Sir Robert Anderson

In Anderson's popular work, *The Gospel and Its Ministry*, a chapter on substitution set forth what should be recognized by now as a familiar Brethren position. He pointed out that the language "bearing sin" is figurative of the Old Testament sin offering, and that "substitution is essentially characteristic of it." Yet, Anderson observed, "scripture never speaks of the death of Christ in its relation to the unbeliever—the unsaved—in language borrowed from the sin-offering."[159] Peter could say, "Christ bore our sins in his body on the tree" when addressing believers (1 Pet 2:24), but Paul did not use this language when addressing unbelievers (e.g., Acts 13:16–41; 17:22–31). As with the blood of the Passover lamb in Exodus, the death of Christ is the righteous basis by which God can cleanse a sinner, yet it is not until the blood has been applied to the sinner that he or she can claim the language of substitution. Anderson acknowledged that the work of Christ has "a great and real aspect to the world," but to declare that substitution applies to the unconverted is "utterly false, and the falsehood is all the more dangerous because of the perverted truth it seems to embrace."[160]

It is not until the sinner believes that "he becomes so thoroughly identified with [Christ] in all His vicarious work, that he can speak of Calvary as though the crucifixion were but yesterday."[161] Yet it is unwarranted to speak to the sinner of substitution before this point. Anderson concludes his discussion as follows:

> There is absolutely no limit to the value of the death of Christ to Godward [sic]; and there is not between the poles a single child of Adam who may not know its power, and receive the reconciliation which it wrought. And on the ground of this accomplished reconciliation, forgiveness is proclaimed to all without reserve or equivocation. But it is only the "*all that believe*" who are justified; and if it be demanded, why, beneath the supremacy of boundless love and almighty power, the few, and not the many should be saved, we can but fall back upon divine sovereignty, and exclaim, "O the depth of the riches both of the wisdom and knowledge of God! how unsearchable are His judgments and His ways past finding out!"[162]

---

159. Anderson, *The Gospel and Its Ministry*, 92.
160. Ibid., 93.
161. Ibid., 97.
162. Ibid., 98–99.

A footnote follows this passage summarizing the dual aspect of the atonement as seen in the two goats of the Day of Atonement, essentially confirming that Open Brethren like Anderson had been influenced by Darby and other Exclusive writers on the matter of substitution and propitiation.

Alexander Marshall

Previous chapters have revealed that when Alexander Marshall left the Evangelical Union in order to join the Brethren, he brought with him a fully formed Arminian theology. Thus he effectively became the voice for unlimited atonement in the movement. In describing Marshall's Morisonian background, Henry Pickering, as we have seen, wrote, "Their main point of cleavage from others was 'the extent of the atonement,' being strong Arminians, or, 'whosoever' men." Pickering added, "This upbringing was manifest in all Alex. Marshall's preaching and writing, and he was ever ready to contend, in a friendly way, for this view of truth."[163] Similarly, in the foreword to Marshall's biography, Pickering said of Marshall, "so firm was his conviction that 'Christ died for all,' that he almost seemed to relish a discussion with one leaning to Calvinistic views."[164]

Marshall's willingness to contend for unlimited atonement is demonstrated in a letter to the editor of *The Golden Lamp*. Marshall found objectionable an answer to the following question from a reader in 1880: "Is it right to say Christ was the propitiation for the whole world?" The editor, Henry Groves, answered that this is precisely what 1 John 2:2 says. Propitiation is Godward and therefore universal; it is the basis on which the gospel goes out to all. Yet in regard to humans, it is conditioned on faith and acceptance. Groves added that it is "wrong to say that the sins of the whole world are propitiated for; that would lead to universalism, a doctrine which Scripture repudiates in the clearest manner."[165]

Marshall rejected this limitation of the atonement. He wrote, "According to this a man cannot know that Christ died for him until he has the assurance of salvation. Hitherto I have believed that a man could not have the assurance of being saved without knowing that Christ died for him."[166]

---

163. Pickering, "Home-calling of a True Gospel Warrior," 411.

164. Hawthorn, *Alexander Marshall*, 4. For an example of this eagerness see the description of Marshall's discussion with the Calvinist A. W. Pink in Pink, *Letters of an Itinerant Preacher*, 42–43.

165. [Groves], "Notes and Replies," 168.

166. Hawthorn, *Alexander Marshall*, 23. Marshall's letter does not appear to have been printed in the *Golden Lamp*.

Marshall did not think that everyone whose sins were atoned for must necessarily be saved. He reasoned that if there was a single sinner for whom Christ did not shed his blood, then it was not possible for such to be saved. In order to preach the gospel, one must declare to the unbeliever that Christ died for his or her sins. Suggesting that Christ died for the elect or simply for "sinners," will not bring peace. "I must believe that He died for my sins, and if it is my duty to believe it, it must be true whether I believe it or not."[167]

Marshall could not accept the idea that there were both universal and particular aspects to the atonement. But again, such an aversion to this duality was part of the Morisonian heritage he brought with him to the Brethren. In the context of specifying the Evangelical Union's position on the extent of the atonement, his biographer stated, "Mr. Marshall was an out-and-out supporter of Dr. Morison."[168] A doctrinal declaration of the Evangelical Union confessed: "We reject the modern dogma of a Double Reference in the atonement—a special and efficacious reference to the elect, a general and inefficacious reference to the non-elect." Such a theological position is simply the ambiguous provision for those who wish to stand with "one foot in Calvinism, and with the other beyond it," but is "destitute of foundation either in Scripture or reason."[169] Thus Marshall allowed no room in his preaching for limited substitution and had no problem, as many other Brethren did, telling the unconverted that Christ died for their sins.[170] He believed the Calvinistic doctrine of the atonement was nothing less than a hindrance to the gospel.[171] In 1927, the year before his death, he was urging readers of *The Witness* to abandon the old Brethren view and embrace an unlimited atonement in which they could freely tell an unbeliever that Christ died for his or her sins.[172]

Presenting the Gospel

The preaching of Brethren evangelists from the revival tradition was not always fully aligned with the leading writers and teachers of the movement.[173] No doubt, some Brethren evangelists were not careful to preserve

167. Ibid., 26.
168. Ibid., 10.
169. Ibid., 11–12.
170. E.g., Marshall, *God's Way of Salvation*, 17, 21; Marshall, *God's Wonderful Love*, 13; Marshall, *Will a God of Love Punish?* 30–31.
171. Marshall, "A Visit," 149.
172. Marshall, "Telling a Sinner," 131.
173. Evidence of this will be provided in chapter 7.

the particularity of substitution, and perhaps some (beyond Marshall) held to unlimited atonement. One of the critics of the Brethren, Thomas Houston—admittedly, not the most reliable source—charged that "numbers of these teachers are Arminian in principle" denying election and maintaining universal atonement. To Houston, Brethren evangelists were typical revival preachers. He complained, "Many of the appeals of Lay revivalist preachers address persons of all classes with the assurance, most positively made, that Christ died for every one of them."[174]

It is difficult to assess the position of revival evangelists among the Brethren on the extent of the atonement, since most of them did not publish much material of a theological nature. We get a glimpse of how evangelist Donald Munro presented the gospel to the unconverted from a letter he wrote to an unbelieving nephew. Munro explained to his nephew that God "LOVES YOU" and gave his Son "that YOU, a lost sinner should not perish but have everlasting life. And in order to save YOU, that beloved Son of God, the Lord Jesus, was lifted up on the Cross, died for poor sinners, died for YOU, bore the punishment due to our sins . . . And by His sin-atoning death on the cross has satisfied God for our sins."[175] It is interesting in this passage that after Munro told his nephew Christ "died for YOU," he switched pronouns when adding, "bore the punishment due to *our* sins." Was the change to the first person plural theologically driven? It is possible, but not conclusive, since a few sentences later he reiterated, "Christ died for your sins"[176]—a phrase many Brethren were uncomfortable saying to an unbeliever. As we have seen, Darby insisted, "It is never said [in Scripture] Christ died for the sins of the world."[177] In his own preaching, he was not opposed to saying that Christ bore "our sins,"[178] since it was the biblical language,[179] but he was often theologically precise in his declarations. In one sermon, for example, he focused on Christ's death for *sinners*: "[God] is calling sinners by a love that has been proved stronger than death. The Son of God went down into the dust of death for sinners; the Son of God went down under the power of Satan for sinners; the Son of God went down under the power of the wrath of God for sinners . . . Christ is risen again, and is alive at the right hand of God. 'All things are ready; come unto the marriage.'"[180]

---

174. Houston, *Plymouthism*, 25–26.
175. Ritchie, *Donald Munro*, 68. Capitalization original.
176. Ibid., 69.
177. Darby, *CW* 21:199.
178. E.g., Darby, *Notes of Addresses*, 3.
179. Darby, *CW*, 19:243.
180. Darby, *Notes of Addresses*, 30.

Darby was not a hyper-Calvinist because he did not hesitate to urge *all* sinners to believe in Christ, but neither did he abandon his Calvinism in the pulpit nor capitulate to a universal atonement, as the following passage indicates: "To you in whom the word of God has not yet taken root, I present Christ as a Saviour. Your sins are between you and the Father. Until these are removed, you cannot have any communion with Him. Christ can remove your sins, and present His blood in their place. Believe in Him, and He will do this ... The Lord direct your hearts to this! May He reveal Christ to all among us who may not yet know Him!"[181]

Not all, however, were so careful in their gospel preaching. In fact, it was Darby's concern over the gospel being rightly preached that led him to publish his article on "Propitiation and Substitution." He opened the piece with these words: "My intercourse with saints, and especially with those who preach, has led me to discover that a good deal of obscurity in their manner of putting the gospel ... arises from not distinguishing propitiation and substitution."[182]

Cautious Particularity among Open Writers

Nevertheless, most Brethren writers and publications in the later part of the nineteenth century, while holding out the availability of the gospel to all and pressing sinners to believe in Christ, were cautious not to suggest that Christ had borne the sins of people who finally perish, but only those of believers. Several final examples from Open Brethren publications will illustrate the point and demonstrate that Alexander Marshall's universal atonement had not gained ascendancy in the movement.

In a popular evangelistic tract, Emily Gosse (1806–57; wife of Philip Gosse and mother of Sir Edmund Gosse) urged her reader to recognize that God's Word "says to each sinner whose ears hear the invitation, 'see the atonement offered for you! Behold the Lamb of God slain to take away the sin of every one who will believe on Him!'" In putting the offer to an individual unbeliever, Gosse did not think it proper to quote the verse precisely: "Behold the Lamb of God who takes away the sin of the world" (John 1:29).[183]

The editor of *The Witness,* John R. Caldwell, writing of how Christ was typified in the Old Testament sin offering, said: "He was the forsaken One, on whom our sins were laid, and who was made sin for us ... who ...

181. Darby, *Notes of Sermons,* 174.
182. Darby, *CW,* 27:318.
183. Gosse, *Narrative Tracts,* 3.

suffered for sins—the Just for the unjust; the Substitute, who took the place and bore the penalty for every sinner that puts his trust in Him."[184] The particularity cannot be missed; Christ is the substitute not for every sinner, but for every sinner "that puts his trust in Him." Likewise, William Laing argued in *The Witness* that the unsaved have no warrant to call Christ their substitute. "When by faith they accept Him, *then*, and not till then, can they truly say, 'He is my Substitute, my Saviour.'"[185]

John Ritchie, editor of *The Believer's Magazine*, made the familiar distinction between the two aspects of the death of Christ. The wider aspect of propitiation vindicates God's righteousness and provides the ground for preaching the gospel to all. The second aspect brings to those who believe blessings such as redemption, the purging of sins through Christ's substitution, and justification. Ritchie observed that "the confusing of these two aspects of the work of Christ leads to many erroneous expressions in presenting the Gospel to sinners and the truth to saints."[186]

When asked if it was right to tell the unconverted that "their sins have all been taken away, and that they have only to believe it," Ritchie responded, "No: it cannot be right to tell the unconverted what is not true. The sins of all the unconverted are upon themselves."[187] He further denounced the idea that Christ has taken away the sins of unbelievers by stating, "Preaching a false Gospel makes hypocrites, and those who make statements such as the above, have much to account for in luring simple souls into refuges of lies." The right course was to preach Christ and allow the Holy Spirit to work through the Word of God. Forgiveness of sins is preached to all on the basis of Christ's death, but only when the sinner believes are his or her sins taken away.[188]

---

184. Caldwell, *Christ in the Levitical Offerings*, 20. In an editor's note to a question on whether or not Isa 53:5–6 applies to unbelievers, Caldwell wrote, "faith alone can say, 'He was wounded for our transgressions . . .'" *W* 8 (1898), 180. Cf. *W* 46 (1916), 27–28.

185. Laing, "Substitution," 28.

186. Ritchie, *Foundation Truths of the Faith*, 34. Ritchie subscribed to the Brethren interpretation of universal purchase, while redemption is limited to those who believe. [Ritchie], "Young Believer's Question Box," (1895) 22. The substitution described in Isaiah 53 is "applicable now to all believers, but not to those who still reject the Saviour." [Ritchie], "Young Believer's Question Box," (1906) 82.

187. [Ritchie], "Young Believer's Question Box," (1897) 46. In a similar way, George Cutting spoke of Christ bearing the believer's sins, but "the Christ-rejecter must bear his own sins in his own person in the lake of fire forever." Cutting, *Safety, Certainty*, 22.

188. Ibid.

Conclusion

This chapter has investigated the question of where nineteenth-century Brethren stood on the question of the extent of the atonement. Were they Calvinistic or Arminian? Based on the evidence presented here, we may conclude that, with the exception of Alexander Marshall and perhaps a few other evangelists, Brethren did not espouse an Arminian version of universal atonement or redemption. While they maintained a universal aspect of the atonement, they consistently denied that Christ bore the sins of unbelievers on the cross—a hallmark of the Arminian position. Furthermore, they were unprepared to tell an unbeliever that Christ died specifically for his or her sins.

At one level, of course, it is not proper to call the Brethren "Calvinists," since they often disavowed the label and accused Calvinism of being too narrow. They seemed to labor under the assumption that Calvinist theology never admitted any universal aspects to the death of Christ, and always saw it in relation to the elect alone. While examples of this extreme position did exist, traditional Calvinism did, in fact, have room to speak of both universal and particular elements in the atonement.[189] William Shedd (1820–94), the nineteenth-century American theologian, while holding to particular redemption, could nevertheless say, "Atonement is unlimited, and redemption is limited." By this he meant that "the sacrifice of Christ is unlimited in its value, sufficiency, and publication, but limited in its effectual application."[190]

The Brethren also advocated universal and particular elements in their doctrine of atonement. But what made their position unique was where they located the universal and particular. It was not in the "sufficient for all, effective for the elect" formula that both particular redemptionists and hypothetical universalists could affirm. Rather, it was in the distinction between universal propitiation and particular substitution. This distinction enabled the preacher to genuinely offer the gospel to all while affirming redemption was effective for all those for whom Christ died. The distinction between propitiation and substitution also gave the Brethren a way of handling biblical texts that were either universal (e.g., 1 John 2:2) or particular (e.g., Eph 5:25) in scope without diminishing the force of either, which is what they believed both Calvinist and Arminian interpretations did.

We must conclude that the particularity within the Brethren position, especially in its denial that Christ bore the sins of the world, places it

---

189. See, for example, the Canons of Dort, II. 3, 5, 8 in Schaff, *Creeds of Christendom*, 3:586–87.

190. Shedd, *Dogmatic Theology*, 743.

within the Calvinist camp, as Arminian opponents such as Alexander Marshall recognized. Nevertheless, it was not typical Calvinism. The position cannot rightly be called particular redemption given its view of propitiation—although there are elements of particular redemption to it. And yet its handling of substitution precludes it from being described as hypothetical universalism—although its emphasis on conditionality is reminiscent of hypothetical universalism. In the end, it is a Calvinistic position, but not easily described by the standard terminology.

It is tempting to view Darby's contribution to the doctrine of the atonement as a creative exercise in systematic theology. However, that would be objectionable to many Brethren—including Darby himself—who believed, in good Brethren fashion, that they had solved the Calvinism/Arminianism divide by simply adhering to Scripture, and thus rising above "the systems of men."

7

"What Must I Do to Be Saved?"

Brethren Perspectives on Saving Faith, Repentance, and Assurance

Ye trembling saints, why longer doubt?
The Saviour's on the throne;
God's Lamb, He suffered for your sins,
The Father's only Son.

Why look within and cry that you
So feebly see Christ's blood?
God ever sees that blood for you;
And who can see like God?

Your thoughts of it may rise or fall,
God's value rests the same:
Henceforth repose your faith on that
Which God sees in the Lamb.

And He declares your sins forgiven,
Yourselves to Him brought near:
In hope of glory then rejoice,
For His love casts out fear.

—William Kelly[1]

---

1. Kelly, *Hymns and Poems*, 24.

Introduction

THE DOCTRINE OF CONVERSION is central to evangelicalism; indeed, in David Bebbington's quadrilateral of evangelical hallmarks, conversionism stands first on the list.[2] In evangelical theology, conversion involves a positive response to the gospel in which individuals repent of sin and trust Jesus Christ for salvation. When the Philippian jailor asked his famous question, "What must I do to be saved?" Paul and Silas answered, "Believe on the Lord Jesus, and thou shalt be saved" (Acts 16:31). This simple articulation of the gospel, however, raises numerous theological questions, such as: What is the nature of saving faith? Can individuals be certain they possess it? And, what place does repentance have in the experience of conversion?

We have seen thus far that the nineteenth-century Brethren movement was largely Calvinistic in its soteriology, and yet this stance is potentially undermined by the fact that critics from the Reformed tradition often took issue with Brethren teaching regarding conversion. Did the Brethren fall outside the spectrum of Calvinism on this central soteriological doctrine? It is the purpose of the current chapter to explore this question.

It should be noted that critics censured the Brethren on a cluster of related theological issues raised by the doctrine of conversion. These included justification, the basis of imputed righteousness, sanctification, prayer and confession, and the role of the Mosaic law in preaching and in the life of the believer. Brethren often did stray from familiar Reformed paths on these topics. For example, while they affirmed that divine righteousness is imputed to believers, they denied that the basis of that imputation was Christ's perfect obedience to the law, as in standard Reformed theology.[3] This was a common target point for Reformed critics.[4] It is impossible to engage

---

2. Bebbington, *Evangelicalism in Modern Britain*, 3, 5–10.

3. For example, William Kelly wrote, "We have no sympathy with the Arminian slur (be it J. Wesley's word or any other's) that 'imputed righteousness is imputed nonsense.' But we do not therefore embrace the hypothesis that imputation means Christ's obedience of the law imputed to us. Scripture grounds it on Christ's obedience up to death—the death of the cross whereon sin was judged and God glorified about it; so that it is God's righteousness to set Christ in heaven and accept us in Him." Kelly, "Rev. A. Moody Stuart on 'Brethren.'" The Brethren did not employ the categories of Covenant Theology typical of Reformed thought. For example, they did not speak of Christ fulfilling the covenant of works violated by Adam at the time of the fall.

4. E.g., [Haldane], *Errors*, 5–12 (1862); Croskery, *Catechism*, 12–13 (1866); Dabney, "Theology of the Plymouth Brethren," 1:187–89 [1872]; Macintosh, *Brethrenism*, 30–32 (1872); Houston, *Plymouthism*, 19–20, (1874); Reid, *Plymouth Brethrenism*, 164–205 (1875); Porteous, *Brethren in the Keelhowes*, 125–35 (1876); Carson, *Heresies*, 40–76 (1883).

all of these issues in this book.[5] Indeed, some of them merit full length treatment in their own right. The present chapter restricts its focus to two topics that bear directly on the doctrine of conversion: the nature of saving faith and the relationship between faith and assurance. Additionally, some consideration will be given to the meaning and place of repentance, since it also impacts the nature of saving faith.

In order to evaluate where the Brethren stood vis-à-vis the Calvinist heritage, it will be useful to have a broad sense of developments within that heritage. We turn first to John Calvin.

The Calvinist Heritage

Saving Faith and Assurance in Calvin

For Calvin, faith was not mere intellectual assent to gospel facts, which he claimed was a common perception.[6] In an important study, Joel Beeke observes, "Like Luther and Zwingli, Calvin said that faith is never merely assent (*assensus*), but involves both knowledge (*cognitio*) and trust (*fiducia*)."[7] Calvin stated, "We shall possess a right definition of faith if we call it a firm and certain knowledge of God's benevolence toward us, founded upon the truth of the freely given promise in Christ, both revealed to our minds and sealed upon our hearts through the Holy Spirit."[8] For Calvin, faith is a deep-seated conviction of both mind and heart. Commenting on Rom 10:10 ("with the heart one believes unto righteousness"), Calvin said, "The seat of faith is not in the head but in the heart . . . Since the word *heart* generally means a serious and sincere affection, I maintain that faith is a firm and effectual confidence, and not just a bare idea."[9]

Yet Calvin's definition also makes assurance part of faith's essence. Calvin asserted, "He alone is truly a believer who . . . relying upon the promises of divine benevolence toward him, lays hold on an undoubted expectation of salvation." Again, "No man is a believer . . . except him who, leaning upon the assurance of his salvation, confidently triumphs over the devil and

---

5. Neatby clarified the Brethren position on some of these matters in Neatby, *History*, 230–36.

6. "Indeed, most people, when they hear this term [faith], understand nothing deeper than a common assent to the gospel history." Calvin, *Institutes*, 3.2.1.

7. Beeke, *Quest for Full Assurance*, 37.

8. *Institutes*, 3.2.8.

9. Calvin, *Epistles of Paul*, 227–28.

death."[10] This strong association of faith and assurance may be explained in part as a reaction against Roman Catholicism's denial that certainty of salvation is even possible. Commenting on 2 Cor 13:5,[11] Calvin wrote:

> This passage serves to prove the assurance of faith, a doctrine which the sophists of the Sorbonne have so corrupted for us that it is now almost uprooted from the minds of men. They hold that it is rash temerity to be persuaded that we are members of Christ and have Him dwelling in us . . . so that our consciences remain perpetually undecided and perplexed. But what does Paul say here? He declares that those who doubt their possession of Christ and their membership in His Body are reprobates. Let us therefore understand that the only true faith is that which allows us to rest in God's grace, not with a dubious opinion but with firm and steadfast assurance.[12]

These strong statements are tempered by Calvin's discussion of the reality of Christian experience, in which the flesh and the Spirit continually battle. He conceded, "While we teach that faith ought to be certain and assured, we cannot imagine any certainty that is not tinged with doubt, or any assurance that is not assailed by some anxiety."[13]

Calvin's perspective is significant because, as we shall see, some writers criticized the Brethren for teaching that assurance is essential to faith.

The Contribution of the Puritans

There was diversity of opinion on the relation of faith and assurance among the early Reformers;[14] however, in the generations that followed, a growing

---

10. Calvin, *Institutes*, 3.2.16.

11. "Examine yourselves, whether ye be in the faith; prove your own selves. Know ye not your own selves, how that Jesus Christ is in you, except ye be reprobates?"

12. Calvin, *The Second Epistle of Paul to the Corinthians*, 173.

13. Calvin, *Institutes*, 3.2.17. For further discussion on Calvin's qualifications see Beeke, *Quest for Full Assurance*, 41–49.

14. While Calvin's position displayed strong similarities to those of Martin Bucer and Peter Martyr Vermigli, others, such as Heinrich Bullinger and Wolfgang Musculus, did not share his outlook. This points to one of the methodological flaws in the work of R. T. Kendall, who argues for a radical discontinuity between Calvin and later Calvinism (Kendall, *Calvin and English Calvinism*). Kendall treats Calvin as a kind of isolated phenomenon and thus fails to account for the diversity that existed in the early Reformed movement. See Letham, "Faith and Assurance," 355–84. Cf. Muller, *After Calvin*, 63–102.

emphasis among the Puritans linked assurance with experience rather than viewing it as part of the essence of faith.

The "Morphology of Conversion"

As Calvinists, the Puritans emphasized divine initiative in salvation; human beings, corrupted by sin, are unable and unwilling to turn to God and embrace the gospel. Nevertheless, God employed certain means to convert sinners, and it was with these means that the Puritans were concerned.[15] They discussed at length the stages through which God normally brought a person in the process of true conversion, developing what Edmund Morgan called "the morphology of conversion."[16] William Perkins (1558–1602), often recognized as "the principle [sic] architect of the young Puritan movement,"[17] was influential in developing this so-called "morphology."[18] In *A Golden Chaine* (1590), Perkins set forth a detailed *ordo salutis* originating in God's decrees and worked out in various steps that issue ultimately in glorification (or damnation in the alternative case).[19] Like much of Perkins's writings, *A Golden Chain* is animated by concerns for practical piety and thus concludes with a section on "the application of predestination." The elect, Perkins maintained, may be sure of their election primarily through two means: the internal

---

15. Simpson identified the "essence of Puritanism" as the "experience of conversion." Simpson, *Puritanism*, 2. The Puritans themselves recognized their contribution on this front. Thomas Goodwin and Philip Nye wrote: "It hath been one of the glories of the Protestant religion that it revived the doctrine of saving conversion, and of the new creature brought forth thereby . . . But in a more eminent manner, God hath cast the honour hereof upon the ministers and preachers of this nation, who are renowned abroad for their more accurate search and discoveries hereof." Foreword to Hooker, *Application of Redemption*, i.

16. Morgan, *Visible Saints*, 66–69. For an insightful discussion of the Puritan doctrine of conversion, as well as the use of conversion narratives see Gribben, *God's Irishmen*, 55–78.

17. Beeke, *Quest for Full Assurance*, 83.

18. See Beeke and Jones, *Puritan Theology*, 587–99.

19. Perkins's work has been variously interpreted. Some (e.g., Basil Hall and R. T. Kendall) see the *Golden Chaine* as the development of a metaphysical structure with a hardened doctrine of predestination at the center. That notion—and others related to the Calvin against the Calvinists theory—has been rejected as a misreading of both Calvin and Perkins. See Muller, *Christ and the Decree*, 132. See also Muller, "Perkins' *A Golden Chaine*," 69–81, and Shaw, "Drama in the Meeting House," 41–72. Beeke argues that though there is development in Perkins's work due to a new pastoral context, there is basic continuity with the Reformers. He concludes, "Perkins's emphases were not foreign to the Reformers. They differed in emphases but not in substance." Beeke, *Quest for Full Assurance*, 98.

testimony of God's Spirit and the evidence of sanctification in one's life. Yet Perkins was careful to reassure the feeble that "if they have faith but as much as a grain of mustard seed and be as weak as a young infant is, it is sufficient to ingraft them into Christ: and therefore they must not doubt of their election because they see their faith feeble and the effects of the Holy Ghost faint within them."[20] This exposition of a Reformed *ordo salutis*, pressed home with pastoral care, encouraged a measure of introspection and self-examination to confirm that one was truly elect. As Hindmarsh notes, "With the 'golden chain' schema, Perkins provided a complete theory of conversion that one could compare with one's own experience."[21]

Perkins's schema of conversion was advanced still further in his casuistical manual, *The Whole Treatise of the Cases of Conscience* (1606). Here he took up the question: "What must a man doe, that he may come into Gods favour, and be saved?"[22] He identified ten stages in the process, the first four being "workes of preparation"—an important concept in the Puritan understanding of conversion—whereas those that follow (5–10) are direct effects of grace.[23] Perkins then summarized the steps of conversion to four: humiliation, faith in Christ, repentance, and new obedience.[24] Conversion was thus broken down into discernible stages wherein an individual "could check his eternal condition by a set of temporal and recognizable signs."[25] Other Puritans writers would follow,[26] so that by the eighteenth century, the Puritan pattern of conversion was a well-established tradition.

More recent scholars have challenged Morgan's notion of a Puritan "morphology of conversion" if perceived as a stereotype that follows an identical sequence in every case.[27] The steps toward conversion could vary.[28] As Hambrick-Stowe notes, "Conversion could be gradual, sudden,

---

20. Perkins, *Work*, 258.

21. Hindmarsh, *Evangelical Conversion Narrative*, 38.

22. Perkins, *William Perkins*, 102.

23. Ibid., 102–3. Beeke and Jones argue that "there was a fundamental unity among Calvin and the Puritans regarding preparation for faith." Beeke and Jones, *Puritan Theology*, 445.

24. For a discussion of the four steps see Shaw, "Drama in the Meeting House," 53–70 and Beeke, *Quest for Full Assurance*, 88–98.

25. Morgan, *Visible Saints*, 66.

26. E.g., Hooker, *Application of Redemption*; Shephard, *Works*, 1:115–237; Sibbes, *Works*, 1:46–47; Flavel, *Works*, 2:3–474.

27. Caldwell, *Puritan Conversion Narrative*, 39–40; Beougher, *Richard Baxter*, 145.

28. Richard Baxter (1615–91), who wrote extensively on conversion, went through much distress in his teens because, as he states, "I could not distinctly trace the Workings of the Spirit upon my heart in that method which Mr. Bolton, Mr. Hooker, Mr.

violent, mild, or scarcely perceptible."[29] Nevertheless, the Puritans considered the process to normally advance along familiar lines. The sequence was not exact, and authors suggested different nuances, but inevitably some preparatory stage was necessary for the individual to be humbled under the guilt of his or her sin.[30] A key element of the preparatory stage was the preaching of the law, which not only brought conviction of sin but destroyed self-righteousness and prepared the soul to be saved by grace.

The Westminster Confession on Assurance

The Puritan "morphology" of conversion was borne out of pastoral concern to test the genuineness of saving faith and warn against false assurance. Full assurance was indeed possible for believers, but the Puritans understood it to be more a *fruit* of faith than part of its essence.[31] This was reflected in the Westminster Confession of Faith (chapter 18). Certainty of salvation was grounded on three things: (1) "the divine truth of the promises of salvation"; (2) "the inward evidence of those graces unto which these promises are made"; and (3) "the testimony of the Spirit of adoption witnessing with our spirits that we are the children of God" (18.2).[32] The Confession then asserted:

> This infallible assurance doth not so belong to the essence of faith, but that a true believer may wait long, and conflict with many difficulties, before he be partaker of it: yet, being enabled by the Spirit to know the things which are freely given him of God, he may, without extraordinary revelation, in the right use of ordinary means, attain thereunto. And therefore it is the duty of everyone to give all diligence to make his calling and election sure; that thereby his heart may be enlarged in peace and

---

Rogers and other Divines describe." Eventually, however, Baxter realized "that God breaketh not all men's hearts alike." Baxter, *Autobiography*, 10–11. Baxter nevertheless upheld a typical schema of conversion. See Baxter, *Practical Works*, 2:588–609. See also Beougher, *Richard Baxter*.

29. Hambrick-Stowe, *Practice of Piety*, 85.

30. For more on Puritan preparation, including an evaluation of the secondary literature, see Beeke and Jones, *Puritan Theology*, 443–61 and Beeke and Smalley, *Prepared by Grace*.

31. Beeke, *Quest for Full Assurance*, 113. For an argument for the continuity between Calvin and the WCF see Ferguson, "Blessèd Assurance," 623–28.

32. The Canons of the Synod of Dort ground assurance on essentially the same three elements, but reverse the order of 2 and 3 (Fifth Head, Art. X.). Schaff, *Creeds of Christendom*, 3:594–95.

joy in the Holy Ghost, in love and thankfulness to God, and in strength and cheerfulness in the duties of obedience, the proper fruits of this assurance: so far is it from inclining men to looseness. (18.3)

It is possible for true believers to have their assurance "shaken, diminished, and intermitted" through negligence, sin and temptation, or even by "God's withdrawing the light of his countenance." Yet they are never "utterly destitute," and assurance may be revived in due time through the means of grace (18.4).

The Eighteenth Century

As noted in chapter 2, the relationship between saving faith and assurance emerged as one of the main issues in the Marrow Controversy (1718–23) in eighteenth-century Scotland. The Church of Scotland Assembly opposed the contents of the recently republished book *The Marrow of Modern Divinity*, originally written by Edward Fisher in 1645. They affirmed, contra *The Marrow*, that assurance is not of the essence of faith, and that "a true believer is not at all times, even when he is acting in faith unto salvation, assured of his present being in a state of grace, and that he shall be saved; but that he may wait long to obtain this assurance."[33] The Assembly believed their position was in concert with the Westminster standards. *The Marrow* supporters countered that the Assembly's position was too narrow and ignored other voices from the Reformed tradition. They affirmed a fundamental agreement between the Westminster standards and the earlier reformers, even if different emphases were present. *The Marrow* men argued that in condemning "ancient" expressions in favor of the "more modern way of describing faith," the Assembly laid "a heavy charge . . . upon our reformers, this and other reformed churches, who generally have defined faith by assurance."[34]

The Marrow supporters made a distinction between two elements of assurance. The first was *fiducia*, or trust, in gospel promises—a resting in Christ and his work for salvation and a confidence that Christ will indeed save those who come to him for salvation. This kind of assurance was an essential dimension of saving faith. But a second kind of assurance included not only the confidence derived from gospel promises, but also from

---

33. Cited in VanDoodewaard, *The Marrow Controversy*, 33. See also Lachman, *The Marrow Controversy*, 9–22, although cf. VanDoodewaard's assessment of how Lachman evaluates the faith/assurance issue in the Marrow controversy (62n13).

34. Cited in VanDoodewaard, *The Marrow Controversy*, 63.

evidence of the Spirit's work in the life of the believer. This assurance varied and was not essential to saving faith.[35]

The Bebbington Thesis

In his history of evangelicalism, David Bebbington argues that the doctrine of assurance was a contributing factor to the emergence of the evangelical movement in the 1730s and, indeed, was what distinguished the new movement from its Puritan heritage. Bebbington suggests that while "the Puritans had held that assurance is rare, late and the fruit of struggle in the experience of believers, the Evangelicals believed it to be general, normally given at conversion and the result of simple acceptance of the gift of God." Bebbington then boldly claims, "The consequence of the altered form of the doctrine was a metamorphosis in the nature of popular Protestantism."[36] Now that believers were certain of their salvation, they could devote their energies to evangelism (Bebbington's "activism") instead of being preoccupied with their personal spiritual status.

Bebbington's thesis has been challenged at a number of points. For example, Garry Williams supplies evidence that John Wesley believed regular self-examination was necessary to avoid self-deception in regard to one's salvation. Yet according to Bebbington, Wesley was one of those responsible for disseminating the more immediate and less introspective understanding of assurance.[37] Furthermore, Wesley's understanding of assurance differed in significant ways from that of Jonathan Edwards, thus undermining "the idea that there was a coherent new doctrine of assurance at the heart of nascent evangelicalism."[38]

Williams also points to the Anglican Calvinist John Newton (1725–1807), whose view of assurance did not fit Bebbington's paradigm.

35. Ibid., 65.

36. Bebbington, *Evangelicalism in Modern Britain*, 43.

37. Williams, "Enlightenment Epistemology," 351–53. Cf. Bebbington, *Evangelicalism in Modern Britain*, 42. Williams concludes, "This is not to deny that assurance was more widely experienced by Wesleyans, but it is to counter Bebbington's argument that the Methodists were freed for their activism by leaving the self-examination of the Puritans behind them" (353).

38. Ibid., 361. After showing the central place of perseverance in good works and the importance of rigorous self-examination in Edwards's doctrine of assurance, Williams suggests, "Perhaps the opposite of Bebbington's view is the case: that a more reserved view of assurance encourages activism in an attempt to provide the evidence that comforts the conscience" (369). For further criticism of Bebbington's position on assurance vis-à-vis Jonathan Edwards see Haykin, "Evangelicalism and the Enlightenment," 55–59.

Newton could say, "Remember that the progress of faith to assurance is gradual. Expect it not suddenly; but wait upon the Lord for it in the way of his appointment."[39] Hindmarsh, in his study of Newton and the English evangelical tradition, demonstrates that during the years 1748–54, Newton wrestled with "the characteristic Puritan preoccupation with assurance: how could he set his conscience at rest before a holy God?"[40] The Puritan spirituality, with its "radical interiority" and "penetrating examination of the heart,"[41] was still very much alive in eighteenth-century evangelicalism.

Sandemanianism

One final piece of background material that has direct bearing on our subject relates to what is known as "Sandemanianism." The movement originated in Scotland in the 1720s under the teaching of John Glas (1695–1773). By the 1730s, several Glasite churches had formed. At this time, Robert Sandeman (1718–71) joined the young movement and married Glas's daughter. In Sandeman the Glasites found an enthusiastic propagator of their views, "being a man of more aggressive and controversial spirit than his father-in-law."[42] Through his publications and travels, Sandeman was responsible for spreading Glasite views in Scotland, England, and New England.[43] As a result, the movement became more commonly known as Sandemanianism, although it could still be referred to as Glasite in Scotland.

While Sandemanianism had a distinctive ecclesiology that displayed some remarkable similarities to the later Brethren movement,[44] it is most remembered for its intellectualist view of faith. Accordingly, saving faith consists solely in mental assent to the facts of the gospel; neither the will nor the affections play any role. As Andrew Fuller summarized, Sandemanian faith consists of "the bare belief of the bare truth."[45] Sandeman clarified that by "bare belief" he did not mean a "hearty persuasion," but mere notional belief. He wrote, "Every one who obtains a just *notion* of the person and

---

39. Cited in Williams, "Enlightenment Epistemology," 371.

40. Hindmarsh, *John Newton*, 63.

41. Ibid., 65.

42. *BDEB*, s.n. "Robert Sandeman."

43. For a history of the movement with particular focus on developments in America, see Smith, *The Perfect Rule*.

44. For the ecclesiological similarities between the Sandemanians and the Brethren see Embley, "Origins," 31–32. Cf. Carter, *Anglican Evangelicals*, 99–100.

45. Fuller, *Complete Works*, 2:566.

work of Christ, or whose *notion* corresponds to what is testified of him, is justified, and finds peace with God simply by that *notion*."[46]

On questions of sin, predestination, and effectual calling, the Sandemanians were Calvinists. Lloyd-Jones said of Glas, "He was not only a Calvinist, he was a very high Calvinist, and thoroughly orthodox in that sense."[47] In Lloyd-Jones's evaluation, a Sandemanian view of the nature of saving faith "can be adopted by Calvinists as well as Arminians."[48] This is significant because, as we shall see, Reformed critics frequently charged the Brethren with a Sandemanian view of faith. Whether or not this was actually the case, we shall evaluate in due course. Even if the Brethren did advocate Sandemanianism, however, this in itself would not disqualify them from the Calvinist fold.

The Nineteenth Century

Before moving to the Brethren context, two episodes in Scotland will illustrate how saving faith and assurance continued to be an issue of debate in the nineteenth century.

As highlighted in chapter 6, John McLeod Campbell is best remembered for his innovative teaching on the atonement. Yet his controversial theological career had its genesis when he began to rethink issues related to the assurance of faith. In 1825 he was ordained as a Church of Scotland minister to the parish of Row in Dumbartonshire. Upon engaging in pastoral work among his parishioners, Campbell discovered "the negative effect of the prevailing theological orthodoxy upon his congregation."[49] Specifically, he noticed that lack of assurance of personal salvation produced people who acted only in the fear of judgment and not out of love for God or holiness. Soon afterward, Campbell urged his people to rest assured of God's "love in Christ to them as individuals, and of their individually having eternal life given to them in Christ" as the first principle of New Testament Christianity.[50] He came to the conclusion that not only was assurance of the essence of faith, but that "unless Christ had died *for all*, and unless the Gospel announced him as *the gift of God to every human being* . . . there was no foundation in the record of

---

46. Cited in ibid., 2:566–67.
47. Lloyd-Jones, *The Puritans*, 171. Cf. *DSCHT*, s.n. "Robert Sandeman," "The basic theology of the movement is Calvinist."
48. Lloyd-Jones, *The Puritans*, 174.
49. Stevenson, *God in Our Nature*, 8.
50. "Extract of a Letter from the Rev. John McLeod Campbell, Minister of Row," (1 January 1831), cited in Stevenson, *God in Our Nature*, 283.

God for the Assurance which I demanded, and which I saw to be essential to true holiness."[51] For Campbell, the basis of assurance was not to be found in searching within for evidences of election, as was commonly believed, but in looking to the cross, where Christ died for all.[52]

Campbell's theology came under intense scrutiny and was opposed by many ministers. In 1831 he was deposed from the ministry of the Church of Scotland by the General Assembly for teaching "the doctrine of universal atonement and pardon through the death of Christ" and "the doctrine that assurance is of the essence of faith, and necessary to salvation."[53] The Assembly judged these doctrines to be contrary to Scripture and the Westminster standards.

Brethren leaders do not appear to have been influenced by Campbell. William Kelly denounced Campbell's mature views on the nature of the atonement as "ruinous departure from revealed truth."[54] Other Brethren writers ignored Campbell altogether. Nevertheless, as we shall see, Brethren evangelists also challenged traditional notions of assurance and encountered opposition for doing so.[55]

A second episode involving debate over the nature of conversion and assurance demonstrates that Calvinists could disagree on these issues. Here we return to the exchange between John Kennedy and Horatius Bonar over the Moody campaign in Scotland (1873–74) described in chapter 3. Kennedy, the traditional Highland Calvinist, raised serious concerns over the prominence of "sudden" conversions. He argued, "The work of conversion includes what we might expect to find detailed in a process . . . If a hearty, intelligent turning to God in Christ be the result of conversion, it is utterly unwarrantable to expect that, as a rule, conversion shall be sudden. Indeed the suddenness is rather a ground of suspicion than a reason for concluding

---

51. Ibid., 284. Emphasis original.

52. Stevenson, *God in Our Nature*, 9. Campbell's friend, Thomas Erskine (1788–1870), bemoaned the lack of assurance among people under the influence of traditional Scottish theology as "the leprosy which has overspread the land." Erskine advanced his own solution to the problem in his highly controversial doctrine of "universal pardon." He went so far as to declare that "personal assurance is necessary to salvation, for personal assurance is nothing more or less than the faith of the Gospel." See Horrocks, *Laws of the Spiritual Order*, 96–101.

53. *The Whole Proceedings*, 1.

54. Kelly, *Lectures on the Day of Atonement*, 171.

55. The controversy over assurance stirred up by Campbell and Erskine, whom traditionalists viewed as untrustworthy or even heretical, may be one reason why some Scottish ministers had no patience with Brethren evangelists who told their listeners that they could be saved and know it immediately.

that the work is God's."⁵⁶ Furthermore, preaching for sudden conversions denied the necessity of repentance, as evidenced for Kennedy by the lack of "law-work" in the Moody mission (that is, the absence of preaching the law for conviction of sin). The sudden conversions that so characterized Moody's campaign suggested to Kennedy that the results produced were more a matter of human manipulation than the sovereign work of God. Genuine conversion wrought by the Holy Spirit would be manifested over time, and "it was presumptive for anyone to pronounce that conversion had occurred simply on the basis of a verbal profession of faith."⁵⁷

In response, Bonar argued that all the conversions recorded in Scripture were sudden, and in affirming them he was simply following "in the footsteps of the apostles."⁵⁸ Bonar struck back at Kennedy's accusations by declaring, "*All conversions must be sudden if they are the work of the Holy Ghost. They who deny such suddenness must believe the process to be in part a human one.*"⁵⁹ He also claimed to have heard many calls to repentance in Moody's preaching, yet Kennedy's insistence that repentance must precede faith "appeared to Bonar to be a dangerous species of 'preparationism,'"⁶⁰ for "repentance which does not come *from believing* must be simply that of the natural conscience."⁶¹ After all, the apostles in the book of Acts preached Christ crucified, and it was this message, not the law, which produced repentance.

Kennedy was also concerned about the campaign's doctrine of assurance, where people were encouraged immediately "to conclude that they are saved because they have so believed."⁶² Subjective assurance for Kennedy was a matter of self-examination; "the accrediting of faith by works which alone can form a basis for the steadfast assurance of having passed from death to life."⁶³ Bonar responded, "'Peace with God,' as the *immediate* result of a believed gospel, is what the apostles preached. 'Peace with God' not as a result of a certain amount of experience or feeling, but as flowing directly

---

56. Kennedy, *Hyper-Evangelism*, 11.
57. Ross, "Calvinists in Controversy," 54.
58. Horatius Bonar, *The Old Gospel* as reprinted in Kennedy and Bonar, *Evangelism*, 64.
59. Kennedy and Bonar, *Evangelism*, 65. Emphasis original.
60. Ross, "Calvinists in Controversy," 56.
61. Kennedy and Bonar, *Evangelism*, 62. Emphasis original.
62. Kennedy, *Hyper-Evangelism*, 20.
63. Kennedy, *A Reply*, 34.

from the light of the cross, is that which we are commanded to preach as the glad tidings of great joy to the sinner."⁶⁴

In defending Moody, Bonar did not believe he was departing from the Reformed tradition; in fact, he appealed to Calvin and other Reformed thinkers (such as Thomas Boston) to demonstrate that his view of faith, repentance, and assurance stood squarely in the Calvinist tradition. He even claimed that the message proclaimed in the Moody campaign "is the teaching of the Westminster Confession and the Shorter Catechism."⁶⁵

The exchange between Kennedy and Bonar suggests that both perspectives had a place in the Calvinist tradition. More broadly, the evidence indicates that genuine conversion and the question of assurance were complex issues within evangelicalism—as David Bebbington himself has come to concede.⁶⁶ While revival preaching did produce a tendency toward instant or sudden conversions,⁶⁷ the Puritan spirituality, with its emphasis on the need for self-examination, still exerted a powerful influence into the nineteenth century. Thus, while personal assurance of salvation was not unusual in the nineteenth century, a number of evangelicals—not least, those in the Reformed tradition—were wary of a kind of immediate assurance based solely on biblical propositions and not borne out by the experience of progressive sanctification. These, again, are the points at which Brethren teaching came under scrutiny.

The Brethren on Conversion

The Brethren believed with other evangelicals that conversion was necessary. One is not a Christian by birth, education, or baptism. "A man becomes a Christian only by being divinely converted."⁶⁸ But what did that entail? Critics frequently targeted the Brethren view of conversion as one problematic feature of their theology. We begin, therefore, by looking at what the critics understood the Brethren to be teaching in regard to conversion, and then we will examine what the Brethren themselves said on the topic.

---

64. Kennedy and Bonar, *Evangelism*, 56. Cf. Ross, *Calvinists in Controversy*, 58.

65. Kennedy and Bonar, *Evangelism*, 86.

66. Bebbington acknowledges that assurance was "a more complex matter than *Evangelicalism in Modern Britain* allows." Bebbington, "Response," 421–22.

67. For Wesley's advocacy of sudden conversions see Pearse, "Soundly Converted?" 231–32.

68. Mackintosh, *Miscellaneous Writings*, 4:4 ("Conversion").

Critics of the Brethren

The Brethren attracted their fair share of critics who were willing to go to print with their strictures against the movement's doctrines and practice.[69] While a number of issues were raised by the critics, we focus here on their objections to Brethren notions of saving faith, repentance, and assurance. It is worth noting that the majority of critics came from the Calvinist tradition,[70] although the Methodists in North America also proved to be vociferous opponents to Brethrenism. The critics are assembled together in this section in order to observe the consistency of their objections in the latter years of the nineteenth century across a wide geographical span. This, in turn, serves as a useful backdrop against which to examine Brethren primary source material.

One of the earliest criticisms of the movement came in 1842 from J. C. Philpot, the Strict Baptist leader. Philpot had an early connection to Darby, having served as tutor to his nephews. Darby even claimed to have been the means of Philpot's conversion.[71] Thus Philpot had some positive things to say about the Brethren, but his primary criticism lay in the movement's faulty view of saving faith. He complained that the Brethren not only set aside the law as a rule of life, but also as "a ministration of condemnation." He wrote, "They do not believe it to be necessary for the law to condemn and curse a sinner, before he can or will come to Christ for mercy and pardon."[72] A sense of guilt and condemnation, therefore, is no prerequisite for the reception of the gospel. Philpot also charged the Brethren with Sandemanianism. "They represent the assurance of faith as the first step in faith; for if faith be a mere assent of the mind to certain facts or evidences, there can be no weak faith where the fact is certain and the evidences clear, as the person of Christ and the truths of the gospel are."[73]

It is important to observe that most of the critics were writing in the post 1859 era, with many works published in the 1870s and beyond.[74] Often the critics' objections stemmed from what they heard from (or about) revival preachers in the movement, who were not always the best represen-

---

69. See Grass, *Gathering to His Name*, 213–28; Coad, *History of the Brethren*, 227–32.

70. Coad comments, "It became the custom in the more respectable Calvinist works of erudition of this period [1870s] to take the odd sniper's long-shot at the Brethren." Coad, *History of the Brethren*, 228.

71. Darby, *Letters*, 3:167. See Stunt, *From Awakening*, 205.

72. Philpot, "Editors' Review," 80.

73. Ibid., 81.

74. See footnote 4 of this chapter for specific dates.

tatives of Brethren thought.[75] For example, the Irish Presbyterian Thomas Croskery was "one of the most indefatigable opponents of Brethrenism,"[76] writing several polemical works against them.[77] Croskery described his perception of the Brethren view of faith as follows: "The Brethren hold the old Sandemanian doctrine, that faith is only belief . . . of God's testimony concerning Christ. They hold likewise that assurance is of the essence of faith. Faith is therefore simply believing 'that Christ died for me' . . . The Brethren, in a word, make the promise, rather than the person of Christ, to be the formal object of faith, while the majority of Christians believe the promise to be the warrant and Christ the object of faith."[78]

True faith was not trust *in* Christ, but accepting biblical propositions *about* Christ, which in turn yielded certainty of salvation: "I believe that I am a believer." Croskery argued that this notion created the real possibility of self-deception and spurious conversions, especially since the Brethren position made self-examination for evidence of spiritual life unnecessary.

On the issue of repentance, Croskery claimed: "It has no place whatever in their *preaching*, except when they warn sinners in this way—'You need not repent—it is not necessary—only come to Christ—repentance hinders the sinner from coming to Christ.'"[79] When Brethren did discuss repentance, according to Croskery, they defined it as merely a change of mind in regard to God—"there is no repentance for *sin* in the Brethren's theology."[80]

William Reid, writing from Edinburgh in 1875, made the rather hyperbolic claim that the Brethren "are opposed to almost every doctrine of Christianity."[81] He complained that they did not speak of "the evil of sin or the necessity of repentance." He claimed that rarely, if ever, was sin presented by the Brethren "as a matter of personal demerit, calling for contrition." He further charged that "repentance, regeneration, the work of the Holy Spirit in the progressive holiness of the saint, are never insisted on; while the doctrine of election, the sovereignty of God, and effectual calling have no recognition whatever."[82]

75. Coad, *History of the Brethren*, 228.

76. Grass, *Gathering to His Name*, 214.

77. Croskery, *Catechism*; Croskery, "The Plymouth Brethren," 48–77; [Croskery], *Plymouth Brethrenism: Its Ecclesiastical and Doctrinal Teachings*; Croskery, *Plymouth-Brethrenism: A Refutation*.

78. Croskery, *Plymouth-Brethrenism: A Refutation*, 108–9.

79. Croskery, *Catechism*, 11.

80. Ibid., 12.

81. Reid, *Plymouth Brethrenism*, v.

82. Ibid., 17.

The Scottish Presbyterian Moir Porteous wrote a popular-level work against the Brethren in the form of a novel. In it he accused the Brethren of espousing an Arminian view of salvation that left out the work of the Holy Spirit—more specifically, that man, "by his own will, co-operates *in giving life* to his soul" and that election is based on the condition "of that voluntary taking of salvation by man himself."[83] Furthermore, faith was reduced to merely "believing what God has said about Jesus." One of the characters opined, "They seem to me to be near of kin to Morrisonians [sic] and Arminians . . . They decide that faith is only an act of the understanding—or, as some call it—a mere intellectual faith. I am afraid they do not remember that 'the devils believe and tremble' . . . We must do more than confess with the mouth that we belong to Christ. We must believe in our hearts if we are to be saved."[84]

The Ulster Presbyterian Thomas Houston acknowledged his debt to the works of Carson,[85] Croskery, and Porteous, and therefore is representative of several critics in his evaluation of Brethren teaching on faith and repentance. He wrote, "Saving faith, according to the Plymouthists and modern Revivalists, is, 'only believing what God has said about Jesus Christ.' They thus make it a mere intellectual act, and a natural gift. Theirs is only the historical faith, such as devils have, when they 'believe and tremble.'"[86] Houston complained that such teaching denies faith is the gift of sovereign grace. He also charged that "there is no more common error among Plymouthists, and a large number of the active agents in modern revivals than that of making the personal *assurance of salvation* to be of the *essence of faith*."[87] According to the "Plymouthists," one should not seek evidence of faith in oneself because works are not necessary to demonstrate faith. He added, "These teachers assert that sinners need only to come to Christ—and that repentance, instead of helping, only hinders their coming. They denounce it, in the strongest terms—calling it 'trash'—'legalism'—'salvation by works.' In their view, Repentance does not consist in contrition of heart,

---

83. Porteous, *Brethren in the Keelhowes*, 159–61. Porteous also included here the notion that Christ died merely to make salvation possible for all, rather than accomplishing actual redemption for the elect.

84. Ibid., 176–77.

85. Carson, *Heresies*. Carson calls Brethrenism "one of the most thoroughly jesuitical systems the world has ever produced;—a system which, in an insidious form, undermines nearly every one of the fundamental doctrines of Christianity as held by our evangelical churches" (6).

86. Houston, *Plymouthism*, 21.

87. Ibid., 22. Houston maintained that assurance is a fruit of saving faith, but not the essence of it.

and godly sorrow for sin—but it is simply a change of mind with respect to the Gospel."[88] Even believers need not seek forgiveness, since all their sins were forgiven through the death of Christ. This point was frequently raised by critics of the Brethren.[89]

A number of critical works were also published in North America. In 1872 the American Presbyterian Robert Dabney wrote a review of Brethren theology. He criticized the movement for "wresting of the doctrine of faith and assurance, and entire depreciation of all subjective marks of a state of grace."[90] If assurance is the essence of faith, as the Brethren insisted, all self-examination and subjective marks of a work of grace in the believer are worthless and absurd. But to elevate the objective work of Christ at the expense of the appropriation of that work in the experience of a believer is to deny the true operations of saving faith. Dabney declared, "The same God who has told us that true faith saves us has also told us that these subjective graces are signs of a saved state."[91]

The charge of Sandemanianism resurfaced in a tract against the Brethren penned by the Canadian clergyman John Nichols. Nichols wrote, "The teaching of the Brethren about faith is deeply tinged with Sandemanianism. With them faith is but an intellectual assent to the doctrines of the Gospel. Christ came to save sinners—that is faith. Christ died for me—that is faith."[92] Furthermore, "Repentance and the agency of the Holy Spirit working out the great purposes of Christian life and character, have no place in their creed."[93]

The preaching of two Brethren evangelists from Scotland, Donald Munro and John Carnie, generated a controversy in South-Western Ontario in 1872–73. The controversy was brought before the public through a series of letters printed in a local newspaper, the *Sarnia Observer*.[94] In a letter to the editor dated February 7, 1873, Mr. George Mill commented

---

88. Ibid., 23. Cf. Croskery, *Catechism*, 11.

89. E.g., Croskery, *Catechism*, 12; Reid, *Plymouth Brethrenism*, 11, 277; *Sarnia Observer* (May 9, 1873), 2.

90. Dabney, "Theology of the Plymouth Brethren," 1:170. The piece originally appeared in *The Southern Presbyterian Review* (January, 1872).

91. Ibid., 1:180.

92. Nichols, *Plymouthism Weighed*, 12.

93. Ibid., 16.

94. The material was collected and edited by Lindsay Reynolds in 1979 under the title, "The Great 'Plymouth Brethren' Controversy in South-Western Ontario, 1872–73." A copy of this material is housed in the United Church of Canada Archives, Toronto, Ontario. An additional copy has been secured by the Emmaus Bible College Library, Dubuque, Iowa. For more on the incident see Stevenson, "Canadian Opposition."

on the meetings held in Warwick, Ontario. He heard the evangelists and was not impressed. "Sinners were never exhorted to repent, but were told again and again that they had nothing to do but believe. We were assured by these gentlemen that when they believed all their sins were pardoned, consequently they never prayed for the forgiveness of sin. Great stress was laid upon being able to tell the exact time when a person was converted, and we were told that if we were not assured that we were saved, we might be assured that we were not saved."[95]

One of the most prominent and vocal opponents of the evangelists was the Rev. James B. Duncan, Presbyterian minister of Forest, Ontario. He wrote several letters that appeared in the *Sarnia Observer* denouncing both the methods and doctrines of Munro and Carnie. He took particular issue with their concept of assurance. "The doctrine of 'perfect Assurance' of salvation, pervades the teachings of Munroe [sic] and Carney [sic]. I question whether they ever preached a sermon in which it did not occupy a prominent place. 'If,' said Munroe one night in our hearing, 'you are not assured of your salvation, conclude that you are not saved; you are on the road to hell!'"[96]

For Duncan, the great mistake of these Brethren was the notion that "assurance is of the nature of saving faith" and is thus "essential to salvation [and] is . . . indispensable to a man's being pardoned and accepted in the sight of God."[97] This was to confuse the assurance of sense (the individual's subjective certainty of his salvation) with the assurance of faith (confidence in God and his word), and thus render meaningless scriptural imperatives to make one's calling and election sure.

Further criticism of Brethren evangelists in Ontario came from Methodists. In 1869 Rev. Edward Dewart castigated Brethren evangelists who had been actively preaching in and around London, Ontario. Among other complaints, Dewart objected to the evangelists' view of faith, which "is merely the reception of an alleged fact by the mind." True saving faith, Dewart countered, "while it pre-supposes the assent of the mind to the truth respecting Christ, is a full trust in the person of a living Saviour."[98] Furthermore, Dewart found it reprehensible that these evangelists told sinners that repentance was unnecessary; that they were only to believe and receive the finished salvation Christ has purchased.

---

95. *Sarnia Observer* (Feb. 7, 1873), 2.
96. Ibid., (April 11, 1873), 2.
97. Ibid., (April 25, 1873), 2.
98. Dewart, *Broken Reeds*, 12–13.

Dewart was not the only Methodist voice objecting to Brethren theology. The president of Canada's leading Methodist institution, Nathanael Burwash, claimed that popular Brethren evangelists reduced the gospel to "an intellectual process" in place of "the deep and regenerative convictions of the Holy Spirit."[99] A Methodist minister in Midland, Ontario, Richard Strachan, was amazed that, according to the Brethren,

> There is no need of contrition for sin, on the part of the sinner, in order to be saved; and no need of prayer for forgiveness, but simply to believe, as if it was possible for a sinner to believe who has not manifested the least degree of penitence. There is nothing said of the true nature of sin, and its exceeding sinfulness... Inquirers, and even persons who are not inquirers, are told that if they simply believe the truth that Jesus died for sinners, they are "saved," and have eternal life.[100]

Strachan further lamented that the Brethren did not teach the need of repentance, and presented saving faith as merely "the assent of the understanding to the testimony of Scripture."[101] Similarly, the American Methodist, Daniel Steele, judged the Brethren to be Sandeman's heirs.[102]

Phyllis Airhart has argued that the Methodists' rejection of the Brethren presentation of conversion is an important factor in understanding why they "either resisted or were ambivalent towards dispensationalism and twentieth-century fundamentalism."[103] But Airhart also notes that the Brethren position was, in part, a response to what they perceived to be errors in the other direction. She reports that Brethren evangelists "disparaged Methodist revivals for requiring a long sorrowing period that led to self-righteousness and made a virtue of feeling."[104] This is an important insight, for certainly some Brethren emphases did constitute reactions to perceived abuses.

---

99. Burwash, *History of Victoria College*, 466–68.

100. Strachan, *Wandering Lights*, 17, 19.

101. Ibid., 23–27.

102. Steele, *Substitute for Holiness*, 100–101.

103. Airhart, "'What Must I Do To Be Saved?'" 375. Airhart is seeking to answer Ernest Sandeen's riddle of why Methodists who embraced dispensationalism felt compelled to sever connections with their denomination. Sandeen, *Roots of Fundamentalism*, 163.

104. Airhart, "'What Must I Do To Be Saved?'" 380, citing "Objections to Methodist Evangelistic Methods," *Christian Guardian* 15 (Feb. 1888), 104.

Evaluating the Critics

One must be wary of accepting the critics' assessment of Brethren theology at face value. Grass cautions, "The teachings which critics so often condemned were not always as widely held within the movement as they asserted."[105] Furthermore, Neatby suggested that many Brethren critics were "generally extremely untrustworthy." He added, "They are commonly passionately prejudiced against the Brethren. For the most part they make the writings of altogether unrepresentative men the basis of their attack, and even these men they have misrepresented."[106] This was certainly the perspective of William Kelly. In response to criticisms of the Brethren, Kelly admitted, "We are in the habit of letting most of these notices pass without a word, especially where their ignorance and coarseness suffice to refute their ill-will; as of Messrs. Carson, Croskery, D. Macintosh, and suchlike."[107] One defender of the Brethren was William Reid, a Presbyterian minister of Carlisle (not to be confused with the William Reid of Edinburgh noted above). He was disturbed by attacks on the Brethren, which he believed had "become so extreme and bold in their misrepresentations as to attack Christianity itself." He therefore wrote "to prove that all the charges of heresies . . . ordinarily preferred against them by their adversaries, are not substantiated."[108] Reid became so persuaded by Brethren teaching that he severed his Presbyterian connections and thereafter associated with the Brethren.[109]

Brethren frequently complained that their critics misrepresented them. John McVicker became the subject of a series of pamphlets after he withdrew as a clergyman in the Eastern Reformed Presbyterian Church—"the strictest of Ireland's dissenting Presbyterian communions"[110]—and joined the Brethren. Among other things, the critics charged him with "holding that Jesus Christ was not made of a woman, and that He is not the believer's righteousness, with denying that believers should confess sin, with denying the obligation of the moral precepts of God's Word . . . with denying repentance, with forbidding Christians to use the Lord's Prayer, with insisting on baptism as necessary to salvation . . . with teaching that men

---

105. Grass, *Gathering to His Name*, 217.

106. Neatby, *History*, 229. Neatby included as examples the critiques by Reid and Carson.

107. Kelly, "Rev. A. Moody Stuart on 'Brethren.'" In a letter to the editor of *The British Herald* (April 1, 1870), Kelly stated, "In general . . . 'Brethren' do not answer attacks made on them, unless they afford a good occasion for stating the truth."

108. [Reid], *Literature and Mission*, 3–4.

109. See Beattie, *Brethren*, 192–93.

110. Gribben, "'The Worst Sect,'" 34.

are saved by believing that they are saved, and not by believing on Christ."[111] McVicker viewed the charges as ridiculous, stating, "We do not hold one of these things, but believe and teach the very opposite."[112]

Alexander Marshall wrote a response to Richard Strachan's negative critique. In the preface, Marshall complained that "Mr Strachan has misunderstood, misinterpreted, misrepresented, and traduced us. He has continued to circulate his book in which false charges are repeated and reiterated, notwithstanding the fact that he has been personally informed that we repudiate doctrines and statements alleged by him to have been taught, held, or made by us."[113]

John Nelson Darby seems to suggest that a number of the attacks launched against the Brethren were in response to "expressions in popular preaching and tracts which overstep scripture."[114] In other words, some Brethren evangelists and popular-level teachers said things that Darby could not endorse as representative of Brethren teaching. His own words here are worth repeating. "Now I have no doubt that, in recent activities, Christians outside and inside 'Brethren' so-called have (in their zeal . . . for winning souls, and delivering them from the state of death in which they were) stated many things less soberly than was right. They have pressed the love of God and the freeness of the gospel in a way which would not bear critical examination. I have no doubt such defects are to be found in their statements."[115]

Evidently, then, the critics did not *always* misrepresent what they heard from Brethren preachers—especially since the post-1859 criticisms found in England, Ireland, Scotland, and North America were so similar. The problem was that a number of these preachers were not the best representatives of Brethren doctrine.

Brethren Perspectives

We come now to analyze Brethren teaching on the nature of saving faith, repentance, and assurance. As with previous chapters, the approach here is both chronological and biographical. We look again at influential writers, teachers, and preachers who had a hand in shaping nineteenth-century

---

111. John G. McVicker, *Salvation by Faith: Set Forth and Vindicated* (1871), cited in Gribben, "'The Worst Sect,'" 35.

112. Ibid.

113. Marshall, *Review*, 2.

114. Darby, *CW* 10:117 (1864).

115. Ibid. This quotation is also cited by Dewart in *Broken Reeds*, 5.

Brethren thought. In order to organize the material in a coherent fashion, the present section also attempts a systematic treatment of the subjects under investigation. Thus we begin with an analysis of Brethren perspectives on saving faith and repentance, and then move to a discussion of the relationship between faith and assurance.

The Nature of Saving Faith and Repentance

As demonstrated above, the Brethren were frequently charged with teaching that the nature of saving faith consists only in mental assent to propositions about the gospel—often called Sandemanianism. They were also accused of either not preaching repentance at all, or diluting it in such a way that it lost its true force. In what follows Brethren views on faith and repentance are evaluated, since they are naturally linked and frequently discussed together in the literature.

John Nelson Darby

Darby rejected Sandemanianism by name. "I admit fully," he wrote, "belief in the truth of scripture may not be saving faith; and it is never the assent of the understanding to propositions. It is not a human thing as Rome makes it; nor mere assent as Sandemanianism would make it."[116] Nevertheless, in defining faith he did not equate it with trust. "I do not believe faith means trust, though I believe trust will infallibly be there if faith is."[117] Darby's separation of faith and trust—making faith more a matter of belief—might open him to the charge of Sandemanianism, but he would not be guilty of the charge. He explained, "True faith is the work of the Holy Ghost in the soul, revealing the object of faith in divine power; so that the heart receives it on divine testimony as divine truth, and a divine fact . . . Faith is the divinely-given perception of things not seen, wrought through the word of God by the Spirit."[118] Again, "Faith is then the real vivid perception of what cannot be known by sight—God, Christ, anything revealed of God, being the object. If there is merely a mental conclusion . . . or assent to a proposition, it is worthless. If it is the revelation of the object of faith to the soul by the Holy Ghost, it is real and living; and this only is true faith."[119]

116. Darby, *CW*, 10:126.
117. Ibid., 125.
118. Ibid., 126.
119. Ibid., 128.

In his discussion of James 2, Darby said, "Faith is a powerful principle, the result of the operation of the Holy Spirit in the heart, a principle which raises it above selfishness and all the base motives of the world, attaching its affections to Christ."[120] Clearly, this amounts to more than mere mental assent to propositions.

Darby's Calvinism informed his view of the place of repentance.[121] For him, faith was a gift of God's grace[122] and thus must precede repentance. Indeed, "all who know what grace is," he asserted, "believe that faith precedes repentance."[123] The unbeliever is unable to repent due to his or her fallen condition. The word of God must enter the soul, revealing the truth and granting the gift of faith, which then brings the person to repentance. An individual "must believe the truth in order to repent. Nothing can be more absurd than putting repentance before faith; for a man then repents believing nothing at all."[124] At the same time, he recognized the vital connection between faith and repentance. He wrote, "You may say that, in one sense, no one can believe fully until he has repented, or repent until he has believed. There must be conviction of sin before forgiveness is received; nor will a sinner ever have conviction of sin until there is something for him to judge sin by, and *that* is what he believes."[125]

Darby understood repentance to be self-judgment of one's sin before God. He wrote, "practical repentance . . . is the estimate a man forms of sin, of his own ways as a sinner, on reflection, through the light of God penetrating into his soul."[126] He was concerned that the revival preaching in his day may have offered a superficial peace to sinners without working true repentance. He argued that in true repentance, "the soul feels it has to do with God responsibly, has failed, been evil, corrupt, without God, is humbled, has a horror of itself and its state; may fear, will surely hope, and eventually, if simple, very soon find peace. But it will say, 'Now mine eye seeth thee, wherefore I abhor myself and repent in dust and ashes.' If there is not this—though the degrees of it may be various, as the form it takes in the soul—there is no true work wrought."[127]

---

120. Darby, *Brief Exposition*, 33.

121. For Darby's view of repentance cf. Dixon, "Pneumatology of John Nelson Darby," 221–25.

122. See for example, Darby, *Synopsis*, 4:426.

123. Darby, *CW*, 10:128.

124. Ibid., 129. Cf. Darby, *Notes and Jottings*, 308–9.

125. Darby, *Notes and Jottings*, 309.

126. Darby, *CW*, 10:224 (1865). Cf. 31:357–58 (1881).

127. Darby, *CW*, 10:226.

He complained that the human-centered character of contemporary preaching undercut the need for repentance: "The peculiar character of much of the gospel preaching nowadays, is, that it presents God as a kind of debtor to the world to save it, and that He must try and get people to pay Him the compliment of believing on Him. Repentance says, 'I am lost, and unless I repent, and believe, I shall be lost entirely.'"[128]

Critics sometimes accused Brethren preachers of minimizing sin; however, that was not true of Darby. In a letter written in 1860 he articulated his approach to evangelistic preaching. While he believed the love of God should have a prominent place, it is love directed to *sinners*. He explained, "All I look for is that the preaching should be such that it should convict of sin, and the impossibility of sin and God going together, so that it should be well understood that there is need of *reconciling*. And here Christ at once comes in, and atonement and righteousness. Holiness precludes all sin from God, righteousness judges it. This I believe the sinner should understand, so that he should know *what love applies to*, yet that love should be fully preached."[129]

By 1876, his views had not changed. He could say, "Both sides of the gospel ought to be preached, and personal conviction of sin too, or repentance only founded on grace."[130] Toward the end of his life, in 1881, he affirmed, "The insisting on real exercise about sin for peace I believe to be useful in these days; there is great looseness and carelessness as to it." He added, "The insisting on reality [sic] of repentance I believe to be timely in these days."[131]

Darby could not endorse some of the contemporary revival preaching. In 1867 he wrote, "In the late revival, not among brethren as much as elsewhere, but generally, there was unscriptural language, I judge, as to repentance and sanctification. The reaction against error over-stepped the bounds of scripture."[132] There is evidence to suggest that he did not always approve the preaching of Brethren evangelists either. In an 1869 lecture from Guelph, Ontario he complained that evangelists were far too willing to accept a superficial kind of faith as legitimate. "But," he corrected, "it is only the deep-rooted seed that God accepts, and that which *brings forth fruit*."[133]

128. Darby, *Notes and Jottings*, 308.
129. Darby, *Letters*, 1:301.
130. Ibid., 3:444.
131. Ibid., 3:167–68.
132. Ibid., 3:380.
133. Darby, *Additional Writings*, 2:266. The lecture was delivered on September 29, 1869.

A few years later, in 1873, he acknowledged that "considerable activity has existed in seeking souls, as in Canada and elsewhere, a good deal independently of our position in these last days, and the character of the gospel had not much connection with it."[134] The comment is not entirely clear, but later in the same piece he complained of "the kind of gospel which knew nothing beyond a soul getting safe, and with little depth of action on the conscience." From Darby's perspective, true preaching must prick the conscience and bring conviction of sin.

On another occasion he lamented "the superficiality of revivalism,"[135] specifically naming the activity of Moody and Sankey. Although he confessed that God's hand was in the work and genuine conversions had occurred, nevertheless he believed it to be "a very shallow work, and encourage[d] shallowness and worldly Christianity." Darby further objected that Moody denied "all grace in conversion"—meaning, the American evangelist upheld human free will and ability, a doctrine he disdained. But he also complained that in Moody's preaching, "None were condemned for their sins, only for not believing—a pretty common notion now." For Darby this was problematic, because it did not deal with a person's conscience before God.[136]

These comments indicate that Darby could not endorse all that the evangelists and revival preachers were saying. Thus it becomes difficult to speak of *the* Brethren view of conversion, or *the* Brethren view of faith and repentance, as some of the Brethren evangelists were advancing notions of the gospel that the most prominent Brethren teachers did not sanction.

Henry William Soltau

In a discussion of the Philippian jailor's great cry, "What must I do to be saved?" (Acts 16:30), Soltau noted, "The apostle did not direct the jailor to pray for salvation . . . neither did Paul tell him that, after much repentance and amendment of life, he might hope in the end to be saved; but he pointed him at once to salvation, present, ready, and immediate, as soon as the poor convicted sinner trusted in the Saviour."[137] This statement provides an example of the message of "instant" salvation that some critics found so objectionable. In context, however, Soltau was not denying the need for repentance. After all, he described the man as a "poor convicted sinner." Soltau had drawn attention earlier in his discussion to the fact that the jailor

---

134. Darby, *Letters*, 2:227.
135. Ibid., 2:334. The letter is dated February 20, 1875.
136. Ibid., 2:328.
137. Soltau, *The Soul and Its Difficulties*, 11–12.

was "aroused to a sense of his lost state" and that his "ruined state" had "burst upon his conscience."[138] Clearly he was under conviction, and this sense of his own sin and need was what prompted him to pose his famous question.

Soltau was challenging the idea that a long period of preparation was necessary before a person could be saved. The jailor "had not to wait in uncertainty for days and weeks; it was not necessary for him to go hither or thither to hear many sermons or discourses; but he simply believed God; that is, he trusted in the Saviour whom God had sent."[139] Indeed, the answer the jailor received ("Believe on the Lord Jesus Christ, and thou shalt be saved") proved the apostle himself preached "immediate" salvation.

C. H. Mackintosh

Mackintosh maintained that true faith is something "wrought in the soul of a sinner, by the power of the Holy Ghost." He explicitly denied that saving faith is simply a matter of intellectual assent to biblical propositions. Indeed, such a position "is fearfully false. It makes the question of faith human, whereas it is really divine. It reduces it to the level of man, whereas it really comes from God."[140]

In 1878 Mackintosh wrote a series of articles on the nature of conversion in which he stressed the deeply rooted character of saving faith.

> A person may be intellectually delighted—almost entranced with the glorious doctrines of grace, a full, free gospel, salvation without works, justification by faith; in short, all that goes to make up our glorious New Testament Christianity. A person may profess to believe and delight in this; he may even become a powerful writer in defence of Christian doctrine . . . and yet the man be wholly unconverted, dead in trespasses and sins, hardened, deceived and destroyed by his very familiarity with the precious truths of the gospel—truths that have never gone beyond the region of his understanding—never reached his conscience, never touched his heart, never converted his soul.[141]

---

138. Ibid., 10.

139. Ibid., 12.

140. Mackintosh, *Notes on the Book of Genesis*, 68. Likewise, in 1884 William Lincoln affirmed, "Assent is not faith. A person may hear, and approve, and in his mind assent, but that is not faith." He decried such a position as part of the "popular and spurious theology of the day." Lincoln, "Is it necessary?" 75.

141. Mackintosh, *Miscellaneous Writings*, 4:17–18 ("Conversion").

Unless there is a work of grace in the heart—not simply assent of the mind—true conversion has not taken place. Mackintosh worried that false conversions were all too common in his day. He contended, "Many profess to be converted, and are accredited as such, who prove to be merely stony-ground hearers. There is no depth of spiritual work in the heart, no real action of the truth of God on the conscience, no thorough breaking with the world." If there is no true repentance, and if there is an ongoing "clinging to earth and nature," then no true work of God has taken place in the soul.[142]

Mackintosh felt the need to sound this warning particularly for evangelists who, in their zeal for converts, may rely too much on "the merely human element" in their work. He complained, "We do not leave the Spirit of God to act . . . There may be too much effort to work on the feelings, too much of the emotional and the sensational." He then suggested, "Perhaps, too, in our desire to reach results . . . we are too ready to accredit and announce, as cases of conversion, many which, alas! are merely ephemeral."[143] Yet this warning ought not to lessen the evangelists' zeal; it should make them more dependent on God and more earnest in prayer.

> We shall feel more deeply the divine seriousness of the work, and our own utter insufficiency. We shall ever cherish the wholesome conviction that the work must be of God from first to last. This will keep us in our right place, that of self-emptied dependence upon God . . . We shall be more on our faces before the mercy-seat . . . in reference to the glorious work of conversion; and then . . . when genuine cases of conversion turn up—cases which speak for themselves, and carry their own credentials with them to all who are capable of judging—then verily shall our hearts be filled with praise to the God of all grace who has magnified the name of His Son Jesus Christ in the salvation of precious souls.[144]

The Calvinistic tone is unmistakeable. This is not to suggest that he endorsed the Puritan morphology, for he claimed, "There are hardly two cases of conversion alike. Some go through exercises of soul before they come to Christ, others after. It is the Christ I reach, and not the way I reach Him, that saves my soul."[145] Neither was he a supporter of the "new measures" often associated with Charles Finney. The apostolic evangelistic efforts in Thessalonica provided the ideal model: "A blessed divine work—all real, the

---

142. Ibid., 19.
143. Ibid.,19–20.
144. Ibid., 20.
145. [Mackintosh], "Correspondence," 195.

genuine fruit of God's Spirit. It was no mere religious excitement, nothing sensational, no high pressure, no attempt to 'get up a revival.'"[146] Furthermore, he viewed the conversion of the Thessalonians as paradigmatic of true conversion, since "there was a complete break with the past, a turning back, once and forever, on their former life and habits; a thorough surrender of all those objects that had ruled their hearts and commanded their energies." What made the Thessalonians' conversion so authentic was the fact that "it was not a mere change of opinion, or the reception of a new set of principles, a certain alteration in their intellectual views." Far more critically, it was the deep conviction that their former manner of life must be abandoned. Thus "there was an out-and-out surrender of that world which had hitherto ruled their hearts' affections; not a shred of it was to be spared."[147]

What is noteworthy here is that Mackintosh clearly embraced a vigorous doctrine of repentance, while at the same time rejecting a mere notional view of saving faith. Yet critics of the Brethren regularly upbraided them for not preaching repentance and for reducing faith to intellectual assent. Mackintosh, the supposed popularizer of Brethren theology, simply does not fit the mold.[148] He recognized, however, that much of the popular evangelism of the time did not preach repentance, and he wrote to combat the practice as a serious error. Ostensibly, preaching repentance introduced a legal requirement that tarnished the luster of the gospel of the grace. To Mackintosh, such an argument was "vanity and folly, or worse," since the Lord himself preached repentance and commissioned his disciples to do the same.[149] He then lamented the current state of gospel preaching in strong terms: "We are inclined to judge that there is a sad lack of depth and seriousness in much of our modern preaching. In our anxiety to make the gospel simple, and salvation easy, we fail to press on the consciences of our hearers the holy claims of truth."[150] He continued:

> We greatly dread the light, airy, superficial style of much of our modern preaching. It sometimes seems to us as if the gospel were brought into utter contempt and the sinner led to suppose that he is really conferring a very great favour upon God in accepting salvation at His hands. Now we most solemnly protest

---

146. Mackintosh, *Miscellaneous Writings*, 4:25 ("Conversion").

147. Ibid., 26–27.

148. Nor did the popular evangelistic tracts of Emily Gosse (1806–57). See for example, Mrs. P. H. Gosse, "The Suicide," in Gosse, *Narrative Tracts*, no. 16.

149. Mackintosh, *Miscellaneous Writings*, 4:7 ("The Great Commission"). He defined true repentance as "the solemn judgment of ourselves, our condition, and our ways, in the presence of God" (9).

150. Ibid., 10

against this. It is dishonouring to God, and lowering His gospel; and . . . its moral effect on those who profess to be converted is most deplorable. It superinduces levity, self-indulgence, worldliness, vanity, and folly. Sin is not felt to be the dreadful thing it is in the sight of God. Self is not judged. The world is not given up. The gospel that is preached is what may be called "salvation made easy" to the flesh—the most terrible thing we can possibly conceive . . . the consequence is, those who profess to be converted by this gospel exhibit a lightness and unsubduedness perfectly shocking to people of serious piety.[151]

Did Mackintosh have Brethren preachers in mind? Certainly they would be included, since he was writing in a Brethren magazine[152] and made no attempt to suggest that only preachers outside the movement fell under his censure. Indeed, his use of the first person—"*our* modern preachers"—may suggest it was those within the movement he had in view.

Brethren evangelists who ignored or minimized repentance were charting their own course; there was nothing inherent in Brethren ecclesiology, eschatology, or dispensationalism that compelled them to do so. As Exclusive Brethren leader C. E. Stuart asserted, "At all times after the fall, and under all dispensations, repentance on the part of fallen man was needful. Dispensational teaching does not do away with it; the fullest grace does not supersede it; for, side by side with the proclamation of forgiveness of sins, the Lord Jesus, when risen, commissioned His apostles to preach it."[153] Like Darby, Kelly, and Mackintosh, Stuart decried the neglect of preaching repentance by the evangelists of his day. "Amid the now widely spread proclamation of God's grace to sinners, is not repentance sometimes overlooked? Is there not too with some a jealousy lest the preaching of it should detract from the freeness of that grace? Such clearly was not the case in apostolic times, nor should it be the case now."[154]

What, then, does true gospel preaching look like? What effects will it display in those who come under its power? Mackintosh explained:

---

151. Ibid., 12.
152. The piece originally appeared in *TNO* 20 (1877).
153. Stuart, "Repentance," 153.
154. Ibid. Stuart believed the apostolic pattern was not repentance "as preparatory to faith, nor faith without repentance; but repentance and faith." Although Stuart was Calvinistic in his view of repentance ("it is God's gift . . . bestowed by the risen and ascended Christ"), he was not in lockstep with the Reformed tradition for he did not view the preaching of the law as necessary to repentance. "Saints before the giving of the law experienced [repentance], as well as Gentiles who never were under it." Ibid.

> Man must take his true place before God, and that is the place of self-judgment, contrition of heart, real sorrow for sin, and true confession. It is here the gospel meets him. The fullness of God ever waits on an empty vessel, and a truly repentant soul is the empty vessel into which all the fullness and grace of God can flow in saving power. The Holy Ghost will make the sinner feel and own his real condition. It is He alone who can do so: but He uses preaching to this end. He brings the Word of God to bear on man's conscience. The Word is His hammer, wherewith He breaks the rock in pieces—His plowshare, wherewith He breaks up the fallow ground.[155]

William Kelly

Of all the Brethren writers, William Kelly was the one who repudiated Sandemanianism by that specific label most explicitly. In a response to a correspondent in the *Bible Treasury*, he rejected the traditional Reformed approach, which viewed repentance as necessarily flowing from preaching the law. Yet he was also careful to reject what he considered to be a greater error. He wrote,

> Others in their desire to set forth the freeness of grace, have fallen into the Sandemanian trap of denying the distinctively moral character of repentance, and thus reduce it to a changed mind about *God*. Whereas grace works so that in faith the eye of the soul looks to Christ as the Saviour, and in repentance that eye looks at self and judges what it is and has done as before God. Faith and repentance are inseparable: if one is divinely given, so is the other; if the repentance is human, the faith is no better.[156]

In Kelly's assessment, an intellectualist view of faith was devoid of the Spirit. "The word without the Spirit of God always ends in intellectualism, Sandemanianism, or rationalism."[157] He employed strong language to denounce what critics of the Brethren often accused them of teaching: "It

---

155. Mackintosh, *Miscellaneous Writings*, 4:12–13 ("The Great Commission").

156. Kelly, "To Correspondents," 176. The same issue (*BT* 12 [1878]) contains a piece by Kelly which strongly advocated preaching repentance. He argued that true repentance brings the conviction of sin in the presence of God so that "we no longer excuse ourselves nor do we desire to do so. The result is confession to God by a conscience which feels itself in His presence . . . while the heart restored desires holiness and the soul feels its responsibility for all that we have done." Kelly, "From Troas to Miletus," 171.

157. Kelly, "Hold Fast," 128.

is granted that there is no true faith without repentance, and that what is commonly called Sandemanianism or Walkerism is in this utterly wrong. All efforts to obliterate repentance, in order to ease or simplify believing in Christ, are false, evil, and dangerous. They slight the work of God in the conscience and reduce faith to intellectualism."[158]

For Kelly, repentance "is a matter of conscience in the light of God, and not a purely intellectual process."[159] Thus in preaching, a call to repentance is essential. In the following passage, Kelly commented on the tendency of evangelists to dilute the nature of faith in the interests of gaining converts. "In urging faith on the lost, repentance is sometimes apparently lost sight of. But there is no true saving faith without repentance. Faith (so-called) without self-judgment is nothing more than the mere assent of the natural mind, not a Spirit-formed faith in the heart . . . When the sun of tribulation arises, this kind of human belief withers away."[160] The concern over what popular evangelists were actually preaching was not infrequently raised by respected Brethren teachers.

Donald Ross

Ross is an important case study, for he was a leading Brethren evangelist. As previously noted (chapter 4), before he joined the Brethren in 1871, Ross led an evangelistic association in the north-east of Scotland which gave him a great deal of experience with revival preaching. After joining the Brethren, he continued as an indefatigable pioneer evangelist.[161]

Ross's own conversion provides some insight into his understanding of salvation. After several days of being troubled in soul, he cried to God for mercy, but found no relief. He concluded that he was lost and could do nothing for his salvation—which he later viewed as an essential lesson that all sinners must learn. Suddenly, his mind was directed to the cross, where he thought of the blood of Jesus Christ being shed on his behalf. His own words tell the rest of the story:

> Instantly I comprehended what SUBSTITUTION meant. The work was done. Christ died for my sins eighteen hundred years ago, and the way of God to me was opened up, and so was my way to God. I closed with Christ there and then as my own personal Saviour. I trusted Him. I received Him. I rested on Him.

158. Kelly, *Christian Worship*, 12.
159. Kelly, *Notes . . . Romans*, 29.
160. [Kelly], "Thoughts on Ephesians," 330.
161. See Ross, *Donald Ross*.

The glorious truth flashed before me, "Christ died for my sins." That is how I was saved.[162]

While this is no mere intellectual assent to propositions, it does reflect the "instant salvation" that Ross and his band of evangelists preached and which so irked the clergy.[163] Although Ross firmly believed that a person could be instantly saved (and sure of it) by trusting in the person and finished work of Christ, he was no proponent of "easy-believism." He denounced "sham conversions" and well-meaning evangelists who "think people are converted when they are not even convicted." He suggested, "A little more knowledge of human nature in its depth of depravity, hypocrisy, and pride would be useful as a preventive in ministering to such."[164] Ross then gave an extended discussion of the nature of conversion, which proved to be more robust than the critics frequently charged.

> If we consider the nature of conversion, we will find it neither a small matter nor an easy matter. It goes to the marrow and intents of the heart. It is a cutting off the old stock and engrafting into Christ, a blasting of a person's chief idol—self, a self-crucifixion, a stripping of every rag of self-righteousness, a making naked, naked, lost, lost [sic], just to be willing to be saved by grace.
>
> This work of cleaning out the foundation is gradual, or it may be abrupt. It may be six months or sixty minutes. When it is abrupt, it is a very hell. Then comes peace—when? When we receive Christ. Out of self into Christ—all our good things thrown overboard, and saved by grace. God does not speak peace before, and never will. It is not peace in the work of the Spirit, or feelings, or in the change in us. True peace is to be found at the Cross, and never anywhere else—a closing with Christ. This is true conversion, and all who do not come this length are still under the curse, and their religion has no root; therefore it will wither as soon as anything turns up to try it.[165]

---

162. Ibid., 22. Donald Munro, had a similar conversion experience. See Ritchie, *Donald Munro*, 15–16.

163. Ross was equally troubled by the lack of gospel preaching in the churches. He wrote, "There are many thousands in our land who never heard the Gospel. Thousands of our kirk-goers never heard God's Gospel, though they may have heard 'Let us seek;' 'Let us be earnest;' 'Let us pray earnestly,' &c., and all that kind of thing, but that is not the Gospel which is the power of God to salvation." [Ross], "Monthly Report," 7.

164. Ross, *Donald Ross*, 25.

165. Ibid., 25–26. Cf. the discussion in [Ross], "Not Feeling but Knowing," 9–12, 18–20, 38–41.

Contrary to what some evangelists were preaching, Ross could say, "It is no evidence of any one being saved that they believe that Christ died for their sins. There are many who believe Christ died for them, or at least say so, who are not saved . . . The evidence of salvation is a new birth, and if there is no new birth there is no salvation."[166]

Donald Munro, a fellow evangelist who worked with and under Ross for many years, testified to the power of his biblical preaching. He claimed that Ross was not "an anecdote preacher" who preyed upon his hearers' natural sympathies, nor did he attempt to intellectually reason them into a profession of salvation with "their consciences never having been awakened or ploughed up by the ploughshare of the Word of God in the hand of the Spirit."[167] This is a significant comment for its insight not only into the character of Ross's preaching, but also into Munro's idea of what evangelistic preaching should be. Munro himself was accused of holding out an intellectualist view of faith, but both he and Ross evidently rejected that position.[168] Ross did not even like the expression "decided for Christ" in connection with conversion because of its intellectualist and Arminian overtones. He wrote,

> Becoming a Christian is not a matter of cold, calculating, intellectual choice. Jesus says, "No man can come to me except the Father who sent me draw him" (John 6:44, 45, 65). The Father who sent the Son has to draw the sinner . . . phrases as he "decided for Christ" or she "decided for Christ" are altogether fleshy, and savour strongly of "moral suasion" and carnal reasonings as to the doctrine only. A professor making use of that phrase in relation to his or her own supposed conversion is to be suspected till full proof is given of the radical change—become a new creature.[169]

Statements like these make the criticisms of those who charged Ross's Northern Evangelistic Society (NES) with teaching propositional faith ring a bit hollow. The Free Church's Hugh McIntosh, in his tract against the NES, claimed its preachers defined faith as, "Believe that you are saved, and then you are saved."[170] It is no wonder that Ross dismissed such criticism as fol-

---

166. [Ross], "Answers to Correspondents," 139.

167. Ross, *Donald Ross*, 103.

168. See the summary of Munro's manner of preaching and view of true conversion—which, according to Ritchie, was strongly Calvinistic—in Ritchie, *Donald Munro*, 10–12.

169. [Ross], "Notes of Questions and Answers," 154.

170. McIntosh, *The New Prophets*, 12. Ritchie described the piece as largely

lows: "The misrepresentations of things said and the positive falsehoods circulated about us, do credit, certainly, to the inventors' imagination, but not to their character."[171] Reformed critics should have had no reason to object to Ross's Calvinistic understanding of conversion.

Edward Dennett

In a brief discussion of Rom 10:10–11,[172] Dennett commented upon the nature of saving faith. Not only did he disavow that faith is simply the mind agreeing with certain facts, but he affirmed the Calvinist position that faith is produced by the Holy Spirit. He wrote, "It is heart belief; that is, a real inward heart conviction, not mere intellectual assent, a faith in God's testimony concerning His beloved Son which is divinely produced by the Holy Spirit."[173]

In an earlier article (1886), Dennett insisted that repentance and faith "should be conjoined in preaching the gospel to sinners." He added, "Whether repentance has been sufficiently insisted on, or whether the essential bond between repentance and faith has been maintained in modern evangelistic preaching, we do not here enquire."[174] Yet the very fact he felt compelled to clarify that his purpose was *not* to address the status of "modern evangelistic preaching" indicates that it was an issue of concern for some.

For Dennett, like Darby, repentance is a self-judgment of one's sin before God. True repentance "involves our hatred of sin, inasmuch as the moment, through grace, we side with God in His judgment upon our deeds . . . When we thus repent, we justify God and condemn ourselves." Such repentance is awakened in the presence of God "when His light, the light of His holiness, reveals sin to us as it appears in His sight."[175]

Despite claiming he would not deal with the question of repentance in modern preaching, he could not resist making the following comment: "Repentance is so little preached, and the forgiveness of sins, or, in other cases,

---

"misrepresentations and stories received from enemies of the work." Ritchie, *Donald Munro*, 54.

171. Ross, *Donald Ross*, 50.

172. "For with the heart man believeth unto righteousness; and with the mouth confession is made unto salvation. For the scripture saith, Whosoever believeth on him shall not be ashamed."

173. Dennett, "Scripture Notes," 35.

174. Dennett, "Simple Christian Truths," 152.

175. Ibid., 154–55.

eternal life, without even raising the question of sin, is so often pressed upon souls—especially in so-called revival preaching—that many appear to be converted with scarcely any exercise as to the state of their souls before God, almost without ever having had the burden of sin upon their conscience."[176] Dennett did not approve of such preaching and considered that those "converted" under this kind of preaching "will have conscience-work as to sin sooner or later."

F. W. Grant

Grant responded directly to the criticism of Daniel Steele in his work against the Brethren, *A Substitute for Holiness, or Antinomianism Revived; or the Theology of the So-Called Plymouth Brethren Examined and Refuted*. Steele charged the Brethren with a view of faith akin to Sandemanianism,[177] to which Grant took considerable exception.

> We do not account that saving faith is "a bare, intellectual, impenitent (!) apprehension" at all. And I boldly challenge Dr. S to prove we do, not by fragmentary quotations from nameless writers, but by honest proof from accepted leaders among us . . . We all believe that a fruitless faith is no faith, and the best proof that Dr. S. has NOT found faith to be defined as a mere intellectual assent in our writings is that he has not produced it. The writings are easily to be found. They are in honest black and white, and know not how to prevaricate or deal falsely in the matter. The charge on Dr. Steele's part is a rash and unworthy charge, and nothing else.[178]

Grant's rebuttal to the charge of Sandemanian faith is significant in its claim that none of the "accepted leaders" among the Brethren held such a position. The vast body of literature these leaders had produced was called as a witness against Steele's charges. Furthermore, Grant rejected Steele's charge that repentance is not necessary to saving faith by stating plainly: "There is no true faith without repentance, no true repentance apart from faith."[179]

Grant's claim is consistent with the evidence considered in this chapter. We have noted, however, that many of these "accepted leaders" were

---

176. Ibid., 157–58.
177. Steele, *Substitute for Holiness*, 100.
178. Grant, *Miscellaneous Writings*, 2:21 ("Christian Holiness").
179. Ibid., 2:18.

themselves critical of evangelists within the movement who were presenting the gospel in ways the Brethren "fathers" did not approve, and who were giving rise to the criticisms of Steele and others.

John R. Caldwell

The industrious Brethren editor sought to distance himself from the notion that faith consists of bare assent to gospel facts—though his position on repentance would not likely assuage the critics. Responding to a question about the meaning of repentance, Caldwell defined it as a change of mind toward God. It is also a change of mind regarding the "dead works" in which the sinner was previously trusting for salvation. He wrote, "This is enough to show that it is something far deeper than a mere mental assent to the truth of the Gospel as to a mathematical problem."[180] It includes a change of plan and attitude toward God. Repentance will inevitably lead to sorrow for sin—but sorrow is the *result* of repentance, not repentance itself.

Toward the end of the century, Caldwell ran in *The Witness* a strong Calvinistic answer to the question, "Is faith in the Lord Jesus Christ (by which we are saved) an involuntary action?" The answer (written by "J. M.") began, "Faith is the voluntary act of the renewed will," but the author clarified that faith is the gift of God, since humanity in its natural condition refuses to come to God.[181] Caldwell added the following editorial comment:

> God never deals with man as a mere machine. His way is so to operate by His Spirit . . . as to show man his guilt and need, and so to make him willing to believe what otherwise, owing to the innate enmity of his heart against God, he would treat with indifference or contempt, and in any case with unbelief. The first motion towards salvation is, therefore, of God's grace, and not of the will of man. But the full guilt of unbelief is charged against the sinner . . . Unbelief is the sin which above all others demonstrates the revolted will [and] the enmity of the carnal mind.[182]

While human responsibility is here maintained, faith is ultimately produced by God's sovereign grace.

---

180. [Caldwell], "Question 164," 48.
181. J. M., "Faith: Is It Involuntary?" 67–68.
182. [Caldwell], "Faith: Is It Involuntary?" 68, editor's note.

James Campbell (1841–1904)

James Campbell was another influential Brethren evangelist whose own ministry was deeply shaped by that of Donald Ross. Campbell labored in Scotland, Ireland, and North America. William Gilmore testified, "I have never known him to speak without sinners being aroused, convicted of sin, and converted to God . . . It was said concerning him 'He was a man who would have made you afraid of sin if he looked at you.'"[183] Gilmore claimed that Campbell "started about forty assemblies" in Northern Ireland.[184]

In 1883 Campbell participated in the Brethren conference in Chicago, which addressed the issue of true conversion in contrast to, as Ritchie put it, "the superficial profession which everywhere abounds."[185] Campbell argued that genuine conversion involves the work of the Holy Spirit penetrating deep into the soul and bringing lasting change. Ritchie reported that "some considered his tests of conversion too severe, and feared that weak and untaught believers might be upset or plunged into darkness, by the strong and searching character of his teaching . . . but no doubt it was greatly needed."[186]

At the Hamilton (Ontario) Conference in January of 1884, Campbell rebuked Brethren preachers for manipulating their hearers with a simplistic faith and a flawed view of conversion.

> Presbyterians have as a rule got a gradual process like the men in 2d Tim. iii and 7. ever learning and never coming to the knowledge of the truth. Methodists have a moment perhaps at the penitent bench, a few happy feelings and they are saved. Baptists are pretty much the same, etc., etc. But there is a more dangerous thing still—we read, John iii. 16, and make them believe because they believe it they are saved. Those deceived by us thus are the most hopeless of any—with the word of God you can soon get a Presbyterian to see the error of his way, but to those who have got the word of God so upon their tongue, it is almost impossible. This thing commenced with Morrisonians [sic], then us, and the sects have copied it.[187]

Campbell's comments indicate that some of the evangelists were indeed guilty of what their critics had charged them with teaching. We have

---

183. Gilmore, *These Seventy Years*, 20.
184. Ibid., 21.
185. Ritchie, *James Campbell*, 58.
186. Ibid.
187. "Notes taken," 44.

seen enough examples of other Brethren writers, however, to conclude that the evangelists reprimanded by Campbell were not broadly representative of Brethren teaching. Nevertheless, examples of the kind of approach that Campbell censured occasionally can be found in Brethren publications. For example, an 1876 article in *God's Glad Tidings* contained the following conversation between a Brethren evangelist and a young woman who was unsure of her salvation:

> "You believe that He died on the cross for us?" "Yes."
>
> "That He bore *all* our sins there?" "Yes."
>
> "That He bore yours as well as mine?" "Yes."
>
> "Well, then, the Lord says, *you are saved*, you *have* eternal life, you have got it *now*."[188]

This exchange demonstrates that some Brethren were capable of teaching an intellectualist notion of faith. The mistake the critics made was in assuming that such a position was normative Brethrenism. But as Grant argued, this was not the view of the most recognized teachers in the movement.

George Cutting

As stated in chapter 4, Cutting's bestselling evangelistic tract, *Safety, Certainty and Enjoyment*, was widely used and had run to eight million copies by 1932. In it he raised the common question, "How may I be sure that I have the right kind of faith?" Cutting answered: "It is not a question of the amount of your faith but the trustworthiness of the person you repose your confidence in."[189] Believing in Christ means distrusting self and safely confiding in Christ, calmly relying on his word, and confidently resting "in the eternal efficacy of His finished work."[190] Reposing, confiding, relying upon, and resting in Christ are expressions incompatible with Sandemanian faith. Nevertheless, Cutting emphasized the object of faith, not its subjective nature. He urged the anxious who doubted the strength of their faith to look outside of themselves. "Faith," he argued, "ever looks outside to a living Person and His finished work, and quietly listens to the testimony of a faithful God about both."[191]

188. I., "Can You Say You Are Saved?" 186.
189. Cutting, *Safety, Certainty*, 13.
190. Ibid., 14.
191. Ibid., 17.

In another tract, Cutting raised the question of whether it is possible to believe with the head but not the heart. "Alas!" he replied, "it is to be feared that there is too much of it." He explained: "To believe on Him in your heart, is simply to believe on Him with the consciousness in your heart, that He alone is the One who can meet your case, and that without Him you will perish for ever; and so to confide in Him. It is more than a mere assent to the historical fact that He died and rose again. It is to see yourself, *without* His precious sacrifice, hopelessly shut up to judgment, and so to believe in Him."[192]

Again, this explicit rejection of an intellectualist version of faith by a respected Brethren evangelist helps us understand why Brethren frequently complained that their critics had misrepresented them.

David Rea (1845–1916)

Henry Pickering, editor of *The Witness*, described Rea's preaching as "spiritual electricity." He claimed that it was worth walking some distance "to hear his burning words of Gospel Grace flowing forth with a natural eloquence, a spiritual penetration, a deepening intensity, and a soul-convicting, soul-awakening, soul-converting force which we have never seen equalled in any of our Gospel halls before or since."[193]

Recounting his own conversion, which occurred in 1869, Rea confessed to being a terrible sinner. Yet not unlike Martin Luther's experience, a fierce thunderstorm arrested him and filled him with fear of the judgment of God. He endured several weeks of "preparation," under deep conviction of sin. He admitted, "I would have given worlds, had I possessed them, to know my sins forgiven."[194] At a Methodist meeting, Rea went forward to the penitent bench and was told that all he needed to do was believe the word of God. Rea persuaded himself that he was saved, but in reality he was not, and shortly thereafter he returned to his sinful ways. One evening, following weeks of anguish, he was lying restlessly on his bed when suddenly the words of 2 Cor 5:20–21[195] "flashed across" his mind. He recalled: "I felt as though I was standing at the Cross on the day that Christ died, and as I gazed upon His pierced hands and side, the words kept sounding in my ears: 'Be ye reconciled to God,' and I thought that Jesus looked down upon me and said: 'Could I give more for you? I have given my life. Will

192. C[utting], *Helps for Enquirers*, 16–17.
193. Pickering, "Home-call of a Warrior," 132.
194. Rea, *Life and Labours*, 19.
195. "Be ye reconciled to God. For he hath made him to be sin for us, who knew no sin; that we might be made the righteousness of God in him."

this not satisfy you?' This was new to me, as I had thought it was I who had to satisfy God."[196]

Immediately he felt the change in his heart and he knew he was saved. This experience deeply shaped his own practice as a preacher. Years later, as a seasoned evangelist, he reflected on the counsel he had initially received at the penitent bench to simply "believe." Rea now considered this to be "an error which thousands make, and which many earnest servants of God make—the mistake of dwelling too much on the word *believe* and failing to put Christ and His Work on the Cross before the anxious soul."[197] Perhaps he had observed other Brethren evangelists make this mistake,[198] but Rea determined he would not. James Hutchinson testified that "Mr. Rea had a wholesome fear of making spurious converts, and discouraged after meetings of the sort in which people are asked to stand up, profess faith, sign covenant cards, and such like. He preached the Word solemnly and faithfully, leaving God to do His own work, which He never fails to do."[199] Revival frequently followed his preaching. And yet we observe for the purposes of the present chapter that Rea always preached for the conviction of sin.[200] Furthermore, he did not urge his hearers to merely believe biblical propositions; he admonished them to trust *Christ* and his finished work.

Alexander Marshall

As previously observed, Marshall is an interesting figure for our study because he held Arminian views, which was unusual for Brethren leaders in the nineteenth century.[201] On the nature of faith, Marshall denied the charge of Sandemanianism. He wrote, "Mr S[trachan] accuses us of representing faith as the 'assent of the understanding to the truth of the Scripture.' A man may 'assent' to all the doctrines of the Scripture and be eternally lost." For Marshall, faith "is the empty hand accepting God's unspeakable gift; the eye of the soul which looks to the Lord Jesus."[202] Some of Marshall's other assertions, however, could be construed in a Sandemanian way. In his widely published tract, *God's Way of Salvation*, he made a distinction between believing a great deal *about* Jesus and believing *on* him for oneself.

196. Rea, *Life and Labours*, 23.
197. Ibid., 20.
198. He had worked on occasion with Alexander Marshall, for example. Ibid., 142.
199. Hutchinson, *Whose Praise Is in the Gospel*, 348.
200. This is a frequent theme in Rea, *Life and Labours*, e.g., 134.
201. *DSCHT*, s.n. "Alexander Marshall."
202. Marshall, *Review*, 7.

Believing Jesus died on Calvary for sinners was not sufficient. Believing Christ died *"on account of your sins"* is what saves.[203] Furthermore, Marshall rejected the idea that there was a right or wrong way to believe. He wrote, "Men may speak about a 'living faith' and a 'dead faith,' a 'saving faith' and an 'intellectual faith,' but Scripture speaks of *believing* what God says. Faith in man and faith in God are the same exercises of mind; the difference is not in the faith, but *in the person* on whom the faith terminates."[204] Here faith is an exercise of the mind. One believes a man who says he is a medical doctor and can therefore treat his illness. Yet when one believes that Jesus died for his sins, he is saved, for *God* has said it. What may narrowly rescue this concept of faith from Sandemanianism is Marshall's insistence that the faith is ultimately in God and not simply in propositions. Yet at other times, Marshall was not so careful. In explaining the gospel to an elderly woman, he told her that the Lord Jesus had paid sin's penalty and that God was satisfied with what Christ had done. Therefore, "the *very moment* she really believed this, that He had taken *her* place and suffered for *her*, she would be saved."[205] On another occasion he wrote, "Paul's Gospel was a Gospel of *facts*, not reasonings. It was not primarily an *offer*, nor an *invitation*, but the *positive statement of accomplished facts* regarding the death, burial, and resurrection of Christ."[206]

Marshall's view of repentance may have given further traction to the Sandemanian accusation, for he taught an intellectualist view of repentance devoid of emotion. He rejected his critic's concept of repentance, which consisted in "penitential sorrow for sin and forsaking of it and crying to God for mercy." From his perspective, this turned repentance into a work and opposed the offer of a free and present salvation. On the basis of the finished work of Christ, sinners should be presented with an immediate salvation, without them needing to "work up" penitential sorrow. Marshall was clearly opposing the traditional Reformed view when he wrote, "if 'penitential sorrow' is a *preparation for salvation*—if it is necessary in order to the obtaining of forgiveness, *Christ has not done enough*."[207] Repentance was a change of mind about self, Christ, sin, and salvation; it had nothing to do with sorrow, although the change of mind will produce sorrow.[208] "When God calls on you to 'repent, and believe the gospel,'" wrote Marshall, "He

---

203. Marshall, *God's Way of Salvation*, 17. Emphasis original.
204. Ibid., 18.
205. Marshall, *Love's Golden Links*, n.p. ("Saved at Seventy").
206. Marshall, "'A Full Gospel,'" 128.
207. Marshall, *Review*, 9. Emphasis original.
208. Ibid., 10.

wishes you to lay aside your wrong thoughts, and believe the glad tidings that He proclaims to you."[209]

Miscellaneous

In an article in *The Christian's Friend*, one writer, identified only as "F. K.," came close to explaining saving faith as intellectual assent. Discussing the character of Abraham's faith, the author wrote, "Many think of faith as a sort of inward feeling or experience, and so, because they do not have these experiences, often wonder whether they have the right faith. But faith is not feeling or experience, but dependence upon what another has said or done."[210] If one enquires of a railway official about the London carriage, faith is trusting the official's word and taking one's seat in the appropriate carriage. No feelings are involved. True faith is simply believing what God has said.

F. K. was evidently conscious that what he was describing was open to the charge of Sandemanianism. Thus he added, "There is such a thing as mere head belief; i.e. the natural intellect acknowledging the truth of God." In contrast to such false faith, genuine faith is captured in Rom 4:3, "Abraham believed *God*." He elaborated: "One may intellectually believe what man says, and a person may be taught about Christ, and believe about Him, just in the same way that he believes there was such a person as Henry VIII., or any other matter of history. When one is really in earnest as to his soul's salvation, and believes what *God* says about Christ, that is not head-belief, but faith in God. Intellectual faith believes what man says; saving faith believes what God says."[211]

It is doubtful this clarification would satisfy his critics, for the author seems to be saying that saving faith consists in believing propositions about Christ; granted, they are reliable propositions because they are made by God, but they are propositions nonetheless.

To summarize, while some Brethren—particularly (some) evangelists influenced by the revivals and zealous for conversions—advanced something akin to Sandemanian faith and repentance, many of the most respected Brethren teachers (and some important evangelists too) strongly rejected that position. Therefore, it must not be assumed, as it often was by the critics, that the Brethren spoke with one voice on the nature of saving faith and repentance.

---

209. Marshall, *God's Way of Salvation*, 23–24.

210. F. K. "Expository Papers," 78.

211. Ibid., 79–80.

Faith and Assurance

There is evidence to indicate some Brethren did, in fact, teach that assurance is of the essence of faith, although not all were prepared to go that far. Some taught that while assurance should be a normative experience for the believer, it is possible to be truly justified and not know it, or at least not be sure of it. Very often the reason a believer lacked assurance was a result of looking internally for evidences of the new birth. The Brethren, however, taught that a believer's assurance is based on what Christ has done, not on what the believer does. They frequently encouraged troubled souls not to look within themselves for evidence of life, but to look to Christ and his finished work.

Darby wrote a fictitious dialogue with a person lacking assurance under the title, "How to Get Peace." He employed this particular genre because it reflected many actual conversations he had engaged in, and he believed this form would help illustrate "the common difficulties of a soul."[212] Darby said to his dialogue partner, "You have not the true knowledge of justification by faith. I do not say you are not justified in God's sight, but your conscience has not possession of it. The Reformers, all of them, went further than I do. They all held that if a man had not the assurance of his own salvation he was not justified at all."[213] Darby was clearly aware of the Reformers' position,[214] but he was unprepared to say that, without assurance, one is not truly justified. He conceded that a man might be genuinely saved but have "no consciousness of it in his own soul."[215]

For Darby, the individual's struggle to gain assurance was bound up with the fact that he was looking for holiness in his own life. Instead, he must look to the finished work of Christ. Darby explained, "You are looking for holiness to get Christ, instead of looking to have Christ to get holiness."[216] When standing before the divine judge, "we need Christ, not progress; righteousness and justification through Him, not help or improvement."[217] Darby identified the problem as confusing the work of the Holy Spirit *in* me with the work of Christ *for* me.

---

212. Darby, *CW*, 10:313 (1867).

213. Ibid.

214. Although he was wrong to say that "all of them" taught assurance was of the essence of faith. See footnote 14 above.

215. This was also the position of William Kelly. See Kelly, *Exposition of the Epistles of John*, 379.

216. Darby, *CW*, 10:315.

217. Ibid., 10:316.

If my soul rests entirely on the work of Christ, and His acceptance, as the One who appears in the presence of God for me,—that is a finished work, and a perfect infinite acceptance . . . Now what men substitute for this, is the examination of the effects of the Spirit in me. Whence I sometimes hope when I see that effect, sometimes despond when I see the flesh working, and having put the work of the Spirit in the place of the work of Christ,—the confidence I am commanded to hold fast never exists, and I doubt whether I am in the faith at all.[218]

Anthony Norris Groves also believed it was essential to focus on Christ and not the fervency of one's pious feelings. He himself had an introspective bent and was frequently burdened by his failures.[219] It is perhaps for this reason that he was so critical of Jonathan Edwards's *Treatise Concerning Religious Affections*. He considered books like Edwards's, which encourage probing self-examination for evidence of genuine spiritual life, to inflict more harm than good. Commenting in his journal, he wrote, "surely it is better to dwell continually on Christ, and if anybody, by contemplating Jesus in all His beauty and perfection of character, does not know whether he loves Him or not, no examination of his affections will show him."[220] Unlike Edwards's dissertation, which tends "to perplex the mind, than clear up its difficulties," Groves preferred books that "lead the soul to the word of Jesus, as the foundation of all stable peace, and the revealed will of Jesus, in all its illimitable purity and love, as the rule of life."[221]

Henry Snell grounded assurance in God's sovereign grace and imputed righteousness, but he acknowledged that not all believers possess this assurance.[222] He advised, "Whenever, dear Christian reader, your soul is assailed with doubts and fears, look at once straight to Jesus—the Lamb as it had been slain . . . Beware of looking within for righteousness; for Christ in the glory is your righteousness . . . Beware of looking at the Spirit's work in you as a ground of justification; for we are justified by the blood of Christ."[223]

Mackintosh likewise taught that assurance is not found in the believer's experience or feelings, but in the infallible word of God. He wrote, "It is not in feelings, not in experiences, not in impressions or convictions, not in reasonings, not in human traditions or doctrines, but simply in the

---

218. [Darby], "Operations of the Spirit of God," 44.
219. Dann, *Father of Faith Missions*, 383.
220. [Groves], *Memoir*, 346.
221. Ibid.
222. Snell, *Streams of Refreshing*, 61–62.
223. Ibid., 66–67.

unchangeable, eternal word of the living God. That word ... can alone impart peace to the mind and stability to the soul.[224] The popular Brethren tract writer, Charles Stanley, concurred:

> If you look at your feelings and your doings for salvation, it is like a person trying to climb a steep mountain of sand—every effort slides him lower. Our poor feelings and our doings are as unstable and shifting as the sand: there is nothing in either for faith to lay hold of. But when faith, looking away from our feelings and doings, takes fast hold of Christ, we are at once on the Rock of Ages. This is the difference between saving faith and all mere spurious faith, which really is only unbelief. If you have obtained the precious faith of God, you look at Christ. If false faith, you are looking at yourself, your feelings and your doings.[225]

While the objective looking to Christ over a subjective looking at self was a common theme in Brethren teaching on assurance, some emphasized that faith necessarily includes assurance. It appears that this teaching came as a reaction to the lack of assurance experienced by many who had been nurtured in Reformed churches. John McVicker maintained that true faith "is not a faith that we can have without knowing it." This position stood in conscious rejection of what he viewed as standard fare in Presbyterianism: "Men tell you to pray, and use means, and wait on ordinances, and assure you that this is the way to Christ. It is the religious way to the pit . . . O Christless ministers, Christless Sunday school teachers, Christless church members, I protest to you, with tears, that you are being directed to the wrong way. It is the way I tried for many years without finding peace."[226]

John Ritchie conceded that it was possible for someone who possessed salvation to lack assurance, but he attributed this to backsliding or bad teaching.[227] The normal state of the believer is to have assurance, because

---

224. Mackintosh, *Miscellaneous Writings*, 4:52–53 ("Ministry of Reconciliation"). Cf. Mackintosh, "Assurance," 281–88. When the believer rests in the finished work of Christ he or she "can be as sure of heaven as though he were already there." Mackintosh, *Miscellaneous Writings*, 4:14 ("Conversion").

225. Stanley, "What a Contrast," 4–5. Cf. Miller, *Meditations on the Grace and Glory*, 81.

226. Cited in Gribben, "'The Worst Sect,'" 36. In a letter to his mother dated July 14, 1859, McVicker described his own experience of saving faith and assurance during the revival in Northern Ireland. At that time he became persuaded "that there is no true faith that does not give assurance of heaven." McVicker, *Selected Letters*, 37–39.

227. He described the errant teaching as follows: "There are preachers, some of them of high rank, in the professing Church, who openly avow their belief that no assurance of salvation is possible in this life; others admit that a favoured few—either

faith, by definition, accepts the work of Christ and the testimony of the Word of God. Ritchie stated the matter bluntly: "To believe God because He speaks, is faith; to doubt Him is unbelief. To ask evidences or signs, either external or internal, is equivalent to saying, 'I cannot take God's bare Word for it, and believe that I am saved, because He says it.' Unbelief asks signs; faith trusts God without them."[228]

Brethren publications often contained accounts of conversations in which an individual who lacked assurance of salvation was exhorted by the Brethren teacher or evangelist to believe in the finished work of Christ and thus experience the certainty of the forgiveness of their sins. Typical here is an article by W. T. P. Wolston (1840–1917), which addressed the question: "Do you hope, or know, that you have eternal life?" Wolston opened with these words: "Most of those to whom I put my query decidedly answer 'I *hope*,' very frequently adding, 'it is impossible to *know*.' If you agree with such a reply, allow me to show you from Scripture that it is not only possible, but actually contemplated by God, that whoever believes in His Son should not only have eternal life, but know that it is possessed even now."[229]

George Cutting stated that he wrote *Safety, Certainty and Enjoyment* "especially for souls desiring before God to be fully and unmistakably SURE of their salvation."[230] Again, the problem was that people were looking to their feelings for certainty of salvation. They may have recognized that Christ's death provided safety, but as they examined their own lives and emotions, they could find no peace. "Ah, there lies your mistake," Cutting declared. "Did you ever hear of a captain trying to find anchorage by fastening his anchor *inside* the ship? Never."[231] The work of the Spirit in sanctification is essential, but "the Spirit does not direct an awakened soul to its own conflicting experiences *as the ground of peace*, but to CHRIST."[232] He counselled his readers: "Listen not to the unstable testimony of inward emotions, but to the infallible witness of the Word of God."[233] Assurance rests upon the

---

those unquestionably *elect*, or of a high degree in Christian virtue—may attain to it, but the ordinary rank and file of believers must 'hope' and 'wait' till the revelations of the great day." Ritchie, *Foundation Truths of the Gospel*, 49.

228. Ritchie, *Foundation Truths of the Gospel*, 46.

229. W[olston], "Do You Hope, or Know?" 213. Cf. P. W., "O God!" 268. While Brethren publications usually record how this teaching led to the conversion of souls, it is clear that not everyone welcomed it. See, for example, Airhart, "What Must I Do to Be Saved?" 378.

230. Cutting, *Safety, Certainty*, 4. Emphasis original.

231. Ibid., 8.

232. C[utting], *Assurance*, 15.

233. Cutting, *Safety, Certainty*, 11.

work of Christ and the promises of Scripture, which announce that those who truly believe in Jesus have eternal life (e.g., John 6:47). In fact, lack of assurance in one who claimed to believe in Christ was tantamount to making God a liar. For Cutting, certainty of salvation was inseparably linked to the character of God, the work of Christ, and the reliability of his word.

Some evangelists, however, were careful to distinguish between saving faith and assurance. Henry Moorhouse, according to his biographer, did not confound "as too many lay-evangelists do, assurance of personal salvation with faith." Moorhouse, it was claimed, dealt wisely with the believer "who doubts not his Lord but himself." The biographer added, "*To believe in Christ is one thing; to know* that *I* believe is another thing."[234] Alexander Marshall would have disagreed. He taught that faith necessarily includes assurance. "Every sinner who believes on the Lord Jesus is BOUND to believe that he is saved. It would indeed be 'great presumption' in anyone to doubt the Word of the living God."[235] Marshall's statements were a calculated response to those who claimed that it was "great presumption" for anyone to claim certainty of salvation. Marshall had little sympathy for doubters. To the one who said: "I believe on Jesus, but I cannot say I am saved," he responded, "Then you are making God a liar; for He again and again asserts that everyone who believes on Jesus has eternal life (John 6:47)."[236]

Donald Ross's Northern Evangelistic Society attracted criticism from Scottish Presbyterians for their position on assurance. Neil Dickson explains, "The society maintained in an extreme form that assurance was of the essence of salvation and therefore individuals who, in the older Scottish manner, expressed uncertainty about their final salvation were deemed not to be regenerate."[237] As noted earlier, "in Highland Evangelicalism a convert was not accepted until his faith had been authenticated by a godly life."[238] According to one account, "In Skye, three years was regarded as a suitable probationary period. By then it would appear whether the convert was a hypocrite ... or a true child of God."[239] As a result, it was not uncommon for Highland Presbyterians to doubt their salvation, or to think that assurance

---

234. Macpherson, *Henry Moorhouse*, 101.

235. Marshall, *God's Way of Salvation*, 22. Emphasis original. To the question "Is it not presumptuous to say that we are saved before we die?" Henry Soltau responded by pointing out that it is not presumption to believe what God says. However, it is the height of presumption to disbelieve God's word. Soltau, *The Soul and Its Difficulties*, 63.

236. Marshall, *God's Way of Salvation*, 27.

237. Dickson, *Brethren in Scotland*, 94.

238. Ross, "Calvinists in Controversy," 59.

239. MacInnes, *The Evangelical Movement*, 217.

of salvation was not even possible.²⁴⁰ John Ritchie wrote of people from Inverurie flocking to hear Ross preach because they were eager "to see and hear the men who said they were 'saved, and sure of it,' so uncommon was it to hear such things from either pulpit or platform then."²⁴¹

In Northern Ireland, James Campbell and James Smith carried on a remarkable gospel ministry in the 1870s that was often bitterly opposed by the clergy.²⁴² On one occasion, a Presbyterian minister preached a sermon "against any one knowing or saying they were saved."²⁴³ Any who taught such "heresy" should be expelled from their town. Campbell and Smith were guilty of preaching this "heresy," and their host was ready to expel them until he saw from 1 John that what they were preaching was true, and he was converted.

Some of the preachers, in countering one extreme (i.e. assurance is not possible), may have gone to another (i.e. assurance is essential). Hugh McIntosh—admittedly, not the most reliable source—claims to have heard NES preachers say, "No man *can* be saved without knowing it." And, "Without assurance there is no salvation." And, "If *you* are not *sure* that you are going to heaven, then *I* am sure you are going to hell."²⁴⁴ Whether the evangelists stated matters in such stark terms, or whether McIntosh's report is a case of critical hyperbole, is unclear. But what *is* clear is that assurance of salvation was part of their message. They could not countenance the sentiment expressed, for example, in the Strict Baptist magazine *The Earthen Vessel* which suggested that assurance is a privilege not all believers receive and "very few enjoy it at all times."²⁴⁵ Ritchie summarized the preaching of the NES evangelists as follows:

> "What did these men preach, that there was such a stir created?"
> Simply the truth of God—the old Gospel of Jesus Christ in fresh

---

240. Cf. Ross, "Calvinists in Controversy," 59.

241. Ritchie in Ross, *Donald Ross*, 157. Cf. [Ross], "A Word to Anxious Ones," 127. The situation was similar in Ireland. See Hutchinson, *Whose Praise Is in the Gospel*, 243.

242. See Beattie, *Brethren*, 288–91.

243. Ritchie, *James Campbell*, 50. Charles Stanley was compelled to write a vigorous rebuttal to a clergyman's assertion that it was unscriptural and indeed, impossible to answer the question "are you saved?" in the affirmative. S[tanley], "Are You Saved?" 184–87; 220–24.

244. McIntosh, *The New Prophets*, 25.

245. "The Assurance of Faith," 106. The author went on to describe "a large body of professing Christians in this day . . . [who] will have nothing to do with doubts and fears about individual and present salvation, and be assured, and be happy, and never fear again." This was the position of many Brethren evangelists, but the author did not view it as normative. He added, "This is the point to which thousands are hoping to come, but they cannot reach it" (153).

and living power, with the definite assurance of present salvation to all who believe and receive it, and the certain damnation of all who reject it. The evangelists brought no new doctrine, but they had the old fundamental truths of ruin by sin, redemption by Jesus Christ, and regeneration by the Holy Ghost burning in them as living realities, and preached them in full confidence that God would use His own Word to do His own work.[246]

Yet even Donald Munro admitted of the NECM evangelists—many of whom would join Ross in the NES, including Munro himself—that "it is quite possible that men whose hearts were on fire, burning with zeal for the salvation of the lost, may not always have spoken or acted in the wisest way."[247]

There was a growing concern among a number of Brethren about the character of evangelistic activity in the closing decades of the nineteenth century.[248] The following comments, published in *The Witness*, expressed the alarm.

In carrying on Gospel work, there is such a thing as an undue anxiety to secure professions of conversion. The result of this is that souls never truly convinced of sin are persuaded to profess . . . but, as there was no depth of conviction, there was no reality of conversion . . . Indeed, this zeal to secure converts is fraught with very serious dangers. It leads *unrepentant* sinners into the delusion that they are *reconciled* to God. It lays the flattering unction to their soul that they are "booked right through for glory," while in reality they are going down to hell with a lie in their right hand . . . If there is to be true conversion to God, there must be true conviction of sin . . . Let us beware lest we attempt to *do the work of the Holy Spirit*.[249]

As a response to concerns over false conversions, some taught that assurance should be based on the experience of sanctification. In an article entitled "Evidences of the New Birth," J. Norman Case wrote, "We can only

---

246. Ritchie, in Ross, *Donald Ross*, 157. The "motto" of the NES was stated as follows in its periodical edited by Ross, *Northern Evangelistic Intelligencer* (Jan. 1, 1872), 6: "Eternal salvation is a free, present, attainable, inalienable, imperishable gift; i.e. any man or woman in this world, be he or she the blackest sinner in it, may, in one moment, be justified for ever, from every charge of sin; and may know, beyond all doubt, that he is justified; and may rest as sure of Eternal Glory as he is certain that in himself he never deserved, and never will deserve, anything but eternal damnation."

247. Ross, *Donald Ross*, 109.

248. See Grass, *Gathering to His Name*, 136.

249. W. S., "Unreal Conversions," 76–77.

have the continuous assurance of our calling as we are growing in grace and in likeness to Christ." Yet he acknowledged that this principle "has been largely ignored among us."[250] Case lamented the state of much of the evangelistic preaching toward the end of the century. He opined:

> In our judgment one of the weakest points in modern evangelism is the little stress that is laid on the work of God in the soul. Who has not mourned over the unsatisfactory nature of much of the popular evangelistic work of the day? Salvation has been degenerated to a proposition in logic, running thus: "God says that Christ died for sinners and all who believe in him have everlasting life. I am a sinner and I believe in Christ, therefore I have everlasting life." Sound enough logic, no doubt, but many of these flippant talkers have never seen their need of believing in Christ, and have simply deceived themselves in thinking that they believe on him. We often hear the expression: "I know that I am saved, for God says it." To many, no doubt, this has proved a soul-emancipating, peace-giving word; but to others, I fear, it has proved a snare and a delusion.[251]

Case agreed that a person should not look to himself as a source of salvation or strength, but he rejected the common Brethren teaching that "a professed child of God must not examine himself to see if he bears the marks of the family." Indeed, Case believed such teaching was "a most foolish and dangerous doctrine."[252] A similar position was taken by William Lincoln in his response to the question: "Is it necessary for a person, in order to be assured of salvation, to know the exact day, hour, and moment of his conversion?" Lincoln outlined several marks of true conversion such as obedience, time, and growth. At the same time he decried the shallowness of popular preaching which often produced spurious conversions.[253]

Evaluation and Conclusion

What we observe from this chapter is a classic case of the pendulum swing. In teaching that assurance was of the essence of faith, Calvin, in the sixteenth century, was reacting to Roman Catholicism's denial that assurance of salvation was even possible. But over time, the basis of assurance in the Reformed tradition shifted its focus to the subjective experience of the

---

250. C[ase], "Evidences of the New Birth," 110.
251. Ibid., 110–11.
252. Ibid., 111.
253. Lincoln, "Is it necessary?" 75–76.

believer. The result was that by the nineteenth century, many who had been nurtured in Reformed churches were taught that it was presumptuous—if not practically impossible—to claim certainty of final salvation. Thus, like Calvin, many Brethren reacted by making assurance part of the essence of faith. Some Brethren, however, rode the pendulum too far and so objectified assurance that experience appeared to be irrelevant. J. Norman Case and others sought to call the Brethren back to a more balanced view.

In the eighteenth century, the Sandemanians reacted to what they considered to be an over-emphasis on the subjective side of faith.[254] However, they went to the opposite extreme of stressing the objective aspects of faith and repentance to the neglect of the subjective reality. The preaching of some Brethren evangelists resembled this emphasis as well, although many of the reputable teachers and evangelists rejected Sandemanianism.

Andrew Fuller observed that traditional Calvinism had a tendency to be excessively introspective. He warned, "If the attention of the awakened sinner, instead of being directed to Christ, be turned inward, and his mind be employed in searching for evidences of his conversion, the effect must, to say the least, be uncomfortable, and may be fatal; as it may lead him to make a righteousness of his religious feelings instead of looking out of himself to the Saviour."[255]

Many Brethren heartily agreed, as was again reflected in their doctrine of assurance. But their perspectives were not just reactionary. Some evangelists were tempted to reduce the gospel to a kind of logical syllogism out of a desire to see more souls saved. While Brethren leaders applauded the evangelists' zeal for souls, they would not sanction a reduced gospel.

There is no doubt that the Brethren displayed their share of theological idiosyncrasies and did depart from some Calvinistic paths. Nevertheless, their teaching on the relationship between faith and assurance was not without precedent in Reformed theology. Indeed, some were not far from the position of Calvin himself. Furthermore, even if some held to a form of Sandemanianism on the nature of saving faith and repentance, that would not disqualify them from reflecting a basic Calvinistic soteriology. Their position on human depravity and the condition of the will, as well as their doctrine of election, placed them squarely—though somewhat uncomfortably—in the Calvinist camp.

---

254. Even Andrew Fuller, while rejecting the Sandemanian extreme, acknowledged there was an imbalance. He wrote, "The attention of Christians appears to have been too much drawn towards what may be called *subjective* religion, to the neglect of that which is *objective*." Fuller, *Complete Works*, 2:564.

255. Fuller, *Complete Works*, 2:564.

8

Evaluation and Conclusion

There are Calvinistic speculations just as much as Arminian. It seems to me that both schemes are beyond question partial and do violence to the truth. The practical lesson is to cherish confidence only in God's word. We may safely rest, as we are bound to rest, in His revelation. The best of men . . . are liable to err; and we must beware lest merely changing names we fall into the old snare of tradition or confidence in man. Our own day presents no better security than another. May we trust to God and the word of His grace, which is able to build us up!

—William Kelly[1]

Summary

THIS BOOK HAS EXPLORED the character of nineteenth-century Brethren soteriology with specific focus on a number of the doctrines central to the Calvinist-Arminian debate. As we bring this study to a conclusion, it is appropriate to summarize our findings. In regard to the condition of humanity after the fall, the Brethren position emphasized the "total ruin of man." Fallen human beings are unwilling and unable to turn to God in faith. Brethren writers consistently denied that fallen people possess "free will";

---

1. Kelly, *Lectures . . . Minor Prophets*, 171.

they consistently affirmed, however, that every person was still morally responsible and accountable before God.

The Brethren espoused the doctrine of unconditional election based on God's sovereign will and *not* on the foreseen faith of the individual. However, they rejected reprobation as unbiblical. People perish for willfully clinging to their sin, not because God has predestined them to damnation. Furthermore, they believed election in no way diminished the urgency of evangelism, and thus the message of salvation should be preached to all. At the same time, Brethren writers stressed that the doctrine of predestination was given for the edification of the saints and should not be broached in evangelistic settings.

On the question of the extent of the atonement, the Brethren advanced a nuanced position. On the one hand, propitiation was universal and Godward; it vindicated God's righteousness and enabled him to offer mercy to all sinners. On the other hand, substitution was particular; Christ bore only the sins of believers. Brethren were unwilling to say to an unbeliever, "Christ bore *your* sins." Yet they did not hesitate to preach the gospel to all, recognizing that through propitiation there was a universal dimension to the death of Christ. Their position could be neatly summarized as follows: "Christ is a *propitiation* for the whole world. He was the *substitute* for His people."[2]

In regard to matters such as saving faith, repentance, and assurance, there was some variation among Brethren leaders. Yet the standard position of reputable leaders disavowed the notion that saving faith consisted merely in intellectual assent to biblical propositions, as in Sandemanianism. True faith was produced by the Holy Spirit and brought deep conviction of sin, along with repentance. They did not advocate a complex "morphology" of conversion with a drawn-out period of "preparation" for salvation. Conversion could be immediate, but if genuine, it was always divinely wrought. Brethren believed that assurance was normative, yet was rooted in the objective work of Christ, not in the subjective experience of sanctification. It was possible for true believers to lack assurance, but in such cases, they were mistakenly looking inward for signs of grace. The solution was realized by looking to Christ and his finished work.

Exceptions to these positions could be found, most notably in Alexander Marshall, the popular Open Brethren evangelist who imported a form of Arminianism into the movement from his close connections with Scottish Morisonianism. Additionally, some revival preachers lacked "theological

---

2. [Mackintosh], "One-Sided Theology," 16.

finesse"[3] and advanced notions about the gospel that Brethren teachers denounced as unrepresentative and out-of-step with the prevailing thought of the movement. By the close of the nineteenth century, these exceptions were still in the minority, although they would gain momentum among Open Brethren as the twentieth century dawned.

In light of the evidence presented throughout this book, we conclude that it is proper to designate nineteenth-century Brethren soteriology as *Calvinistic*. The term is used advisedly, since Brethren leaders never claimed to embrace *Calvinism* per se, nor would they call themselves *Calvinists*. They believed that Calvinism as such amounted to a human system and included elements that could not be supported by the Bible. Nevertheless, the emphasis on the total ruin of human beings—including the impotence of the unregenerate will to turn to God—and the consistent stress on the sovereignty of God in redemption makes the use of the adjective *Calvinistic* entirely appropriate to characterize Brethren soteriology.

Primary Features of Brethren Calvinistic Soteriology

The delicacy with which Calvinistic terminology must be employed illustrates the independent spirit of the Brethren position. We may thus identify three primary features that contributed to their particular brand of Calvinistic soteriology: unsystematic, biblicist, and evangelistic. This is not to suggest that these features were altogether unique to the Brethren, but at least in the case of the first two, the fervency with which they professed these principles seemed to outshine other groups. The unsystematic and biblicist approach to doctrine was for many Brethren a badge of honor. Furthermore, these three features, taken together, help capture something of the ethos of the movement through the nineteenth century.

Dogmatically Unsystematic and Non-Creedal

First, Brethren soteriology was neither systematic nor confessional; that is, it was not tied to the structure of a particular theological system and claimed no loyalty to any confession of faith or creed. Reformed theologians often rooted their soteriology in the categories of Covenant Theology, as, for example, the following statement from the Westminster Larger Catechism demonstrates: "God doth not leave all men to perish in the estate of sin and misery, into which they fell by the breach of the first covenant, commonly

---

3. Coad, *History of the Brethren*, 170.

called the Covenant of Works; but of his mere love and mercy delivereth his elect out of it, and bringeth them into an estate of salvation by the second covenant, commonly called the Covenant of Grace."[4]

Although Darby could express his appreciation for the way the Thirty-Nine Articles handled the doctrine of election, the Brethren generally opposed systems of divinity and confessions on principle. They believed that such human products inevitably supplant the authority of Scripture.[5] Mackintosh captured the essence of the Brethren sentiment when he wrote: "Men might as well attempt to confine the ocean in buckets of their own formation as to confine the vast range of divine revelation within the miserable enclosures of human systems of doctrine. It cannot be done, and it ought not to be attempted. Better far to fling aside all systems of theology and schools of divinity, and come like a little child to the eternal fountain of holy scripture, and there drink in the living teachings of God's Spirit."[6]

An 1834 essay in *The Christian Witness* argued that the tendency to construct systematic views of religion was an error "dishonourable to God." The problem with systematizing notions of "God's sovereignty and man's responsibility," for example, is that invariably the end product amounts to mere human opinion, which is only "awkwardly and artificially referred to the Bible rather than really based upon it."[7] Moreover, the attempt to systematize "will frequently evince its unscriptural character by the adoption of a *name*."[8] Thus Brethren steadfastly rejected the *name* "Calvinist."

In 1843, John Eliot Howard published a refutation of an Arminian tract by the future Evangelical Union leader, John Guthrie. Howard's Calvinistic response made generous use of Martin Luther's *Bondage of the Will*, yet he also claimed that his desire "was only to drink water with joy out of the pure well-springs of Scripture, and to cast systematic theology to the owls and bats."[9]

Since they felt no loyalty to Calvinism as a system, they felt free to reject elements of it wherever they believed that tradition deviated from Scripture—although they did not always demonstrate a sophisticated

---

4. Question 30. Cf. WCF 7.2–3.

5. [Ross], "Salvation," 44.

6. [Mackintosh], "One-Sided Theology," 12. In another place, he warned that if earnest souls "are turned from Jesus to theology—from the heart of a loving, pardoning God to the cold and withering dogmas of systematic divinity, it is impossible to say where they may end; they may take refuge either in superstition on the one hand, or in infidelity on the other." Mackintosh, *Miscellaneous Writings*, 4:28–29 ("Glad Tidings").

7. [Brenton], "Thoughts on System in Religion," 310.

8. Ibid., 311. Emphasis original.

9. Howard, *"New Views,"* 24.

understanding of the Reformed tradition, and often fell prey to caricatures of historic Reformed teaching on doctrines such as reprobation, human responsibility, and the free offer of the gospel.[10] Neatby, who wrote the first history of the movement, concluded: "In systematic divinity [the Brethren] were weak, and their history shows the perilous character of the weakness. But the Bible, in a wonderful way, was a living book to them."[11]

Radically Biblicist

Second, the unsystematic and somewhat eclectic nature of Brethren soteriology was driven by its radical biblicism. In other words, their principled opposition to theological systems arose out of a commitment to the sole authority of the Bible. Brethren writers, for example, displayed no appetite for speculation over the order of divine decrees. Nor did they exhibit a sense of dependence on theologians or theological traditions; their stated loyalty was always to Scripture. Darby expressed appreciation for reformers such as Luther and Calvin, but he refused to tie himself to them. If they were presented to him as a standard of truth, he would reject them "with indignation." "They were not inspired," Darby explained. "Their teachings are not the word of God." He respected "the gifted men," but they "would become a horror to me if they were in any way substituted for, or made to compete with, the word of God." He believed Luther and Calvin were used by God to recover vital truth, but at the same time he was convinced the systems they developed were tainted with error. Thus he exclaimed, "Do not bring their doctors or their systems to me as authority. You are trenching on the authority of the word of God."[12] On another occasion he declared: "A system takes the place of godly subjection to the word. And alas! this is suited to a decline of spirituality. As [subjection to the word] becomes feeble, the exercise of mind, and the play of the mere natural feelings, become a necessary ailment. But to the soul, fresh in its spirituality, the word of God (and oh! how can it be otherwise?) has more sweetness in its least statements (for they come from God) than any indulgence whatever of the mental powers."[13]

In the Brethren outlook, being party to a system meant that one could not be true to the whole of Scripture. Again, William Kelly criticized both

10. E.g., Kelly, *Great Olivet Prophecy*, 15.

11. Neatby, *History*, 331–32. In Neatby's evaluation, "The abjuration of 'system' was the special boast of the Brethren, and it has proved their ruin" (331). I develop this theme further in Stevenson, "The Brethren and Systematic Theology."

12. Darby, *CW*, 7:205–6 (1858–59; second edition 1867).

13. Ibid., 11:38 (1845).

Calvinism and Arminianism because "like other systems they are in part true and in part false—true in what they believe of scripture, false in yielding to human thoughts outside scripture." He then declared, "Happy those, who are content as Christians with the truth of God and refuse to be partisans on either side of men! Our wisdom is to have our minds open to all scripture, refusing to go a hair-breath farther."[14] This sentiment expresses the essence of Brethren methodology with respect to soteriological questions. They refused to draw upon creeds, confessions, theologians, or traditions to shape their thought; the full range of Scripture alone was definitive. This, they believed, always kept them biblically balanced and guarded them against the extremes to which both Calvinists and Arminians were wont to go.

The biblicist nature of Brethren soteriology is further illustrated in the way Charles Stanley responded to a question regarding what he believed about the doctrine of election. "All that God has spoken," he replied. This included John 3:16 ("God so loved the world . . .") *and* Eph 1:4 ("[God] hath chosen us in him before the foundation of the world"). Stanley maintained, "The Arminian seems to believe only one of these truths; the Calvinist only the other, I surely believe both." Again, the Bible was the determinative factor, not party systems. Nevertheless, Stanley's Calvinistic soteriology was irrepressible, prompting him to add, "The gospel supper was ample, and all were invited, but all refused. Then infinite, sovereign grace compels some, even the most hell-deserving to come in. Oh, the riches of His grace!"[15]

For some writers, radical biblicism meant that any attempt to harmonize theological tensions was unnecessary and wrongheaded. "A disposition to reconcile every thing, to systematize every thing," Brenton asserted, "must lead to failure."[16] Mackintosh concurred and refused to theologize over the question: How can those who are dead in trespasses repent? He wrote,

> Our Lord knows better than all the theologians in the world what ought to be preached. He knows all about man's condition—his guilt, his misery, his spiritual death, his utter helplessness, his total inability to think a single right thought, to utter a single right word, to do a single right act; and yet He called upon men to repent. This is quite enough for us. It is no part of our business to seek to reconcile seeming differences. It may

---

14. Kelly, *Notes . . . Romans*, 220.

15. Stanley, "Doctrines of the Salvation Army," 11.

16. [Brenton], "Thoughts on System in Religion," 311. He confessed, "There are things to be joined, but God must join them; there are difficulties to be reconciled, but *we* cannot solve the problem. Inattention to this fact is the secret of that abortive process by which man stepping out of his own line would forestall his Maker" (312).

seem to us difficult to reconcile man's utter powerlessness with his responsibility; but "God is His own interpreter, and He will make it plain."[17]

Apparently, any attempt to harmonize human inability and responsibility would be to cast doubt on the sufficiency of Scripture, or to assume finite minds can tread with the infinite. The path of fidelity was simply to embrace the mystery and accept both truths as written.

The inclination to eschew systematic theology in favor of the purity of Scripture was attributable in part to the influence of Romanticism on the Brethren movement.[18] In reaction to the rationalism of the Enlightenment, Romanticism stressed imagination, mystery, and emotion.[19] By the 1830s, the evangelical movement was appropriating some of the values of Romanticism. Among other things, this led to exalting faith over reason, with a keen sense of God's hand in human affairs. It also involved elevating the simplicity of the Word of God over rational systems of theology.[20] The Brethren were not the only evangelicals to display these ideals, but the impulse to exalt Scripture over every other source and authority tended to be stronger among them than other evangelicals. Thus Bebbington labelled the Brethren as "extremists" in their devotion to the Bible. Yet this extreme commitment to Scripture is what preserved their conservative orthodoxy when others who absorbed the spirituality of Romanticism drifted into "doctrinal vagueness."[21] For Bebbington, consequently, Brethren may rightly be dubbed "evangelicals of the evangelicals."[22]

As observed in chapter 5, Brethren historian Harold Rowdon has argued that a radical appropriation of the principle of *Sola Scriptura* was the defining feature of Brethrenism.

> We shall not go very far astray if we come to the conclusion that the thing above everything else which distinguished the early Brethren was the absolute priority which they accorded

17. Mackintosh, *Miscellaneous Writings*, 4:5 ("The Great Commission"). Cf. [Ross], "Questions and Answers," 153–54.

18. See Stevenson, "Brethren and Systematic Theology."

19. See Bebbington, "Place of the Brethren Movement." On pages 248–60, Bebbington illustrates the ways in which Romanticism was evident in Brethren thought and practice. He argues that "Brethren approximated to the ideal type of Romantic evangelicals—radical, intense, quixotic." See also Grass, *Gathering to His Name*, 10–12.

20. Although Bebbington argues that aversion to metaphysical systems of theology was also part of the Enlightenment reaction to scholasticism. Bebbington, *Evangelicalism in Modern Britain*, 57–58.

21. Bebbington, "Place of the Brethren Movement," 252–53.

22. Ibid., 260.

to the Word of God ... It may be objected that this is no more than the Reformation principle of *Sola Scriptura* which was also avowed by contemporary evangelicals as their lode star. But, just as Anabaptists of the sixteenth century chided the Reformers with failure to be sufficiently radical in their application of Scripture to the problems of the church in their day, so nineteenth-century Brethren belaboured contemporary evangelicals for their failure to be consistent biblicists. Here, if anywhere, is the essential principle of the Brethren. For man-made tradition they cared not a hoot: Scripture, on the other hand, was the voice of God.[23]

Whether or not radical biblicism was the central principle of Brethrenism, as Rowdon here argues, is open to discussion.[24] What is clear, however, is that radical biblicism shaped Brethren soteriology, allowing it to stand independently from the Reformed tradition even while endorsing a number of Reformed doctrines. Neatby described the biblicism of Brethren soteriology somewhat hyperbolically when he wrote, "They did not master the truths of salvation in a logical concatenation; they saw them. Inference was nothing; immediate perception everything ... Where logical Puritan divinity was anxious to explain, Darby only cared to feel."[25]

Although the Brethren claimed to stand above human systems of theology, they inevitably developed their own systematic approach to Scripture. This is readily observed in the way they handled the extent of the atonement. By making careful distinctions between propitiation and substitution, as well as purchase and redemption—even if these distinctions were not obvious from the biblical text itself—they were able to balance universal and particular elements in their doctrine of the atonement. Furthermore, Darby's Calvinistic soteriology informed his understanding of the larger framework of redemptive history. Each successive dispensation up to the cross demonstrated the "total ruin of man" and the absolute necessity of the sovereignty of divine grace. His ecclesiology, likewise, was characterized by belief in the "ruin" of the church, a conviction rooted in his Calvinist anthropology.[26]

---

23. Rowdon, *Who Are the Brethren?* 33–34. Cf. Rowdon, "The Problem of Brethren Identity," 174.
24. See Grass, *Gathering to His Name*, 84–85.
25. Neatby, *History*, 331.
26. Grass, "The Church's Ruin," 100.

Passionately Evangelistic

Finally, the Calvinistic soteriology of nineteenth-century Brethren was passionately evangelistic. Soteriology was not simply a theological conundrum to be debated in an ivory tower; it was the message of salvation to be proclaimed from the pulpit, in the open air, and under the evangelist's tent. It was to be distributed through gospel tracts and shared in personal conversations.[27] Both streams of the movement produced active itinerant evangelists and popular literature that pressed the lost to be saved—and to be sure of it. Such intense activism sometimes resulted in a superficial account of the gospel, which Brethren teachers felt compelled to correct. On the other hand, devotion to Scripture meant that even popular evangelists such as Donald Ross and Charles Stanley were concerned with doctrinal precision in their articulation of the gospel.

As practitioners of evangelism, the Brethren did not consider it appropriate in evangelistic settings to disclose the deeper theological truths that lay behind the simple gospel message. They were conscious that the Reformed tradition sometimes led anxious souls to agonize over whether or not they were part of the elect, and whether Christ had died for them. The Brethren practice was to preach the good news to sinners without perplexing their hearers with questions about election. Mackintosh stated, "We believe it to be of the utmost importance for the anxious enquirer to know that the standpoint from which he is called to view the cross of Christ, is not the standpoint of election, but of conscious ruin. The grace of God meets him as a lost, dead, guilty sinner, not as an elect one."[28] This perspective did not undermine the doctrine of election; it merely put it in its proper place. He then clarified, "The gospel meets us as lost, and saves us; and then, when we know ourselves saved, the precious doctrine of election comes in to establish us in the fact that we can never be lost."[29] They did not attempt to skirt questions about election,[30] but neither did they find it necessary to trouble unbelievers with complex matters of doctrine.

Of course, the Brethren were not unique in their passion for evangelism. The most visible and outspoken defender of Calvinism in the nineteenth century, Charles Spurgeon, was also arguably the greatest evangelist

---

27. Grass suggests that the priority of evangelism intensified after 1859. "From being a movement whose most obvious distinguishing characteristic was perhaps the intense discussion of theological issues, Open Brethren became a movement whose primary *raison d'être* was evangelism." *Gathering to His Name*, 131.

28. Mackintosh, *Miscellaneous Writings*, 4:24 ("Glad Tidings").

29. Ibid., 26.

30. E.g. Stanley, "Election," 1–38.

of the nineteenth century.³¹ Yet it is often suggested by those of a more Arminian persuasion that commitment to Calvinistic soteriology undermines the urgency of evangelism. Perhaps few other groups illustrate the fallacy of that assumption more than nineteenth-century Brethren. They admitted no incompatibility between a strong doctrine of the sovereignty of grace in salvation and indefatigable evangelism. It was their ecclesiastical descendants, primarily among the Open Brethren, who grew weary of the tensions and abandoned much of their Calvinistic heritage in the twentieth century. The influence of Alexander Marshall and other revival evangelists eventually turned the tide. Yet the non-confessional and biblicist nature of Brethren thought provided Marshall (and others of his persuasion) an equal place at the table. As the "chief men" passed off the scene, these voices of a different tone would eventually win the day. It is also true that Calvinism was in decline among evangelicals generally in the early decades of the twentieth century, but it is unclear to what extent this broader milieu affected Brethren thought. In any case, the development of Brethren soteriology in the twentieth century is an area that merits further exploration. Perhaps future researchers will be able to pick up where the present thesis leaves off.³²

Conclusion

As we draw this study to a close, it may go without saying that in the history of theology, the Brethren have rarely been mistaken for outstanding exemplars of Reformed thought, and neither have they claimed to be. Today, many in the Calvinist tradition think of the Brethren as little more than the progenitors of dispensationalism, an approach to the Bible often judged to be antithetical to Reformed theology. There may even be an assumption that Brethren teaching is shot-through with Arminianism (or at least, anti-Calvinist proclivities), and there are plenty of examples from twentieth and twenty-first-century Brethren to substantiate that impression. However, this book has argued that "the doctrines of grace"—that inimitable idiom for Calvinistic soteriology—may indeed be found in an unexpected place: the forgotten annals of nineteenth-century Brethren thought.

---

31. See Nettles, *Living By Revealed Truth*, 279–315.

32. Other aspects of Brethren soteriology call for further research, such as their doctrine of justification and imputation, both of which attracted criticism. A study of evangelistic sermons and tracts would help establish whether or not there was a distinctive Brethren approach to the gospel and its proclamation.

Bibliography

Adamson, William. *The Life of the Rev. James Morison, D.D.* London: Hodder & Stoughton, 1898.

Airhart, Phyllis D. *Serving the Present Age: Revivalism, Progressivism, and the Methodist Tradition in Canada.* Montreal: McGill-Queen's University Press, 1992.

———. "'What Must I Do To Be Saved?' Two Paths to Evangelical Conversion in Late Victorian Canada." *CH* 59 (Sept. 1990) 372–85.

Akenson, Donald Harman. *Discovering the End of Time: Irish Evangelicals in the Age of Daniel O'Connell.* Montreal: McGill-Queen's University Press, 2016.

Allison, Gregg R. *Historical Theology: An Introduction to Christian Doctrine.* Grand Rapids: Zondervan, 2011.

Anderson, Robert. *The Entail of the Covenant or the Saviour's "Little Ones."* London: Pickering & Inglis, n.d.

———. *The Gospel and Its Ministry: A Handbook of Evangelical Truth.* 13th ed. London: Nisbet, 1907.

Armstrong, Brian G. *Calvinism and the Amyraut Heresy: Protestant Scholasticism and Humanism in Seventeenth-Century France.* Madison: University of Wisconsin Press, 1969.

"The Assurance of Faith: and How to Obtain It." *Earthen Vessel* 21 (1865) 106, 153.

Augustine. "A Treatise on the Predestination of the Saints." Translated by Peter Holmes and Robert Ernest Wallis. In *Nicene and Post-Nicene Fathers*, edited by Philip Schaff, First Series, vol. 5, 494–519. 1887. Reprinted, Peabody, MA: Hendrickson, 1994.

B. "'The Called of Jesus Christ.'" *Echoes of Service* (1892) 105–6.

———. "'The Elect of God.'" *Echoes of Service* (1892) 129–30.

Baird, Thomas. "The Original Fall and Incorrigible Depravity of Man." *W* 38 (1908) 111–12.

The Barley Cake.

Bass, Clarence B. "The Doctrine of the Church in the Theology of J. N. Darby with Special Reference to Its Contribution to the Plymouth Brethren Movement." PhD diss., University of Edinburgh, 1952.

Bavinck, Herman. "The Future of Calvinism." *The Presbyterian and Reformed Review* 5.17 (January 1894) 1–24.

Baxter, Richard. *The Autobiography of Richard Baxter.* Edited by J. M. Lloyd Thomas. London: Dent, 1931.

———. *The Practical Works of Richard Baxter*. Vol. 2. 1846. Reprinted, Morgan, PA: Soli Deo Gloria, 2000.

Baylis, Robert. *My People: The History of Those Christians Sometimes Called Plymouth Brethren*. Wheaton, IL: Shaw, 1995.

Beattie, David J. *Brethren: The Story of a Great Recovery*. Kilmarnock, UK: Ritchie, 1940.

Bebbington, David W. "Calvin and British Evangelicalism in the Nineteenth and Twentieth Centuries." In *Calvin and His Influence, 1509–2009*, edited by Irena Backus and Philip Benedict, 282–305. Oxford: Oxford University Press, 2011.

———. *The Dominance of Evangelicalism: The Age of Spurgeon and Moody*. Downers Grove, IL: InterVarsity, 2005.

———. "Evangelical Conversion, c. 1740–1850." *SBET* 18.2 (2000) 102–27.

———. "Evangelicalism." In *The Blackwell Companion to Nineteenth-Century Theology*. Edited by David Fergusson, 235–50. Chichester, UK: Wiley-Blackwell, 2010.

———. *Evangelicalism in Modern Britain: A History from the 1730s to the 1980s*. 1989. Reprinted, New York: Routledge, 1993.

———. *Holiness in Nineteenth-Century England*. Carlisle, UK: Paternoster, 2000.

———. "The Place of the Brethren Movement in International Evangelicalism." In *The Growth of the Brethren Movement: National and International Experiences*, edited by Neil T. R. Dickson and Tim Grass, 241–60. Milton Keynes, UK: Paternoster, 2006.

———. "Response." In *The Advent of Evangelicalism: Exploring Historical Continuities*, edited by Michael A. G. Haykin and Kenneth J. Stewart, 417–32. Nashville: B & H, 2008.

———. *Victorian Religious Revivals: Culture and Piety in Local and Global Contexts*. Oxford: Oxford University Press, 2012.

Beeke, Joel R. *Living for God's Glory: An Introduction to Calvinism*. Orlando: Reformation Trust, 2008.

———. *The Quest for Full Assurance: The Legacy of Calvin and His Successors*. Edinburgh: Banner of Truth, 1999.

Beeke, Joel R., and Mark Jones. *A Puritan Theology: Doctrine for Life*. Grand Rapids: Reformation Heritage, 2012.

Beeke, Joel R. and Paul M. Smalley. *Prepared by Grace, for Grace: The Puritans on God's Ordinary Way of Leading Sinners to Christ*. Grand Rapids: Reformation Heritage, 2013.

The Believers Hymn Book. London: Pickering & Inglis, [1884].

Bellett, George. *Memoir of the Rev. George Bellett, M.A.* London: Masters, 1889.

Bellett, J. G. *Brief Notes on the Epistle to the Ephesians*. Reprinted, Denver: Wilson Foundation, n.d.

———. *Miscellaneous Papers*. London: Allan, n.d.

———. *On the Gospel of John*. New York: Loizeaux, n.d.

———. *The Patriarchs: Being Meditations upon Enoch, Noah, Abraham, Isaac, Jacob, Joseph, Job; the Canticles, Heaven and Earth*. London: Morrish, n.d.

———. *Paul's Apostleship and Epistles*. Kilmarnock, UK: Ritchie, n.d.

———. *Short Meditations*. London: Morrish, 1887.

———. *Showers upon the Grass*. London: Morrish, 1865.

Bellett, L. M. *Recollections of the Late J. G. Bellett*. London: Rouse, 1895.

B[ennet], W. H. "Regeneration and Election." *W* (1894) 132.

———, ed. *Robert Cleaver Chapman of Barnstaple*. Glasgow: Pickering & Inglis, 1903.

Beougher, Timothy K. *Richard Baxter and Conversion: A Study of the Puritan Concept of Becoming a Christian*. Fearn, UK: Mentor, 2007.
Bettenson, Henry and Chris Maunder, eds. *Documents of the Christian Church*. 3rd ed. Oxford: Oxford University Press, 1999.
Bevan, Frances. *John Wesley*. 5th ed. London: Holness, n.d.
———. *Prayers and Promises: Timeless Gospel Stories*. Fearn, UK: Christian Focus, 2005.
———. *Three Friends of God: Records from the Lives of John Tauler, Nicholas of Basle, Henry Suso*. New York: Loizeaux, n.d.
———. *William Farel*. 2nd ed. London: Holness, [1883].
Blackburn, W. M. *History of the Christian Church from Its Origins to the Present Time*. Cincinnati: Hitchcock & Walden, 1879.
Blacketer, Raymond A. "Definite Atonement in Historical Perspective." In *The Glory of the Atonement: Biblical, Theological, and Practical Perspectives*, edited by Charles E. Hill and Frank A. James III, 304–23. Downers Grove, IL: InterVarsity, 2004.
Blocher, Henri. "The Atonement in John Calvin's Theology." In *The Glory of the Atonement: Biblical, Theological, and Practical Perspectives*, edited by Charles E. Hill and Frank A. James III, 279–303. Downers Grove, IL: InterVarsity, 2004.
Boettner, Loraine. *The Reformed Doctrine of Predestination*. Phillipsburg, NJ: Presbyterian and Reformed, 1932.
Bonar, Horatius. *The Everlasting Righteousness, or How Shall Man Be Just with God?* London: Nisbet, 1873.
———. *The Old Gospel: Not "Another Gospel" but the Power of God unto Salvation: A Reply to Dr. Kennedy's Pamphlet "Hyper-Evangelism."* Edinburgh, 1874.
Bowen, Desmond. *History and the Shaping of Irish Protestantism*. New York: Lang, 1995.
———. *The Protestant Crusade in Ireland, 1800–70: A Study of Protestant-Catholic Relations between the Act of Union and Disestablishment*. Dublin: Gill & Macmillan, 1978.
Bray, Gerald. *God Has Spoken: A History of Christian Theology*. Wheaton, IL: Crossway, 2014.
[Brenton, L. C. L.]. "Thoughts on System in Religion." *CWit* 1 (1834) 310–12.
The British Hearld.
Brown-Lawson, Albert. *John Wesley and the Anglican Evangelicals of the Eighteenth Century*. Edinburgh: Pentland, 1994.
Buchanan, Andrew D. "Brethren Revivals 1859–70." B.A. diss., University of Stirling, 1990.
Bulteel, H. B. *A Sermon on 1 Corinthians 2.12 Preached before the University of Oxford at St. Mary's on Sunday Feb. 6, 1831*. Oxford, 1831.
Bunyan, John. *The Works of John Bunyan*. Vol. 2. Glasgow: Blackie & Son, 1855.
Burnham, Jonathan D. *A Story of Conflict: The Controversial Relationship between Benjamin Wills Newton and John Nelson Darby*. Carlisle, UK: Paternoster, 2004.
Burton, Edward. *Remarks upon a Sermon Preached at St. Mary's on Sunday February 6th, 1831*. Oxford, 1831.
Burwash, Nathanael. *The History of Victoria College*. Toronto: Victoria College Press, 1927.
C., J. T. "Thoughts on Part of 1st John ii. 2." *The Gospel Herald* 5 (1837) 5–11.
Caldwell, John R. *Because Ye Belong to Christ*. Glasgow: Pickering & Inglis, 1899.
———. *Christ in the Levitical Offerings*. Glasgow: Pickering & Inglis, n.d.

[———]. "Election." *W* 18 (Oct 1888) 159–60.
[———]. "Faith: Is It Involuntary?" *W* 8 (1898) 68, editor's note.
———. *Foundations of the Faith Once for all Delivered to the Saints*. Glasgow: Pickering & Inglis, 1903.
[———]. "Question 164." *NW* 14 (1884) 48.
[———]. "Question 189." *NW* 15 (1885) 32.
[———]. "Question 275." *W* 17 (1887) 192.
[———]. "Question 496." *W* 5 (May 1895) 84.
Caldwell, Patricia. *The Puritan Conversion Narrative: The Beginnings of American Expression*. Cambridge: Cambridge University Press, 1983.
Callahan, James Patrick. *Primitivist Piety: The Ecclesiology of the Early Plymouth Brethren*. Lanham, MD: Scarecrow, 1996.
Calvin, John. *Calvin's Calvinism: Treatises on the Eternal Predestination of God and the Secret Providence of God*. Translated by Henry Cole. 1856. Reprinted, Grand Rapids: Reformed Free Publishing, n.d.
———. *The Epistles of Paul to the Romans and Thessalonians*. Translated by Ross MacKenzie. Grand Rapids: Eerdmans, 1973.
———. *Institutes of the Christian Religion*. Edited by John T. McNeill. Translated by Ford Lewis Battles. Philadelphia: Westminster, 1960.
———. *The Second Epistle of Paul to the Corinthians, and the Epistles to Timothy, Titus and Philemon*. Translated by T. A. Smail. Grand Rapids: Eerdmans, 1964.
"Calvinism Not the Whole of Christianity." *The Morning Watch* 3 (1831) 369–83.
Cameron, Nigel M. de S., ed. *Dictionary of Scottish Church History and Theology*. Downers Grove, IL: InterVarsity, 1993.
Campbell, J. McLeod. *The Nature of the Atonement*. Reprinted, Grand Rapids: Eerdmans, 1996.
The Canons of the Councils of Orange. http://www.reformed.org/documents/canons_of_orange.html.
Carey, William. *An Enquiry into the Obligations of Christians to Use Means for the Conversion of the Heathen*. Leicester, 1792.
Carson, D. A. *How Long, O Lord? Reflections on Suffering and Evil*. 2nd ed. Grand Rapids: Baker, 2006.
Carson, James C. L. *The Heresies of the Plymouth Brethren*. London: Houlston & Sons, 1883.
Carson, John T. *God's River in Spate: The Story of the Religious Awakening of Ulster in 1859*. Belfast: Presbyterian Church in Ireland, 1958.
Carter, Grayson. *Anglican Evangelicals: Protestant Secessions from the Via Media, c. 1800–1850*. Oxford: Oxford University Press, 2001.
Carwardine, Richard. *Transatlantic Revivalism: Popular Evangelicalism in Britain and America 1790–1865*. 1978. Reprinted, Milton Keynes, UK: Paternoster, 2006.
C[ase], J. N. "According to God's Good Pleasure. *OR* 11 (1898) 145–49.
———. "Evidences of the New Birth." *OR* 1 (1888) 109–13, 121–24.
Cassian, John. "The Third Conference of Abbot Chaeremon." Translated by Edgar C. S. Gibson. In *Nicene and Post-Nicene Fathers*, edited by Philip Schaff, Second Series, vol. 11, 422–35. 1894. Reprinted, Peabody, MA: Hendrickson, 1994.
Chadwick, Owen. "Arminianism in England." *Religion in Life* 29.4 (1960) 548–55.
Chapman, Robert C. *Choice Sayings: Being Notes of Expositions of the Scriptures*. Glasgow: Pickering & Inglis, 1914.

---. *Hymns and Meditations*. 3rd ed. Glasgow: Pickering & Inglis, n.d.
---. "Self-will and Sovereign Grace." *W* 5 (1895) 113–14.
Cheyne, Alexander C. "The Place of the Confession through Three Centuries." In *The Westminster Confession in the Church Today*, edited by Alasdair I. C. Heron, 17–27. Edinburgh: Saint Andrew Press, 1982.
---. *The Transforming of the Kirk: Victorian Scotlands [sic] Religious Revolution.* Edinburgh: Saint Andrew Press, 1983.
Clark, R. Scott. *Recovering the Reformed Confession: Our Theology, Piety, and Practice.* Phillipsburg, NJ: P & R Publishing, 2008.
Clarke, Matthew Austin. "A Critical Examination of the Ecclesiology of John Nelson Darby." PhD thesis, University of Gloucestershire, 2009.
Clifford, Alan C. *Calvinus: Authentic Calvinism, a Clarification.* 2nd ed. Norwich: Charenton Reformed Publishing, 2004.
Clipsham, E. F. "Andrew Fuller and Fullerism: A Study in Evangelical Calvinism." *BQ* 20.3 (July 1963) 99–114.
Coad, F. Roy. *A History of the Brethren Movement: Its Origins, Its Worldwide Development and Its Significance for the Present Day.* 2nd ed. Exeter, UK: Paternoster, 1976.
---. *Prophetic Developments: With Particular Reference to the Early Brethren Movement.* Pinner, Middlesex: Christian Brethren Research Fellowship, 1966.
Coates, C. A. *An Outline of the Epistle to the Romans.* London: Morrish, n.d.
Coffey, John. "Puritanism, Evangelicalism and the Evangelical Protestant Tradition." In *The Advent of Evangelicalism: Exploring Historical Continuities*, edited by Michael A. G. Haykin and Kenneth J. Stewart, 252–77. Nashville: B & H, 2008.
Cole, W. H. *Reminiscences of the Plymouth Meeting of "Brethren."* Sheringham: Roche, n.d.
Collinson, Patrick. "England and International Calvinism 1558–1640." In *International Calvinism 1541–1715*, edited by Menna Prestwich, 197–223. Oxford: Oxford University Press, 1985.
"The Coming, and the Day, of the Lord." *BT* 3 (April 1860) 59.
Coppedge, Allan. *John Wesley in Theological Debate.* Wilmore, KY: Wesley Heritage Press, 1987.
Cragg, Gerald R. *The Church and the Age of Reason 1648–1789.* London: Penguin, 1960.
---. *From Puritanism to the Age of Reason.* Cambridge: Cambridge University Press, 1950.
Craik, Henry. *Biblical Expositions, Lectures, Sketches of Sermons.* Edited by W. Elfe Tayler. London: Morgan & Chase, 1867.
Cramp, J. M. *Baptist History from the Foundation of the Christian Church to the Present Time.* 1871. Reprinted, Watertown, WI: Baptist Heritage Publications, 1987.
Critchlow, Anne-Louise. "William Kelly and the Inspiration of Scripture." *BHR* 6 (2010) 37–53.
Crocker, Robert. *Henry More, 1614–1687: A Biography of the Cambridge Platonist.* Dordrecht: Kluwer, 2003.
Croskery, Thomas. *A Catechism on the Doctrines of the Plymouth Brethren.* 5th ed. London: Nisbet, 1866.
---. "The Plymouth Brethren." *The Presbyterian Quarterly and Princeton Review* 1 (1872) 48–77.
[---]. *Plymouth Brethrenism: Its Ecclesiastical and Doctrinal Teachings; with a Sketch of Its History.* London: Hodder & Stoughton, 1874.

———. *Plymouth-Brethrenism: A Refutation of Its Principles and Doctrines*. London: Mullan & Son, 1879.

Cross, Edwin. *The Irish Saint and Scholar: A Biography of William Kelly*. London: Chapter Two, 2004.

———. *The Life and Times of Charles Henry Mackintosh: A Biography*. London: Chapter Two, 2011.

Cross, F. L., and E. A. Livingstone, eds. *The Oxford Dictionary of the Christian Church*. 3rd ed. Oxford: Oxford University Press, 2005.

Crowley, Edward. *The Plymouth Brethren (So Called): Who They Are—Their Creed—Mode of Worship, Etc., Explained in a Letter to His Friends and Relations*. Ottawa: Loveday, 1871.

Crutchfield, Larry V. *The Origins of Dispensationalism: The Darby Factor*. Lanham, MD: University Press of America, 1992.

C[utting], Geo[rge]. *Assurance without Presumption*. London: Tract Depot, n.d.

———. *"Good in Every Man." Is it True according to God?* Stamford: "Tidings" Office, n.d.

———. *Helps for Enquirers on the Subject of Faith*. Lancing, Sussex: Kingston Bible Trust, n.d.

———. *Safety, Certainty and Enjoyment*. Oak Park, IL: Bible Truth Publishers, n.d.

———. *Why Does Man Hate the Bible?* London: Tract Depot, n.d.

D., J. S. "Question 314." *W* 19 (1889) 47 Ans. B.

Dabney, Robert L. "Theology of the Plymouth Brethren." In *Discussions of Evangelical Theology*. Vol. 1. 1890. Reprinted, London: Banner of Truth, 1967.

Dallimore, Arnold. *George Whitefield: The Life and Times of the Great Evangelist of the Eighteenth-Century Revival*. Vol. 1. Edinburgh: Banner of Truth, 1970.

———. *George Whitefield: The Life and Times of the Great Evangelist of the Eighteenth-Century Revival*. Vol. 2. Edinburgh: Banner of Truth, 1980.

Daniel, Curt. *The History and Theology of Calvinism*. Dallas: Scholarly Reprints, 1993.

Dann, Robert Bernard. *Father of Faith Missions: The Life and Times of Anthony Norris Groves*. Milton Keynes, UK: Authentic Media, 2004.

———. *The Primitivist Ecclesiology of Anthony Norris Groves: A Radical Influence on the Nineteenth-Century Protestant Church in Britain*. Victoria, BC: Trafford, 2007.

———. "The Primitivist Missiology of Anthony Norris Groves (1795–1853): A Radical Influence on Nineteenth-Century Protestant Mission." PhD diss., University of Liverpool, 2006.

Darby, John Nelson. *Additional Writings of J. N. Darby*. 2 vols. Jackson, NJ: Present Truth Publishers, 2006.

———. *Brief Exposition of the Epistle of James*. 2nd ed. London: Morrish, n.d.

———. *The Collected Writings of J. N. Darby*. Edited by William Kelly. 34 vols. Kingston-on-Thames: Stowe Hill Bible and Tract, n.d.

———. *Exposition of the Epistle to the Romans*. London: Morrish, n.d.

———. "Has Fallen Man a Free Will?" Reprinted in *Christian Truth for the Household of Faith* 11 (December 1958) 252.

———. Letter [to T. Douglas]. CBA 5540 (406), n.d.

———. *Letters of J. N. D.* 3 vols. Kingston-on-Thames: Stow Hill Bible and Tract, n.d.

———. *Letters of J. N. Darby: Supplement from French*. 2 vols. Chessington: Bible and Gospel Trust, 2014.

———. *Meditations on the Epistle to the Romans*. London: Morrish, n.d.

———. *Notes and Comments on Scripture.* 7 vols. Reprinted, Sunbury, PA: Believers Bookshelf, 1971.

———. *Notes and Jottings from Various Meetings with J. N. Darby.* Kingston-on-Thames, UK: Stow Hill Bible and Tract, n.d.

———. *Notes of Addresses.* 2 vols. London: Morrish, n.d.

———. *Notes of Sermons.* Rev. ed. London: Morrish, n.d.

[———]. "The Operations of the Spirit of God." *CWit* 4 (1837) 42–52.

———. Papers of John Nelson Darby. CBA JND/2/39, 1871–73.

———. *Spiritual Songs.* 3rd ed. London: Carter, 1900.

———. *Synopsis of the Books of the Bible.* Rev. ed. 5 vols. Cleveland: Union Gospel Press, 1942.

———. "Utter Ruin the Ground of Complete Blessing." *Words of Faith* 2 (1883) 258–59.

Dates of J. N. Darby's Collected Writings. Chessington, UK: Bible and Gospel Trust, 2013.

Daubeny, Charles. *Vindiciae Ecclesiae Anglicanae: in which Some of the False Reasonings, Incorrect Statements, and Palpable Misrepresentations, in a Publication Entitled, "The True Churchmen Ascertained" by John Overton, A.B. Are Pointed Out.* London, 1803.

Davidson, John. "Reformation and the Brethren." *Reformation Today* 12 (Nov.–Jan. 1972–73) 2–11.

Davis, M. M. "Making Our Election Sure." *W* 5 (1895) 147–48.

Davis, Thomas J. "Images of Intolerance: John Calvin in Nineteenth-Century History Textbooks." *CH* 65:2 (1996) 234–48.

———. "Rhetorical War and Reflex: Calvinism in Nineteenth-Century Popular Fiction and Twentieth-Century Criticism." *CTJ* 33 (1998) 443–56.

Deck, James G. *Hymns and Sacred Poems.* 2nd ed. London: W. H. Broom and Rouse, 1889.

Dennett, Edward. *Fundamental Truths of Salvation: Being Helps for the Anxious and for Young Believers.* London: Morrish, 1876.

———. "Scripture Notes." *CF* 16 (1889) 35.

———. "Simple Christian Truths: Repentance and Faith." *CF* 13 (1886) 152–58.

———. *The Step I Have Taken: Being Letters to a Friend, on Taking His Place with "Brethren."* 1875. Reprinted, Addison, IL: Bible Truth Publishers, 1982

"The Depravity of Man." *A Voice to the Faithful* 21 (1887) 340–52.

de Silva, J. W. *Calvinism: "Bitter for Sweet."* Kilmarnock, UK: Ritchie, 2014.

Dewart, Edward Hartley. *Broken Reeds; or, the Heresies of the Plymouth Brethren Shown to Be Contrary to Scripture and Reason.* Toronto: Wesleyan Conference Office, 1869.

Dickson, Neil T. R. *Brethren in Scotland 1838–2000: A Social Study of an Evangelical Movement.* Carlisle, UK: Paternoster, 2002.

———. "'A Darbyite Mystic': Frances Bevan (1827–1909)." In *Bible and Theology in the Brethren Movement*, edited by Neil T. R. Dickson and T. J. Marinello. Troon: Brethren Archivists and Historians Network, forthcoming.

———. "The Howards: Global, Cultural, and Religious Influence." In Gerald T. West, *From Friends to Brethren: The Howards of Tottenham—Quakers, Brethren, and Evangelicals*, edited by Tim Grass, 1–21. Troon: Brethren Archivists and Historians Network, 2016.

Dickson, Neil T. R. and Tim Grass, eds. *The Growth of the Brethren Movement: National and International Experiences.* Milton Keynes, UK: Paternoster, 2006.

Dixon, Larry Edward. "The Pneumatology of John Nelson Darby (1800–1882)." PhD diss., Drew University, 1985.

The Doctrinal Declaration of the Conference of the Evangelical Union, Reviewed and Brought to the Test of Scripture. Edinburgh: Paton & Ritchie, 1862.

"The Doctrine of Reprobation." *The Gospel Herald* 9 (1880) 178–79.

Donnelly, John Patrick. *Calvinism and Scholasticism in Vermigli's Doctrine of Man and Grace.* Studies in Medieval and Reformation Thought 18. Leiden: Brill, 1976.

Douglas, J. D. *The New International Dictionary of the Christian Church.* Grand Rapids: Zondervan, 1978.

Drummond, Andrew L. and James Bulloch. *The Church in Victorian Scotland, 1843–1874.* Edinburgh: Saint Andrew Press, 1975.

Dunlap, David. *Limiting Omnipotence: The Consequence of Calvinism: A Study of Crucial Issues in Reformed and Dispensational Theology.* Port Colborne, ON: Gospel Folio Press, 2004.

D[yer], H[enry]. "Christ as 'Door' and as 'Good Shepherd.'" *Golden Lamp* 3 (1880) 193–98.

———. "'Other Sheep I Have.'" *Echoes of Service* (1885) 83–84.

E., E. "I Want to Believe that I Am an Elect Vessel of Mercy." *Earthen Vessel* 5 (1849) 286.

Eaton, Kent. "Beware the Trumpet of Judgement! John Nelson Darby and the Nineteenth-Century Brethren." In *The Coming Deliverer: Millennial Themes in World Religions*, edited by Fiona Bowie, 119–62. Cardiff: University of Wales, 1997.

Edwards, John. *Veritas Redux: Evangelical Truths Restored.* London, 1707.

Edwards, Jonathan. *Freedom of the Will.* Edited by Paul Ramsey. New Haven: Yale University Press, 1957.

Edwards, Paul, ed. *The Encyclopedia of Philosophy.* New York: Macmillan, 1967.

Ehlert, Arnold D. *Brethren Writers: A Checklist with an Introduction to Brethren Literature and Additional Lists.* Grand Rapids: Baker, 1969.

Elliot-Binns, L. E. *The Early Evangelicals: A Religious and Social Study.* London: Lutterworth Press, 1953.

Elmore, Floyd Saunders. "A Critical Examination of the Doctrine of the Two Peoples of God in John Nelson Darby." ThD diss., Dallas Theological Seminary, 1997.

Embley, Peter L. "The Early Development of the Plymouth Brethren." In *Patterns of Sectarianism: Organisation and Ideology in Social and Religious Movements*, edited by Bryan R. Wilson, 213–43. London: Heinemann, 1967.

———. "The Origins and Early Development of the Plymouth Brethren." PhD diss, St. Paul's College, Cheltenham, 1966.

Ensor, Peter. "Justin Martyr and Penal Substitutionary Atonement." *EQ* 83.3 (2011) 217–32.

Erskine, Thomas. *The Doctrine of Election and Its Connection with the General Tenor of Christianity, Illustrated from Many Parts of Scripture, and Especially from the Epistle to the Romans.* London: James Duncan, 1837.

Evans, James Joyce, ed. *Memoir and Remains of the Rev. James Harington Evans, Late Minister of John-Street Chapel.* 2nd ed. London: Nisbet, 1855.

Faber, George Stanley. *Thoughts on the Calvinistic and Arminian Controversy.* London: Rivington, 1804.

"The Fall of Man." *TNO* 33 (1890) 320–326.

"The Falling Asleep of Dr. Case." *Echoes of Service* 42 (May 1913), 193.
Feinberg, John S. *No One Like Him: The Doctrine of God*. Wheaton, IL: Crossway, 2001.
Ferguson, Fergus. *A History of the Evangelical Union from Its Origin to the Present Time*. Glasgow: Morison, 1876.
Ferguson, Sinclair. "'Blesséd Assurance, Jesus Is Mine'? Definite Atonement and the Cure of Souls." In *From Heaven He Came and Sought Her: Definite Atonement in Historical, Biblical, Theological, and Pastoral Perspective*, edited by David Gibson and Jonathan Gibson, 607–31. Wheaton, IL: Crossway, 2013.
———. *The Whole Christ: Legalism, Antinomianism, and Gospel Assurance—Why the Marrow Controversy Still Matters*. Wheaton, IL: Crossway, 2016.
Ferguson, Sinclair B. and David F. Wright. *New Dictionary of Theology*. Downers Grove, IL: InterVarsity Press, 1988.
Fesko, J. V. *The Theology of the Westminster Standards: Historical Context and Theological Insights*. Wheaton, IL: Crossway, 2014.
A Few Hymns and Some Spiritual Songs Selected 1856, for the Little Flock. Rev. ed. London: Morrish, 1903.
Field, David P. *Rigide Calvinism in a Softer Dresse: The Moderate Presbyterianism of John Howe, 1630–1705*. Edinburgh: Rutherford House, 2004.
Findlay, J. F., Jr. *Dwight L. Moody: American Evangelist, 1837–1899*. Grand Rapids: Baker, 1969.
Finney, Charles G. *Lectures on Systematic Theology*. Edited by J. H. Fairchild. 1878. Reprinted, South Gate, CA: Colporter Kemp, 1944.
Fiske, John. *The Beginnings of New England; or the Puritan Theocracy in Its Relations to Civil and Religious Liberty*. 1902. Reprinted, Boston: Houghton, Mifflin, 1889.
Flavel, John. *The Works of John Flavel*. Vol. 2. 1820. Reprinted, Edinburgh: Banner of Truth, 1968.
Fleming, Kenneth C. "Inglis Fleming: Understudy to the 'Chief Men.'" *Emmaus Journal* 15 (2006) 109–25.
Fletcher, John. *The Works of the Reverend John Fletcher*. Vol. 2. 1833. Reprinted, Salem, OH: Schmul, 1974.
Fromow, George H. *B. W. Newton and Dr. S. P. Tregelles: Teachers of the Faith and Future*. 2nd ed. London: Sovereign Grace Advent Testimony, 1969.
Fry Manuscript. MSS of history, letters, and recollections of B. W. Newton. Transcribed and edited by A. C. Fry and F. W. Wyatt, n.d. CBA 7049.
Fuller, Andrew. *The Complete Works of the Rev. Andrew Fuller*. 3 vols. Edited by Joseph Belcher. London, 1845. Reprinted, Harrisonburg, VA: Sprinkle, 1988.
Fuller, Andrew Gunton. *Andrew Fuller*. London: Hodder & Stoughton, 1882.
Garrett, James Leo, Jr. *Baptist Theology: A Four-Century Study*. Macon, GA: Mercer University Press, 2009.
Gerstner, John H. *Wrongly Dividing the Word of Truth: A Critique of Dispensationalism*. Brentwood, TN: Wogemuth & Hyatt, 1991.
Gibson, David, and Jonathan Gibson, eds. *From Heaven He Came and Sought Her: Definite Atonement in Historical, Biblical, Theological, and Pastoral Perspective*. Wheaton, IL: Crossway, 2013.
Gill, John. *The Cause of God and Truth*. 1735–38. Reprinted, London: 1855.
Gilmore, William. *These Seventy Years*. Kilmarnock, UK: John Ritchie, n.d.
Goddard, John Howard. "The Contribution of John Nelson Darby to Soteriology, Ecclesiology, and Eschatology." ThD diss., Dallas Theological Seminary, 1948.

Godfrey, William Robert. "Tensions within International Calvinism: The Debate on the Atonement at the Synod of Dort, 1618–1619." PhD diss., Stanford University, 1974.

Gosse, P. H. (Mr & Mrs). *Narrative Tracts.* London: Morgan & Scott, n.d.

Goulding, Christopher. *A Series of Letters on Divine Subjects.* London: Bensley, 1814.

Grant, F. W. *Atonement in Type, Prophecy, and Accomplishment.* New York: Loizeaux, n.d.

———. *Christian Holiness; Its Roots and Fruits: A Review of Dr. Steele's "Antinomianism Revived."* New York: Loizeaux, n.d.

———. *Leaves from the Book: Being Miscellaneous Papers for the Household of Faith.* New York: Loizeaux, n.d.

———. *Miscellaneous Writings of F. W. Grant.* 3 vols. New York: Loizeaux, n.d.

———. *The Numerical Bible: Hebrews to Revelation.* Neptune, NJ: Loizeaux, 1902.

[———]. "Some Further Notes on the Day of Atonement." *Help and Food for the Household of Faith* 3 (1885) 25–28.

———. "The Sovereignty of God in Salvation." *Help and Food for the Household of Faith* 2 (1884) 163–70; 180–87.

Grass, Timothy George. "The Church's Ruin and Restoration: The Development of Ecclesiology in the Plymouth Brethren and the Catholic Apostolic Church, c. 1825–c. 1866." PhD thesis, King's College, London, 1997.

———. *Edward Irving: The Lord's Watchman.* Milton Keynes, UK: Paternoster, 2011.

———. *Gathering to His Name: The Story of Open Brethren in Britain and Ireland.* Milton Keynes, UK: Paternoster, 2006.

———. *Generations: British Brethren Mission to Spain, 1834–1990.* Ramsey, UK: Thornhill Media, 2011.

———. "The Quest for Identity in British Brethren Historiography: Some Reflections from an Outsider." In *The Growth of the Brethren Movement: National and International Experiences,* edited by Neil T. R. Dickson and Tim Grass, 11–27. Milton Keynes, UK: Paternoster, 2006.

———. "Thomas Dowglass (1806–57)—Evangelist." *BAHNR* 4 (2006) 2–21.

———. "Undenominationalism in Britain, 1840–1914." In *Grounded in Grace: Essays to Honour Ian M. Randall,* edited by Pieter J. Lalleman, Peter J. Morden, and Anthony R. Cross, 69–84. London: Spurgeon's College, 2013.

———, ed. *Witness in Many Lands: Leadership and Outreach among the Brethren.* Troon, UK: Brethren Archivists and Historians Network, 2013.

Green, Jay, ed. *The Five Points of Calvinism in a Series of Letters by Horatius Bonar, Andrew Fuller, John Calvin, John Gill, Thomas Goodwin, Jonathan Edwards.* Grand Rapids: Sovereign Grace, 1971.

Gribben, Crawford. *God's Irishmen: Theological Debates in Cromwellian Ireland.* Oxford: Oxford University Press, 2007.

———. *The Irish Puritans: James Ussher and the Reformation of the Church.* Darlington, UK: Evangelical Press, 2003.

———. *John Owen and English Puritanism: Experiences of Defeat.* Oxford: Oxford University Press, 2016.

———. "'The Worst Sect that a Christian Man Can Meet': Opposition to the Plymouth Brethren in Ireland and Scotland, 1859–1900." *Scottish Studies Review* 3 (2002) 34–53.

Groves, Anthony N. *Journal of a Residence at Bagdad.* London: Nisbet, 1832.

[Groves, Harriet Baynes]. *Memoir of the Late Anthony Norris Groves containing extracts from his Letters and Journals.* Compiled by his widow. 2nd edition. London: Nisbet, 1857.

G[roves], Henry. "The Day of Atonement: Its Godward and Manward Aspects." *Golden Lamp* 2 (1879) 265–73.

[―――]. "Notes and Replies." *Golden Lamp* 1 (1878) 143–44.

[―――]. "Notes and Replies." *Golden Lamp* 3 (1880) 168.

Grudem, Wayne. *Systematic Theology: An Introduction to Biblical Doctrine.* Grand Rapids: Zondervan, 1994.

Gundry, Stanley N. *Love Them In: The Life and Theology of D. L. Moody.* Grand Rapids: Baker, 1976.

H., W. "Suggestions for Reconciling the Arminian and Calvinist." *CO* 17 (1818) 211–14.

[Haldane, A.]. *Errors of the Darby and Plymouth Sect.* 2nd ed. London: Nisbet, 1862.

Hall, Percy Francis. *Discipleship: or Reasons for Resigning His Naval Rank and Pay.* 2nd ed. London: Nisbet, 1835.

Hambrick-Stowe, Charles E. *Charles G. Finney and the Spirit of American Evangelicalism.* Grand Rapids: Eerdmans, 1996.

―――. *The Practice of Piety: Puritan Devotional Disciplines in Seventeenth-Century New England.* Chapel Hill: University of North Carolina Press, 1982.

Hamilton, Ian. *The Erosion of Calvinist Orthodoxy: Drifting from the Truth in Confessional Scottish Churches.* Fearn, Mentor, 2010.

Hamilton, William. *An Inquiry into the Scriptural Character of the Revival of 1859.* 1866. Reprinted, Hudsonville, MI: Reformed Book Outlet, 1993.

Hampton, Stephen. *Anti-Arminians: The Anglican Reformed Tradition from Charles II to George I.* Oxford: Oxford University Press, 2008.

Harris, J. L. *Antinomianism and Legalism: What Is the Rule for Christian Conduct?* Reprinted, London: Chapter Two, 1997.

―――. *Law and Grace: Being Notes of Lectures on the Epistle to the Galatians.* London: Yapp and Hawkins, n.d. www.stempublishing.com/authors/JL_Harris/JLH_Law_Grace1.html.

Hart, D. G. *Calvinism: A History.* New Haven: Yale University Press, 2013.

Harvey, Bonnie. *George Müller: Man of Faith.* Uhrichsville, OH: Barbour, 1998.

Harvey, James. "Donald Ross: A Soteriological Retrospective." *Impact '59* (December 2009) 1–70. http://impact59.files.wordpress.com/2010/01/donald-ross-soteriological-retrospective-dec09.pdf.

Hatch, Nathan O. *The Democratization of American Christianity.* New Haven: Yale University Press, 1989.

Hawker, Robert. *The Works of the Rev. Robert Hawker, D.D.* Vol. 10. London: Palmer, 1831.

Hawthorn, John. *Alexander Marshall: Evangelist, Author, and Pioneer.* London: Pickering & Inglis, [1929].

Hayden, Roger. *Continuity and Change: Evangelical Calvinism among Eighteenth-Century Baptist Ministers Trained at Bristol Academy, 1690–1791.* Chipping Norton: Lynn, 2006.

―――. *English Baptist History and Heritage.* 2nd ed. Didcot: Baptist Union of Great Britain, 2005.

Haykin, Michael A. G. "Evangelicalism and the Enlightenment: A Reassessment." In *The Advent of Evangelicalism: Exploring Historical Continuities*, edited by Michael A. G. Haykin and Kenneth J. Stewart, 37–60. Nashville: B & H, 2008.

Haykin, Michael A. G. and Mark Jones, eds. *Drawn into Controversie: Reformed Theological Diversity and Debates within Seventeenth-Century British Puritanism*. Reformed Historical Theology, vol. 17. Göttingen: Vandenhoeck & Ruprecht, 2011.

Haykin, Michael A. G. and Kenneth J. Stewart, eds. *The Advent of Evangelicalism: Exploring Historical Continuities*. Nashville: B & H, 2008.

Helm, Paul. *Eternal God: A Study of God without Time*. Oxford: Clarendon, 1988.

———. *Calvin and the Calvinists*. Edinburgh: Banner of Truth, 1982.

———. "Calvin, A. M. Toplady and the Bebbington Thesis." In *The Advent of Evangelicalism: Exploring Historical Continuities*, edited by Michael A. G. Haykin and Kenneth J. Stewart, 199–220. Nashville: B & H, 2008.

———. *The Providence of God*. Downers Grove, IL: InterVarsity Press, 1994.

Hempton, David and Myrtle Hill. *Evangelical Protestantism in Ulster Society 1740–1890*. London: Routledge, 1992.

Henzel, Ronald M. "Darby, Dualism and the Decline of Dispensationalism." M.A. thesis, Wheaton College Graduate School, 2002.

Heron, Alasdair I. C., ed. *The Westminster Confession in the Church Today*. Edinburgh: Saint Andrew Press, 1982.

Hindmarsh, D. Bruce. *The Evangelical Conversion Narrative: Spiritual Autobiography in Early Modern England*. Oxford: Oxford University Press, 2005.

———. *John Newton and the English Evangelical Tradition: Between the Conversions of Wesley and Wilberforce*. 1996. Reprinted, Grand Rapids: Eerdmans, 2001.

———. "The Reception of Jonathan Edwards by Early Evangelicals in England." In *Jonathan Edwards at Home and Abroad: Historical Memories, Cultural Movements, Global Horizons*, edited by David W. Kling and Douglas A. Sweeney, 201–21. Columbia: University of South Carolina, 2003.

Hogg, David S. "'Sufficient for All, Efficient for Some': Definite Atonement in the Medieval Church." In *From Heaven He Came and Sought Her: Definite Atonement in Historical, Biblical, Theological, and Pastoral Perspective*, edited by David Gibson and Jonathan Gibson, 75–95. Wheaton, IL: Crossway, 2013.

Holmes, Andrew R. *The Shaping of Ulster Presbyterian Belief and Practice, 1770–1840*. Oxford: Oxford University Press, 2006.

Holmes, Frank. *Brother Indeed: The Life of Robert Cleaver Chapman "Barnstaple Patriarch."* London: Victory, 1956.

Hooker, Thomas. *The Application of Redemption*. 1657. Reprinted, Ames, IA: International Outreach, 2008.

Hopkins, Mark. *Nonconformity's Romantic Generation: Evangelical and Liberal Theologies in Victorian England*. Carlisle, UK: Paternoster, 2004.

Horrocks, Don. *Laws of the Spiritual Order: Innovation and Reconstruction in the Soteriology of Thomas Erskine of Linlathen*. Carlisle, UK: Paternoster, 2004.

Horton, Michael. *The Christian Faith: A Systematic Theology for Pilgrims on the Way*. Grand Rapids: Zondervan, 2011.

Houston, Thomas. *Plymouthism and Revivalism: or, the Duty of Contending for the Faith in Opposition to Prevailing Errors and Corruptions*. 2nd ed. Belfast: Aitchison, 1874.

Howard, I. E. *"New Views," Compared with the Word of God.* 2nd ed. London: Groombridge, 1843.
Huebner, R. A. *Free-will? or Not of Him that Willeth? Does Man Have Free Moral Agency or Is He Morally Dead in Trespasses and Sins, Needing Sovereign Quickening?* Morganville, NJ: Present Truth, 1988.
———. *God's Sovereignty and Glory in the Election and Salvation of Lost Men.* Jackson, NJ: Present Truth, 2003.
———. *The Work of Christ on the Cross and Some of Its Results: Propitiation, Substitution, the Righteousness of God, Etc.; What Is for the World and What Is for the Believer?* Morganville, NJ: Present Truth, 2002.
Hunt, Dave. *What Love Is This? Calvinism's Misrepresentation of God.* Rev. ed. Bend, OR: Berean Call, 2004.
Hutchinson, J. G. *Whose Praise Is in the Gospel: A Record of One Hundred and Nine Irish Evangelists.* Glasgow: Gospel Tract Publications, 2002.
I. "Can You Say You Are Saved?" *God's Glad Tidings* 5 (1876) 184–87.
Ingenuus. "Conciliatory Remarks on the Calvinistic Controversy." *CO* 17 (1818) 8–12.
Ironside, H. A. *A Historical Sketch of the Brethren Movement.* Rev. ed. Neptune, NJ: Loizeaux, 1985.
Jeffrey, Kenneth S. *When the Lord Walked the Land: The 1858–62 Revival in the North East of Scotland.* Carlisle, UK: Paternoster, 2002.
Jeffery, Steve, Michael Ovey, and Andrew Sach. *Pierced for Our Transgressions: Rediscovering the Glory of Penal Substitution.* Wheaton, IL: Crossway, 2007.
Jewett, Paul K. *Election and Predestination.* Grand Rapids: Eerdmans, 1985.
Johnson, James E. "Charles G. Finney and a Theology of Revivalism." *CH* 38.3 (1969) 338–58.
Jones, John Morgan and William Morgan. *The Calvinistic Methodist Fathers of Wales.* 2 vols. Translated by John Aaron. Edinburgh: Banner of Truth, 2008.
K., F. "Expository Papers on the Romans." *CF* 4 (1877) 298–300.
K., H. "Remarks on Romans IX. 19." *The Evangelical Magazine* 14 (1806) 257–59.
K., I. "A Morsel of the Bread of Life." *GS* 5 (July 1839) 152–53.
Kelly, William. "The Archdeacon of Durham on Certain Religious Errors." *BT* 9 (1872) 96.
———. "The Catholic Apostolic Body, or Irvingites." *BT* 18 (1890) 93–95.
———. *Christian Worship.* Reprinted, London: Chapter Two, 2004.
———. *The Day of Atonement.* London: Race, 1925.
[———]. "The Early Chapters of Genesis." *BT* 19 (1893) 209–211.
———. *The Epistles of Peter.* London: Hammond, n.d.
———. *An Exposition of the Acts of the Apostles.* 3rd ed. London: Hammond, 1952.
———. *An Exposition of the Epistles of John the Apostle.* London: Weston, 1905.
———. *An Exposition of the Gospel of John.* London: Race, 1923.
———. *An Exposition of the Gospel of Luke.* Edited by E. E. Whitefield. London: Pickering & Inglis, n.d.
———. "From Troas to Miletus." *BT* 12 (1878) 169–74.
———. *The Gospel of God.* London: T. Weston, n.d.
———. *The Great Olivet Prophecy of the Lord Jesus Christ.* London: Hammond, n.d.
———. "Hold Fast that which Thou Hast." *BT* ns 12 (1918) 125–28.
———. *Hymns and Poems of William Kelly.* London: Chapter Two, 2005.
[———]. "The Intermediate State." *BT* NS 3 (1900) 80.

———. *Lectures Introductory to the Study of the Acts, The Catholic Epistles, and the Revelation*. 1870. Reprinted, Winschoten, Netherlands: Heijkoop, 1970.

———. *Lectures Introductory to the Study of the Minor Prophets*. 5th ed. London: Hammond, n.d.

———. *Lectures on the Church of God*. London: Morrish, n.d.

———. *Lectures on the Day of Atonement*. Rev. ed. London: Weston, 1902.

———. *Lectures on the Epistle of Paul, the Apostle to the Colossians*. London: Morrish, n.d.

———. *Lectures on the Epistle of Paul, the Apostle to the Ephesians*. London: Morrish, n.d.

———. *Lectures on the Gospel of Matthew*. Rev. ed. New York: Loizeaux, 1911.

———. *Lectures on the New Testament Doctrine of the Holy Spirit*. Rev. ed. London: Morrish, 1913.

———. *Notes on the Epistle of Paul, the Apostle, to the Romans*. London: Morrish, 1873.

———. *Notes on the First Epistle of Paul the Apostle to the Corinthians*. London: Morrish, 1878.

———. *Notes on the Second Epistle of Paul the Apostle to the Corinthians, with a New Translation*. London: Morrish, 1882.

———. "Purchase and Redemption." *BT* ns 6 (1907) 261–65, 280–84.

———. *The Purpose of God for His Sons and Heirs*. London: Weston, 1906.

———. "The Rev. A. Moody Stuart on 'Brethren.'" www.stempublishing.com/authors/kelly/7subjcts/moodystr.html.

———. "Scripture Queries and Answers." *BT* (April 1905) 254.

———. "The 'Strange Doctrine' on Propitiation." December 1899. http://www.stempublishing.com/authors/kelly/7subjcts/ces_prop.html.

———. "Synoptical Study of the Gospels." *The Christian Annotator* 3:61 (1856) 207.

[———]. "Thoughts on Ephesians." *BT* 16 (1887) 329–31.

———. "To Correspondents." *BT* 12 (1878) 176.

Kendall, R. T. *Calvin and English Calvinism to 1649*. 2nd ed. Milton Keynes, UK: Paternoster, 1979.

Kennedy, J. *Hyper-Evangelism: "Another Gospel" though a Mighty Power: A Review of the Recent Religious Movement in Scotland*. 7th ed. London: Houlston, 1875.

———. *A Reply to Dr. Bonar's Defence of Hyper-Evangelism*. Edinburgh: Lyon & Gemmell, 1875.

Kennedy, John and Horatius Bonar. *Evangelism: A Reformed Debate*. Portdinorwic, Wales: James Begg Society, 1997.

Kimbro, Reginald C. *The Gospel According to Dispensationalism: A Doctrinal Survey of the System that Permeated Fundamentalism*. Toronto: Wittenburg, 1995.

King, Henry M. "The Plymouth Brethren." *Baptist Review* 3 (1881) 438–65.

Krapohl, Robert H. "A Search for Purity: The Controversial Life of John Nelson Darby." PhD diss, Baylor University, 1988.

Kuyper, Abraham. *Lectures on Calvinism*. Grand Rapids: Eerdmans, 1931.

Lachman, David C. *The Marrow Controversy*. Edinburgh: Rutherford House, 1988.

Laing, William. "Substitution." *W* 18 (1888) 27–28.

Lang, G. H. *An Ordered Life: An Autobiography*. London: Paternoster, 1959.

Larsen, Timothy, ed. *Biographical Dictionary of Evangelicals*. Downers Grove, IL: InterVarsity Press, 2003.

———. "'Living by Faith': A Short History of Brethren Practice." *BAHNR* 1 (1998) 67–102. Reprinted in *Emmaus Journal* 12 (2003) 277–315.

———. *A People of One Book: The Bible and the Victorians*. Oxford: Oxford University Press, 2011.

Letham, Robert. "Faith and Assurance in Early Calvinism: A Model of Continuity and Diversity." In *Later Calvinism: International Perspectives*, edited by W. Fred Graham, 355–84. Kirksville, MO: Sixteenth Century Journal Publishers, 1994.

———. *The Westminster Assembly: Reading Its Theology in Historical Context*. Phillipsburg, NJ: P & R Publishing, 2009.

Lewis, Donald M., ed. *Blackwell Dictionary of Evangelical Biography, 1730–1860*. Oxford: Blackwell, 1995.

———. *Lighten Their Darkness: The Evangelical Mission to Working-Class London, 1828–1860*. New York: Greenwood, 1986.

Lichtenstein, Aharon. *Henry More: The Rational Theology of a Cambridge Platonist*. Cambridge: Harvard University Press, 1962.

Lincoln, William. "Is it necessary for a person, in order to be assured of salvation, to know the exact day, hour, and moment of his conversion?" *NW* 14 (1884) 73–76.

———. *Lectures on the Epistle to the Ephesians*. Kilmarnock, UK: Ritchie, n.d.

———. *Lectures on the Epistles to the Thessalonians*. Kilmarnock, UK: Ritchie, n.d.

———. *Lectures on the First and Second Epistles of Peter*. Kilmarnock, UK: Ritchie, n.d.

———. "Notes on Ephesians." *BC* 4 (November 1884) 167–72, 177–81.

Lineham, Peter J. "The Significance of J. G. Deck 1807–1884." *Christian Brethren Research Fellowship Journal* 107 (November 1986) 13–34.

Livingston, James C. *Religious Thought in the Victorian Age: Challenges and Reconceptions*. London: Continuum, 2006.

Lloyd-Jones, D. Martyn. *Preaching and Preachers*. Grand Rapids: Zondervan, 1971.

———. *The Puritans: Their Origins and Successors*. Edinburgh: Banner of Truth, 1987.

Lucas, Sean Michael. "Charles Finney's Theology of Revival: Moral Depravity." *The Master's Seminary Journal* 6:2 (1995) 197–221.

Luther, Martin. *The Bondage of the Will*. Translated by J. I. Packer and O. R. Johnston. Grand Rapids: Revell, 1957.

M., J. "Faith: Is It Involuntary?" *W* 8 (1898) 67–68.

———. "Human Depravity." *Baptist Magazine* 24 (1832) 381–83.

MacInnes, John. *The Evangelical Movement in the Highlands of Scotland, 1688 to 1800*. Aberdeen: Aberdeen University Press, 1951.

Macintosh, Duncan. *Brethrenism; or the Special Teachings, Ecclesiastical and Doctrinal, of Brethren, or Plymouth Brethren; Compiled from Their Own Writings. With Strictures*. 3rd ed. London: Houlston & Sons, 1872.

Mackintosh, C. H. "'Accepted' and 'Acceptable.'" *TNO* 17 (1874) 246–50.

———. "Assurance." *TNO* 22 (1879) 281–88.

[———]. "Correspondence." *TNO* 21 (1878) 195–96.

[———.] "Glad Tidings." *TNO* 10 (1867) 1–8, 21–25, 41–49, 61–67, 81–89.

———. "'God for Us.'" *TNO* 16 (1873) 29–39, 57–68.

———. "The Great Commission." *TNO* 20 (1877) 1–11, 29–38, 57–65, 85–93, 113–21, 141–51, 169–83, 197–206.

[———]. "Landmarks and Stumblingblocks." *TNO* 6 (1863) 141–48, 176–78.

———. *Miscellaneous Writings of C. H. M.* 6 vols. New York: Loizeaux, 1898.

———. *Notes on the Book of Genesis*. New York: Loizeaux, 1880.

[———]. "One-Sided Theology." *TNO* 19 (1876) 10–16.
[———]. "Responsibility and Power." *TNO* 17 (1874) 57–63.
———. *Short Papers*. 2 vols. Sunbury, PA: Believers Bookshelf, 1975.
MacLeod, David J. "Walter Scott: A Link in Dispensationalism between Darby and Scofield?" *Bibliotheca Sacra* 153 (1996) 155–78. Reprinted in *Witness in Many Lands: Leadership and Outreach among the Brethren*, edited by Tim Grass, 111–31. Troon: Brethren Archivists and Historians Network, 2013.
MacLeod, James Lachlan. *The Second Disruption: The Free Church in Victorian Scotland and the Origins of the Free Presbyterian Church*. East Linton: Tuckwell Press, 2000.
Macleod, John. *Scottish Theology in Relation to Church History since the Reformation*. 2nd ed. Edinburgh: Publications Committee of the Free Church of Scotland, 1946.
Macpherson, John. *Henry Moorhouse: The English Evangelist*. Kilmarnock, UK: Ritiche, n.d.
———. *The Life and Labours of Duncan Matheson: The Scottish Evangelist*. London: Morgan & Scott, 1910.
Marsden, George M. *Jonathan Edwards: A Life*. New Haven: Yale University Press, 2003.
———. *Fundamentalism and American Culture: The Shaping of Twentieth-Century Evangelicalism 1870–1925*. New York: Oxford University Press, 1980.
Marshall, Alexander, ed. *Cleansed, Clothed, Crowned*. Glasgow: Pickering & Inglis, n.d.
———. "Dr Andrew Bonar." *W* 25 (1895) 47–49.
———. "'A Full Gospel.'" *W* 41 (1911) 127–28.
———. *God's Way of Salvation*. 1888. Reprinted, Chicago: Moody, n.d.
———. *God's Wonderful Love: The Gospel in Miniature*. London: Pickering & Inglis, n.d.
———, ed. *A Great Ransom*. Glasgow: Pickering & Inglis, n.d.
———, ed. *Heard Round the Globe*. Glasgow: Pickering & Inglis, n.d.
———. "Hindrances to Progress in the Gospel." *W* 35 (1905) 149–51, 167–68, 182–85.
———. *"Holding Fast the Faithful Word." or Whither Are We Drifting?* Glasgow: Pickering & Inglis, [1908].
———. "The Life of Dwight L. Moody." *W* 31 (1901) 42–45, 58–60.
———, ed. *Love's Golden Links*. Glasgow: Pickering & Inglis, n.d.
———. "Power Gone." *W* 21 (1891) 11–12.
———. *Review of "Reverend" R. Strachan's Book Entitled "Wandering Lights: A Stricture on the Doctrines and Methods of Brethrenism."* Glasgow: The Witness Office, n.d.
———, ed. *The Royal Refuge*. Glasgow: Pickering & Inglis, n.d.
———. "The Soul-winner (C. H. Spurgeon)." *W* 26 (1896) 22–25.
———. "Shall We Preach Law or Grace?" *W* 54 (1924) 300–301.
———. *Straight Paths for the Children of God*. Sacramento, CA: Bible House Press, n.d.
———. "Telling a Sinner that Christ Died for Him." *W* 57 (1927) 131.
———. "A Visit to the Inner and Outer Hebrides." *W* 49 (September 1919) 149.
———. *Will a God of Love Punish Any of His Creatures for Ever?* London: Pickering & Inglis, n.d.
———. "Work in the Highlands." *W* 41 (1911) 176–77.
Martyn, Henry. *Sermons, by the Late Rev. Henry Martyn, B.D*. Boston, 1822.
Mathison, Keith A. *Dispensationalism: Rightly Dividing the People of God?* Phillipsburg, NJ: P & R Publications, 1995.
M'Clintock, John and James Strong, eds. *Cyclopædia of Biblical, Theological, and Ecclesiastical Literature*. 1879. Reprinted, Grand Rapids: Baker, 1970.

McDowell, Ian. "The Influence of the 'Plymouth Brethren' on Victorian Society and Religion." *EQ* 55.4 (1983) 211–22.
McFarlane, Graham W. P. *Christ and the Spirit: The Doctrine of the Incarnation according to Edward Irving*. Carlisle, UK: Paternoster, 1996.
McInelly, Brett C. *Textual Warfare and the Making of Methodism*. Oxford: Oxford University Press, 2014.
McIntosh, Hugh. *The New Prophets: Being an Account of the Operations of the Northern Evangelistic Society*. Aberdeen: Milne, 1871.
McKee, John. "Revivals, Revivalism and Calvinism with Special Reference to Ireland." In *Ebb and Flow: Essays in Church History in Honour of R. Finlay G. Holmes*. Edited by W. Donald Patton, 87–100. Belfast: Presbyterian Historical Society of Ireland, 2002.
McKim, Donald, ed. *Encyclopedia of the Reformed Faith*. Louisville: Westminster John Knox, 1992.
McLaren, Ross Howlett. "The Triple Tradition: The Origin and Development of the Open Brethren in North America." M.A. thesis, Vanderbilt University, 1982. Edited and reprinted in the *Emmaus Journal* in four parts: 4 (1995) 169–208; 5 (1996) 57–87 and 161–203; 6 (1997) 129–50.
McVicker, J. G. *Selected Letters with Brief Memoir of J. G. M'Vicker*. Edited by Max Reich. London: Office of Echoes of Service, 1902.
Miley, John. *Systematic Theology*. 2 vols. 1893. Reprinted, Peabody, MA: Hendrickson, 1989.
Miller, Andrew. *Meditations on the Grace and Glory of the Blessed God as Seen in the Gospel of the Old and New Testaments*. Glasgow: Pickering & Inglis, n.d.
———. *Meditations on the Song of Solomon*. Oak Park, IL: Bible Truth Publishers, n.d.
———. *Miller's Church History: From First to Twentieth Century*. Grand Rapids: Zondervan, 1964.
Miller, Basil. *George Muller: A Man of Faith*. 4th ed. Grand Rapids: Zondervan, 1941.
Mills, Brian and Patrick Sookhdeo. "Revival and the Brethren." *The Harvester* 57 (September 1978) 262, 265
The Missionary Echo.
"Modern Antinomianism." *The Eclectic Review* 22 (1824) 508-28.
Moncreiff, G. R., ed. *Remains of Thomas Byrth, Rector of Wallasey*. London, 1851.
Moody, William R. *The Life of Dwight L. Moody*. New York: Fleming H. Revell, 1900.
Moore, Jonathan D. *English Hypothetical Universalism: John Preston and the Softening of Reformed Theology*. Grand Rapids: Eerdmans, 2007.
———. "The Extent of the Atonement: English Hypothetical Universalism versus Particular Redemption." In *Drawn into Controversie: Reformed Theological Diversity and Debates within Seventeenth-Century British Puritanism*, edited by Michael A.G. Haykin and Mark Jones, 124–61. Göttingen: Vandenhoeck & Ruprecht, 2011.
Morden, Peter. J. *Offering Christ to the World: Andrew Fuller (1754–1815) and the Revival of Eighteenth Century Particular Baptist Life*. Carlisle, UK: Paternoster, 2003.
Morgan, Edmund S. *Visible Saints: The History of a Puritan Idea*. Ithaca, NY: Cornell University Press, 1963.
Morison, James. "Apology for those Evangelical Doctrines which Maintain and Establish the Freeness of the Grace of God to All." *The Evangelical Repository* 1 (Sept. 1862) 1–80.

———, et al. *The Worthies of the Evangelical Union Being the Lives and Labours of Deceased Evangelical Union Ministers*. Glasgow: Morison, 1883.

M[uir], T. D. W. "Mr. John Gill." *OR* 34 (1921) 17–20.

Müller, George. *Jehovah Magnified*. Bristol: Bible and Tract Depot, 1876.

———. *A Narrative of Some of the Lord's Dealings with George Müller*. 6th ed. London: J. Nisbet, 1860.

———. *Sermons and Addresses*. Bristol: Mack, 1898.

Muller, Richard A. *After Calvin: Studies in the Development of a Theological Tradition*. Oxford: Oxford University Press, 2003.

———. *Calvin and the Reformed Tradition: On the Work of Christ and the Order of Salvation*. Grand Rapids: Baker Academic, 2012.

———. *Christ and the Decree: Christology and Predestination in Reformed Theology from Calvin to Perkins*. Grand Rapids: Baker Academic, 2008.

———. "How Many Points?" *CTJ* 28 (1993) 425–33.

———. "Perkins' *A Golden Chaine*: Predestinarian System or Schematized *Ordo Salutis?*" *Sixteenth Century Journal* 9 (1978) 69–81.

———. "Philip Doddridge and the Formation of Calvinistic Theology in an Era of Rationalism and Deconfessionalization." In *Religion, Politics and Dissent, 1660–1832: Essays in Honour of James E. Bradley*, edited by Robert D. Cornwall and William Gibson, 65–84. Farnham, UK: Ashgate, 2010.

———. "The Placement of Predestination in Reformed Theology: Issue or Non-Issue?" *CTJ* 40 (2005) 184–210.

———. *Post-Reformation Reformed Dogmatics: The Rise and Development of Reformed Orthodoxy, ca. 1520 to ca. 1725*. Vol. 4, *The Triunity of God*. Grand Rapids: Baker, 2003.

Murray, Iain H. *The Forgotten Spurgeon*. 2nd ed. Edinburgh. Banner of Truth, 1973.

———. *The Life of Arthur W. Pink*. Rev. ed. Edinburgh: Banner of Truth, 2004.

———. *Spurgeon v. Hyper-Calvinism: The Battle for Gospel Preaching*. Edinburgh: Banner of Truth, 1995.

Murray, John. "Calvin, Dort, and Westminster on Predestination—A Comparative Study." In *Crisis in the Reformed Churches: Essays in Commemoration of the Great Synod of Dort, 1618–1619*, edited by Peter Y. De Jong, 183–194. Grand Rapids: Reformed Fellowship, 1968

Murray, John J. "The Marrow Controversy: Thomas Boston and the Free Offer." In *Preaching and Revival*, 34–56. London: Westminster Conference, 1984.

Naylor, Peter. *Calvinism, Communion and the Baptists: A Study of English Calvinistic Baptists From the Late 1600s to the Early 1800s*. Milton Keynes, UK: Paternoster, 2003.

———. *Picking Up a Pin for the Lord: English Particular Baptists from 1688 to the Early Nineteenth Century*. London: Grace Publications, 1992.

Neatby, William Blair. *A History of the Plymouth Brethren*. 2nd ed. London: Hodder & Stoughton, 1902.

———. "Mr. William Kelly as a Theologian." *The Expositor* 4.19 (July, 1907) 70–86.

Nebeker, Gary Lynn. "The Hope of Heavenly Glory in John Nelson Darby (1800–1882)." PhD diss., Dallas Theological Seminary, 1997.

Needham, Geo[rge] C. *Recollections of Henry Moorhouse, Evangelist*. Chicago: Revell, 1881.

Nettles, Thomas J. "Andrew Fuller (1754–1815)." In *The British Particular Baptists 1638–1910*, vol. 2, edited by Michael A. G. Haykin, 96–141. Springfield, MO: Particular Baptist Press, 2000.

———. *By His Grace and for His Glory: A Historical, Theological and Practical Study of the Doctrines of Grace in Baptist Life*. Rev. ed. Cape Coral, FL: Founders, 2006.

———. "John Wesley's Contention with Calvinism: Interactions Then and Now." In *The Grace of God, the Bondage of the Will*, vol. 2, edited by Thomas R. Schreiner and Bruce A. Ware, 297–322. Grand Rapids: Baker, 1995.

———. *Living by Revealed Truth: The Life and Pastoral Theology of Charles Haddon Spurgeon*. Fearn: Mentor, 2013.

———. "The Passion and Doctrine of Andrew Fuller in *The Gospel Worthy of All Acceptation*." *SBJT* 17.2 (2013) 20–42.

Newberry, Thomas. "God's Will, and Man's Independency." *BM* 4 (1894) 125.

[Newton, Benjamin Wills]. "Doctrines of the Church in Newman Street." *CWit* 2 (1835) 111–28, *121–*28.

———. *An Erroneous Mode of Stating the Gospel Considered*. 1877. Reprinted, London: Cottey, 1933.

[———]. "On the Propitiation of Christ." *CWit* 1 (1834; 2nd ed., 1837) 32–35.

———. *Salvation by Substitution*. 3rd ed. London: Collins, 1909.

Nichols, James. *Calvinism and Arminianism Compared in Their Principles and Tendency*. London: Nichols, 1824.

Nichols, John. *Plymouthism Weighed in the Balances*. Montreal: Drysdale, n.d.

Nockles, Peter Benedict. *The Oxford Movement in Context: Anglican High Churchmanship, 1760–1857*. Cambridge: Cambridge University Press, 1994.

Noel, Napoleon. *The History of the Brethren*. Edited by William F. Knapp. 2 vols. Denver: Knapp, 1936.

Noll, Mark. *The Rise of Evangelicalism: The Age of Edwards, Whitefield and the Wesleys*. Downers Grove, IL: InterVarsity, 2003.

The Northern Intelligencer.

"Notes Taken at Hamilton Conference, Jan. 1884." *BC* 4 (March 1884) 33–46.

Nuttall, Geoffrey F. "Calvinism in Free Church History." *BQ* 22.8 (October 1968) 418–28.

———. "Northamptonshire and *The Modern Question*: A Turning-Point in Eighteenth-Century Dissent." *JTS* 16.1 (1965) 101–23.

O'Donnell, Jean. *John Venn and the Friends of the Hereford Poor*. Almeley: Logaston, 2007

Oliver, Robert W. *History of the English Calvinistic Baptists, 1771–1892*. Edinburgh: Banner of Truth, 2006.

Olson, Roger E. *Arminian Theology: Myths and Realities*. Downers Grove, IL: InterVarsity Press, 2006.

Our Record.

Overton, John. *The True Churchmen Ascertained, or an Apology for those of the Regular Clergy of the Establishment, who are Sometimes Called Evangelical Ministers: Occasioned by Several Modern Publications*. York, 1801.

Owen, John. *The Works of John Owen*. Edited by William H. Goold. Vol. 10. 1850–53. Reprinted, London: Banner of Truth, 1967.

Owles, J. A. "Assurance and Life." *W* 34 (1904) 50–51.

Oxford Dictionary of National Biography. http://www.oxforddnb.com.

Packer, J. I. *A Quest for Godliness: The Puritan Vision of the Christian Life.* Wheaton, IL: Crossway, 1990.

———. "What Did the Cross Achieve? The Logic of Penal Substitution." *Tyndale Bulletin* 25 (1974) 3–45.

Patterson, F. G. "Editor's Preface." In J. N. D[arby], *On the Eternity of Punishment; and the Immortality of the Soul*, edited by F. G. Patterson, v–xv. London: Allan, 1870.

Patterson, Mark Rayburn. "Designing the Last Days: Edward Irving, the Albury Circle, and the Theology of *The Morning Watch*." PhD thesis, King's College, London, 2011.

Patton, W. Donald, ed. *Ebb and Flow: Essays in Church History in Honour of R. Finlay G. Holmes.* Belfast: Presbyterian Historical Society of Ireland, 2002.

Pearse, Meic. "Soundly Converted?" In *Mission and Meaning: Essays Presented to Peter Cotterell*, edited by Antony Billington, Tony Lane, and Max Turner, 230–41. Carlisle, UK: Paternoster, 1995.

Pelikan, Jaroslav. *The Emergence of the Catholic Tradition (100–600).* Vol. 1 of *The Christian Tradition: A History of the Development of Doctrine.* Chicago: University of Chicago Press, 1971.

Perkins, William. *The Work of William Perkins.* Edited by Ian Breward. Berkshire: Sutton Courtenay, 1970.

———. *William Perkins, 1558–1602, English Puritanist: His Pioneer Works on Casuistry: "A Discourse of Conscience" and "The Whole Treatise of Cases of Conscience."* Edited by Thomas F. Merrill. Nieuwkoop: de Graaf, 1966.

Peterson, Robert L. *Robert Chapman: A Biography.* Neptune, NJ: Loizeaux, 1995.

[Philpot, J. C.]. "Address to Our Spiritual Readers." *GS* 26 (1860) 10–11.

———. "Editors' Review: The Christian Witness." *GS* 8 (1842) 77–84.

———. *William Tiptaft: Minister of the Gospel.* 1867. Reprinted, Leicester: Oldham & Manton, 1972.

Pickering, Henry, ed. *Chief Men among the Brethren.* 1918. Reprinted, Neptune, NJ: Loizeaux, 1996.

———. "Home-Call of Sir Robert Anderson, K.C.B., LL.D." *W* 48 (1918) 100.

———. "Home-call of a Warrior." *W* 46 (1916) 132.

———. "Home-calling of a True Gospel Warrior." *W* 58 (1928) 411–12.

Pink, Arthur W. *Letters of an Itinerant Preacher 1920–1921.* Edited by Richard P. Belcher. Columbia, SC: Richbarry, 1994.

———. *Letters from Spartanburg 1917–1920.* Edited by Richard P. Belcher. Columbia, SC: Richbarry, 1993.

Piper, John. *A Camaraderie of Confidence: The Fruit of Unfailing Faith in the Lives of Charles Spurgeon, George Müller, and Hudson Taylor.* Wheaton, IL: Crossway, 2016.

Porteous, J. Moir. *Brethren in the Keelhowes; or, Brethrenism Tested by the Word of God.* London: Simpkin, Marshall, 1876.

Psalms and Hymns and Spiritual Songs. Wooler: Central Bible Hammond Trust, 1978.

Rack, Henry D. *Reasonable Enthusiast: John Wesley and the Rise of Methodism.* 3rd ed. London: Epworth, 2002.

Randall, Ian M. *Evangelical Experiences: A Study in the Spirituality of English Evangelicalism 1918–1939.* Carlisle, UK: Paternoster, 1999.

———. "'Ye Men of Plymouth': C. H. Spurgeon and the Brethren." In *Witness in Many Lands: Leadership and Outreach among the Brethren,* edited by Tim Grass, 73–90. Troon: Brethren Archivists and Historians Network, 2013.
Raven, F. E. *Ministry.* Vol. 3. Kingston-on-Thames: Stow Hill Bible and Tract Depot, n.d.
Rawson, David. "Barton Hall, Hereford: A History." *BHR* 7 (2011) 43–67.
Rea, Tom. *The Life and Labours of David Rea, Evangelist.* Glasgow: Hulbert, 1925.
Reid, John. *F. W. Grant: His Life, Ministry, and Legacy.* Plainfield, NJ: John Reid Book Fund, 1995.
[Reid, William]. *Literature and Mission of the So-Called Plymouth Brethren, or an Attempt at a Just Estimate of Their Testimony to the Revealed Truth of God.* London: Nisbet, 1875.
Reid, William. *Plymouth Brethrenism Unveiled and Refuted.* Edinburgh: Oliphant, 1875.
Rennie, Ian S. "Aspects of Brethren Spirituality." In *Alive to God: Studies in Spirituality Presented to James Houston,* edited by J. I. Packer and Loren Wilkinson, 190–209. Downers Grove, IL: InterVarsity, 1992.
Reynolds, Lindsay. "The Great "Plymouth Brethren" Controversy in South Western Ontario, 1872–1873." The United Church of Canada Archives.
Ritchie, John. *Contested Truths of the Word.* Kilmarnock, UK: Ritchie, 1917.
———. *Donald Munro: A Servant of Jesus Christ.* Kilmarnock, UK: Ritchie, n.d.
———. "Election." *BM* 13 (1912) 76–78, 91–92.
———. *Foundation Truths of the Faith.* Kilmarnock, UK: Ritchie, n.d.
———. *Foundation Truths of the Gospel: Twelve Bible Readings.* 2nd ed. Kilmarnock, UK: Office of The Believer's Magazine, 1904.
———. *James Campbell: A Servant of Jesus Christ.* Kilmarnock, UK: Ritchie, n.d.
[———]. "The Young Believer's Question Box." *BM* 3 (1893) 70.
[———]. "The Young Believer's Question Box." *BM* 5 (1895) 22.
[———]. "The Young Believer's Question Box." *BM* 7 (1897) 46.
[———]. "The Young Believer's Question Box." *BM* ns 7 (1906) 82.
Roach, Adrian. *The Little Flock Hymn Book: Its History and Hymn Writers.* Morganville, NJ: Present Truth, 1974.
Ross, C. W. *Donald Ross: Pioneer Evangelist of the North of Scotland and United States of America.* Kilmarnock, UK: Ritchie, n.d.
[Ross, Donald]. "Answers to Correspondents." *BC* 2 (1882) 139–40.
[———]. "The Atonement." *OR* 9 (1896) 24–27.
———. "A Clear Statement." *W* 69 (1939) 5–6.
[———]. "Counter Truths of Scripture." *NI* 17 (1873) 66–70.
[———]. "Creamery." *BC* 2 (1882) 110.
[———]. "His Own Blood." *BC* 5 (1885) 115–16.
———. "Loose Him, and Let Him Go." *NEI* 1, 2 (1872) 5–6, 14.
———. "The Lord's Work." *NEI* 8 (1872) 59.
[———]. "Monthly Report." *NEI* 1 (1872) 7.
———. *The More Excellent Way.* London: Central Bible Truth Depot, n.d.
[———]. "Not Feeling but Knowing." *BC* 2 (1882) 9–12, 18–20, 38–41.
[———]. "Notes of Questions and Answers." *BC* 5 (1885) 153–54, 184–85.
———. *Our Responsibilities as Christians.* Kilmarnock, UK: John Ritchie, n.d.
[———]. "Question 14." *BC* 1 (May 1881) 79–80.
———. "Question 23." *BC* 1 (July 1881) 111–12.

———. "Question 91." *BC* 5 (October 1885) 153–55.

———. "Question 96." *BC* 5 12 (December 1885) 184.

[———]. "Questions and Answers." *OR* 14 (October 1901) 153–54.

[———]. "Salvation, How Attained." *NEI* 6 (June 1872) 44.

[———]. "A Word to Anxious Ones." *NI* (August 1874) 127.

Ross, Kenneth R. "Calvinists in Controversy: John Kennedy, Horatius Bonar and the Moody Mission of 1873–74." *SBET* 9:1 (1991) 51–63.

Rouse, J. J. *Pioneer Work in Canada*. Kilmarnock, UK: John Ritchie, 1935.

Rouwendal, Pieter L. "Calvin's Forgotten Classical Position on the Extent of the Atonement: About Sufficiency, Efficiency, and Anachronism." *WTJ* 70 (2008) 317–35.

Rowdon, Harold H. "The Brethren Concept of Sainthood." *VE* 20 (1990) 91–102.

———. "The Early Brethren and Baptism." *VE* 11 (1979) 55–64.

———. *The Origins of the Brethren 1825–1850*. London: Pickering & Inglis, 1967.

———. "The Problem of Brethren Identity in Historical Perspective." In *Piero Guicciardini 1808–1886: Un Riformatore Religioso Nell'Europa Dell'Ottocento*, edited by Lorenzo Giorgi and Massimo Rubboli, 159–74. Firenze: Leo S. Olschki Editore, 1988.

———. "Secession from the Established Church in the Early Nineteenth Century." *VE* 3 (1964) 76–88.

———. *Who Are the Brethren and Does It Matter?* Exeter, UK: Paternoster, 1986.

Rupp, Ernest Gordon. *Religion in England 1688–1791*. Oxford: Clarendon, 1986.

Rupp, E. Gordon and Philip S. Watson, trans. and eds. *Luther and Erasmus: Free Will and Salvation*. Philadelphia: Westminster, 1969.

Ryken, Philip Graham. *Thomas Boston as Preacher of the Fourfold State*. Carlisle, UK: Paternoster, 1999.

Ryle, J. C. *Light from Old Times*. London, n.p., 1890.

S., W. "Unreal Conversions," *W* 8 (1898) 76–77.

Sandeen, Ernest R. *The Roots of Fundamentalism: British and American Millenarianism, 1800–1930*. 1970. Reprinted, Grand Rapids: Baker, 1978.

The Sarnia Observer.

Schaff, Philip, ed. *The Creeds of Christendom*. 6th ed. 3 vols. 1931. Reprinted, Grand Rapids: Baker, 2007.

Schneider, Michael. "'The Extravagant Side of Brethrenism': The Life of Percy Francis Hall (1801–84)." In *Witness in Many Lands: Leadership and Outreach among the Brethren*, edited by Tim Grass, 17–44. Troon: Brethren Archivists and Historians Network, 2013.

Schreiner, Thomas R. "Does Scripture Teach Prevenient Grace in the Wesleyan Sense?" In *The Grace of God, the Bondage of the Will*, vol. 2, edited by Thomas R. Schreiner and Bruce A. Ware, 365–82. Grand Rapids: Baker, 1995.

Schwarz, Berthold. *Leben im Sieg Christi: Die Bedeutung von Gesetz und Gnade für das Leben des Christen bei John Nelson Darby*. Giessen: Brunnen, 2007.

Scott, Thomas. *The Articles of the Synod of Dort and Its Rejection of Errors: with the history of events which made way for that Synod, as published by the authority of the States-General; and the documents confirming its decisions*. Utica, NY: Williams, 1831.

———. *Remarks on the Refutation of Calvinism by George Tomline*. 2 vols. Philadelphia: Woodward, 1817.

Scott, Walter. *Exposition of the Revelation of Jesus Christ*. London: Pickering & Inglis, n.d.
Sell, Alan P. F. *Defending and Declaring the Faith: Some Scottish Examples 1860–1920*. Exeter, UK: Paternoster, 1987.
———. *The Great Debate: Calvinism, Arminianism, and Salvation*. Grand Rapids: Baker, 1983.
Sellers, Ian. *Nineteenth-Century Nonconformity*. London: Arnold, 1977.
Shaw, Ian J. *High Calvinists in Action: Calvinism and the City, Manchester and London, c.1810–1860*. Oxford: Oxford University Press, 2002.
Shaw, Mark R. "Drama in the Meeting House: The Concept of Conversion in the Theology of William Perkins." *WTJ* 45 (1983) 41–72.
Shedd, William G. T. *Dogmatic Theology*. Edited by Alan Gomes. 3rd ed. Phillipsburg, NJ: P & R, 2003.
Shephard, Thomas. *The Works of Thomas Shepard*. Vol. 1. Reprinted, Ligonier, PA: Soli Deo Gloria, 1991.
[Short, Rendle]. *The Principles of Open Brethren*. Glasgow: Pickering & Inglis, n.d.
Shuff, Roger N. *Searching for the True Church: Brethren and Evangelicals in Mid-Twentieth-Century England*. Milton Keynes, UK: Paternoster, 2005.
Sibbes, Richard. *The Works of Richard Sibbes*. Vol. 1. 1862. Reprinted, Edinburgh: Banner of Truth, 1973.
Simeon, Charles. *Horae Homileticae*. Vol. 1. London: Holdsworth & Ball, 1832.
Simpson, Alan. *Puritanism in Old and New England*. Chicago: University of Chicago Press, 1955.
Sinnema, Donald. "Calvin and the Canons of Dordt (1619)." *Church History and Religious Culture* 91 (2011) 87–103.
Smeaton, George. *The Doctrine of the Atonement as Taught by Christ Himself*. 2nd ed. Edinburgh: T. & T. Clark, 1871.
Smith, Jay E. "The Theology of Charles Finney: A System of Self-Reformation." *Trinity Journal* 13 (1992) 61–93.
Smith, John Howard. *The Perfect Rule of the Christian Religion: A History of Sandemanianism in the Eighteenth Century*. Albany: State University of New York Press, 2008.
Soltau, Henry W. *The Holy Vessels and Furniture of the Tabernacle*. 1851. Reprinted, Grand Rapids: Kregel, 1971.
———. *The Soul and Its Difficulties: A Word to the Anxious*. London: Yapp, n.d.
———. *The Tabernacle, the Priesthood, and the Offerings*. London: Morgan & Scott, n.d.
S[nell], H. H. "Atonement." *CF* 11 (1884) 118–25.
———. *The Collected Writings of H. H. Snell*. Jackson, NJ: Present Truth, 2003.
———. *Streams of Refreshing from the Fountain of Life*. 4th ed. London: Broom, 1877.
Spellman, W. M. *The Latitudinarians and the Church of England, 1660–1700*. Athens: University of Georgia Press, 1993.
Spurgeon, C. H. *An All-Round Ministry: Addresses to Ministers and Students*. 1900. Reprinted, Edinburgh: Banner of Truth Trust, 1960.
———. *Autobiography: Volume 1: The Early Years 1834–1859*. Rev. ed. Edinburgh: Banner of Truth, 1962.
———. *Autobiography: Volume 2: The Full Harvest 1860–1892*. Rev. ed. Edinburgh: Banner of Truth, 1973.

———. *Metropolitan Tabernacle Pulpit*. Vol. 14. London: Passmore & Alabaster, 1869.

———. "The Present Positoin of Calvinism in England." *The Sword and the Trowel* (Feb. 1874) 49–53.

Spurr, John. "'Latitudinarianism' and the Restoration Church." *Historical Journal* 31 (1988) 61–82.

———. *The Restoration Church of England, 1646–1689*. New Haven: Yale University Press, 1991.

Stanley, Charles. "Are You Saved? The Churchman's Answer to the Question." *TNO* 28 (1885) 184–87, 220–24.

———. *The Atoning Death of the Son of God*. Reprinted, Addison, IL: Bible Truth Publishers, 1979.

———. *"C. S." Tracts*. 6 vols. Morrish, n.d.

———. "The Doctrines of the Salvation Army Compared with Scripture." In *"C. S." Tracts*. Vol. 6. London: Morrish, n.d.

———. "Election." In *"C. S." Tracts*. Vol. 5. London: Morrish, n.d.

———. "Free Will." *TNO* 33 (1890) 19–26, 29–36.

———. *On the Epistle to the Romans*. London: Morrish, 1885.

———. *Plain Words to Ritualists on Their Way to Rome*, No. 2, *Baptismal Regeneration: The Council of Trent Tested by the Word of God*. London: Morrish, n.d.

———. *The Way the Lord Hath Led Me; or, Incidents of Gospel Work*. London: Morrish, n.d.

———. "What a Contrast." *Railway Tracts* no. 7. London: Morrish, n.d.

Steele, Daniel. *A Substitute for Holiness or, Antinomianism Revived; or, the Theology of the So-Called Plymouth Brethren Examined and Refuted*. 3rd ed. 1887. Reprinted, New York: Garland, 1984.

Stephen, Leslie and Sidney Lee, eds. *Dictionary of National Biography*. 22 vols. Reprinted, Oxford: Oxford University Press, 1967–68.

Stevenson, Mark R. "The Brethren and Systematic Theology: Outspoken Objectors; Unconscious Practitioners." In *Bible and Theology in the Brethren Movement*, edited by Neil T. R. Dickson and T. J. Marinello. Troon: Brethren Archivists and Historians Network, forthcoming.

———. "Canadian Opposition to Brethren Evangelists: The Great 'Plymouth Brethren' Controversy in South-Western Ontario, 1872–73." In *Brethren and Mission*, edited by Neil T. R. Dickson and T. J. Marinello, 241–50. Troon: Brethren Archivists and Historians Network, 2016.

———. "The Doctrines of Grace in an Unexpected Place: Nineteenth-Century Brethren Soteriology." *In Writing* 123 (2013) 4–17.

———. "Early Brethren Leaders and the Question of Calvinism." *BHR* 6 (2010) 2–33.

———. "Whose Theology Is This? Dave Hunt's Misrepresentation of Calvinism." *Emmaus Journal* 15.1 (2006) 3–44.

Stevenson, Peter K. *God in Our Nature: The Incarnational Theology of John McLeod Campbell*. Carlisle, UK: Paternoster, 2004.

Stewart, Kenneth J. "The Points of Calvinism: Retrospect and Prospect." *SBET* 26 (Autumn 2008) 187–203.

———. *Restoring the Reformation: British Evangelicalism and the Francophone "Réveil" 1816–1849*. Milton Keynes, UK: Paternoster, 2004.

———. "The Strange Reemergence of the "Points" of Calvinism in England: 1700–1820." Unpublished paper, n.d.

———. *Ten Myths about Calvinism: Recovering the Breadth of the Reformed Tradition.* Downers Grove, IL: InterVarsity, 2011.
Stokes, George T. "John Nelson Darby." *Contemporary Review* 48 (1885) 537-52.
Stoney, J. B. *Ministry.* Vol. 5. Kingston-on-Thames: Stow Hill Bible and Tract Depot, 1964.
———. "The Objective and Subjective." in *Ministry.* Vol. 8. 1896. Reprinted, Lancing: Kingston Bible Trust, n.d.
Strachan, R. *Wandering Lights: A Stricture on the Doctrines and Methods of Brethrenism.* Toronto: Briggs, [1880].
Strivens, Robert. "The Thought of Philip Doddridge in the Context of Early Eighteenth-Century Dissent." PhD thesis, University of Stirling, 2011.
Stuart, C. E. *An Outline of St. Paul's Epistle to the Romans.* 2nd ed. London: E. Marlborough, 1900.
———. "Propitiation." *CF* 7 (1880) 244-51, 274-77.
———. "Repentance and the Preaching of It." *BT* 7 (1868) 153-55.
———. "Substitution." *CF* 11 (1884) 297-306.
———. *Tracings from the Gospel of John; or, Records of the Incarnate Word.* London: Marlborough, n.d.
Stunt, Timothy C. F. *Early Brethren and the Society of Friends.* Pinner: C.B.R.F. Publications, 1970.
———. *The Elusive Quest of the Spiritual Malcontent: Some Early Nineteenth-Century Ecclesiastical Mavericks.* Eugene, OR: Wipf & Stock, 2015.
———. *From Awakening to Secession: Radical Evangelicals in Switzerland and Britain 1815-35.* Edinburgh: T. & T. Clark, 2000.
———. "John Nelson Darby: Contexts and Perceptions." In *Protestant Millenialism, Evangelicalism and Irish Society, 1790-2005,* edited by Crawford Gribben and Andrew R. Holmes, 83-98. Basingstoke, UK: Palgrave Macmillan, 2006.
———. "John Nelson Darby—The Scholarly Enigma." *BAHNR* 2 (2003) 70-74.
———. "Trinity College, John Darby and the Powerscourt *Milieu.*" In *Beyond the End: The Future of Millennial Studies,* edited by Joshua Searle and Kenneth G. C. Newport, 47-74. Sheffield: Sheffield Phoenix, 2012.
Stunt, W. T., et al. *Turning the World Upside Down: A Century of Missionary Endeavour.* 2nd ed. Bath, UK: Echoes of Service, 1973.
Summerton, Neil. "The Theology of George Müller." In *Bible and Theology in the Brethren Movement,* edited by Neil T. R. Dickson and T. J. Marinello. Troon: Brethren Archivists and Historians Network, forthcoming.
Sweetnam, Mark and Crawford Cribben. "J. N. Darby and the Irish Origins of Dispensationalism." *JETS* 52 (September 2009) 569-77.
The Sword and the Trowel.
Tayler, W. Elfe, ed. *Passages from the Diary and Letters of Henry Craik of Bristol.* London: Shaw, 1866.
Things New and Old.
Thomas, G. Michael. *The Extent of the Atonement: A Dilemma for Reformed Theology from Calvin to the Consensus.* Carlisle, UK: Paternoster, 1997.
Thompson, Joseph. "The Influence of D. L. Moody on Irish Presbyterianism." In *Ebb and Flow: Essays in Church History in Honour of R. Finlay G. Holmes.* Edited by W. Donald Patton, 119-40. Belfast: Presbyterian Historical Society of Ireland, 2002.

Thuesen, Peter J. *Predestination: The American Career of a Contentious Doctrine.* New York: Oxford University Press, 2009.
Tillotson, John. *The Works of the Most Reverend Dr. John Tillotson, Volume 8: Sermons on Several Subjects and Occasions.* London, 1757.
Tomline, George. *A Refutation of Calvinism.* 3rd ed. London: Cadell & Davies, 1811.
Toon, Peter. *The Emergence of Hyper-Calvinism in English Nonconformity, 1689–1765.* London: Olive Tree, 1967.
Toplady, Augustus. *The Works of Augustus Toplady, B.A. 1794.* Reprinted, Harrisonburg, VA: Sprinkle, 1987.
Torrance, Thomas F. *Scottish Theology: From John Knox to John McLeod Campbell.* Edinburgh: T. & T. Clark, 1996.
T[rench?], G. F. "Substitution in Relation to the Unconverted." *W* 8 (1898) 179–80.
Trotter, W. *A Full Christ for Empty Sinners: Thoughts on John vi. 1865.* Reprinted, London: Carter, 1896.
———. "Man's Will and God's Grace." *BT* 14 (1883) 362–64; 373–75.
[———]. "No Man Becomes a Child of God by an Act of His Own Will." *Present Testimony* 8 (1856) 306–18.
———. *The Origin of (So Called) Open-Brethrenism.* Lancing: Kingston Bible Trust, n.d.
———. *Plain Papers on Prophetic and Other Subjects.* Rev. ed. New York: Loizeaux, n.d.
Trueman, Carl R. *The Claims of Truth: John Owen's Trinitarian Theology.* Carlisle, UK: Paternoster, 1998.
Turner, W. G. *John Nelson Darby.* London: Hammond, 1944.
———. *Unknown and Well Known: A Biography of John Nelson Darby.* Rev. ed. Edited by Edwin N. Cross. London: Chapter Two, 2006.
Tyacke, Nicholas. *Anti-Calvinists: The Rise of English Arminianism c. 1590–1640.* Oxford: Clarendon, 1990.
Tyerman, Luke. *The Life and Times of the Rev. John Wesley, M.A.* 6th ed. Vol. 1. London: Hodder & Stoughton, 1890.
———. *The Life of the Rev. George Whitefield.* 2 vols. London: Hodder & Stoughton, 1876.
van Asselt, Willem. "Christ's Atonement: A Multi-Dimensional Approach." *CTJ* 38 (2003) 52–67.
VanDoodewaard, William. *The Marrow Controversy and Seceder Tradition: Atonement, Saving Faith, and the Gospel Offer in Scotland (1718-1799).* Grand Rapids: Reformation Heritage, 2011.
van 't Spijker, Willem. "Bucer's Influence on Calvin: Church and Community." In *Martin Bucer: Reforming Church and Community*, edited by D. F. Wright, 32–44. Cambridge: Cambridge University Press, 1994.
———. "Prädestination bei Bucer und Calvin: Ihre gegenseitige Beeinflussung und Abhängigkeit." In *Calvinus Theologus*, edited by Wilhelm Neuser, 85–111. Neukirchen: Neukirchener Verlag, 1976.
Veitch, Thomas Stewart. *The Story of the Brethren Movement.* London: Pickering & Inglis, [1933].
Venn, Henry, ed. *The Life and a Selection from the Letters of the Late Henry Venn.* 4th ed. London: Piccadilly, 1836.
Vlach, Michael J. "Penal Substitution in Church History." *The Master's Seminary Journal* 20.2 (2009) 199–214.

W., P. "O God! That I Might Know My Sins Forgiven." *Gospel Messenger* 1 (1885) 266–69.

Walker, John. *Essays and Correspondence, Chiefly on Scriptural Subjects, by the Late John Walker.* Vol. 1. Edited by William Burton. London: Longman, 1838.

———. *Seven Letters to a Friend on Primitive Christianity; in which Are Set Forth the Faith and Practice of the Apostolic Churches.* 1819. Reprinted, London: Kempster, 1874.

Wallace, Dewey D., Jr. *Puritans and Predestination: Grace in English Protestant Theology, 1525–1695.* Chapel Hill: University of North Carolina Press, 1982.

———. *Shapers of English Calvinism, 1660–1714: Variety, Persistence, and Transformation.* Oxford: Oxford University Press, 2011.

Walsh, John, Colin Haydon, and Stephen Taylor. *The Church of England c. 1689–c. 1833: From Toleration to Tractarianism.* Cambridge: Cambridge University Press, 1993.

Ward, John Percy. "The Eschatology of John Nelson Darby." PhD thesis, University of Gloucestershire, 2009.

Warfield, Benjamin Breckinridge. *The Works of Benjamin B. Warfield.* Vol. 5, *Calvin and Calvinism.* 1931. Reprinted, Grand Rapids: Baker, 1991.

———. *The Works of Benjamin B. Warfield.* Vol. 9, *Studies in Theology.* 1932. Reprinted, Grand Rapids: Baker, 1991.

Watts, Michael. *The Dissenters: From the Reformation to the French Revolution.* Oxford: Clarendon, 1978.

Weremchuk, Max S. *John Nelson Darby.* Neptune, NJ: Loizeaux, 1992.

Wesley, John. *The Works of John Wesley.* Vol. IV. 1872. Reprinted, Peabody, MA: Hendrickson, 1984.

———. *The Works of John Wesley.* Vol. V. 1872. Reprinted, Peabody, MA: Hendrickson, 1984.

———. *The Works of John Wesley.* Vol. VII. 1872. Reprinted, Peabody, MA: Hendrickson, 1984.

———. *The Works of John Wesley.* Vol. X. 1872. Reprinted, Peabody, MA: Hendrickson, 1984.

West, Gerald T. *From Friends to Brethren: The Howards of Tottenham—Quakers, Brethren, and Evangelicals.* Edited by Tim Grass. Troon: Brethren Archivists and Historians Network, 2016.

———. "John Eliot Howard: From Friend to Brother." In *The Growth of the Brethren Movement: National and International Experiences*, edited by Neil T. R. Dickson and Tim Grass, 35–48. Milton Keynes, UK: Paternoster, 2006

Whelan, Irene. *The Bible War in Ireland: The 'Second Reformation" and the Polarization of Protestant-Catholic Relations, 1800–1840.* Madison: University of Wisconsin Press, 2005.

Whitby, Daniel. *A Discourse Concerning the True Import of the Words Election and Reprobation and the Things Signified by Them in the Holy Scripture.* 4th ed. London: Rivington, 1817.

Whitefield, George. *Letters of George Whitefield: For the Period 1734–1742.* 1771. Reprinted, Edinburgh: Banner of Truth, 1976.

———. *The Works of the Reverend George Whitefield, M.A.* Vol. 4. London, 1771.

The Whole Proceedings before the Presbytery of Dumbarton, and Synod of Glasgow and Ayr, in the Case of the Rev. John M'Leod Campbell, Minister of Row. Greenock: Lusk, 1831.

"Whose Faith Follow." *BM* (July 2006) 215.
Wilberforce, Robert Isaac and Samuel Wilberforce. *The Life of William Wilberforce*. Vol. 3. London: Murray, 1838.
Williams, Edward. *A Defence of Modern Calvinism: Containing an Examination of the Bishop of Lincoln's Work, Entitled a* Refutation of Calvinism. London: Black, 1812.
Williams, Garry J. "Enlightenment Epistemology and Eighteenth-Century Evangelical Doctrines of Assurance." In *The Advent of Evangelicalism: Exploring Historical Continuities*, edited by Michael A. G. Haykin and Kenneth J. Stewart, 345–74. Nashville: B & H, 2008.

———. "Penal Substitutionary Atonement in the Church Fathers." *EQ* 8.3 (2011) 195–216.

The Witness.
Wolffe, John. *The Expansion of Evangelicalism: The Age of Wilberforce, More, Chalmers and Finney.* Downers Grove, IL: InterVarsity, 2007.
W[olston], W. T. P. "Do You Hope, or Know, that You Have Eternal Life?" *God's Glad Tidings* 5 (1876) 213–18.
Wood, Darren Cushman. "John Wesley's Use of the Atonement." *Asbury Journal* 62.2 (2007) 55–70.
Yeager, Jonathan. "The Roots of Open Brethren Ecclesiology: A Discussion of the Nature of the Church Compared to the Ecclesiology of the Darbyite Brethren, 1825–1848." ThM thesis, Regent College, 2006.

General Index

Aaron, 177
Abraham, 124, 243
Adam, 68, 71, 79, 81, 86–88, 90, 98–99, 193, 202n3
Adamson, William, 59, 102, 106, 108, 158, 191
Airhart, Phyllis D., 220, 247
Akenson, Donald Harman, 2n3, 3n14, 8n37, 39, 119n37
Alleine, Joseph, 19
Allison, Gregg R., 113n6, 166n7
America. *See* United States
Amyraldianism, 20n17, 174
Amyraut, Moïse, 174–75
Anabaptists, 260
Anderson, Sir Robert, 9, 95, 155–56, 193–94
Anglicanism. *See* Church of England
Anselm, 166
Arles, Synod of, 69
Arminianism, 1, 4, 16, 18–19, 24, 26–27, 29–33, 35–37, 41, 43–52, 59–63, 66, 71–74, 76, 78, 90, 102, 105–6, 117–18, 120, 125, 128, 130, 138, 141, 145–46, 148, 152, 156–58, 162–64, 167, 172–77, 180, 185, 187–90, 199–200, 202n3, 211, 217, 234, 253–54, 258, 262
Arminius, Jacob, 16, 18, 89
Armstrong, Brian G., 175n55
assurance, 27–29, 38, 194, 254; *see* chapter 7
atonement, 20, 27–28, 34, 36, 39n138, 41, 46–48, 59–60, 129, 254, 260; *see* chapter 6; (*see also* governmental theory of the atonement)
Augustine, 16–17, 68–69, 89, 135, 160
Augustinianism, 68–70, 83, 155n248

Baird, Thomas, 110
baptism, 22n29, 98, 118n30, 129, 158, 214, 221
Baptists, 43–45, 60, 65–66, 94, 238
   General Baptists, 29, 31, 130
   Particular Baptists, 29–30, 37, 39–40, 54n65, 58, 72, 130
   Strict Baptists, 56, 58, 130n109, 136n136, 215, 249
Baring, George, 53
Barnstaple, 54n65, 86, 129–30
Bass, Clarence B., 3n13
Baxter, Richard, 19, 175, 206–7n28
Baxterian, 30, 37
Baylis, Robert, 11
Beattie, David J., 86n102, 127n81, n85, 143n176, 221n109, 249n242
Beatty, Lisa, xii
Bebbington, David, xi, 2n5–6, 9, 5n22, 17, 24, 31, 40n146–147, 43, 44n4, 45, 48n27, 49, 49n37, 51n44, 63n117, 65n129, 66n133, 103–4n216, 116n18, 163n293, 166–67, 175n58, 202, 209, 214, 259
Beeke, Joel R., 203, 204n13, 205n17–19, 206n23–24, 207n30–31
Bellett, George, 85

Bellett, John Gifford, 7n32, 83n82, 85, 117n21, 124-25, 134n125
Bennet, W. H., 86n109, 87n110, 130n112, 131n113, 115, 159n273
Beougher, Timothy K., 206n27, 206-207n28
Bethesda Chapel (Bristol), 11, 54n65, 87, 191n148
Bevan, Emma Frances, 149-50
Beza, Theodore, 114
biblicism, 61, 116, 164, 255, 257-60, 262
Blackburn, William M., 13
Blacketer, Raymond A., 172
Blocher, Henri, 166
Bolton, Robert, 206n28
Bonar, Horatius, 62-63, 179, 212-14
Book of Common Prayer, 44
Boston, Thomas, 27n61, 28, 214
Boston (USA), 71, 144-45
Bowen, Desmond, 51n46
Brady, Gary, xii
Bray, Gerald, 166n7
Brenton, Sir L. Charles L., 8n35, 256n7, 258
Brewer, Charles, 127-28
Brine, John, 30
Bristol, 11, 30, 54, 87, 191
Britain, 5, 11, 17, 31, 33, 38, 63, 72, 115, 146
Brookes, James H., 154-55
Brown, James Baldwin, 65
Brown, John, 59
Bruce, F. F., 105
Bucer, Martin, 57, 70, 114, 120, 204n14
Bullinger, Heinrich, 114, 204n14
Bulteel, Henry Bellenden, 54-58, 119-20, 123, 134, 136, 176
Bunyan, John, 18, 22
Burnham, Jonathan D., 3n15, 13, 41n149, 53n61, 55n71, 74, 56n77, 57n83, 90n131, 123n58, 134n123, 136n136
Burton, Edward, 56-57, 120
Burwash, Nathanael, 220
Byrth, Thomas, 55-56

Caldecott, William, 125-26

Caldwell, John R., 10, 106, 109-110, 152-53, 176n59, 197-98, 237
Caldwell, Patricia, 206n27
Callahan, James Patrick, 3n13, 12-13
Calvin, John, 16n2, 17, 21, 34, 36-38, 49, 64-65, 70, 113-16, 160, 166-167n9, 171n37, 172n39, 203-4, 205n19, 206n23, 207n31, 214, 251-52, 257
Calvinism, on the term "Calvinism," 1, 16-17, 25n48, 37-38, 40-42, 45-46, 113-14, 161, 171-172n37, 255; five points of, 18, 25-26, 40, 47-48, 85, 138; inadequacy of the acronym TULIP, 4n19
High Calvinism, 37-38, 41-42, 46-47, 50-58, 63, 66, 123, 126, 128, 134, 136, 141, 155, 176, 211
Hyper-Calvinism. See hyper-Calvinism
Moderate Calvinism, 12, 30-31, 37, 41-42, 45-51, 54, 57, 61, 65-66, 117, 141
Strict Calvinism, 13, 20, 37-38, 40-42, 54, 58
Cambridge Platonists, 20
Campbell, James, 118n31, 158n268, 238-39, 249
Campbell, John McLeod, 60n101, 168-70, 211-12
Canada, xiii, 5, 104, 106, 150, 157, 161, 218-20, 226
Carey, William, 43n3
Carne, James, 54
Carnie, John, 104, 218-19
Carson, D. A., 156n254
Carson, James C. L., 202n4, 217, 221
Carson, John T., 64
Carter, Grayson, 7, 38, 45n15-16, 46n18, 50-52, 53n60, 54n65, 55, 56n80, 57, 58n88, 119n34, 37, 128n95, 129n97, 210n44
Carter, Joel, xii
Carthage, Council of (418), 68
Carwardine, Richard, 72n22, 73n28
Caryl, Jospeh, 28n69

GENERAL INDEX

Case, J. Norman, 158n268, 160–62, 250–52
Cassian, John, 69
Catholic Apostolic Church, 6, 171n36
Christian Brethren Archive, (CBA), xii, 8n36
Cennick, John, 32, 34, 149
Chadwick, Owen, 18n7, 23
Chalmers, Thomas, 61
Chapman, Robert Cleaver, 53n60, 54n65, 86–87, 128–31, 165
Charles II, 18n7, 19
Cheyne, A. C., 59n94, 61
Chicago (USA), 79, 153, 238
China, 161
Church of England (Anglicanism; Established Church), 18–19, 23–25, 26n56, 36–37, 44–46, 48, 50–54, 56–58, 64n123, 119–20, 135
Clarke, Matthew Austin, 3n13, 80n66
Clifford, Alan, 175n55
Clipsham, E. F., 40n141
Coad, F. Roy, 3n14, 11, 52n57, 63, 96, 153, 154n239, 215n69–70, 216n75, 255n3
Coates, C. A., 159n272
Coffey, John, 20n16
Cole, Henry, 16n2
Cole, W. H., 123
Collinson, Patrick, 114n10, n12
compatibilism, 75–76n42, 156
Congregationalism, (also Independents) 29–30, 39n133, 44n4, 45, 60, 64–65
Coppedge, Allan, 33n100
Covenant theology, 202n3, 255–56
Cowan, Thomas, 54n65
Coyle, William, xii
Cragg, Gerald R., 18–19, 23
Craik, Henry, 11, 54n65, 87–88, 131–33
Cranmer, Thomas, 18
Cravillion, Elizabeth, xii
creeds and confessions, Brethren rejection of, 92, 102, 116, 146, 191, 218, 255–60, 262
Critchlow, Anne-Louise, 80n71
Cromwell, Oliver, 18
Croskery, Thomas, 202n4, 216–18, 221

Cross, Edwin, xi, 9n40–41, 80, 83n82, 91n138, 97n173, 98n181, n186, 154n241, 186n116
Crutchfield, Larry V., 3n12
Cunningham, William, 61n108
Cutting, George, 100–101, 198n187, 239–40, 247–48

Dabney, Robert L., 202n4, 218
Dale, R. W., 64–65
Dallimore, Arnold, 26n54, 33n98, n101, 34n107, n111, 35n117
Dann, Robert Bernard, 3n13, n16, 7, 54n64, 126n75, 245n219
Darby, John Nelson, 3, 8–9, 52n57, 57, 63, 90, 222, 257; on assurance, 244–45; on the atonement, 170–71, 176–81, 196–97, 200; on election/predestination, 119–22; on fallen human nature/will, 74–80; on saving faith and repentance, 223–26; on reprobation, 120, 122
Darwinism, 65, 73n30
Daubeny, Charles, 44
Davenant, John, 175
Davidson, John, 4n21
Davis, M. M. 152n232
Davis, Thomas J., 115n16
Dawson, William, 92
de Silva, J. W., 4n20
Deck, James G., 13n64
Delaune, William, 25n47
Dennett, Edward, 94–95, 235–36
Denny, Edward, 165
Dewart, Edward Hartley, 219–20, 222n115
Dickson, Neil T. R., xi, 5n23, 11, 58n92, 60n100, 63n117, 88n121–n123, 96n166, 101, 149, 152n231, n233, 153, 158n267, 160n275, 248
Dispensationalism, 3, 12–14, 74, 79–80, 220, 230, 260, 262
dissent (see also Nonconformists), 12n56, 19, 20n17, 22–23, 29–31, 37, 40, 46, 50–51, 59, 221
Dixon, Larry E., 3n15, 5n24, 224n121
Doddridge, Philip, 30–31

Dort (also spelled Dordt or Dordrecht), Synod (and/or Canons) of, 18, 22, 36n123, 40, 44n7, 70–71, 114, 163n292, 172–73, 174n53, 175n57, 185n114, 199n189, 207n32
Drummond, Henry, 128
du Moulin, Pierre, 175
Dublin, 51, 52n57, 85
Duncan, James B., 104–5, 219
Dunlap, David, 4n20, 80n67
Dyer, Henry, 143–44, 181n88

ecclesiology, 3, 6, 12–13, 52n57, 61, 74, 80, 94, 138n148, 164, 210, 230, 260
Edinburgh, 59, 114, 216, 221
Edwards, John, 25
Edwards, Jonathan, 25n49, 26, 39–40, 71–72, 209, 245
election, doctrine of, *see* chapter 5
Elmore, Floyd Saunders, 3n15
Embley, Peter L., 12, 53n61, 127n84, 210n44
Emmaus Bible College, xii, 8n36, 218n94
England, 1, 5, 17–20, 23–24, 25n48, 33, 36, 39n140, 44n4, 51–58, 65, 98, 114n10, 143, 150, 161, 210, 222
Enlightenment, the, 2, 27, 29, 49, 259
Ensor, Peter, 167n10
Erasmus, 16, 70, 89
Erskine, Ebenezer, 27n61
Erskine, Ralph, 27n61
Erskine, Thomas, 60n101, 73, 169–71, 212n52, n55
eschatology, 3, 94, 138n148, 230
Established Church (of England). *See* Church of England
Evangelical Revival, 23–24, 31–36, 49n32, 62
evangelism, 2, 61–62, 66, 72–73, 96–97, 101, 103, 133, 147, 159, 161, 163–64, 166, 191, 209, 229, 251, 254, 261–62
evangelists, (*see also* preaching), Brethren evangelists, 2, 9, 11, 63, 96–111, 118, 212, 218–20, 249n245, 261–62; popular Brethren evangelists not always aligned with Brethren leaders, 96, 162, 195–96, 222, 225–26, 228–30, 232, 234, 236–39, 241, 243, 250, 252
Evans, James Harington, 53n60, 128–29

Faber, George Stanley, 49–50
Fairbairn, Donald, xi
faith, nature of, *see* chapter 7
Farel, William, 149
Feinberg, John S., 75n42, 156n254
Ferguson, Fergus, 60n100, 106
Ferguson, Sinclair, 27n61, 207n31
Fesko, J. V., 175n56
Finney, Charles Grandison, 59–60, 72–73, 89, 102, 167–68, 228
Fish, Jack, xi
Fisher, Edward, 27, 208
Fiske, John, 115
Flavel, John, 18, 206n26
Fleming, Inglis, 112
Fleming, Kenneth C., xi, 112n1
Fletcher, John, 37
Fletcher, Khellan, xii
foreknowledge, 41, 112–13, 117–18, 120–21, 124, 140, 148, 156, 158, 161
Foster, I. T., 60, 157n261
Fowler, Edward, 21n22
Frame, John, 163n292
Fromow, George H., 136n135
Fuller, Andrew, 30, 37–40, 43, 72, 210–11, 252

Garrett, James, 40
Geisler, Norman, 6
General Baptists. *See* Baptists
Geneva, 25n48, 58n87, 114–15
George, Timothy, 26–27
Gerstner, John H., 14n66, 80n67
Gill, John (Baptist), 26–27, 30, 33n100, 39
Gill, John (Brethren), 144–45
Gilmore, William, 238
Gipp, Henry, 127–28
Glanvil, Joseph, 21n22

GENERAL INDEX

Glas, John, 210–11
Glasgow, 60–61, 106
Goddard, John, 5
Godfrey, William Robert, 172n39
Gomarus, Franciscus, 16
Goodwin, Thomas, 205n15
Gosse, Emily, 197, 229n148
Gottschalk, 16
governmental theory of the atonement, 39n138, 167n15, 177n70, 188
Grant, F. W., 1, 10, 79, 150–52, 187–91, 192, 236–37, 239
Grass, Tim, ix, xi, 3–4, 6–11, 44n7, 50n42, 52n57, 53n61, 54n65, 63n117, 74n32, 80, 83n82, 86, 87n114, 92n145, 96, 100–101, 116, 125, 129n99, 130n109, 143n176, 147, 155n246, 159n274, 170n30–31, 176n60, 215n69, 216n76, 221, 250n248, 259n19, 260n24, n26, 261n27
Gribben, Crawford, xi, 3n12, 23n36, 51n46, 109, 205n16, 221n110, 222n111, 246n226
Griffiths, Dr. & Mrs. J., 127
Grotius, Hugo, 167n15
Groves, Anthony Norris, 2, 7, 9, 11, 16, 52n57, 125–26, 130, 137n141, 148n202, 171n34, 176, 245
Groves, Henry, 182–83, 194
Grudem, Wayne, 117n22
Guelph, Ontario, 225
Gundry, Stanley N., 13n64, 154–55
Guthrie, John, 88–89, 106, 177n177, 256

Hall, Basil, 205n19
Hall, Percy Francis, 127–28, 181–82
Hall, Robert, Jr., 30n80, 39n140
Hambrick-Stowe, Charles E., 206–7
Hamilton, Ian, 59n94, 60n98
Hamilton, Ontario, 238
Hamilton, William, 64n120, 145n186
Hampton, Stephen, 24–25
Harris, Howel, 32, 34
Harris, James Lampen, 10, 118, 123
Harrisburg, Pennsylvania, 146
Hart, D. G., 17n5, 27n60

Harvey, James, 5–6, 101–2, 103n211, 144n180, n183
Haweis, Thomas, 37
Hawker, Robert, 54–55, 58
Hawthorn, John, 61n102, 105n226, 106, 157n260, 158, 159n271, 162n288, 194n164, n166
Hayden, Roger, 29n73, n76, 31n91
Haykin, Michael A. G., 31n93, 49n34, 166n5, 209n38
Helm, Paul, 36–37, 75n42, 156n254
Henn, Silas, 64
Henzel, Ronald M., 3n12
Hereford, 127–28
Herendeen, I. C., 109n248
Hervey, James, 26n56, 37
Hill, Rowland, 37
Hincmar, 16
Hindmarsh, D. Bruce, 39n140, 41, 72n19, 206, 210
Hog, James, 27n61
Holmes, Andrew R., 51n45
Holmes, Frank, 128n94, 129n98, 130n109, n111
Hooker, Thomas, 205n15, 206n26, n28
Hopkins, Mark, 65n132
Horrocks, Don, 60n101, 73n29, 169n27–28, 170n29, 212n52
Horton, Michael, 22n28, 117n24, 168n17
Houston, Thomas, 118, 196, 202n4, 217
Howard, John Eliot, 67, 88–89, 176–77, 256
Howe, John, 19–20
Huebner, Roy A., 6, 79–80
Hunt, Dave, 6, 14n67
Huntington, William, 50
Hussey, Joseph, 30
Hutchinson, James G., 241, 249n241
hyper-Calvinism, 7, 12, 22, 27, 29–30, 33n100, 37–43, 46–47, 50–54, 56, 58, 62–63, 72, 83, 109n248, 117, 123n62, 133, 136n136, 138, 141, 150, 152, 155n248, 158n264, 159, 174, 176, 184n108, 185, 197

hypothetical universalism, 20n15, 28n65, 173n45, 174–75, 190, 199–200

imputed righteousness, 4, 37, 42, 171, 202, 245, 262n32
Independents. *See* Congregationalism
India, 182
infralapsarianism, 21–22, 117, 153, 163n292
Inverurie, 249
Ireland, 1, 2n3, 5, 11, 17, 33n104, 46, 51, 221–22, 238
Ironside, H. A., 79, 150, 181n87
Irving, Edward, 170–71
Israel, 110, 143, 145, 151, 169

Jabini, Frank, xii
Jeffrey, Kenneth S., 63n117
Jewett, Paul K., 113
Johnson, Graham, xii, 88n123
Johnston, O. R., 70
Jones, Mark, 205n18, 206n23, 207n30
justification, 4, 23, 41–42, 57, 66, 100, 120, 154n242, 158n264, 166–67, 179, 190, 193, 198, 202, 211, 227, 244–45, 250n246, 262n32

Kelly, Thomas, 52
Kelly, William, 9, 253, 257–58; on assurance, 244n215, on the atonement, 170–71, 181n87, 183–85; on election/predestination, 140–42; on fallen human nature/will, 80–83; on imputed righteousness, 202n3; on saving faith and repentance, 231–32; on reprobation, 141–42
Kendall, R. T., 175n55, 204n14, 205n19
Kennedy, John, 61–63, 212–14
Kilmarnock, 59–60, 102
Kimbro, Reginald C., 14n66
Krapohl, Robert H., 3n15

Lachman, David C., 28n68, 208n33
Laing, William, 181n88, 198
Lalleman, Pieter, xi
Lambeth Articles, 21
Lampen, Robert, 125n73

Larsen, Timothy, 3n17, 116n19
Latimer, Hugh, 135
Latitudinarianism, 20–21
Laud, William, 16
Letham, Robert, 18n8, 204n14
Lincoln, William, 147–49, 227n140, 251
Lineham, Peter J., 13n64
Livingston, James C., 73n30
Lloyd-Jones, D. Martyn, 14n66, 211
Lombard, Peter, 172
London, xi–xii, 30, 50n43, 54, 65, 88, 112n1, 125, 128, 243
London (Ontario), 219
London Baptist Confession, 21n27; Second London Baptist Confession, 29
Lucas, Sean Michael, 73
Luther, Martin, 16, 70, 80, 89, 95, 135, 203, 240, 256–57
Lutheran, 57, 120

McDowell, Ian, 13n64
McFarlane, Graham W. P., 170n30
Macintosh, Duncan, 202n4, 221
McIntosh, Hugh, 234, 249
Mackintosh, Charles Henry, 9, 256, 258–59; on assurance, 245–46; on the atonement, 186–87; on fallen human nature/will, 83–85, 108; on election/predestination, 136–40, 157, 261; on saving faith and repentance, 227–31; on reprobation, 139–40
McKee, John, 51n45, 64
McLaren, Ross H., 11, 96n168
Maclean, John, 182
MacLeod, David J., xi–xii, 3n12
Macleod, John, 27n59, 61n108
Macpherson, John, 144n184, 154n243, 155n244, 248n234
McVicker, John G., 118n31, 182–83, 221–22, 246
Manchester, xii, 8n36, 153
Marinello, Thomas, xi–xii
Marrow Controversy, 27–28, 208–9
Marsden, George M., 74
Marshall, Alexander, 60–61, 63, 98n108, 222, 254, 262; on assurance, 248; on the atonement, 194–97,

199–200; on fallen human nature/will, 105–111; on election/predestination, 157–59, 162, 164; on saving faith and repentance, 241–43
Martyn, Henry, 134
Matheson, Duncan, 102, 103n209, 144
Mathison, Keith A., 14n66
Maurice, Matthias, 39n133
Melanchthon, Philip, 120
Methodism/Methodists, 14n66, 31, 48, 51, 79n63, 90n135, 92–94, 167, 188, 209n37, 215, 219–20, 238, 240; Calvinistic Methodists, 32, 150
Midlane, Albert, 166
Miley, John, 167
Mill, George, 218–19
Miller, Andrew, 96–97, 246n225
Miller, Basil, 87n113
Milner, Isaac, 49
missions/missionary, 2, 3, 32, 37, 40, 62, 86, 96n169, 110n252, 126, 143–44, 161–62, 182
Moderate Calvinism. *See* Calvinism
Moody D. L., 2–3, 61–63, 74n33, 79, 108n247, 153–55, 212–14, 226
Moore, Jonathan D., 20n15, 28n65, 173n45, 174n50, n52, 175n56
Moorhouse, Henry, 3, 153–55, 248
Morden, Peter J., 30n78, n80, 37n126, 39n134, 40n146
More, Hannah, 49
Morgan, Edmund, 205–6
Morison, James, 59–61, 88–89, 102, 105–8, 158, 191, 195
Morisonianism, 60, 102–3, 105, 144, 157–58, 164, 191, 194–95, 217, 238, 254
Mostert, Adam, xii
Müller, George, 2, 9, 11, 54n65, 87–88, 131–33, 176, 191n148
Muller, Richard A., 16n2, 30n83, 31n86, 114, 171n37, 172n39, 173n47, 174n50–51, n53, 175, P204n14, 205n19
Munro, Donald, 9, 11, 63, 104–5, 111, 144, 146, 159, 196, 218–19, 233n162, 234, 250

Murray, Iain H., 22n32, 50n43, 58n89, 64n124, 65, 109n248, 174n48
Murray, John, 114n13
Murray, John J., 28n68
Musculus, Wolfgang, 114n10, 204n14

Naylor, Peter, 30n79, 39n138
Neatby, William Blair, 11–12, 42n151, 51n50, 52, 92, 176n60, 203n5, 221, 257, 260
Nebeker, Gary Lynn, 3n15
Needham, George C., 3n11, 153n237, 154–55
Nettles, Thomas J., 35n113, 36n122, 39n134, n136, 40n145, 65n132, 262n31
Newberry, Thomas, 75n40
Newton, Benjamin Wills, 10, 13, 55–56, 58, 90–91, 112n2, 118, 123, 134–36, 176
Newton, John, 37, 209–210
Nichols, James, 26, 46
Nichols, John, 218
Noel, Napoleon, 91n137, 94n157, 186n116, 188n134
Noll, Mark, 35
Nonconformists (*see also* dissent), 18, 23n36, 50, 65
North America, 5, 10–11, 79, 96, 101, 145–46, 150, 215, 218, 222, 238
North-East Coast Mission (NECM), 101–2, 105, 144, 250
Northern Evangelistic Society (NES), 101, 105, 234, 248–50
Northern Ireland (*see also* Ulster), 238, 246n226, 249
Nuttall, Geoffrey F., 39n133, 40n144, 47n22, 50n39
Nye, Philip, 205n15

Oakland, California, 109
Oliver, Robert W., 29n75, 30n76, 38n131, 39n135n, n138, 58n89
Olson, Roger E., 118n27, 167n15
Ontario, 106, 161–62, 218–20, 225, 238
Orange, Council of (529), 68–69
Overton, John, 44
Owen, John, 18, 23n36, 120n39, 173n46, 184n108

Oxford, 10, 25n47, 53–58, 90, 119, 123, 134, 136, 176

Packer, J. I., 70, 167
Paget, Elizabeth (Bessie), 125–26, 129–30
Particular Baptists. *See* Baptists
Passmore, John, 20
Patterson, F. G., 81n72
Paul, 81, 123, 137, 144, 157, 178, 193, 202, 204, 226, 242
Payne, E. A., 40
Pearse, Meic, 214n67
Pelagianism, 25, 41, 50, 68–69, 73, 76, 89, 90, 97, 101, 120, 123n58; (*see also* semi-Pelagianism)
Pelagius, 16, 68–69
Pelikan, Jaroslav, 69n3
Perkins, William, 18, 205–6
perseverance, 18, 25, 32, 34, 36–37, 41, 103, 132, 135–36, 176n64, 209n38
Peterson, Robert L., 86n101, n103, n106, 128n94, 129, 130n106, n110, n112
Philpot, J. C., 46–47n20, 56, 118, 215
Pibworth, Nigel, xi
Pickering, Henry, 15n69, 61n104, 63n118, 95n162, 106, 107n235, 157, 194, 240
Pink, A. W., 109, 159, 194n164
Piper, John, 87n113
Plainfield, New Jersey, 150
Plymouth, 1, 7, 10, 53–55, 58n87, 90, 112n2, 123, 125, 127, 182
Porteous, J. Moir, 13n65, 202n4, 217
prayer, 86, 103, 106–7, 133, 156, 202, 219–21, 226, 228, 233n163, 246
preaching, Brethren (*see also* evangelists), 63, 84, 86, 89, 96–98, 100, 103–7, 118, 127–28, 133, 137, 144–47, 152–56, 160–61, 163, 175–76, 178, 183–84, 187, 191–92, 195–99, 216, 218–19, 222–26, 229–36, 238, 240–41, 249–52, 254, 261
predestination, doctrine of, *see* chapter 5

Presbyterianism/Presbyterians, 19, 20n17, 29, 44n4, 51, 59–61, 64, 104–5, 118, 154, 216–19, 221, 238, 246, 248–49
propitiation, 6, 167, 173, 174n53, 176n62, 177–81, 183–89, 191–92, 194, 197–200, 254, 260
Protestantism, 16, 25n48, 51, 70, 116, 205n15, 209
Puritans/Puritanism, 16, 18–21, 36, 61n108, 115, 204–7, 209–210, 214, 228, 260

Quakers, 88–90, 135

Rack, Henry, 34, 36n120
Ramsey, Paul, 26n55
Randall, Ian, xi, 2n10, 7n31
Raven, F. E., 159n272
Rawson, David, 127–28
Rea, David, 240–41
Reformation/Reformers, Protestant, 17, 25n48, 28, 44, 57, 70, 89, 114–16, 119–20, 149, 166, 167n10, 172, 204, 205n19, 208, 244, 257, 260
regeneration, 12, 71, 93, 98, 104, 129, 135, 158, 216, 220, 248, 250
Reid, John, 14n68, 79n63, 150n214, 151n218
Reid, William (Carlisle), 221
Reid, William (Edinburgh), 202n4, 216, 218n89, 221
Rennie, Ian, 7, 54
repentance, 28, 30, 38–42, 72, 84, 138, 169–70; *see* chapter 7
reprobation, 6, 19, 21–22, 25, 31, 33n100, 35, 41–42, 46, 48, 117–18, 120, 122, 126, 139–41, 143, 148, 152n227, 153, 155, 160, 163, 254, 257
Restoration, the, 17–24, 25n52, 43
revival, 51n45, 59, 72, 195–96, 214–15, 217, 220, 224–26, 232, 236, 241, 243, 254, 262
Revivals of 1859–60, 2, 9, 11, 63–64, 96, 144–45, 246n226

Evangelical Revival. *See* Evangelical Revival
revivalism, 62, 72, 226, 229
Reynolds, Lindsay, 218n94
Ridley, Nicholas, 135
Ritchie, John, 10, 74n31, 95n160, 104, 105n224, 159–60, 196n175, 198, 233n162, 234n168, n170, 238, 246–47, 249–50
Roman Catholicism, 204, 223, 251
Romanticism, 2, 259
Rouwendal, Pieter L., 172n41
Rowdon, Harold H., 1, 7n32, 8n33, 11–12, 51n47, 53n61, 92n145, n147, 94, 116, 118n30, 119n37, 127n83, n86, 182n92, 259–60
Rowland, Daniel, 32
Rupp, E. Gordon, 23–24, 29n74, 30n82, 70n8
Rush, John, xii
Ryken, Philip Graham, 28n68
Ryland, John Jr., 30n80, 39n140, 40
Ryle, J. C., 64n123

sanctification, 41, 53, 78, 129, 135, 202, 206, 214, 225, 247, 250–51, 254
Sandeen, Ernest R., 220n103
Sandeman, Robert, 210–11, 220
Sandemanianism, 210–11, 215–16, 218, 220, 223, 231–32, 236, 239, 241–43, 252, 254
Sankey, Ira D., 226
Sarnia, Ontario, 218–19
Savoy Declaration, 21n27, 29
Schneider, Michael, 127n80
Schreiner, Thomas R., 71n17
Schulz, Jonathan, xii
Schwarz, Berthold, 3n15
Scotland, 5, 11, 17, 27–28, 58–61, 63, 73, 96, 101–2, 105, 144, 157, 159, 168, 173, 208, 210–12, 217–18, 222, 232, 238, 248, 254
   Highlands/Highlanders, 59, 61–63, 109n248, 159, 212, 248
Scott, A. J., 176n63
Scott, Thomas, 26n56, 44–45, 47–48, 114n13, 117n26
Scott, Walter, 3n12, 185n112

Second London Baptist Confession, 29
Sell, Alan P. F., 23n36, 32, 61n109, 62–63, 66n134
Sellers, Ian, 13n64
semi-Pelagianism, 69, 97, 107 (*see also* Pelagianism)
Shaw, Ian J., 38, 50n43, 54n62
Shaw, Mark R., 205n19, 206n24
Shedd, William G. T., 199
Shephard, Thomas, 206n26
Shuff, Roger N., xi, 2n7–8
Sibbes, Richard, 206n26
Simeon, Charles, 49, 116n18
Simpson, Alan, 205n15
Sinnema, Donald, 114n13
Skepp, John, 30
Smeaton, George, 170n32
Smith, James, 249
Smith, Jay E., 73n27
Smith, John Howard, 210n43
Snell, H. H., 91–92, 245
Soltau, Henry William, 181–82, 226–27, 248n235
Spain, 86
Spellman, W. M., 20n21
Spurgeon, C. H., 2n10, 22, 58, 64–65, 86, 115, 261
Spurr, John, 19–21
Stanley, Charles, 10, 91n138, 97n178, 98–100, 105, 142–43, 181, 246, 249n243, 258, 261
Steane, Edward, 40
Steele, Daniel, 79n63, 121n44, 188, 220, 236–37
Stevenson, Mark R., 4n20, 41n148, 55n73, 84n87, 90n134, 96n168, 105n221, 125n70, 134n122, 138n148, 155n246, 218n94, 257n11, 259n18
Stevenson, Peter K., 60n101, 168n18, 169n26, 211n49–50, 212n52
Stewart, Kenneth J., xi, 4n19, 16n2, 25n48, n52–53, 31n93, 42n152, 49n32, 114–15, 166n5
Stoney, J. B., 159n272
Strachan, Richard, 106–7, 220, 222
Strict Baptists. *See* Baptists
Strivens, Robert, 30–31

Stuart, C. E., 159, 181n87, 230
Stunt, Timothy C. F., xi, 2n4, 7, 10n47, 45n15, 53, 56n76–77, n81, 57n83, 58n87, 85n95, 88n122, 90n132–133, 119n37, 125, 127n89, 128, 215n71
substitution (atonement), 6, 39n138, 60n101, 166–67, 169–71, 176–81, 183–85–189, 192–200, 232, 254, 260
Summerton, Neil, xi, 133n133
supralapsarianism, 21, 22n28, 38, 42, 117, 126, 148, 163n292
Sutcliff, John, 30n80, 39n140
Sweetnam, Mark, 3n12
Swiss Réveil, 7, 58n87
synergism (in salvation), 69n, 97, 107
systematic theology/divinity, 5, 8, 49–50, 73, 80, 116, 129, 137–38, 148, 155, 163, 168, 180, 186, 191–92, 200, 255–60

Tayler, W. Elfe, 88n116, 132n116, 133n121
Teignmouth, 131–32
Thompson, Ryan D., xii
Thuesen, Peter J., 113, 162n291
Tillotson, John, 21–23
Tinder, Donald, xi
Tomline, George Pretyman, 26, 44–47
Toon, Peter, 22n31, 30n77, 38n131, 50n39
Toplady, Augustus M., 26n56, 36–37, 43
Torrance, Thomas F., 27n59, 60n101
Tregelles, Samuel Prideaux, 112–13
Trent, Council of, 98
Trinity, the, 29, 53, 129n97, 161
"Triple Tradition," 11, 96n168
Trotter, William, 80n65, 92–94
Trueman, Carl R., 23n36
TULIP, inadequacy of the acronym for Calvinism, 4n19
Turner, W. G., 79
Tyacke, Nicholas, 18n7
Tyerman, Luke, 23n33, 33
Tyler, Sue, xi

Ulster (see also Northern Ireland), 51, 63–64, 96, 118, 217
Unitarianism, 29, 31, 44n4
United Kingdom, 40, 182
United States, (also America), 5, 26, 33, 71, 74n33, 79, 113, 115, 137, 145, 150, 153–54, 210n43
universal/free gospel offer, 22, 28, 30, 34–35, 37–42, 58, 62, 72, 84, 97, 178, 150, 180, 185, 188–90, 199, 254
universalism, 188–90, 194, 200
Ussher, James, 175

van Asselt, Willem, 166n8
VanDoodewaard, William, 27n60, n63–64, 28n66, n70, 208n33–34
van 't Spijker, Willem, 114n9
Vaughan, Edward Thomas, 54n63
Veitch, Thomas Stewart, 79n62
Venn, Henry, 37, 47
Venn, John, 127–28
Vermigli, Peter Martyr, 57, 114, 120, 204n14
Vlach, Michael J., 167n10

Wales, 32
Walker, John, 51–52
Walkerites, 51–53, 232
Wallace, Dewey D., Jr., 17n3, 19, 20n15, 23n36, 25n52
Ward, John Percy, 3n14
Warfield, Benjamin B., 70n9
Warner, Richard, 53
Watts, Graham, xi
Watts, Michael, 29n72, n74, 30n81–82
Weremchuk, Max S., 85n96
Wesley, Charles, 34
Wesley, John, 16, 23n33, 26, 31–36, 43, 52, 62, 71, 136, 149–50, 167n13, 202n3, 209, 214n67
Wesleyan, 31, 37n125, 48, 51, 75, 209n37
Western Schism, 51–54, 128
Westminster Catechisms, 27–28, 102, 144, 175n56, 191, 208, 212, 214, 255–56

Westminster Confession of Faith (WCF), 18, 20–21, 27–29, 31, 58–59, 71, 173, 175n56, 191, 207–8, 212, 214
Whelan, Irene, 33n104
Whitby, Daniel, 25–27, 46n19
Whitefield, George, 16, 23n33, 26, 32–36, 43, 62, 71, 149
Wigram, George V., 10, 58n87, 118
Wilberforce, William, 54

Wilkins, John, 21n22
Wolffe, John, 45
Wolston, W. T. P., 247
Wood, Darren C., 167n13
Wright, Stephen, xi

Yapp, William, 127, 182
Yeager, Jonathan, 3n13

Zwingli, Ulrich, 70, 203

Scripture Index

Genesis	154, 160	1:11–13	77n52
		1:13	77, 92, 99
		1:29	187, 197
Exodus	193	3:16	146, 153, 159, 238, 258
Leviticus		3:27	123
		5:40	77
16	177–78, 188, 192	6	93, 159n272
		6:37	93–94
		6:44	76–77, 99, 108, 121, 234
Isaiah			
53	198n186	6:45	234
53:5–6	198n184	6:47	248
		6:65	234
Ezekiel	149	10	181n88
Matthew		**Acts**	213
4:16	87	2:43	156
13:44	180, 192	3:19	58n90
25	140n157	13	144
25:34	139	13:16–41	193
		13:48	142, 146, 156–57
		16:30–31	202, 226–27
Luke		17:22–31	193
15:23	97	17:30	138
18:10–14	91		
		Romans	81n73
John	77n52	3:11	77
		4	124
1:1	131	4:3	243
1:9	71	5:6	82

Romans (continued)

8:6–7	77
8:7	95
8:29	120–21, 140
9	121n45, 122, 139
9:10–11	146
9:21	122
9:22	122
9:23	122
10:10–11	235
10:10	203
16:7	157

1 Corinthians

1:1–3	134n126
2:12	56
15	178
15:50–58	81

2 Corinthians

5:20–21	240
13:5	204

Galatians

1	123

Ephesians

1	140, 146, 148
1:4	140, 148, 157, 158n266, 258
1:5	131
1:6	131
2	148
2:1–3	81–82
2:1	90, 108, 141, 145
2:8–9	82
2:8	128
3	148
4	148
5	148
5:25	199

1 Thessalonians

1:4	147
1:9	229

2 Thessalonians

2:13	131, 147
2:13–14	156

1 Timothy

1:15	182
2:4	138

2 Timothy

3:7	238

Hebrews

9:26	192
13:7	14

James

1:18	77, 92
2	224

1 Peter

	140
1:2	148
2:24	184, 193
3:18	198

2 Peter

2:1	179–80, 185n111, 192
3:9	122n51, 138

1 John

	249
2:2	178, 194, 199

Revelation

	154, 160
13:8	139

www.ingramcontent.com/pod-product-compliance
Lightning Source LLC
Chambersburg PA
CBHW050621300426
44112CB00012B/1608